Guide for In-House Counsel

Practical Resource to Cutting-Edge Issues

Leslie A. Berkoff, Editor

AMERICAN BAR ASSOCIATION
Business Law Section

Cover design by Catherine Zaccarine.

Page layout by Quadrum Solutions.

Printed in the United States of America.

23 22 21   5 4 3 2

ISBN: 978-1-64105-394-5

Discounts are available for books ordered in bulk. Special consideration is given to state bars, CLE programs, and other bar related organizations. Inquire at Book Publishing, ABA Publishing, American Bar Association, 321 N. Clark Street, Chicago, Illinois 60654-7598.

www.ShopABA.org

Table of Contents

Chapter 8:   The Impact of the Automatic Stay   171

Introduction to the Guidebook

In-house counsel are regularly confronted with a variety of issues to consider, analyze, provide direction for, and decide, often at the same time. The expanse of legal topics and issues has grown exponentially over the years. In fact, there are many areas of the law which I suspect cross the desks of in-house counsel that were not even in existence, or perhaps were only in their infancy, when many counsel attended law school (certainly I can attest to a similar experience); by way of example, cybersecurity law, personal and corporate data privacy, as well as the growth of mediation, are just a few areas of the law which come to mind. Given that some of these topics may not have been within in-house counsel's educational training and/or even their ordinary daily legal frame of reference, we developed this guidebook to assist in-house counsel in addressing these and many other hot topic issues.

The goal and purpose of this guidebook is to provide counsel with a fundamental outline of key issues as well as allow them to garner a basic understanding of certain subject matter. Each chapter covers and highlights the key issues that arise within a particular area of the law and then provides guidance on the key points or issues which may arise; these are identified throughout the book as practice pointers. While we presume that it is more than likely that in-house counsel will eventually tap into experienced outside counsel who possesses more in-depth knowledge in a particular subject area, the information in this guidebook is intended to provide in-house counsel with a baseline of knowledge. The goal is to in the first instance assist and facilitate in-house counsel with the identification of a particular issue or concern. Thereafter, to assist in-house counsel in the subsequent selection of appropriate outside counsel or experts by having a fundamental understanding of what issues are at play in particular area of the law. Finally, by providing in-house counsel with an initial understanding of the fundamental issues at play in a specific area, counsel can then have a more meaningful discourse with outside counsel or an expert in regard to the particular issue which has been presented.

In selecting the topics for this book, I covered what I perceive to be the hot and critical topics facing in-house counsel given the kinds of issues and situations arising in companies today. While not every company will encounter every issue that is covered in this book, I believe that by and large a good number of these chapters will provide useful over time.

In identifying authors to participate in this publication, time and effort was spent to find leading lawyers in each particular field. The contributing authors are well recognized each in their own right, many writing and speaking on their discrete topics frequently whether it is for the American Bar Association or other nationally recognized organizations.

It has been an absolute pleasure serving as an Editor-in-Chief of this book. Having the opportunity to work with so many distinguished professionals who freely gave of their time and effort has been truly rewarding. In addition to the authors, I thank the ABA and in particular Rick Paszkiet for his never-ending support and guidance in this process.

Leslie A. Berkoff

Editor-in-Chief

Chapter 1

Attorney-Client Privilege for the In-House Attorney

By Samantha R. Johnson

The concept of insulating and protecting communications with counsel is at the heart of the attorney-client relationship, yet what truly is a privileged communication and how it can be easily lost is somewhat misunderstood. The goal of this chapter is to outline the principles, identify the pitfalls, and provide practical advice.

Privileges protect certain confidential communications between parties from voluntary or compelled discovery. The attorney-client privilege is the oldest recognized privilege; its purpose is "to encourage full and frank communication between attorneys and their clients and thereby promote broader public interests in the observance of law and administration of justice."[1] The privilege not only protects the lawyer's advice to the client, but also encourages the client to provide sufficient information to permit the lawyer to render sound legal advice to the client.[2]

The essential elements of the privilege were succinctly set forth in *United States v. United Shoe Machinery Corp.*[3]

---

1. Upjohn Co. v. United States, 449 U.S. 383, 389, 101 S. Ct. 677, 682, 66 L. Ed. 2d 584 (1981).
2. *Upjohn*, 449 U.S. at 390 ("[T]he privilege exists to protect not only the giving of professional advice to those who can act on it but also the giving of information to the lawyer to enable him to give sound and informed advice.").
3. 89 F. Supp. 357, 358–59 (D. Mass. 1950).

The [attorney-client] privilege applies only if:

(1) the asserted holder of the privilege is or sought to become a client;
(2) the person to whom the communication was made (a) is a member of the bar of a court, or his subordinate and (b) in connection with this communication is acting as a lawyer;
(3) the communication relates to a fact of which the attorney was informed (a) by his client (b) without the presence of strangers (c) for the purpose of securing primarily either (i) an opinion on law or (ii) legal services or (iii) assistance in some legal proceeding, and not (d) for the purpose of committing a crime or tort; and
(4) the privilege has been (a) claimed and (b) not waived by the client.

The burden of establishing applicability of the attorney-client privilege falls on the party asserting it.[4] Particularly in the in-house context, where counsel's role involves participation in general business strategy and problem-solving, every communication to or from in-house counsel is not privileged. This chapter explores the elements of the attorney-client privilege with special attention to the issues that confront in-house attorneys.

I. THE CORPORATION AS CLIENT—WHO HOLDS THE PRIVILEGE?

The concept of "corporate personhood" dates back to medieval times, with some commentators noting that the Catholic church was likely the first "corporation" as that term is understood today.[5] A corporation itself cannot act; it relies on human actors (officers, directors, employees, agents) to carry out the corporation's business. Although corporations are in theory "artificial creatures" of the law and not individuals, the attorney-client privilege applies even when the client is a corporation.[6]

However, the corporate attorney-client privilege belongs to the corporation, not to an individual officer, director, employee, or agent (corporate representative) of the corporation, and an individual corporate representative has no power to either assert the corporation's privilege or to prohibit the corporation from waiving it.[7] The privilege remains with the corporation despite changes in corporate structure, ownership, or control. Ultimately, a corporate representative who decides to assert or waive the privilege

---

4. United States v. Ruehle, 583 F.3d 600, 607 (9th Cir. 2009) (citations omitted).

5. Nina Totenberg, *When Did Companies Become People? Excavating the Legal Evolution*, NPR, July 28, 2014, https://www.npr.org/2014/07/28/335288388/when-did-companies-become-people-excavating-the-legal-evolution.

6. *Upjohn*, 449 U.S. at 389–90 (citing United States v. Louisville & Nashville R. Co., 236 U.S. 318, 336, 35 S. Ct. 363, 369, 59 L. Ed. 598 (1915)).

7. *See, e.g.*, Zielinski v. Clorox Co., 270 Ga. 38, 40, 504 S.E.2d 683 (1998).

may not be the person who communicated with the attorney on the corporation's behalf and may not have participated in the attorney-client communication at issue.[8]

A. "Control Group" and "Subject Matter" Tests

Courts use two tests to determine whether a communication to an attorney by a corporation is privileged. The "control group test"[9] (the minority view) provides that the privilege attaches if the corporate representative who is making the communication is in the position to control or even to take a substantial part in a decision about any action that the corporation may take upon the advice of the attorney.[10] The representative making the communication:

> must be shown to either have the authority to obtain professional legal services on behalf of the organization or to act on advice rendered pursuant to a request made under such authority . . . . Generally, only someone relatively high on the corporate ladder will qualify. Communications with underlings who may make internal recommendations to their superiors but who are not themselves authorized to make the final decision will remain unprivileged.[11]

In adopting the control group test, the Supreme Court of Illinois pointed out that "the labels or titles of the employees are not determinative; rather, the actual duties or responsibilities delegated to these individuals determine their status as decision makers." An employee whose advisory role to top management in a particular area is such that a decision would not normally be made without his or her advice or opinion, and whose opinion in fact forms the basis of any final decision by those with actual authority, may be considered part of the control group.[12]

The "subject matter test" was adopted by the Supreme Court in *Upjohn Co. v. United States*,[13] applies to all cases pending in federal courts, and has subsequently been adopted by a majority of state courts. The subject matter test provides that communications will be protected when the communications are (1) made by employees to counsel at the direction of corporate superiors; (2) in order to secure legal advice; (3) concerning matters within the scope of the employees' corporate duties; (4) where the employees themselves were aware that they were questioned so that the corporation could obtain

---

8. Shari Claire Lewis, *The Ins and Outs of Attorney-Corporate-Client Privilege*, For the Defense, July 2010, at 70.

9. This test was disfavored in *Upjohn*, but is still used in some state courts (Alaska, Hawaii, Illinois, Maine, New Hampshire, Oklahoma, Rhode Island, South Dakota, Texas).

10. City of Philadelphia v. Westinghouse Elec. Corp., 210 F. Supp. 483, 485 (E.D. Pa. 1962).

11. Osborne v. Johnson, 954 S.W.2d 180, 184 (Tex. App. 1997) (internal quotations and citations omitted).

12. Consolidation Coal Co. v. Bucyrus-Erie Co., 89 Ill. 2d 103, 119–20, 432 N.E.2d 250, 257–58 (1982).

13. *Id.*

legal advice; and (e) the communications were kept confidential since the time they were made.[14] In *Upjohn*, the Supreme Court observed:

> In the corporate context, however, it will frequently be employees beyond the control group . . . who will possess the information needed by the corporation's lawyers. Middle-level and indeed lower-level employees can, by actions within the scope of their employment, embroil the corporation in serious legal difficulties, and it is only natural that these employees would have the relevant information needed by corporate counsel if he is adequately to advise the client with respect to such actual or potential difficulties.[15]

B. *"Upjohn* Warnings"

In most cases, the interests of a corporation and its corporate representatives are in sync. When interests diverge, however, it creates a significant conflict of interest for counsel. If an attorney representing the corporation also represents an individual corporate representative, the corporation cannot disclose information even when it might be in the corporation's best interest to do so. Similarly, a corporate representative who is represented by the corporation's counsel may have the right to waive the privilege even when it would be disadvantageous to the corporation to do so.

An example of these pitfalls is illustrated by the case of *United States v. Ruehle*[16] wherein the Ninth Circuit considered whether the chief financial officer of a publicly traded corporation could claim the attorney-client privilege (and thus shield himself from criminal prosecution) in a case involving backdating of stock options. The board of directors of Broadcom Corporation, a publicly traded semiconductor company, hired an outside law firm to conduct an internal review of the company's stock option granting practices in anticipation of an inquiry by the Securities and Exchange Commission (SEC) and potential shareholder lawsuits. The board's audit committee, of which CFO William Ruehle was a member, planned for the involvement of the company's outside auditors from Ernst & Young, LLP, and made it clear that the board intended to turn over information obtained through the investigation to the auditors, to fully cooperate with the government, and to self-report any problems with the company's financial statements if necessary. As CFO, Ruehle was charged with primary responsibility for Broadcom's financial affairs, including accurately and completely reporting the company's stock option granting processes and ensuring compliance with reporting to, and record keeping for, the government. Ruehle participated in a number of meetings in May and June 2006 with the attorneys hired by the board and provided information and statements to them. Subsequent to these meetings, the outside attorneys advised Ruehle to retain his own counsel to advise him individually. He did so, but remained heavily involved in the internal review and was privy to the reports of outside counsel to the audit committee.

---

14. Acosta v. Target Corp., 281 F.R.D. 314 (N.D. Ill. 2012) (citing *Upjohn*, 449 U.S. at 394–95).
15. *Upjohn*, 449 U.S. at 390–91.
16. 583 F.3d 600 (9th Cir. 2009).

In June 2008, Ruehle was indicted by a California grand jury on charges of conspiracy, securities and wire fraud, and other violations. The government sought disclosure of Ruehle's statements to, and communications with, the company's outside counsel, but Ruehle claimed that he was entitled to the protection of the individual attorney-client privilege. The Ninth Circuit concluded that those communications were not protected because they were not "made in confidence," but rather for the purpose of disclosure to outside auditors. The Ninth Circuit stated:

> Ruehle readily admits his understanding that all factual information would be communicated to third parties, which undermines his claim of confidentiality to support the privilege. Ruehle's subjective shock and surprise about the subsequent usage of the information he knew would be disclosed to third-party auditors—e.g., information subsequently shared with securities regulators and the Justice Department now used to support a criminal investigation and his prosecution—is frankly of no consequence here.[17]

Ruehle's situation underscores the need for attorneys representing a corporation (whether in-house counsel or outside counsel) to clearly define their role as attorneys for the corporation and not for the individual representatives (even if those representatives are senior officers of the corporation).

The concept of an "*Upjohn* warning" or "corporate *Miranda*" warning arose out of the need for corporate counsel to protect against conflicts of interest in representing the corporation while gathering information from corporate representatives. Although there is no set form for an *Upjohn* warning, the warning generally provides that:

(1) The lawyer represents only the company and not the witness personally;
(2) The lawyer is collecting facts for the purpose of providing legal advice to the company;
(3) The communication is protected by the attorney-client privilege, which belongs exclusively to the company, not the witness;
(4) The company may choose to waive the privilege and disclose the communication to a third party, including the government; and
(5) The communication must be kept confidential, meaning that it cannot be disclosed to any third party other than the witness's counsel.[18]

Counsel should note in a contemporaneous file note or memorandum summarizing the witness meeting that an *Upjohn* warning was given; some attorneys also require the witness to sign a written warning. A sample *Upjohn* warning prepared by the Association of Corporate Counsel[19] is provided at Appendix A.

---

17. *Id.* at 611.

18. Gregory R. Jones, *The Need for Enhanced Upjohn Warnings After Yates,* Feb. 17, 2016, https://www.mwe.com/~/media/files/experience/health-care-resource-center/yates-memorandum/the-need-for-enhanced-upjo.pdf.

19. Association of Corporate Counsel, *Example of an Upjohn Warning Used In Internal Investigations*, http://www.acc.com/chapters/del/upload/DrinkerBiddle-Sample_Upjohn_Warning-HANDOUT.pdf.

Counsel should be careful to provide clear *Upjohn* warnings. The Fourth Circuit warned against the confusion that could be created by "watered-down warnings" in *In Re Grand Jury Subpoena*.[20] In that case, AOL retained an outside law firm to assist in an internal investigation into the company's relationship with PurchasePro, Inc. AOL's general counsel and the outside attorneys interviewed several corporate employees as part of the investigation. In-house and outside counsel interviewed Kent Wakeford, a manager in the company's Business Affairs division, on six occasions. During the third interview, AOL's general counsel finally provided a version of an *Upjohn* warning, stating "We represent the company. These conversations are privileged, but the privilege belongs to the company and the company decides whether to waive it. If there is a conflict, the attorney-client privilege belongs to the company." The outside attorneys apparently also informed Wakeford that they represented AOL, but that they "could" represent him as well so long as there was no conflict, and that he could retain his own counsel as well. In interviews with another employee, identified only as John Doe 1, AOL's general counsel stated, "We represent the company. These conversations are privileged, but the privilege belongs to the company and the company decides whether to waive it. You are free to consult with your own lawyer at any time." Again, outside counsel stated that they could also represent John Doe 1 until such time as there appears to be a conflict of interest. The SEC deposed Wakeford and John Doe 1 as part of the government's investigation of AOL and PurchasePro's relationship. Wakeford and John Doe 1 both were represented by personal counsel, and both asserted the attorney-client privilege as it related to their discussions with AOL's attorneys.

The Fourth Circuit held that the privilege did not apply, and stated that Wakeford and John Doe 1 could not have believed that the company attorneys represented them personally. The court issued an admonition regarding the watered-down warnings, although it pointed out the pitfalls when counsel is not sufficiently clear in drawing the line between representation of the corporation and representation of the corporate representatives:

> We note, however, that our opinion should not be read as an implicit acceptance of the watered-down "*Upjohn* warnings" the investigating attorneys gave the appellants. It is a potential legal and ethical mine field. Had the investigating attorneys, in fact, entered into an attorney-client relationship with appellants, as their statements to the appellants professed they could, they would not have been free to waive the appellants' privilege when a conflict arose. It should have seemed obvious that they could not have jettisoned one client in favor of another. Rather, they would have had to withdraw from all representation and to maintain all confidences. Indeed, the court would be hard pressed to identify how investigating counsel could robustly investigate and report to management or the board of directors of a publicly-traded corporation with the necessary candor if counsel were constrained by ethical obligations to individual employees. However, because we agree with the district court that the appellants never

---

20.   415 F.3d 333 (4th Cir. 2005).

entered into an attorney-client relationship with the investigating attorneys, they averted these troubling issues.[21]

It may be necessary in some cases for counsel to take a *Miranda*-warning approach and specifically indicate to the witness that there is the possibility of criminal charges or prosecution. Under section 18 U.S.C. § 1519,[22] prosecutors can charge a corporate employee with obstruction of justice when an employee lies or tampers with evidence during an internal corporate investigation.

> Courts have found that Section 1519 applies in three scenarios: when there is a federal investigation, when the defendant anticipates there will be a pending federal investigation, or when there is no pending federal investigation. Therefore, whether there is a federal investigation pending is irrelevant to a Section 1519 violation. Even where there is only an internal corporate investigation, a violation may arise where a defendant tampers with documents with the 'intent to impede, obstruct, or influence' the investigation.[23]

Government prosecutors are increasingly using this statute to prosecute employees who alter or destroy documents or who lie to corporate counsel during investigations.

In addition to the standard *Upjohn* warning, in-house counsel should consider informing the employee of potential criminal consequences of lying or destroying documents during an internal investigation, advise the employee of the right to remain silent and to have his or her own attorney, and allow the employee to make an informed decision on the nature and accuracy of the information he or she provides to the investigating attorney.[24]

II.   LEGAL ADVICE VERSUS BUSINESS ADVICE—WHAT COMMUNICATIONS ARE PROTECTED?

A.   Privilege Protects Communications, Not Facts

The attorney-client privilege protects disclosure only of *communications*; it does not protect disclosure of the underlying *facts* by those who communicated with the attorney. The client cannot be compelled to answer the question, "What did you say or write

---

21.   *Id.* at 340.

22.   The statute provides: "Whoever knowingly alters, destroys, mutilates, conceals, covers up, falsifies, or makes a false entry in any record, document, or tangible object with the intent to impede, obstruct, or influence the investigation or proper administration of any matter within the jurisdiction of any department or agency of the United States or any case filed under title 11, or in relation to or contemplation of any such matter or case, shall be fined under this title, imprisoned not more than 20 years, or both."

23.   Sehyung Daniel Lee, *The Benefits of a Miranda-Type Approach to Upjohn Warnings*, ABA Section of Litigation Commercial & Business, Apr. 30, 2012, http://apps.americanbar.org/litigation/committees/commercial/articles/spring2012-0412-benefits-miranda-warning-upjohn-warnings.html (citing United States v. Yielding, 657 F.3d 688 (8th Cir. 2011)).

24.   *Id.*

to the attorney?" but may not refuse to disclose any relevant fact within the client's knowledge merely because the client incorporated a statement of such fact into his or her communication to his or her attorney.[25] For example, the fact that a client is meeting with an attorney for the purposes of obtaining legal advice, as well as the general subject matter of the meeting, is not necessarily privileged information. Records of dates, places, or times of meetings, the names of attendees at the meetings, and communications between attorney and client (although not the content of those communications) are also not within the scope of the attorney-client privilege.[26]

B. Communication Must Be To or From an Attorney Acting in That Capacity

In the corporate context, it is often difficult to apply the attorney-client privilege to communications between in-house corporate counsel and those who personify the corporate entity because modern corporate counsel have become involved in all facets of the enterprises for which they work. In-house legal counsel participates in and renders decisions about business, technical, scientific, public relations, and advertising issues, as well as purely legal issues. Courts require a clear showing that the attorney was acting in his or her professional legal capacity before cloaking documents in the privilege's protection.[27]

Corporations often employ lawyers in roles other than specifically in-house legal counsel. For example, many lawyers serve as chief executive officers, chief human resource officers, and compliance officers in corporations. The attorney-client privilege cannot be invoked simply because an employee has a juris doctorate. The communication at issue *must* be directed to an employee working in that role as a legal advisor to the corporation in order for the privilege to apply.

In *Casey v. Unitek Global Services, Inc.*,[28] the Eastern District of Pennsylvania addressed the issue of the application of the attorney-client privilege when the employee was not acting in a traditional legal capacity. Carolyn Casey, the vice president of safety and risk for Unitek, complained that she was paid less than her male colleagues and that she was sexually harassed. She e-mailed a written complaint regarding repeated harassment by one of her superiors in 2013 and was terminated within minutes of sending her complaint. Casey had a law degree from Widener University; however, she had not been hired at Unitek as an attorney. In her position as vice president of risk and safety, she led the risk-management and safety departments. Those departments were separate from and not reportable to Unitek's general counsel. Ms. Casey primarily managed insurance claims in litigation against Unitek, which involved acting as Unitek's registered agent

---

25. *Upjohn*, 449 U.S. at 395–96 (citing Philadelphia v. Westinghouse Electric Corp., 205 F. Supp. 830, 831 (E.D. Pa. 1962)).

26. Meade v. Gen. Motors, LLC, 250 F. Supp. 3d 1387, 1391 (N.D. Ga. 2017).

27. *In Re* Vioxx Products Liability Litig., 501 F. Supp. 2d 789, 797 (E.D. La. 2007) (citing PAUL R. RICE, 1 ATTORNEY-CLIENT PRIVILEGE IN THE UNITED STATES § 11.9, at 78–79 (Thomson West 2d. ed. 1999)).

28. 2015 WL 539623 (E.D. Pa. Feb. 9, 2015).

for service of process, retaining and managing outside counsel, and participating in litigation update meetings. The district court held that "[w]hile Ms. Casey's performance of this function may make her position look quasi legal the cases were not assigned to her office because she was an attorney. Rather, she took charge of these claims because the insurance policies which she negotiated and oversaw would indemnify Unitek for any loss . . . . There can be no doubt that Ms. Casey's legal training assisted her greatly in this aspect of her position, but Unitek points to no evidence that it sought Ms. Casey's legal advice or opinion with regard to any of the insurable claims."[29]

C. Communication Must Be for the Purpose of Securing or Providing Legal Advice

The attorney-client privilege attaches when the purpose of the communication is for the purpose of securing legal advice or assistance. The privilege also provides a derivative protection to responsive communications from attorney to the client to the extent that those communications reveal the content of prior confidential communications from the client.[30]

Some courts employ a "but for" test in determining whether privilege applies, i.e., the communication is only privileged if it would not have been made *but for* the client's need for legal advice or services. Courts employing this test apply the attorney-client privilege strictly in order to prevent attorneys from using the privilege as a shield to thwart discovery.[31]

A majority of courts look to whether the "primary purpose" of the communication was for purposes of legal advice:

> The test for the application of the attorney-client privilege to communications with legal counsel in which a mixture of services are sought is whether counsel was participating in the communications primarily for the purpose of rendering legal advice or assistance. Therefore, merely because a legal issue can be identified that relates to on-going communications does not justify shielding them from discovery. The lawyer's role as a lawyer must be primary to [his or her] participation . . . . Only if the attorney is "acting as a lawyer"—giving advice with respect to the legal implications of a proposed course of conduct—may the privilege be properly invoked. In addition, if a communication is made primarily for the purpose of soliciting legal advice, an incidental request for business advice does not vitiate the attorney-client privilege.[32]

---

29. *Id.* at *3.
30. United States *ex rel.* Baklid-Kunz v. Halifax Hospital Medical Center, 2012 WL 5415108 (M.D. Fla., Nov. 6, 2012) (citations omitted).
31. Leonen v. Johns-Manville, 135 F.R.D. 94, 99 (D.N.J. 1990) (citing First Chicago Int'l v. United Exchange Co., Ltd., 125 F.R.D. 55 (S.D.N.Y. 1989)).
32. *Vioxx*, 501 F. Supp. 2d at 798–99 (internal citations omitted).

The context in which the communication occurs is helpful, but it is not always determinative. The attorney-client privilege may apply when a corporation seeks advice about a threatened or pending lawsuit. If a company conducts an internal investigation, regardless of whether the investigation was conducted pursuant to a company compliance program required by statute or regulation, or was otherwise conducted pursuant to company policy, the privilege will apply only if one of the significant purposes of the internal investigation was to obtain or provide legal advice.[33]

A communication is not automatically privileged because counsel was in the room when the communication occurred or because counsel was copied on an e-mail or memorandum.[34] Courts note that the problem of determining whether a communication is privileged "has been exacerbated by the advent of e-mail that has made it so convenient to copy legal counsel on every communication that might be seen as having some legal significance at some time, regardless of whether it is ripe for legal analysis. But one cannot properly claim the protection of the attorney-client privilege by simply copying an attorney on an e-mail."[35]

> The purpose of the communication must be the obtaining or providing of legal advice, not a business discussion. A business that gets marketing advice from a lawyer does not acquire a privilege in the bargain. The attorney-client privilege protects only communications related to the giving or seeking of legal advice; funneling other communications past an attorney will not make them privileged. Where a document is prepared for simultaneous review by legal and non-legal personnel and legal and business advice is requested, it is not primarily legal in nature and is therefore not privileged. However, documents communicating legal advice to non-legal personnel are within the attorney-client privilege, as well as documents reflecting discussions among executives of legal advice. Thus the mere fact that a document is sent to many non-legal and few legal personnel is not determinative of whether it is privileged. The principal consideration is the nature of the document: whether it primarily requests or gives legal or business advice. Thus, the privilege does not apply to an e-mail "blast" to a group of employees that may include an attorney, but where no request for legal advice is made and the input from the attorney is business-related and not primarily legal in nature.[36]

33. *In re* Kellogg Brown & Root, Inc., 756 F.3d 754, 760 (D.C. Cir. 2014).

34. *Vioxx*, 501 F. Supp. 2d at 807 ("A proponent of privilege "cannot reasonably expect [the court] to make this assessment for it on either a document-by-document basis or universally through a presumption that everything in-house counsel comments upon is legal advice.").

35. *Meade*, 250 F. Supp. 3d at 1392–93.

36. *Acosta*, 281 F.R.D. at 321.

III. CONFIDENTIALITY OF COMMUNICATIONS

In order to invoke the attorney-client privilege, the client must intend that that the communications are confidential in nature.

The burden is on the party claiming privilege to demonstrate that confidentiality was expected in the handling of the communications and that the party was reasonably careful to keep the confidential information protected from general disclosure.[37] Where the company does not take any significant precautions to prevent the disclosure of privileged materials, including failing to undertake a manual privilege review, a court may find that those materials are not privileged.[38] Failure to lodge a timely and specific objection to the production of a communication may result in a waiver of the claimed privilege.[39] In *Coastal States Gas Corp. v. Dept. of Energy*, the District of Columbia Circuit Court held that the attorney-client privilege was not demonstrated where the party made no attempt to protect the memoranda within the agency, admitted it did not know who had access to the documents, and allowed copies of the allegedly privileged documents to be circulated to other offices, filed, and kept for future use.[40]

In the corporate context, communications may be disseminated to those with a "need to know" in connection with their duties within the organization without destroying the confidentiality. The scope of an individual's employment is highly relevant to the question of maintenance of confidentiality.[41] However, dissemination must be confined to those with a "need to know," and appropriate warnings on forwarding, copying, or other forms of republication or reproduction should be provided, either on the face of documents themselves or from policies identifying the need to maintain confidentiality.[42] Knowing disclosure to a third party almost invariably surrenders the privilege. The privilege is waived if the communications are disclosed to employees who did not need access to that communication.[43] Therefore, keeping tighter controls over who has access to information, and avoiding large group e-mails, is advisable.

IV. ASSERTING THE PRIVILEGE

A party asserting the attorney-client privilege bears the burden of asserting all essential elements. In *Acosta v. Target Corporation*,[44] the United States District Court

---

37. *Id*. at 322.

38. *Baklid-Kunz*, 2012 WL 5415108, at 10 (citations omitted).

39. *Id*.

40. *Acosta*, 281 F.R.D. at 322 (citing Coastal States Gas Corp. v. Dept. of Energy, 617 F.2d 854, 863 (D.C. Cir. 1980)).

41. *Id*. at 322.

42. Henry S. Bryans, *Employed Lawyers and the Attorney-Client Privilege: Parsing the Trade-offs*, 47 U. Tol. L. Rev. 109, 116 (2015) (citations omitted).

43. *Acosta*, 281 F.R.D. at 321–22.

44. 281 F.R.D. 314 (N.D. Ill. 2012).

for the Northern District of Illinois summarized the requirements for withholding communications pursuant to Federal Rule Civil Procedure 26(b)(5)(A):

> When a party withholds information otherwise discoverable by claiming that the information is privileged or subject to protection as trial preparation material, the party must:
> (i) expressly make the claim; and
> (ii) describe the nature of the documents, communications, or tangible things not produced or disclosed—and do so in a manner that, without revealing information itself privileged or protected, will enable other parties to assess the claim.

Generally, these requirements are met by serving a privilege log listing each separate, withheld document and identifying for each the date, author, all recipients along with their capacities, the document's subject matter, purpose for production, and a specific explanation of why the document is immune from discovery. Privilege logs are generally accompanied by an explanatory affidavit from counsel. Documents (including e-mails, text messages, voicemails, etc.) must be listed separately because the claim of privilege must be made and sustained on a question-by-question or document-by-document basis. Blanket claims of privilege are not permitted.[45]

The privilege log must describe the nature of the withheld material in a manner that, without revealing information itself privileged or protected, will enable other parties and the court to assess the validity of the claimed privilege. A privilege log must be tailored to allow the reviewing court and the other party or parties to evaluate the validity of the claimed privilege. The log should contain explanatory information about the actual contents of the documents at issue, but boilerplate language regarding the contents is not sufficient.[46]

Courts are divided on the manner in which e-mails should be specified in privilege logs, particularly in the case of corporations. Some courts compare an e-mail chain to a single conversation and require only the most recent to be listed. Other courts believe that a proper analysis of privilege requires more detail, and therefore each e-mail in the chain must be identified and described. If the sender and/or recipient(s) at an e-mail address cannot be adequately identified, it may be impossible to determine whether the privilege is properly asserted. If listing only the recipients of the last e-mail in a chain fails to disclose everyone to whom an allegedly privilege communication has been sent, the listing may not be adequate.[47]

---

45. *Id.* at 319–20.
46. *Meade,* 250 F. Supp. 3d at 1396.
47. *Acosta,* 281 F.R.D. at 320.

V. WAIVER

A. Corporation Is the Holder of the Privilege and Therefore Able to Waive It

As the holder of the attorney-client privilege, a corporation can also waive that privilege. As previously discussed, given that a corporation is an inanimate entity, it must act through its agents. For solvent corporations, the power to waive the corporate attorney-client privilege rests with the corporation's management and is normally exercised by its officers and directors.[48] The corporation's officers, directors, and managers must exercise the privilege in a manner consistent with their fiduciary duty to act in the best interests of the corporation and not of themselves as individuals.

When new officers, directors, or managers take control of a corporation, the authority to assert and waive the corporation's attorney-client privilege passes to the new management as well. New officers, directors, and managers may waive the attorney-client privilege with respect to communications made by former officers, directors, managers, and employees. The replaced or displaced managers may not assert the privilege over the wishes of current managers, even as to statements that the former managers or employees might have made to counsel concerning matters within the scope of their corporate duties.[49]

B. Voluntary Waiver

Any voluntary disclosure of information to a third party waives the attorney-client privilege, regardless of whether such disclosure later turns out to be harmful.[50] Voluntary waiver most often arises in two contexts: where the corporation raises the advice of counsel defense or where the corporation waives the privilege to obtain cooperation credit from the United States Department of Justice.

1. Advice of Counsel Defense

A person or entity may assert the advice of counsel defense in response to criminal charges of a specific intent crime (to negate the required intent) or in a civil case to demonstrate good faith or lack of intent for an intentional tort. To assert an advice of counsel defense, the person or entity must prove the following factors: (1) the person or entity sought counsel's advice in good faith; (2) the person or entity disclosed all pertinent information to counsel; (3) the person or entity acted on counsel's advice in good faith; and (4) the attorney was competent in the particular area of law and disinterested in the

---

48. Commodity Futures Trading Comm'n v. Weintraub, 471 U.S. 343, 348, 105 S. Ct. 1986, 85 L.Ed.2d 372 (1985).

49. *Id.* at 348–49 (the Supreme Court also held that, for a bankrupt corporation, the privilege passes to the appointed bankruptcy trustee).

50. *Ruehle*, 583 F.3d at 612.

matter.[51] Use of the defense puts the advice given by counsel "in issue." As the Southern District of New York stated in *S.E.C. v. Wyly*:[52]

> A client who claims that he acted on advice of counsel cannot use the privilege to prevent inquiry into the communications that the client and lawyer had about that advice. There is a compelling notion that the adversary cannot be stonewalled by the simultaneous assertion of the [advice of counsel] defense and the privilege. Put another way, the attorney-client privilege can be used to shield information, but it cannot be used as a sword against the adversary. If the rule were otherwise, a claim of reliance on counsel would be immune from a showing that, in fact, the defendant had received overwhelming advice to the contrary, or that the lawyers' advice was in fact based on misinformation coming from the client. The common-law rule, providing for a subject matter waiver when the client interposes an advice of counsel defense, has been codified by Federal Rule of Evidence 502(a) (providing for subject matter waiver when a disclosure of privileged information is intentional and the disclosed and undisclosed information "ought in fairness to be considered together").

2. Cooperation Credit

A corporation may also choose to waive the attorney-client privilege in order to gain cooperation credit from the United States Department of Justice (DOJ). In 2015, Sally Quillian Yates, then deputy attorney general of the Department of Justice, issued a memorandum entitled "Individual Accountability for Corporate Wrongdoing," colloquially known as the "Yates Memo." The Yates Memo updates the DOJ's Principles of Federal Prosecution of Business Organizations, contained within the United States Attorney's Manual (the principal internal policy guide for DOJ attorneys).[53] Unlike the memoranda that preceded it, the Yates Memo specifically focused on seeking out "bad actors" within corporations, stating "[o]ne of the most effective ways to combat corporate misconduct is by seeking accountability from the individuals who perpetrated the wrongdoing. Such accountability is important for several reasons: it deters future illegal activity, it incentivizes changes in corporate behavior, it ensures that the proper parties are held responsible for their actions, and it promotes the public's confidence in our justice system."[54]

---

51. Katrice Bridges Copeland, *In-house Counsel Beware!*, 39 Fordham Urb. L.J. 391, 430 (2012).

52. S.E.C. v. Wyly, No. 10 CIV. 5760 SAS, 2011 WL 3366491, at *2 (S.D.N.Y. July 27, 2011), *modified on reconsideration sub nom.* S.E.C., Inc. v. Wyly, No. 10 CIV. 5760 SAS, 2011 WL 3841591 (S.D.N.Y. Aug. 18, 2011), *and modified on reconsideration sub nom.* S.E.C., Inc. v. Wyly, No. 10 CIV. 5760 SAS, 2011 WL 4055408 (S.D.N.Y. Aug. 19, 2011).

53. Ty E. Howard & Todd Presnell, *In-House Counsel: Protecting the Privilege in a Post-Yates Memorandum World*, 21 The Corporate Counselor 3 (June 2016), *available at* https://presnellonprivileges.files. wordpress.com/2016/06/corporate-counselor-article-june-2016-corp.pdf.

54. Sally Quillian Yates, *Individual Accountability for Corporate Wrongdoing*, Memorandum for All United States Attorneys, Sept. 9, 2015, *available at* https://www.justice.gov/archives/dag/file/769036/ download.

The Yates Memo set out six steps to strengthen the DOJ's pursuit of individual corporate wrongdoing:

(1) To qualify for *any* cooperation credit, a company must disclose all relevant facts about culpable individuals;

(2) Criminal and civil investigations will focus on individuals from the start;

(3) Criminal and civil investigators should routinely communicate;

(4) Absent extraordinary circumstances, DOJ will not release individuals from liability as apart of a corporate resolution;

(5) Corporate case should not be resolved unless individual cases can be resolved before the statute of limitations;

(6) In civil cases, attorneys should focus on individuals and determine whether to bring suit regardless of ability to pay.

Although the Yates Memo does not specifically address waiver of the attorney-client privilege, a corporation hoping to obtain cooperation credit from the DOJ must consider whether to waive the privilege in order to hang responsibility on certain individuals and save itself from civil and criminal penalties. It may not be possible for corporations to disclose all relevant facts about individual actors without disclosing information obtained in ostensibly privileged interviews. Additionally, when a corporation conducts an investigation with a plan to disclose that information to the government, the expectation of confidentiality in attorney-client communications may be destroyed.

C. Involuntary Waiver

When a corporation uses the privilege in an offensive (rather than defensive) manner, that use can result in a waiver of the privilege. Courts generally hold that a party cannot use the attorney-client privilege as both a sword and a shield.[55]

Both the attorney-client and work-product privileges may be waived if a party puts the privileged communication at issue by relying on it to support a claim or defense. Such a waiver may be implied in circumstances where it is called for in the interests of fairness, such as when a party attempts to use the privilege both as a shield and a sword. In other words, a party cannot partially disclose privileged communications or affirmatively rely on privileged communications to support its claim or defense and then shield the underlying communications from scrutiny by the opposing party. A defendant may not use the privilege to prejudice his opponent's case or to disclose some selected communications for self-serving purposes.[56]

---

55. Casey v. Unitek Global Services, Inc., 2015 WL 539623 (E.D. Pa. 2015) (citations and internal quotations omitted).

56. Koumoulis v. Indep. Fin. Mktg. Grp., Inc., 295 F.R.D. 28, 40 (E.D.N.Y. 2013), *aff'd*, 29 F. Supp. 3d 142 (E.D.N.Y. 2014) (citations and internal quotations omitted).

In *Casey v. Unitek Global Services, Inc.*, discussed previously in Part II, the district court disallowed the application of the attorney-client privilege where Unitek attempted to use the privileged communications as a complete defense to Ms. Casey's lawsuit. Unitek sought a protective order, claiming that communications involving Ms. Casey (including ones that could be used to prove her claims of harassment and discrimination) were covered by the attorney-client privilege. If Unitek were successful in withholding the documents pursuant to a protective order, Ms. Casey would have been prevented from obtaining any discovery to prove her case. Unitek waived the privilege by attempting to use it to block Ms. Casey's claims.[57]

Privilege may also be waived as a sanction for improper conduct, including failure to produce a proper privilege log.

> The court may impose as a sanction the waiver of privilege for cases of unjustifiable delay, inexcusable conduct, and bad faith in responding to discovery requests by improperly withholding documents on the basis of privilege, and failing to provide an adequate privilege log in compliance with Rule 26. [There is an] abundance of district court case law holding that a party claiming privilege is obliged to produce a privilege log and its failure to do so means the privilege is waived.[58]

VI.   CONCLUSION—"IT'S DIFFERENT IN-HOUSE"

In-house counsel occupy a valuable role within a corporation as trusted advisors on both legal and business matters. As corporate gatekeepers, in-house attorneys are often called upon to investigate, educate, litigate, and mitigate. Protecting client confidentiality is one of the highest ethical duties of an attorney, and understanding the parameters of the attorney-client privilege allows corporate counsel to safeguard the best interests of the corporation.

---

57.   2015 WL 539623 at *8.
58.   *Meade*, 250 F. Supp. 3d at 1393–94 (citations and internal quotations omitted).

Appendix A:
Example of an *Upjohn* Warning Used in Internal Investigations

We are conducting an investigation for the Company into certain events related to [INSERT RELEVANT ISSUE IN GENERAL TERMS]. We believe that you may have facts and/or documents that may be relevant to our investigation and we appreciate you meeting with us.

To be clear, we serve as counsel to the Company. We are not your personal counsel and cannot give you legal advice. If you wish to obtain separate counsel, we will reschedule this interview so that you may do so.

In addition, your communications with us, as part of this investigation, are confidential and protected by, among other things, the attorney-client privilege. As the Company is our client, the attorney-client privilege belongs solely to the Company. Accordingly, the Company, in its sole discretion, may elect to waive the privilege and reveal your communications with us to third parties, including the government.

As part of this investigation, we are interviewing a number of employees to gain a better understanding of the relevant issues. The fact that we are conducting this investigation does not mean the Company believes that any current or former employee has engaged in improper or illegal conduct. It simply is the process through which the Company ensures that it maintains the highest standards of corporate integrity. Your candor and honesty are critical to our ability to effectively conduct our investigation. To maintain the integrity of this investigation, we request that you keep our conversations today confidential. We appreciate your cooperation.

May we continue?

Chapter 2

Internal Corporate Investigations

By Elizabeth S. Fenton, Michelle N. Lipkowitz,
Mark A. McGrath, and John Levitske

*Internal corporate investigations may become necessary for a variety
of reasons. Therefore, new in-house lawyers should be aware of areas in
which internal investigations may be warranted and the considerations
and steps to take when conducting an internal investigation. Even though
such investigations vary depending on the particular conduct involved,
whether regulatory agencies are already involved, and the industry, certain
considerations carry through all internal investigations.*

Behavior that does not comply with expectations, company assets that may not be fully
under control, and disagreements regarding reported figures are common issues that
give rise to internal corporate investigations. White-collar enforcement activities at
the Securities and Exchange Commission (SEC),[1] the Department of Justice (DOJ),[2]

---

1. The SEC brought 754 enforcement actions in 2015. *See* https://www.sec.gov/news/press-release/2017-210.

2. Deputy Attorney General Rod J. Rosenstein, Remarks at the American Conference Institute's 20th Anniversary New York Conference on the Foreign Corrupt Practices Act (May 9, 2018), *available at* https://www.justice.gov/opa/speech/deputy-attorney-general-rod-j-rosenstein-delivers-remarks-american-conference-institutes ("In 2017, Main Justice Fraud Section prosecutors convicted 234 individuals. The Section also concluded 10 corporate resolutions. The 2017 results exceed the prior year in both the number of convictions and monetary sanctions.").

and other federal and state agencies continue to be a focus of government resources. Accordingly, for in-house lawyers, a sound understanding of when to initiate and how to conduct an internal investigation, including related responsibilities and pitfalls, is necessary to sufficiently fulfill their fiduciary duties to the organization.

The effects of internal investigations into potential violations of the law may play as significant a role in representing an institution as key acquisitions or bet-the-company litigation. Increased regulatory focus and pursuit of individual wrongdoers, including attorney "gatekeepers," has become a key deterrent feature of enforcement programs that in-house lawyers must consider when faced with both civil and criminal investigations. The 2017 SEC Enforcement Annual Report notes: "In the six months since Chairman Clayton took office, pursuing individuals has continued to be the rule, not the exception. One or more individuals have been charged in more than 80 percent of the standalone enforcement actions the Commission has brought."[3] This trend is not expected to abate. If criminal liability is a possibility, the stakes are very high indeed.

The subject matter of internal investigations is broad and may range from employment issues or financial fraud to bribery and data breaches. Each stage of an internal investigation is critical, including:

- the decision to commence;
- whether to use internal or external resources;
- identifying and protecting sources of information;
- hiring the right experts to guide the process;
- establishing clear roles and scope;
- executing the investigative plan;
- determining the level of communication with stakeholders;
- evaluating what to do with the investigation's results, and
- implementing remedial measures.

Self-disclosure to the government is often encouraged, and where such a disclosure is made, negotiation over the consequences is also a nuanced and specialized area. In short, if the subject is important enough to warrant an internal investigation, the consequences of making an error in judgment at any of these stages may threaten the corporation's reputation, its share price, balance sheet, and in some cases the liberty of the involved employees.

I.   SUBJECT MATTERS INVOLVED IN CORPORATE INTERNAL INVESTIGATIONS

General counsel might need to initiate internal investigations concerning a variety of subjects. Even as the current administration scales back some enforcement activities,

---

3. SEC 2017 Annual Report, at 2, *available at* https://www.sec.gov/files/enforcement-annual-report-2017.pdf.

state and local regulatory bodies, shareholders, and other stakeholders remain interested in compliance with laws of all sorts and remain steadfast in their pursuit.[4] Various areas remain ripe for enforcement and litigation that may require internal investigations and potential self-disclosure as issues arise.

Although not exhaustive, the following subject matters are commonly associated with internal investigations.

A. Employment

Many issues where internal investigations may be warranted begin as employment disputes. What may appear to be a personality conflict between a manager and an employee can turn into individual litigation over employment discrimination on the basis of race, gender, or other protected class. More rarely, possible criminal issues involving fraud or theft may be unearthed. If a problem appears to be a contained employment matter, the internal investigator should keep his or her eyes and ears open as to whether other issues may be involved.

B. Cybersecurity and Theft of Intellectual Property

Data privacy has become a hot-button issue across all business sectors. Commodity hacking and malware are the modern version of highway robbery. In some cases, a disgruntled employee, former employee, or customer is behind a hack. Data breaches from within cause disruption, morale issues, and financial loss.

Other data breaches involve outsiders—some from foreign countries. In those cases, even if the wrongdoer is a domestic or foreign individual or entity, the corporation may still face criminal or civil exposure if its safeguards are found to be inadequate. Social media adds yet another layer of complexity, as does the growing number of whistleblowers who stand ready and willing to go to the government.

In the face of a data breach, an internal investigation is an effective way not only to troubleshoot and avoid future issues, but also to confirm that the issue was truly external, that the corporation did have adequate controls in place, and that the point of data exposure was contained or mitigated. An internal investigation may lead to additional training of employees, enhanced security measures, and identification of vulnerabilities that could be problematic in future hacks.

If the corporation did not have adequate controls in place, a plan to remediate will be critical if criminal liability is on the horizon. Data breaches involving customers often require additional disclosures, many of which are regulated by both state and federal law. Although those laws are beyond the scope of this chapter, in-house counsel should be aware of these laws so that the disclosures are timely and accurate.

---

4. *See* John F. Savarese, et al., White Collar and Regulatory Enforcement: What to Expect in 2018, https://wp.nyu.edu/compliance_enforcement/2018/01/29/white-collar-and-regulatory-enforcement-what-to-expect-in-2018/ (describing continuing unpredictability in enforcement).

In addition to these kinds of incidents, theft or misuse of company-issued equipment and intellectual property is also a potential source of criminal liability. An internal investigation may be warranted to determine whether the company's systems for protecting laptops, thumb drives, smartphones, and other devices are adequate. Does the company use encryption, for example? Are trade secrets and other intellectual property protected? What are the policies when employees leave? Does the business conduct regular audits or stress tests to confirm controls are adequate? If the company outsources much of its IT function, what do the service providers do to ensure data is protected? Insurers, regulators, customers and shareholders will want to know what the corporation's policies are (and in the event of a problem, what the remedial plan is), and customer notice may be required in certain instances. Internal investigations and resulting corrective actions can help organizations to identify control gaps and better prepare for, prevent, and respond to future incidents to reduce risk and potential legal exposure. Again, customer notice may also be required in certain of these incidents.

C. Securities

Charged with enforcing the federal securities laws, the SEC has historically maintained a vigorous enforcement program to combat wrongdoing, compensate harmed investors, and maintain confidence in the integrity and fairness of the capital markets. Enforcement inquires have become a common occurrence even when organizations and individuals act with pure intentions. Enforcement inquiries are not to be taken lightly, and in-house lawyers should be vigilant to respond in a prompt and informed manner. Retaining experienced counsel, calling the SEC immediately to understand the nature of the inquiry, preserving relevant records, looking at potential insurance coverage, and determining whether the SEC inquiry itself should be disclosed are all critical first steps.

Internal investigations around enforcement inquiries are common, and organizations often benefit from the advice not only of experienced counsel, but of accounting experts with expertise handling such matters as well. Familiarity with the SEC enforcement process, knowledge of applicable law and investigative best practices, and credibility of both lawyers and accounting experts with the SEC is vital to obtaining the most effective outcome. SEC inquiries can begin as discrete issues that may expand into broader questions regarding financial reporting and disclosure practices. Related investigations often take years to complete and pose potentially high-stakes ramifications to organizations, management, and individuals. Thoughtful consideration and assessment from in-house lawyers early and often throughout the process is necessary.

An internal investigation often proves to be an integral component of the successful representation of an organization under investigation by the SEC because it can provide facts and information regarding potential legal exposure, financial reporting or disclosure issues, and a determination as to whether action (or inaction) of employees necessitates personnel changes. Internal investigations also often identify deficiencies in the organization's internal controls and procedures. Addressing such deficiencies in a timely and proactive manner may positively influence future potential monetary penalties should the SEC decide to bring (and win) civil enforcement proceedings against the organization.

D. Corruption

High-stakes government enforcement matters in the areas of bribery and corruption represent another area that often necessitates some level of internal investigation. Organizations that run afoul of the Foreign Corrupt Practices Act (FCPA), the UK Bribery Act, and other similar laws in foreign jurisdictions may present unique challenges to in-house attorneys attempting to wrap their arms around the potential violations of laws, concerns relating to books and records or internal controls, and related risks and potentially costly impacts on their businesses. The dual elements of the FCPA in particular, dealing with bribery of foreign officials and accounting transparency requirements, were designed to facilitate parallel criminal and civil enforcement. The in-house lawyer must be mindful of the two different standards involved.

Internal investigations are often necessary in corruption-related investigations to identify the facts and circumstances underlying allegations to determine whether improper activities occurred. Investigative procedures may include electronic data capture and analysis, document review, witness interviews, examination of activity contained in the underlying books and records, data analytics, and related presentations and communications to regulators.

E. Consumer Protection

Allegations from regulators or individuals regarding unfair, deceptive, and fraudulent business practices represent additional subject matter that in-house lawyers often encounter. "Do Not Call" lists, fair debt collection, home lending, product safety, and labeling issues are just a few of the subjects that arise in this realm. In addition to the Federal Trade Commission (FTC),[5] and particularly the Bureau of Consumer Protection, many states also have agencies devoted to consumer protection. These agencies investigate fraud and unfair business practices, and enforce the laws and regulations relating to those issues. Corporations may become implicated in such an investigation on a whistleblower report, a consumer complaint, or by a zealous enforcer. Upon learning of a potential consumer protection issue, a corporation should evaluate whether an internal investigation is merited. The analysis will depend on how widespread the issue is, how serious it is, and what potential fines or statutory penalties may be involved. In addition, the FTC, the DOJ Antitrust Division, and state agencies also enforce antitrust laws intended to protect consumers. Internal investigations are especially warranted in these kinds of matters because many antitrust laws provide for treble damages, making violations an expensive prospect.

F. Environmental

Environmental and related worker-safety issues also may be the subject of internal investigations. The Occupational Safety and Health Act (OSHA), the Clean Water Act,

---

5. *See generally* www.ftc.gov.

the Clean Air Act, and state regulations governing environment and safety are a few of the laws that may be implicated. Whistleblowers, inspectors, and private citizens all are sources of reporting. Retention of scientific experts at an early stage to assist with the investigation often makes sense once a company learns of an environmental or safety issue.

II. WAYS LEGAL DEPARTMENTS LEARN OF ISSUES THAT MAY WARRANT INVESTIGATION

There are numerous ways for issues warranting investigation to arrive at the doorstep of the legal department. In addition to whistleblowers, regulatory oversight, management reviews, internal and external audits, employee tips, and law enforcement, many businesses now have compliance hotlines to which employees or third parties may report suspected wrongdoing or noncompliance with laws. The results of regular internal compliance or information technology reviews are other ways the legal department might learn about potential issues that introduce potential risk to the organization, necessitating further examination.

The sections below provide additional descriptions regarding some of the more common ways in which in-house lawyers may be alerted to potential issues.

A. Whistleblowers

The use of internal investigations has become much more widespread and commonplace since the adoption of the Sarbanes-Oxley Act in 2002 (SOX) and the Dodd-Frank Act in 2010 (Dodd-Frank), largely due to additional rules, requirements, and protections afforded by those laws. Rules promulgated under SOX and Dodd-Frank laid the groundwork to more meaningfully incentivize individuals, including employees, former employees, and third parties, to proactively provide information to regulators relating to violations of law, and afforded them related protections. Bounty programs awarding millions of dollars to whistleblowers who provide original information that leads to the successful enforcement by the SEC encourage these individuals to share information that may result in an award worth many times their current earning potential.

Such programs have benefited the SEC and whistleblowers alike, as evidenced by a substantial increase in the number of tips received by regulators, monetary sanctions paid, and awards received by whistleblowers. The SEC's FY 2017 Whistleblower Report[6] identified approximately 4,500 tips received, $975 million in total monetary sanctions paid to the government, and $50 million awarded to whistleblowers in 2017. Similar bounty programs exist at, among others, the Commodity Futures Trading Commission (CFTC), DOJ, Occupational Health and Safety Administration (OSHA), and the Department of Health and Human Services. Given that whistleblowers have

---

6. 2017 Annual Report to Congress: Whistleblower Program, at 2, *available at* https://www.sec.gov/files/sec-2017-annual-report-whistleblower-program.pdf.

proven to be one of the government's strongest weapons in the fight against fraud, in-house lawyers should continue to expect whistleblower activity as a meaningful source of potential issues. Whether the whistleblower has any basis for his or her claim, an internal investigation of appropriate scope and scale should be conducted promptly upon learning of the allegation(s) to ferret out the facts. This type of investigation can be especially sensitive if the whistleblower is still employed, who become emboldened if he or she perceives the corporation is retaliating.

B. Government Inquiry or Investigation

In some instances, in-house lawyers will learn of potential issues from governmental agencies. Such notices may or may not involve information obtained from a whistleblower. The foregoing examples assume that the corporation has not received notice that an outside investigation is already underway. In the unfortunate event that a governmental agency issues an information request before the business initiates an internal investigation, an internal investigation may still be necessary and appropriate. A search warrant, a grand jury subpoena, an administrative audit, an informal inquiry, or another type of agency request often serves as the reason for initiating an internal investigation. As discussed in greater detail below, most agencies will look closely at the business' internal controls, its compliance program, and similar remedial measures to evaluate fines, sentencing, and sanctions. Thus, a defensible and thorough internal investigation may be beneficial.

C. Independent Auditors

Independent auditors sometimes identify issues during an audit to be further researched by the organization. When an auditor raises concerns, an internal investigation may be appropriate depending on the nature and materiality of the potential issue. Congress has enacted comprehensive laws to address financial reporting problems: the Sarbanes-Oxley Act of 2002[7] and the Dodd-Frank Wall Street Reform and Consumer Protection Act of 2010.[8] These kinds of internal investigations can also be very sensitive because they frequently involve members of the C-suite. As discussed below, special committees of the board may be appropriate to avoid criminal or civil liability down the road.

---

7. Pub. L. 107-204, *available at* https://www.gpo.gov/fdsys/pkg/PLAW-107publ204/html/PLAW-107publ204.htm.

8. Pub. L. 111-203, *available at* https://www.gpo.gov/fdsys/pkg/PLAW-111publ203/html/PLAW-111publ203.htm.

III.   INTERNAL INVESTIGATIONS: THE MECHANICS

A.   Is an Internal Investigation Necessary?

The determination of whether to conduct an internal investigation is an important consideration with potentially wide-ranging ramifications. In-house lawyers should dedicate sufficient time and critical thought to this decision, including considerations such as:

- whether the company has some duty to investigate (e.g., federal regulation or statute; material to the financial statements);
- whether regulators are aware of the issue (or whether they likely to become involved) and how they will view the company's decision;
- whether there is reason to believe a significant problem exists;
- whether potential misconduct and violations are attributable to the actions of senior management or whether senior management was aware of such conduct;
- whether the issue is expected to have wide-ranging impact; and
- whether investigating (or not investigating) will send a particular message to employees and other stakeholders.

Additional factors to consider may revolve around potential criminal or civil liability, customer relations, reputational issues, and shareholder concerns. If the corporation trades publicly, a litmus test is often whether the issue may be viewed to have a material effect on the consolidated financial statements. If so, the prospect of an internal investigation becomes more likely. If the concern potentially rises to the level of criminal liability, serious thought must be given to conducting an internal investigation.

Corporations may use an internal investigation as a way to control the facts around an issue, protect attorney-client privilege and work product, set a tone internally and externally, evaluate and preserve potential defenses, or position itself for a more lenient sentence or monetary penalties if criminal conduct is discovered. Additional benefits to conducting an investigation include the limitation of civil claims, deterrence of future misconduct, improved morale and productivity, and demonstration that senior management takes such matters seriously and has fulfilled fiduciary duties of care. Business leaders who use the fact of an internal investigation to implement a strong compliance and remediation program show good corporate citizenship that should make the business stronger in the long run.

As S. Jack Balagia, Jr. and Jason D. Vendel have written in their chapter on the in-house perspective in *Internal Corporate Investigations*:

> Conducting an internal investigation can be time-consuming, intrusive, and expensive, and the in-house lawyer must be prepared to justify it to the client. The client may be skeptical, but with the prospect of disgorgement of ill-gotten gains, criminal fines equal to double those gains . . . , and even debarment from government contracts, the need for companies to conduct thorough and credible internal investigations can hardly be disputed. Well-counseled and sophisticated

clients will accept this, especially if they can recognize the fundamental purposes and consequences of conducting an appropriate investigation.[9]

Despite the foregoing, a full-blown internal investigation is not always necessary. If, upon learning of an issue, the in-house lawyer can quickly determine that the complaint or report lacks merit (for example, a disgruntled employee is overreacting), no further action may be required. In other cases, an issue may appear to be valid and once an investigation is begun, the investigator may learn early on that the problem can be isolated and contained without further probing. Examples include baseless allegations or asset misappropriation schemes, such as theft of company assets, payments to nonapproved vendors, or expense reimbursement fraud, that do not materially impact the company's financial statements. In such cases, isolated procedures applied by company personnel will oftentimes suffice, assuming the company has confidence in its overall internal control and reporting structure.

B. Should Corporate Counsel "Outsource" the Internal Investigation?

Having made the decision to conduct an internal investigation, in-house counsel next face the decision of whether to use internal or external resources to conduct interviews, collect and review documents, report to senior management, communicate with regulators (if applicable), and recommend next steps.

Some considerations relevant to the decision about whether to "outsource" include:

- financial impact of the potential issue
- complexity of the potential issue
- specialized skill set of potential investigators
- how far up the management ladder the issue may go
- whether the legal department has sufficient resources to conduct the investigation quickly (especially where the government may evaluate penalties based on timeliness of response, or where there is potential for repeat misconduct in the near future);
- cost;
- possibly better chance of maintaining privilege;
- likelihood that government will eventually become involved

In-house counsel should keep close tabs on the investigation regardless of whether internal or external resources are used.

---

9. S. Jack Balagia, Jr. & Jason D. Vendel, *An Overview of Internal Investigations from the In-House Perspective, in* INTERNAL CORPORATE INVESTIGATIONS 448 (Brad D. Brian, Barry F. McNeil & Lisa J. Demsky, eds. 4th Ed. 2017).

1. When to Use Internal Resources

If the issue is relatively small and contained, internal personnel, whether from the legal department, human resources, or the business unit, may well be the best way to go. Likewise, if the company appears to be the victim of an employee's crime, at least beginning with internal resources often makes sense. Internal personnel know the business, company policies, and fellow personnel, and they can hit the ground running to resolve an isolated issue quickly. They can also conduct the investigation with less disruption to operations and possibly more discretion because employees do not see outside counsel coming in to the business. If there is a person within the company who has the skill, experience, time, and training to conduct the investigation effectively, impartially, and thoroughly, in-house counsel may wish to proceed without bringing in outsiders. In some cases, the ability of internal resources to maintain attorney-client privilege and work-product protection may be more difficult, but the lower cost of using existing employees may outweigh these concerns.

2. When to Hire Outside Counsel

If the issue is more complex, likely to be of interest to regulators, has a potentially material impact on the financial reporting or disclosure requirement of the company, or carries with it possible criminal exposure, then corporate counsel should seriously consider outsourcing the investigation to a law firm. Many lawyers in private practice who specialize in internal investigations, securities law, and white-collar criminal defense have prior experience within government agencies. That experience assists them in knowing how the government might view certain facts. In addition, outside investigators often have already established a level of credibility with prosecutors or regulators, which enables them to negotiate more effectively on the scope of discovery, the scheduling of deadlines and witness interviews, grand jury appearances, and the scope of document productions. They often may be in a better position to negotiate a better outcome at sentencing as well. Outside counsel may also obtain better fact-finding results from senior management, who do not have a prior relationship with the investigator as the in-house lawyer might. They also may have specialized experience in preparing reports and disclosures.

In-house counsel should often look beyond the corporation's usual lawyers and firms when choosing professionals to lead the investigation. Existing partner law firms may very well be independent and have valuable historical knowledge of the business, but their independence may be questioned; therefore, the risk exists that the company could perform and incur substantial time and costs associated with an investigation only to have the regulator or trier of fact reject the results. In addition, when outside counsel retains financial and/or technology experts, as a practical matter, they stand a better chance of protecting attorney-client privilege and work-product protection. In-house lawyers should be aware that the financial cost to the company of using external resources can be considerable. In cases where substantial fines or criminal liability are possible, however, the cost of not using them can be far greater.

If the government is already aware of the issue, corporate counsel should consider how much involvement the government will require in the process, and what the impact on the attorney-client privilege will be. If the government is already involved, the privilege may be difficult to maintain. The government may also decide to conduct its own investigation by requesting documents and meeting with potential witnesses.

When the government is not yet involved, the ability to preserve attorney-client privilege and work-product protection is one important reason to outsource the investigation. If there is an inkling that the company benefited from an employee's actions, and it appears government or civil suits could follow, using outside counsel, often with other experts, is the best way to protect the privilege. Although attorney-client and work-product privileges apply to in-house counsel, privilege does not apply to facts, only to communications made for the purpose of rendering legal advice. After the fact (and with opposing counsel and a judge in the mix), it can be difficult to separate legal communications from business advice. Privilege also does not apply to communications made to facilitate a crime or fraud.[10]

Another point to keep in mind regarding privilege and work product is that foreign jurisdictions do not necessarily recognize it (either at all or to the same extent as in the United States). Accordingly, where the investigation, the potential wrongdoer, and the company are located are pertinent. For example, many countries, including some in Europe, do not extend the privilege to in-house lawyers. In many countries in Asia, there is no formal recognition of the privilege, but outside counsel may have a better claim to it than in-house counsel. Therefore, it is critical to evaluate the privilege laws of every country where the investigation may lead.

3. Traits of a Good Investigator

Regardless of whether in-house counsel keeps the investigation truly "internal" or enlists the assistance of outside investigators, there are certain traits any investigator should have: neutrality, objectivity, passion, discretion, and of course knowledge regarding applicable aspects of law are key. In addition, the ability to listen and to ask tough questions about uncomfortable subjects are important skills. An effective investigator will know enough about the business, regulatory environment, and legal issues involved to ask the right questions and to follow-up when there are inconsistencies or missing pieces.

4. Bringing Subject Matter Experts into the Investigation

Akin to the importance of using specialized legal resources to lead complex investigations is ensuring the involvement of appropriate subject matter experts. As Barry F. McNeil and Brad D. Brian have written, company resources may be the best place to start:

---

10. *See* United States v. Lentz, 419 F. Supp. 2d 820, 830 (E.D. Va. 2005).

Many internal investigations deal with complex questions that only specialists can address. Auditors, engineers, and specialized technicians can provide invaluable assistance. Because these individuals can be found within the company, their participation will have the added benefit of reducing the cost of the internal investigation.[11]

However, just as with the outsourcing of the investigation to outside counsel, it may make sense to bring in outside subject-matter expertise. This is especially the case when the potential liability is large. Outside experts may have experience and credibility working at, and with, the enforcing government agencies. In addition to benefits associated with the credibility that such experts may have with regulators and other third parties with a vested interest in the investigation (e.g., independent auditors or board members), the experts can be a valuable source of knowledge and best practices related to forming and executing the investigative plan, applying creative and efficient investigative techniques, and considering and assessing remedial actions. Specialized expertise that often proves valuable on complex investigations may include financial, accounting, technology, and data, among others. Identifying and retaining experts at the earliest possible stage of the investigation is critical.

In the recent case of *In re Kellogg Brown & Root, Inc.*,[12] the Court of Appeals for the District of Columbia recently reaffirmed this principle:

> Some of the COBC documents in this case involve communications from an investigator, acting at the direction of in-house counsel, to an attorney who is in-house counsel. In such a circumstance, the investigator effectively steps into the shoes of the attorney. . . . *Linde Thomson Langworthy Kohn & Van Dyke, P.C. v. Resolution Trust Corp.*, 5 F.3d 1508, 1514 (D.C. Cir. 1993) ("The attorney-client privilege undeniably extends to communications with one employed to assist the lawyer in the rendition of professional legal services.") (internal quotation marks omitted); *see also United States v. Kovel*, 296 F.2d 918, 921 (2d Cir.1961) (holding that the attorney-client privilege covers communications from a client to an attorney's non-lawyer employee) . . . .

5.   A Note about Special Committees

In larger corporations, an issue may be so important to the finances, operation, or management of the business that it warrants the appointment of a special committee of the board of directors. Note that the board appoints the special committee, not management. Significant accounting or public reporting issues, government investigations into antitrust violations, whistleblower or other allegations involving senior management, and the like may require that the officers and directors separate themselves from the investigation to

---

11.   Barry F. McNeil & Brad D. Brian, *Overview: Initiating an Internal Investigation and Assembling the Investigative Team, in* INTERNAL CORPORATE INVESTIGATIONS, *supra* note 9, at 17.

12.   796 F.3d 137, 149 (D.C. Cir. 2015).

maintain independence. In such circumstances, the general guidelines discussed here apply, with several additional considerations.

In-house counsel must be vigilant in avoiding conflicts of interest. As noted above, corporate counsel may want to bring in an outside counsel to represent the committee who is not the company's usual counsel to bring a new and wholly independent point of view into the equation. Working with outside counsel, corporate counsel should articulate the mandate and authority of the special committee. The special committee, among other things, must be able to engage specialists to advise the committee, analyze the facts, and assist with presentations to the board. Care should be taken in preparation of any minutes of meetings of the special committee, and it should be assumed that such minutes will not be privileged. The result of the investigation is typically a report to the board of directors (either written or oral) and then a determination as to what, if any, next steps must be taken.

C. Conducting the Investigation

After making the decision to conduct an internal investigation, in-house counsel should immediately take steps to lay the groundwork for a defensible process. This begins with the selection of qualified resources to serve on the investigative team and establishing privileges. Considerations should include whether to use outside counsel and supporting subject matter experts, as described previously in this chapter. The reporting lines for the investigative team should be made clear, whether to in-house counsel for the organization, select members of management, or a board committee. This important determination will have implications on the scope, timing, and perceived independence and credibility of the investigation. In-house counsel should also notify the senior management team, unless the investigation involves a member of it, and identify whether there is insurance coverage relating to the issue, and whether notice to the carrier is appropriate. If there is a chance of press coverage, general counsel should notify corporate press relations to prevent surprises. As soon as these foundational decisions have been made, the investigative team can begin to plan for and protect the integrity and credibility of investigative procedures and results.

1. Formulating the Plan

In-house counsel should schedule an introductory meeting or call with the lead investigator or investigative team to discuss generally the issue under investigation, the key players, the timing, any known important documents, and the objectives of the investigation. To afford better certainty about the privileged nature of the investigation, the client should send the investigator a written request "clearly stat[ing] the client's desire for an investigation for purposes of receiving legal advice and that the attorney and investigative team should keep confidential any findings or other information related to the investigation."[13]

---

13. Balagia & Vendel, *supra* note 9, at 453.

The legal department and outside counsel should work together to develop a written plan for the investigation. The plan should set forth the goals and scope of the investigation and a timeline to execute. Like board minutes, the plan need not detail every last issue or identify strategic considerations, but should be a road map to confirm everyone is on the same page, outline responsibilities and lines of reporting, and prevent misunderstandings. The plan might include a list of potential witnesses, a schedule of interviews, and identification of documents and data to be collected and reviewed.

The plan should be a "living document" and flexible in the sense that if new questions are raised during the document review and witness interview process, the contemplated procedures can be adapted to expand the scope. Depending on the nature of the investigation, the general counsel may want to issue a memorandum to all or some employees that the investigation is happening to minimize uninformed speculation and prevent surprise in the event of press coverage. Consideration may also be warranted to determine whether certain valuable customers or vendors should be alerted.

If the issue requires retention of nonlawyer outside experts, the outside law firm typically engages those experts because it is the best way to preserve privilege and work-product protection. The engagement agreement, which should be in writing, should specify that the outside expert is being retained to consult with the attorney providing legal advice, that the expert is being directed by the attorney, and that the work is being performed in anticipation of legal and/or regulatory proceedings. If there is no outside law firm, in-house counsel should use an engagement letter that establishes a prima facie case for privilege. Language that the legal department is hiring the expert for the primary or predominant purpose of consulting on anticipated litigation is helpful. In all events, outside experts should be cautioned not to create written materials without consulting with counsel, and that all such writings should bear a notation that they were prepared at the direction of counsel.

If the internal investigation is conducted in parallel to a government investigation, either civil or criminal, the decision of how much to communicate and share with the government and whether to self-disclose are important considerations that should be revisited throughout the investigation.

2. Document Collection and Review

In-house counsel should identify and preserve all potential sources of relevant information as early as possible. Doing this discreetly can be a challenge, but the cost of not doing so and risking spoliation of evidence is high.

Litigation hold notices should be issued to employees with potentially relevant information. The hold notice should give some description of the types of documents (electronic, hard copy, texts, voice mails, and social media) to be preserved. The hold notice may also instruct employees to search hard copy files and e-mail folders for relevant documents. Consideration should also be given to ceasing standard document destruction policies until the issue is behind the company to ensure potentially relevant information is not accidentally destroyed by the organization in the normal course of business. If there is accounting or bookkeeping software that is often dynamic, the legal department likely must involve specialized collection techniques. It is also often advisable to forensically image computer hard drives, phones, and other devices and maintain a clear chain of custody to avoid possible litigation challenges down the road.

A separate plan and checklist for collection of documents is helpful when information is located in many places and when there are numerous custodians. General categories of documents are often relevant, such as policies, personnel files, and information from prior investigations concerning similar subject matters. For larger, more complex investigations involving potential financial reporting and disclosure, management reports, internal audit reports, and board committee minutes are often valuable. Outside vendors can assist with maintaining chain of custody for documents to ensure they have not been tampered with, providing support for document review platforms, and applying technology-assisted review to the document population to identify clusters of key words, de-duplicate, and pre-tag potentially privileged documents. The investigative team should be aware of, and comply with, any cross-border data privacy rules, such as the European Union's General Data Protection Regulation (GDPR).[14]

The document review process can range from simple to complex, depending principally on volume, the complexity of the issue under investigation, and the presence of foreign-language documents. Sometimes the universe of documents is small enough that one or two lawyers can handle the review. More often, however, a team of reviewers (whether within the outside law firm or outsourced to a vendor) must review the documents. The best practice for such reviews is to create a protocol document that gives the review team an overview of the subject matter, guidance on what may be privileged, and issue or topic tags to use for coding documents. Selecting the most appropriate review platform and technology can also meaningfully increase the efficiency, throughput, and cost effectiveness of a review.

An electronic database is useful because it is searchable in many ways (by key word, by custodian, by date, etc.). Depending on time constraints, the investigator should be able to use documents to assist in the interviewing process. Even if things are moving quickly, searches and analytics may allow the investigator to identify some key documents before conducting interviews.

3. Interviewing Witnesses

It is difficult to overstate the importance of witness interviews to the internal investigation process. The interviews constitute the investigators' best chance to determine the severity of the problem, the credibility of the parties, and whether the issue under investigation is limited in scope or pervades the corporate culture. The investigation team should work with the legal department to develop an order for interviews, ensuring that the witnesses make adequate time in their schedule so that interviews are not rushed or cut off before completion to ensure all available information is properly gathered. Optimally, interviews will take place in person, rather than by videoconference or phone. In-person interviews permit the investigator to assess body language, nervousness, and credibility.

---

14. General Data Protection Regulation, *available at* https://eur-lex.europa.eu/legal-content/EN/TXT/?uri=CELEX%3A32016R0679.

The investigator should also be mindful of his or her own body language because it may impact the witness' comfort level in being forthcoming with information.

If time permits, counsel should develop a script or outline of interview questions aligned to applicable documents. If government entities are involved investigating potential violations of law, counsel may want to research public records to determine what the government has focused on in investigations involving similar fact patterns. Governmental agencies issue press releases after an administrative or cease and desist order, conviction, or agreed-upon settlement that identifies the facts that led to the order, conviction, or resolution, including any mitigating facts.

Counsel should *always* begin the interview by giving clear "*Upjohn*" warnings. These warnings are required to protect the organization's attorney-client privilege. Under Model Rule of Professional Conduct 1.13, Organization as Client, "[a] lawyer employed or retained by an organization represents the organization acting through its duly authorized constituents." According to the Supreme Court case of *Upjohn v. United States*[15] and its progeny, an organization can claim privilege as to communication by its duly authorized constituents to counsel, but only if counsel makes clear to that constituent that counsel represents the organization at the outset of the communication. As Balagia and Vendel have written:

> [T]he employee should be informed about some of the implications of the attorney's corporate representation:
> - That although the conversation is privileged, the privilege belongs to the corporation, not the employee
> - That it is the corporation's prerogative whether to waive the privilege, not the employee's
> - That the corporation can decide to waive the privilege and divulge the substance of the interview to anyone it chooses, including government enforcement authorities[16]

In addition to the *Upjohn* warnings, the interviewer should explain the process and notify the witness that he or she can retain his or her own counsel and that the topics discussed in the interview should remain confidential. The attorney should also remind the employee to be truthful, and that the consequences of not being truthful may result in disciplinary action from the employer as well as individual civil and/or criminal liability.

Although the attorney should not be wedded to the interview outline or script for the interview, having one ensures that all the key topics are covered with each witness. Avoid "legalese" and use plain language. Begin with open-ended questions and then circle in on more detailed questions. Documents should come after the open-ended questions, and the toughest questions should be reserved for the end. As the interviews progress, counsel should update the script or outline to reflect new findings.

---

15. 449 U.S. 383 (1981).
16. Balagia & Vendel, *supra* note 9, at 456.

If a witness is not cooperative, work to keep the witness in the room and try to develop a rapport. Remind the witness that he or she is required by the employer to participate. If the employer has a policy on cooperation in internal investigations, which some employers do, it is helpful to have a copy handy. However, the investigator may ultimately have to end the interview. Documenting what happened in such instances is important.

The interview location may vary depending on the nature of the investigation. Although employees' schedules are disrupted the least by conducting interviews at a corporate location, discretion may dictate that interviews take place at the law firm. Off-site interviews may make the witness less distracted as well. In some cases, witnesses know who the other witnesses are and having simultaneous or overlapping interviews makes sense. In other cases, the risk of one witness influencing another is too great, and witnesses should not know about other witnesses' interviews.

If budgets permit, having two interviewers in the room is encouraged and valuable. One can take notes and observe nonverbal cues while the other listens. This also permits corroboration of witness statements and shorter breaks between interviews. If having two investigators is not viable, the investigator should schedule the interviews so that he or she has time between them to digest information, note key statements, reassess the situation, adjust interview outlines, and locate documents.

The interview notes should reflect who is in the room during the interview, that *Upjohn* instructions were given, and the start and end times. If it is important to get an exact quotation from a witness, take the time to get it right. The investigator can explain to the witness that the notes will be kept confidential and disclosed under only limited circumstances. If the investigator has impressions of the witness' credibility or demeanor, it may make sense to keep those notes separate from the "factual" summary. Some practitioners prefer one integrated interview summary with a disclaimer at the beginning that it is not a verbatim report, but rather a summary of factual information provided by the witness with the interviewer's observations and impressions.

Sometimes during the course of an investigation, and rarely during the course of a single interview, it becomes clear that the witness and the corporation have such divergent interests that the investigator should remind the witness that he or she represents the corporation and recommend that the witness retain separate counsel.[17] When this happens, the investigator must draw on his or her experience, judgment, and common sense to decide how to proceed.

In cases where an investigation crosses international borders, there are several practices to keep in mind. First, hiring local counsel can be invaluable. They can provide translation services, assist U.S. counsel in understanding local culture, and highlight any local laws that differ from U.S law and that will impact the interview process and potentially the investigation.

---

17. MODEL RULES OF PROF'L CONDUCT R. 1.13(f), cmt. 10; MODEL RULES OF PROF'L CONDUCT R. 4.3.

4. Keeping Stakeholders Updated

As the investigation proceeds, in-house counsel and appropriate members of the investigative team should regularly provide updates to the board and other interested parties (possibly the government, auditors, and securities counsel). The investigation should be comprehensive and credible, but should not drag out indefinitely. Not only does it become more expensive as it drags out, the government and other stakeholders may conclude that the business did not sufficiently prioritize the investigation and potential corrective and remedial actions. At the penalty stage, the government considers such issues.

5. Reporting the Findings

When the investigation concludes, the next step is typically the preparation of an investigative report and an investigative file. In a small or especially sensitive situation, an oral report may be appropriate. The report should include a summary and/or timeline of the situation, including allegations that have been either corroborated or disproven, credibility assessments, an analysis of relevant legal issues, and identification of root cause and corrective actions taken. The written report will also often include an executive summary and a description of the investigative process.

In many instances, the report will summarize existing compliance efforts and recommend additional remedial action, such as additional training for certain employees, hiring additional or better qualified resources, disciplinary action, policy revisions, better controls, adopting a code of conduct, or creating a reporting system. The investigative report need not go into extensive detail on any of these items, but the recommendations should be tailored to the issues identified during the investigative process. To the extent the investigation has uncovered additional areas of concern, those areas may be addressed here, but can also be addressed separately. If outside experts have been retained to assist in the investigation, their input will be helpful to incorporate into the report.

As with the preparation of expert reports in litigation, the author of the report may want to use care in creating multiple versions of the report. As discussed below, in many cases the report may at some point become part of the government's record or discoverable in parallel or derivative litigation; as such, the report should be worded with care and attention to detail.

Once the report is prepared, the next step is to present it internally as appropriate. The board of directors will often be the audience for the report when it concerns misconduct by high-level employees. If the misconduct occurred at a lower level of the company's structure, the audience may be executives. The confidentiality of the report should be emphasized to anyone receiving it, both for preservation of morale and protection of privilege.

IV. SELF-DISCLOSURE OF INVESTIGATIVE FINDINGS

Assuming the government is not already aware of the subject matter of the internal investigation, the next step is to determine whether to disclose the issue. The government, including the DOJ and SEC, rewards self-disclosure in assessing fines, penalties, and sentencing recommendations.[18] The advantages of self-disclosure are so strong in terms of charging decisions that self-disclosure should be seriously considered if criminal liability in a possibility. When the government evaluates what sanction to impose on the corporation and/or any employees, it looks closely at how cooperative the corporation was and how effective its remedial plan is. For criminal cases, a company generally faces potential criminal liability for the criminal conduct of its employees whenever the employees' acts are for the company's benefit. If the corporation's response to an employee's criminal conduct is a rapid and thorough investigation followed by a comprehensive corrective plan (and often the willingness to pay a large fine), the company may even be able to obtain a deferred prosecution agreement (DPA) or, even better, a nonprosecution agreement (NPA). As the use of DPAs and NPAs became more prevalent, the DOJ announced various guidance documents to assist corporate counsel in evaluating what to do after learning of employees' criminal conduct. A 1999 Memorandum, "Bringing Criminal Charges Against Corporations,"[19] which is referred to as the Holder Memorandum after then-Deputy Attorney General Eric Holder, set forth the following factors for corporate prosecution:

- the gravity and kind of offense involved
- how pervasive the wrongdoing in the company
- whether the company had a history of similar conduct
- the company's voluntary, timely, and thorough disclosure (including waiver of attorney-client privilege)
- the existence and efficacy of a compliance program
- remedial measures
- the collateral consequences of enforcement activity (e.g., disproportionate harm to nonculpable persons such as other employees and shareholders)

Over the years, the message of the Holder Memorandum has been refined multiple times to incentivize cooperation, remediation, and to the dismay of many, the waiver of the attorney-client privilege.

In 2015, then Deputy Attorney General Sally Quillian Yates announced the "Individual Accountability for Corporate Wrongdoing"[20] initiative, which guided corporations to focus their internal investigations on individuals, to make comprehensive disclosures about their investigation into individuals, and to encourage civil attorneys to focus on individuals in their litigation. More recently, Deputy Attorney General Rod Rosenstein announced in May 2018 that the DOJ had established a Working Group on Corporate Enforcement and Accountability and that, although he would not issue

---

18. U.S. Department of Justice, Offices of the U.S. Attorneys, U.S. Attorneys' Manual § 9-28.300(A)(6), § 9-28.700, § 9-28.800, § 9-28-900.

19. Memorandum from Deputy Attorney General Eric Holder, Jr., Bringing Criminal Charges Against Corporations (June 16, 1999).

20. Memorandum from Deputy Attorney General Sally Quillian Yates, Individual Accountability for Corporate Wrongdoing (Sept. 9, 2015).

a "Rosenstein Memo," the U.S. Attorneys' Manual would now include guidance on evaluating corporate criminal wrongdoing.[21] Among other things, the new policy announced by Rosenstein still rewards disclosure, cooperation, and remediation, but is intended to foster cooperation and nonduplication across government agencies such as the SEC, CFTC, Federal Reserve, FDIC, OCC, and OFAC as well as with international law enforcement authorities.

Given the various guidance from the DOJ and SEC, in-house counsel must evaluate at what point self-disclosure to the government may be appropriate. The decision should be made in consultation with senior management and outside counsel. It will depend on the nature of the findings, whether the business has a sound plan for remediation, and how the regulatory agency looks at self-disclosures and in particular the role of timing (this may differ from agency to agency and from federal to state or local).

The most significant consideration, however, is the risk that the regulators will find out from a whistleblower, a competitor, or a business partner. As noted previously, the incentives for whistleblowers are strong. With respect to business partners, "knowledge of a company's activities may stem from its partners' own participation in the alleged wrongdoing."[22] With respect to competitors, they "may have dealt with some of the same questionable counterparties or may have been solicited to participate in the same corrupt scheme."[23] In addition, both domestic and international regulatory agencies increasingly cooperate with each other in investigating corporate wrongdoing.[24]

If self-disclosure is appropriate, the first step is generally a conversation (often in person) between the regulating agency and outside counsel. If self-disclosure to the government is in your company's future, and outside counsel has not already been retained, now is the time. There are many practitioners who specialize in these kinds of discussions, have relationships with regulators, and can advise on the content and timing of self-disclosures. The Foreign Corrupt Practices Act is one of many areas where the government has considered self-disclosures in the assessment of fines and penalties.

For publicly traded companies, federal securities laws also impose obligations to disclose certain information in documents filed with the SEC. Outside expertise is likely needed to determine when and what to disclose. Even if no binding authority requires disclosure, consider whether the investigation and the facts underlying the investigation represent "material information" that a reasonable investor would consider important to making an investment decision. If not disclosed and later determined to be material, the information could expose the company to civil liability.

Once the decision to disclose is made, the company should cooperate fully with the government and offer to provide periodic updates. A key question is whether to waive the attorney-client privilege. As explained above, the DOJ's position on the role

---

21. Deputy Attorney General Rod J. Rosenstein, Remarks at the American Conference Institute's 20th Anniversary New York Conference on the Foreign Corrupt Practices Act (May 9, 2018), *available at* https://www.justice.gov/opa/speech/deputy-attorney-general-rod-j-rosenstein-delivers-remarks-american-conference-institutes.

22. Balagia & Vendel, *supra* note 9, at 462.

23. Balagia & Vendel, *supra* note 9, at 462.

24. Balagia & Vendel, *supra* note 9, at 462-63.

waiver plays in assessing penalties have swung a bit over time. Although DOJ and SEC attorneys are not authorized to demand a waiver, they will want a fulsome report of what the internal investigation uncovered. The risk of waiver will depend, in large part, on whether civil litigation is anticipated. Most courts that have evaluated the question have determined that corporations cannot waive the privilege relative to government criminal or civil proceedings and then withhold the same information in shareholder or antitrust class-action litigation.

In some instances, the company should consider identifying additional relevant misconduct uncovered during investigation if doing so will avoid closer scrutiny at a later date. These are judgment calls that require input from the business and from the lawyers. In some instances, disclosure to customers or vendors may also be either required or be appropriate. Again, it makes sense at this point to bring in specialized expertise to assist in sending the right message at the right time to avoid liability and financial and reputational harm.

V. CONCLUSION

Internal investigations are commonplace in the corporate world and have increasingly become an important aspect of the work of many legal departments. Although the subject matter of these investigations may vary, the considerations and processes to conduct them are more static. The outcomes can be meaningful and far-reaching, potentially impacting the reputation and financial well being of the company and its employees. The stakes are even higher where criminal liability might be involved. Creating a defensible process and being thorough in the accumulation of evidence, in the review of documents, and in the interviewing of witnesses will greatly assist the company in dealing with government authorities, consumers, vendors, and employees, and concluding the issues at the core of the investigation.

Whether they work with outside counsel or manage the process internally, in-house counsel is vital to the success of any internal investigation. At all times, however, in-house lawyers must remain aware of, and act in accordance with, their ethical obligations as lawyers, as well as in their "crucial gatekeep[ing]"[25] role with respect to corporate compliance. Recent cautionary tales of lawyers who stepped over the line and participated in their clients' fraud, obstruction of justice, or other crimes are fortunately still the exception. The suggestions discussed herein will assist the in-house lawyer in developing a sound understanding of when to initiate, and how to conduct, an internal investigation where there may be noncompliant employee behavior, company assets not fully under control, or disagreements regarding reported figures.

---

25. Christopher Cox, U.S. Securities and Exchange Commission, Address to the 2007 Corporate Counsel Institute (Mar. 8, 2007), *available at* https://www.sec.gov/news/speech/2007/spch030807cc.htm.

Chapter 3

Conducting a Sexual Harassment Investigation: A Practical Guide

By Katherine A. Lemire and Amy R. Foote

The goal of this chapter is to provide an overview to in-house counsel of the various laws and factual identifiers surrounding one of the nation's hot-button issues currently: sexual harassment. The "Me Too" movement has raised in the public's consciousness. This chapter hopes to do the same so that counsel is prepared to handle concerns in this area.

I.   INTRODUCTION

The issue of sexual harassment in the workplace is at the forefront of the nation's collective conversation. This watershed moment is prompting leaders of many organizations—corporate, nonprofit, and governmental—to evaluate and improve workplace standards and culture.

According to a report prepared by the Equal Employment Opportunity Commission (EEOC) Select Task Force on the Study of Harassment in the Workplace,[1] workplace harassment—whether based on sex, race, disability, age, ethnicity, national origin, color, or religion—"remains a persistent problem." Furthermore, workplace harassment,

---

1.   Equal Emp't Opportunity Comm'n, Report of the Co-Chairs of the Select Task Force on the Study of Harassment in the Workplace (2016), https://www.eeoc.gov/eeoc/task_force/harassment/upload/report.pdf.

particularly sexual harassment, often goes unreported, and therefore is not addressed. As a consequence, many organizations may have serious undisclosed sexual harassment problems.

If media coverage, ranging from CNN to the *Wall Street Journal* and other #MeToo-inspired reporting, represents an accurate bellwether, the likelihood your organization will encounter claims of workplace sexual harassment is growing.

The better prepared you are, the safer your organization and employees. A basic grasp of the federal rules governing sexual harassment is essential. Understanding the applicable laws specific to your local jurisdiction (state and municipal) is also a must. This is particularly true for those jurisdictions, such as New York State and New York City, with more stringent rules than those provided in the federal framework. Knowing your company's policies regarding sexual harassment is also necessary.

This chapter will outline applicable law governing workplace sexual harassment, provide tangible steps to protect your company and its employees in the event of a workplace sexual harassment allegation, and provide suggestions for proactively preventing sexual harassment in the workplace.

II.   APPLICABLE LAW

Although the dominance of sexual harassment cases in the headlines is new, the applicable laws are not. Numerous layers of federal, state, and local laws provide employees the right to be free from sexual discrimination and harassment.

Title VII of the Civil Rights Act of 1964 prohibits workplace discrimination on the basis of race, color, national origin, religion, and sex.[2] Specifically, Title VII makes it "an unlawful employment practice for an employer . . . to discriminate against any individual with respect to his [or her] compensation, terms, conditions, or privileges of employment, because of such individual's race, color, religion, sex, or national origin."[3] Title VII applies to employers with 15 or more employees, including federal, state, and local governments.[4] The Supreme Court has held that the prohibition against sex discrimination reaches sexual harassment in the workplace,[5] including same-sex workplace harassment.[6]

The EEOC defines sexual harassment as "[u]nwelcome sexual advances, requests for sexual favors, and other verbal or physical conduct of a sexual nature when (1) submission to such conduct is made either explicitly or implicitly a term or condition of an individual's employment, (2) submission to or rejection of such conduct by an individual is used as the basis for employment decisions affecting such individual, or (3) such

---

2.   42 U.S.C. § 2000e *et seq.*

3.   *Id.* § 2000e-2(a)(1).

4.   *Id.* § 2000e(b).

5.   Meritor Sav. Bank, FSB v. Vinson, 477 U.S. 57, 64 (1986).

6.   Oncale v. Sundowner Offshore Servs., Inc., 523 U.S. 75, 79 (1998).

conduct has the purpose or effect of unreasonably interfering with an individual's work performance or creating an intimidating, hostile, or offensive working environment."[7]

Almost every state has enacted state-specific sexual harassment statutes that, in many cases, follow federal law. In some cases, however, both state and municipal laws may provide expanded protection to employees. In New York State, for example, every employee is entitled to a working environment free from sexual harassment pursuant to the New York Human Rights Law, regardless of the size of the employer.[8] New York State and New York City laws provide for broader damages than federal law; specifically, they provide for unlimited compensatory damages,[9] and New York City allows for punitive damages.[10]

It is important to note that the EEOC and the United States Courts of Appeals for the Second and Seventh Circuits recently have held that discrimination on the basis of sexual orientation is a form of sex discrimination, reversing previous holdings that sexual orientation discrimination is not a form of sex discrimination.[11] The Supreme Court has not yet addressed the issue.

The EEOC and federal courts recognize two forms of sexual harassment under Title VII: *quid pro quo* and hostile work environment. These terms do not appear in the text of Title VII; however, the EEOC and federal courts have interpreted Title VII to include harassing behavior that has a tangible impact on employment (*quid pro quo*) and an intangible impact (hostile work environment).[12] The terms "*quid pro quo*" and "hostile work environment" illustrate the distinction between cases involving a threat that is carried out and offensive conduct in general.[13] For offensive conduct in general to be actionable, it must be severe or pervasive.[14]

A. *Quid Pro Quo* Harassment

Quid pro quo harassment occurs when the "submission to or rejection of [unwelcome sexual] conduct by an individual is used as the basis for employment decisions affecting such individual . . . "[15] When a plaintiff proves that a tangible employment action resulted from a refusal to submit to a supervisor's sexual demands, he or she establishes that the employment decision itself constitutes a change in the terms and conditions of employment and is actionable under Title VII.[16] A tangible employment action is a significant change in employment status, such as hiring, firing, failing to

---

7. 29 C.F.R. § 1604.11(a) (2018).
8. NYCLS Exec. § 292(5) (2018).
9. *Id.* § 296 (2018); NYC Admin. Code 8-101 *et seq.* (2018).
10. N.Y.C. Admin. Code 8-502 (a) (2018).
11. Zarda v. Altitude Express, Inc., 2018 U.S. App. LEXIS 4608 (2d Cir. Feb. 26, 2018); Hively v. Ivy Tech Cmty. College of Ind., 853 F.3d 339, 339 (7th Cir. 2017); Baldwin v. Foxx, 2015 EEOPUB LEXIS 1905, 116 FEOR (LRP) 2, EEOC (IHS) 120133080 (E.E.O.C. July 16, 2015).
12. Meritor Sav. Bank, FSB v. Vinson, 477 U.S. 57, 64-66 (1986); 29 C.F.R. § 1604.11(a)(3) (2018).
13. Burlington Indus. v. Ellerth, 524 U.S. 742, 753 (1998).
14. *Ellerth*, 524 U.S. at 753-54.
15. 29 C.F.R. § 1604.11(a) (2018); *see also Ellerth*, 524 U.S. at 751.
16. *Ellerth*, 524 U.S. at 753-54.

promote, reassignment with significantly different responsibilities, or a decision causing a significant change in benefits.[17] A tangible employment action is "the means by which the supervisor brings the official power of the enterprise to bear on subordinates" and requires an official act of the enterprise.[18]

B. Hostile Work Environment

A plaintiff may establish a violation of Title VII without showing an economic effect on the plaintiff's employment by proving that discrimination based on sex has created a hostile or abusive work environment.[19] For sexual harassment to be actionable under a hostile work environment claim, the harassment "must be sufficiently severe or pervasive 'to alter the conditions of [the complainant's] employment and create an abusive working environment.'"[20]

A hostile work environment exists when unwelcome sexual conduct "unreasonably interfer[es] with an individual's job performance" or creates an "intimidating, hostile, or offensive working environment."[21] For a hostile work environment claim, conduct does not need to result in a tangible employment action (such as discharge, demotion, or an undesirable reassignment); however, that conduct must be so "severe or pervasive" that it creates an abusive working environment.[22]

Off-color jokes, sexually suggestive compliments about bodies or apparel, unwelcome and insistent invitations, vulgar language, overly familiar touching, standing inappropriately close, and conversations about or innuendoes to sex acts or sexuality qualify as forms of harassment. They can be conveyed verbally and via text message, e-mail, photographs, and social media posts. When such actions are common in a workplace, they can form a hostile work environment.

C. Defining Sexual Harassment

The EEOC's *Policy Guidance on Current Issues of Sexual Harassment* provides extensive guidance on defining sexual harassment, including the following sections quoted below:[23]

Determining Whether Sexual Conduct Is Unwelcome

Because sexual attraction may often play a role in the day-to-day social exchange between employees, "the distinction between invited, uninvited-but-welcome, offensive-but-tolerated, and flatly rejected"[24] sexual advances may well be

---

17. *Id.* at 761.
18. *Id.* at 762.
19. *Meritor*, 477 U.S. at 66.
20. *Id.* at 67 (citing Henson v. Dundee, 682 F.2d 897, 904 (11th Cir. 1982)).
21. 29 C.F.R. § 1604.11(a) (2018); *see also Meritor*, 477 U.S. at 66-67.
22. *Ellerth*, 524 U.S. at 754.
23. EEOC Notice N-915-050, Policy Guidance on Current Issues of Sexual Harassment (Mar. 1990).
24. *Id.* (citing Barnes v. Costle, 561 F.2d 983, 999 (D.C. Cir. 1977) (MacKinnon J., concurring)).

difficult to discern. But this distinction is essential because sexual conduct becomes unlawful only when it is unwelcome. . . . When confronted with conflicting evidence as to welcomeness, the Commission looks "at the record as a whole and at the totality of circumstances . . . ," 29 C.F.R. § 1604.11(b), evaluating each situation on a case-by-case basis. When there is some indication of welcomeness or when the credibility of the parties is at issue, the charging party's claim will be considerably strengthened if she made a contemporaneous complaint or protest. . . . When welcomeness is at issue, the investigation should determine whether the victim's conduct is consistent, or inconsistent, with her assertion that the sexual conduct is unwelcome.

Determining Whether a Work Environment Is "Hostile"

In determining whether harassment is sufficiently severe or pervasive to create a hostile environment, the harasser's conduct should be evaluated from the objective standpoint of a "reasonable person."

. . .

Unless the conduct is quite severe, a single incident or isolated incidents of offensive sexual conduct or remarks generally do not create an abusive environment.

. . .

When the alleged harassment consists of verbal conduct, the investigation should ascertain the nature, frequency, context, and intended target of the remarks. Questions to be explored might include:

- Did the alleged harasser single out the charging party?

- Did the charging party participate?

- What was the relationship between the charging party and the alleged harasser(s)?

- Were the remarks hostile and derogatory?

D. Employer Liability

An employer will be held vicariously liable under Title VII for *quid pro quo* sexual harassment committed by a supervisor, and there is no defense available to employers.[25] Further, "[a]n employer is subject to vicarious liability to a victimized employee for an actionable hostile environment created by a supervisor with immediate (or successively

---

25. *Ellerth*, 524 U.S. at 760-61.

higher) authority over the employee."[26] However, if no tangible employment action is taken, a defending employer may raise an affirmative defense to liability or damages, subject to proof by a preponderance of the evidence.[27] The affirmative defense is comprised of two necessary elements: (1) reasonable care by the employer to prevent and promptly correct any sexually harassing behavior, and (2) unreasonable failure by the harassed employee to take advantage of any preventative or corrective opportunities provided by the employer or otherwise avoid the harassment.[28] No affirmative defense is available when the supervisor's harassment culminates in a tangible employment action, such as discharge, demotion, or undesirable reassignment.[29] Further, no affirmative defense is available if the harassing employee holds a high rank in the company, which makes him or her the employer's "alter ego."[30]

Sexual harassment allegations can serve to expose multiple layers of culpability within an organization. Although an allegation and investigation may focus on one perpetrator, in court the accused's behavior may be portrayed as an extension of the company's culture. Executive leadership and high-level managers may be portrayed as having tacitly allowed harassing behavior from not only employees, but also clients and outside consultants and vendors. In such instances, high-level management and the company itself may have exposure to liability.

Laws may vary among jurisdictions. Regardless of the locale, however, it is imperative to take essential certain steps when investigating sexual harassment allegations. Decisions made at the beginning of a sexual harassment investigation—whether considerate or careless, systematic or sloppy—can serve to enhance or diminish the potential of a swift and successful resolution, perhaps even avoiding litigation. Poor decisions may pave the way for a costly and drawn-out legal saga resulting in unwanted headlines, alienated clients, public protests, and a social media crisis, significantly impacting your company's reputation. Knowing the applicable laws, adhering to internal rules and regulations, and following the tips below will help you avoid a bungled investigation or litigation.

Under federal law (and most state laws), an employer has a duty to take all reasonable steps to prevent sexual harassment from occurring.[31] Reasonable steps may include:

- adopting and disseminating an anti-harassment policy;
- establishing an employee-friendly reporting procedure (and providing a reporting channel separate from chain-of-command);
- monitoring employee behavior;
- conducting periodic training;
- treating all reports of harassment in a serious manner;
- conducting prompt, thorough, and impartial investigations;

---

26. *Id.* at 765.
27. *Id.*; Faragher v. City of Boca Raton, 524 U.S. 775, 807 (1998).
28. *Ellerth*, 524 U.S. at 765; *Faragher*, 524 U.S. at 808.
29. *Ellerth*, 524 U.S. at 765.
30. *Id.* at 758.
31. 29 C.F.R. § 1604.11(f) (2018).

- taking appropriate remedial action based on the findings of the investigations; and
- protecting employees from retaliation.

III. ESSENTIAL STEPS FOR CONDUCTING WORKPLACE SEXUAL HARASSMENT INVESTIGATIONS

Successful internal investigations will help identify and stop unwanted behavior, and will serve to maintain legal compliance with federal and local employment laws. A solid investigation will also lay the groundwork for a defense to harassment claims and related damages, especially if conducted in conjunction with a reliable channel for reporting. Effective investigations will also help defend against civil litigation and can ward off government enforcement actions. Well-run internal investigations can also serve to protect your company's reputation and enhance employee morale, recruitment, and retention.

The law requires a prompt, thorough, and impartial investigation.[32] The longer an organization or its leaders or managers have known about a harassment claim without taking action, the increased exposure down the road if litigation commences. Consider carefully any decision to conduct your investigation internally. There may be many potential conflicts of which you are unaware when initiating the investigation. An internal investigation may seem cost-efficient, but you could pay significantly for that decision in the long-run. Consider carefully whether there are potential conflicts of interest raised by the party conducting the investigation. For example, engaging the attorney who drafts your employee contracts may pose a conflict of interest. A wiser choice might be to engage someone with no history of interfacing with your employees.

Successfully investigating alleged harassment within your organization can be thorny in itself, but a sensitive situation can be compounded by otherwise easily avoided mistakes. Implementing these important steps will allow you to act quickly, avoid critical mistakes, and reach the best possible resolution.

A. Take Control Quickly

Hear a rumor? Don't wait. Act immediately. If you are in-house counsel and an allegation surfaces, take action quickly. Even a mere rumor places the onus on the employer to act on the allegation and conduct an investigation. On the other hand, stalling in response to complaints and failing to initiate an investigation could expose your organization to liability. Being proactive not only helps satisfy your legal obligations, it also sends a signal that you take harassment allegations seriously. Employee morale could suffer if employees learn about allegations and believe the employer is nonresponsive or has ignored a long-term situation despite repeated complaints.

---

32. EEOC Notice 915.002, Enforcement Guidance on Vicarious Employer Liability for Unlawful Harassment by Supervisors (June 18, 1999).

There is no requirement that a "formal" complaint must be made or that a complaint must be in writing. There is also no requirement that an employee must complain through the chain-of-command or that a complainant identify herself or himself.

Do not dismiss an allegation simply because it originates from a single source. Likewise, do not underestimate the potential veracity of a rumor. Create a record about what you heard and what you did to address the allegations as soon as possible.

B. Maintain Confidentiality

There are multiple reasons for limiting the number of people who know about allegations and the investigation. First, the subject of the allegation can suffer a tarnished reputation if it turns out he or she is exonerated. Confidentiality also reduces the likelihood of future litigation by the falsely accused. Second, the complainant is vulnerable and must be shielded from possible retaliation. In addition, the reputation of a complainant can be tarnished in the course of an investigation. Moreover, an investigation will fare better if conducted in a discreet manner: employees may be franker if they believe their interviews will not be the subject of office gossip, and potential witnesses may be more truthful if they are approached without advance knowledge of an on-going investigation.

Note, however, that the need for confidentiality should not be confused with the message to employees that encourages whistleblowers or other reporting of allegations. Also, even though you want to maintain confidentiality of the investigation to the extent possible, do not guarantee strict confidentiality to any participants in the investigation. There will be certain circumstances in which disclosure of facts will be necessary (for example, a person accused of sexual harassment must be informed of the nature of the allegations).

C. Preserve, Collect, and Analyze Relevant Documents

The duty to preserve company documents based on the existence of pending, threatened, or reasonably foreseeable litigation is mandated by law. Moreover, documentary evidence is often the most reliable source of facts and also serves to refresh witness memory. In-house or outside counsel should take affirmative steps to plan, implement, and monitor document preservation in the event of anticipated litigation. Document hold orders should be issued and compliance should be monitored. A sample document hold order is included in Appendix B. In addition, evidence on company IT systems should be preserved. In addition to e-mail, relevant evidence might include video or audio recordings. You should strive to mitigate the potential for destruction of evidence, which may occur if word gets out about the investigation. You should also take steps to preserve documents outside the purview of the company, such as social media posts, as well as photographs and texts messages that might be stored on employer-issued devices. Ensuring the extraction and preservation of vital potential proof of harassment also protects your firm against allegations of not fully cooperating or, worse, a cover-up.

Be aware that key electronic evidence is sometimes lost unintentionally through routine server maintenance and data purges. Whether your company uses servers or cloud-based storage, ensure that evidence will be preserved and not destroyed in this manner. Working closely with someone in your IT department or an outside IT consultant can help in recovering digital evidence that was otherwise deleted, including e-mail deleted from computers and smart phones but stored on servers.

In addition, you may decide to engage an outside IT consultant in order to gather evidence in an expert and confidential manner. At the same time, an internal senior and trusted IT manager must be briefed to assist in efforts to recover digital evidence. Be mindful not to alert the entire IT staff to the existence of the investigation and the underlying allegations.

D. Know Your Internal Policies and Procedures

If you are in-house counsel, review all relevant company policies and procedures even before a harassment issue surfaces. Update your sexual harassment prevention policy as necessary to comply with relevant federal, state, and/or local laws. Before initiating an investigation, thoroughly review your firm's policies and procedures, including personnel policies, hiring contracts, and nondisclosure agreements. Review the specific rules and regulations disclosed to employees during hiring and through routine training. Review also the rights afforded by employment contracts. If the organization is unionized, know the relevant provisions of applicable collective bargaining agreements.

A complete understanding of internal rules will protect the company from the perception that it violated employee rights and help establish a legally sound roadmap for the investigation. In most companies, employee e-mail accounts are the property of the company, and you should ensure that your employee manuals make this clear while noting that the company has the right to review all e-mails.

Be aware of any signed agreements specific to the complainant or the subject of the complaint, including employee and nondisclosure agreements. In addition, review your company's applicable insurance policies: some insurance policies require early notification of any potential wrongdoing that may subject the company to legal claims.

If the employer is a publicly traded company, additional actions and disclosures may be warranted. Depending on the seriousness of the allegations and the potential impact on stock value, crisis management may also be necessary.

E. Select an Investigator

In an effort to contain costs, organizations sometimes resist bringing in outside help. At the same time, using an outside firm may ensure the investigation will be objective. Moreover, an outside firm should have expertise in interviewing witnesses and evaluating credibility, as well as the resources to conduct forensic exams of electronic devices. If the allegations involved many people within the company, you may have no choice but to bring in an outside firm to conduct the investigation.

The investigator you choose must be perceived as credible, unbiased, and independent. You may choose to retain expert investigative help by hiring a law firm or an investigative firm, or a combination of the two. The advantages to retaining a law firm are the benefits of attorney-client privilege confidentiality and resources to conduct an investigation while mindful of applicable law. On the other hand, an investigative firm can also be retained through outside counsel, which may serve to cover the investigative firm's work with the same attorney-client privilege protections, while also containing costs. Moreover, an investigative firm can bring to the table professionals with extensive experience in this work.

Whether a law firm or an investigative firm, be sure to hire people with experience in reviewing sexual harassment claims. Sexual harassment investigations require particular sensitivity and experience in dealing with particular witnesses, such as employees who have been subjected to harassment for extended periods of time but have not been comfortable coming forward. A person who has been sexually harassed might be embarrassed or blame herself or himself, resulting in a reluctance to discuss what happened. Moreover, a person who has been sexually harassed might have multiple reasons to hold back on important facts, including fear of retribution and a concern that he or she will not be deemed credible. A good investigator should be able to unpeel the layers of information with sensitivity, thoroughness, and efficiency. Needless to say, learning of important facts later could cause serious problems if the case advances to litigation.

F. Create an Investigative Plan

The investigative plan (which could be oral or written, depending on the circumstances of the investigation) should be flexible and should consider the need to retain expert investigative help while also protecting attorney-client privilege. The plan should determine the scope of the investigation by taking into consideration the nature and gravity of the allegation, the source and circumstances under which allegations are received, and available corroborative evidence. The plan should ensure that the investigation be conducted as promptly as reasonably possible and that all appropriate witnesses are interviewed and all relevant documents and other evidence is collected and reviewed. The plan should also provide for the documentation of the investigation and, if necessary, a formal report.

G. Interview Witnesses

The investigation plan should identify individuals the investigator intends to interview, including the complainant, alleged harasser, and other relevant witnesses, including those in whom the complainant may have confided. The plan should consider the order in which witnesses are examined and the timing of third-party witness interviews. Analysis of documents may impact timing of interviews: documents can serve to refresh witness memory or challenge a witness who may be less than truthful. The investigation plan should also determine how interviews will be memorialized, with options ranging from formal memoranda to detailed notes.

H. Ensure No Retaliation

The law protects from retaliation not only those who have been sexually harassed, but also those who report harassment allegations. Every effort should be made to ensure that no actions by other employees or managers could be portrayed as retaliatory in nature. Retaliation can include not only termination and demotion, but also exclusion from meetings, reduction in resources, and artificially poor performance reviews. You should ensure through close monitoring and educating staff that the complainant has not suffered and will not suffer retaliation.

IV.   CREATING A HARASSMENT-FREE WORKPLACE

Going forward, ensure your organization maintains a workplace free from sexual harassment. These six steps will help.

1.   **Set the tone at the top of the organization.** Effective prevention efforts must begin at the highest level of management. Leadership and accountability are crucial, and no system of training, monitoring, or reporting is likely to succeed in preventing harassment in the absence of genuine and public buy-in from the top levels of any organization.

2.   **Utilize strong policies with clear principles.** Institute strong policies and procedures to support the clear principles set by senior management, with clear reporting lines. Implement policies and procedures that govern what employees should do if they encounter harassment. In addition to making the reporting process clear, include alternative reporting channels to allow complainants to bypass immediate supervisors. Conduct compliance reviews and evaluate policies and procedures periodically and update them as necessary based on the needs of the organization.

3.   **Train your employees.** Develop tailored workplace training that sets the standard for respectful behavior at work. Effective training can reduce workplace harassment, but it must also serve as one component within a broader culture in which harassment is deemed unacceptable. Consider that training is an ongoing process, not a one and done.

4.   **Establish and enforce anti-retaliation policies.** Through close monitoring and educating staff, ensure that employees who report harassment will not be subjected to retaliation through close monitoring and education of staff.

5.   **Communicate with your employees.** Make it clear that all employees have a role to play in keeping the workplace safe and free of harassment.

6.   **Ensure equal opportunities.** In order to maintain a workplace free of harassment, all employees must have equal opportunities to succeed, including through mentoring, advising, and promotion. A wide range of employees should be included in decision-making processes and in shaping the culture of the workplace.

In closing, below are a few highlights from the EEOC's chart of risk factors for sexual harassment in the workplace. If you recognize any of these red flags in your workplace, please bookmark this chapter. You may need to revisit it sooner than anticipated.

Homogenous workforce: Historic lack of diversity in the workplace. Employees in the minority can feel isolated and may actually be, or at least appear to be, vulnerable to pressure from others. Employees in the majority might feel threatened by those they perceive as "different" or "other," or might simply be uncomfortable around others who are not like them.

"Rough and tumble" or single-sex-dominated workplace cultures: Remarks, jokes, or banter that are crude, "raunchy," or demeaning. Employees may be viewed as weak or susceptible to abuse. Abusive remarks or humor may promote workplace norms that devalue certain types of individuals.

Young workforces: Significant number of teenage and young-adult employees.

Young employees may lack the self-confidence to resist unwelcome overtures or challenge conduct that makes them uncomfortable. Young employees may be more susceptible to being taken advantage of by coworkers or superiors, particularly those who may be older and more established in their positions.

Workplaces with significant power disparities. Supervisors may feel emboldened to exploit low-ranking employees. Low-ranking employees may be less likely to understand complaint channels (language or education/training insufficiencies). Undocumented workers may be especially vulnerable to exploitation or the fear of retaliation.

Appendix A:
EEOC Sexual Harassment Checklists

Checklist One: Leadership and Accountability[33]

The first step for creating a holistic harassment prevention program is for the leadership of an organization to establish a culture of respect in which harassment is not tolerated. Determine if the leadership of your organization has taken the following steps:

- Leadership has allocated sufficient resources for a harassment prevention effort.
- Leadership has allocated sufficient staff time for a harassment prevention effort.
- Leadership has assessed harassment risk factors and has taken steps to minimize those risks.

Based on the commitment of leadership, determine if your organization has the following components in place:

- A harassment prevention policy that is easy-to-understand and that is regularly communicated to all employees.
- A harassment reporting system that employees know about and is fully resourced and which accepts reports of harassment experienced and harassment observed.
- Imposition of discipline that is prompt, consistent, and proportionate to the severity of the harassment, if harassment is determined to have occurred.
- Accountability for mid-level managers and front-line supervisors to prevent and/or respond to workplace harassment.
- Regular compliance trainings for all employees so they can recognize prohibited forms of conduct and know how to use the reporting system.
- Regular compliance trainings for mid-level managers and front-line supervisors so they know how to prevent and/or respond to workplace harassment.

Bonus points if you can confirm these statements:

- The organization conducts climate surveys on a regular basis to assess the extent to which harassment is experienced as a problem in the workplace.
- The organization has implemented metrics for harassment response and prevention in supervisory employees' performance reviews.

---

33. EEOC Checklists for Employers, Checklist One: Leadership and Accountability, https://www.eeoc.gov/eeoc/task_force/harassment/checklist1.cfm.

- The organization conducts workplace civility training and bystander intervention training
- The organization has partnered with researchers to evaluate the organization's holistic workplace harassment prevention effort.

Checklist Two: An Anti-Harassment Policy[34]

An anti-harassment policy is a key component of a holistic harassment prevention effort. Determine if your anti-harassment policy contains the following elements:

- An unequivocal statement that harassment based on *any* protected characteristic will not be tolerated.
- An easy-to-understand description of prohibited conduct, including examples.
- A description of a reporting system—available to employees who experience harassment as well as those who observe harassment—that provides multiple avenues to report, in a manner easily accessible to employees.
- A statement that the reporting system will provide a prompt, thorough, and impartial investigation.
- A statement that the identity of an individual who submits a report, a witness who provides information regarding a report, and the target of the complaint, will be kept confidential to the extent possible consistent with a thorough and impartial investigation.
- A statement that any information gathered as part of an investigation will be kept confidential to the extent possible consistent with a thorough and impartial investigation.
- An assurance that the employer will take immediate and proportionate corrective action if it determines that harassment has occurred.
- An assurance that an individual who submits a report (either of harassment experienced or observed) or a witness who provides information regarding a report will be protected from retaliation from co-workers and supervisors.
- A statement that any employee who retaliates against any individual who submits a report or provides information regarding a report will be disciplined appropriately.
- Is written in clear, simple words, in all languages commonly used by members of the workforce.

Checklist Three: A Harassment Reporting System and Investigations[35]

A reporting system that allows employees to file a report of harassment they have experienced or observed, and a process for undertaking investigations, are essential components of a holistic harassment prevention effort.

---

34. EEOC Checklists for Employers, Checklist Two: An Anti-Harassment Policy, https://www.eeoc.gov/eeoc/task_force/harassment/checklist2.cfm.

35. EEOC Checklist for Employers, Checklist Three: A Harassment Reporting System and Investigations, https://www.eeoc.gov/eeoc/task_force/harassment/checklist3.cfm.

Determine if your anti-harassment effort contains the following elements:

- A fully-resourced reporting process that allows the organization to respond promptly and thoroughly to reports of harassment that have been experienced or observed.
- Employer representatives who take reports seriously.
- A supportive environment where individuals feel safe to report harassing behavior to management.
- Well-trained, objective, and neutral investigators.
- Timely responses and investigations.
- Investigators who document all steps taken from the point of first contact and who prepare a written report using guidelines to weigh credibility.
- An investigation that protects the privacy of individuals who file complaints or reports, individuals who provide information during the investigation, and the person(s) alleged to have engaged in harassment, to the greatest extent possible.
- Mechanisms to determine whether individuals who file reports or provide information during an investigation experience retribution, and authority to impose sanctions on those who engage in retaliation.
- During the pendency of an investigation, systems to ensure individuals alleged to have engaged in harassment are not "presumed guilty" and are not "punished" unless and until a complete investigation determines that harassment has occurred.
- A communication of the determination of the investigation to all parties and, where appropriate, a communication of the sanction imposed if harassment was found to have occurred.

Checklist Four: Compliance Training[36]

A holistic harassment prevention effort provides training to employees regarding an employer's policy, reporting systems and investigations. Determine if your organization's compliance training is based on the following structural principles and includes the following content:

Structural Principles

- Supported at the highest levels.
- Repeated and reinforced on a regular basis.
- Provided to all employees at every level of the organization.
- Conducted by qualified, live, and interactive trainers.
- If live training is not feasible, designed to include active engagement by participants.
- Routinely evaluated and modified as necessary.

---

36. EEOC Checklist for Employers, Checklist Four: Compliance Training, https://www.eeoc.gov/eeoc/task_force/harassment/checklist4.cfm.

Content of Compliance Training for All Employees

- Describes illegal harassment, and conduct that, if left unchecked, might rise to the level of illegal harassment.
- Includes examples that are tailored to the specific workplace and the specific workforce.
- Educates employees about their rights and responsibilities if they experience conduct that is not acceptable in the workplace.
- Describes, in simple terms, the process for reporting harassment that is experienced or observed.
- Explains the consequences of engaging in conduct unacceptable in the workplace.

Content of Compliance Training for Managers and First-line Supervisors

- Provides easy-to-understand and realistic methods for dealing with harassment that they observe, that is reported to them, or of which they have knowledge or information, including description of sanctions for failing to use such methods.
- Provides clear instructions on how to report harassing behavior up the chain of command, including description of sanctions for failing to report.
- Encourages managers and supervisors to practice "situational awareness" and assess the workforces within their responsibility for risk factors of harassment.

Note: These checklists are meant to be useful tools in thinking about and taking steps to prevent harassment in the workplace and responding to harassment when it occurs. They are not meant to convey legal advice or to set forth legal requirements relating to harassment. Checking all of the boxes does not necessarily mean an employer is in legal compliance; conversely, the failure to check any particular box does not mean an employer is not in compliance.

Appendix B:
Sample Document Hold Order

Attorney-Client Communication

Privileged and Confidential

[SAMPLE]

URGENT – PLEASE REVIEW THIS LEGAL HOLD NOTICE

**DO NOT DESTROY ELECTRONIC INFORMATION OR PAPER RECORDS
OF ANY KIND
THAT MAY BE RELEVANT TO THIS MATTER**

TO: [Relevant Parties]

DATE:

REGARDING: [Description of matter]

Please be advised that [your organization] reasonably anticipates commencement of litigation involving [description of matter].

Applicable laws and rules require you to preserve all Potentially Relevant Information (as defined below) and any failure to comply could result in severe penalties against [your organization]. To protect your interests and fulfill any legal obligations, it is necessary to preserve all Potentially Relevant Information immediately.

The affirmative and continuing duty to preserve and maintain all Potentially Relevant Information applies both to hard-copy documents and electronically stored information ("ESI"). **Accordingly, it is vitally important that you retain and preserve all Potentially Relevant Information, whether paper, electronic, or otherwise, wherever located.**

Potentially Relevant Information as used in this Notice includes all records, communications, and data, including memoranda, letters, spreadsheets, databases, calendars, telephone logs, computer disks, E-mails (including attachments), audiotapes, videotapes, CDs, DVDs charts, handwritten notes, drafts, files, archives, and other material related in any way to [description of the matter].

All Potentially Relevant Information should be preserved regardless of whether it is stored in your paper files, on your computer, on removable electronic media, or in some other format or location (including your home).

Effective immediately, it is critical that you do not delete, over-write, or otherwise alter or destroy any documents or files (print or electronic) that may contain Potentially Relevant Information. The obligation to retain and preserve Potentially Relevant Information applies to Potentially Relevant Information that currently exists or is created in the future. Therefore, you should preserve all existing Potentially Relevant Information and continue to preserve information in the future. If your business practices involve the routine destruction, recycling, relocation, or mutation of documents or files that may contain Potentially Relevant Information, please (1) halt such business practices; (2) sequester or remove such material from that business practice; or (3) arrange for the preservation of complete and accurate duplicates or copies of such material, suitable for later discovery.

In addition, please note the following concerning the preservation of Potentially Relevant Information:

- E-Mail and ESI: Preserve relevant E-mail and electronic information of any kind (i.e., any information created, stored, accessible, or that uses or can use computer technology). Also, do not delete any potentially relevant E-mail (or attachments to any E-mail) in any inbox, outbox, delete box, or other location, or any potentially relevant E-mail that may be sent or received in the future.
- Duplicate Records: All duplicate copies of potentially relevant records should be preserved.
- "Non-Official" Files: You should not distinguish between "official" company files and "personal' or other "non-official" files for purposes of preserving Potentially Relevant Information. All Potentially Relevant Information should be preserved, including any files or copies of files that employees may have in addition to "official" or "company" files, including any files stored off-site.
- Backup Tapes and Offline Data: You should preserve backup tapes and offline data. Backup tapes (especially if used for disaster recovery purposes) and offline data, may not be reasonably accessible, but may still contain Potentially Relevant Information.
- Other Possible Sources: All sources of Potentially Relevant Information should be included in your preservation efforts, including, for example, any laptops, PCs, handheld devices (such as BlackBerry devices), or other devices such as USB drives. In addition, you should preserve any Potentially Relevant Information on network shared drives, individual user drives, local E-mail servers, self-created CDs or DVDs, and home computers, if applicable.

In the future, we may collect some or all of the Potentially Relevant Information from you as necessary. Until then, please continue to protect and preserve all of this information.

Chapter 4

Mediation and Arbitration: How to Prepare Your Company and Yourself

By Elizabeth J. Shampnoi

This chapter is intended to provide an overview of the most important considerations for in-house counsel when evaluating the use of mediation and/or arbitration pre- and post-dispute; the strategic drafting of clauses; and best practices when handling a matter internally or working with outside counsel. Given the broad nature of disputes a business might face, counsel should also consult the applicable substantive and procedural law surrounding the nature of the dispute (i.e., employment, commercial, construction, consumer, class actions, etc.) as well as industry standards involving mediation and arbitration, which are beyond the scope of this chapter.

I. INTRODUCTION

Disputes arise in the ordinary course of business despite best efforts, practices, and intentions. When disputes arise, they are costly and often negatively impact a business's bottom line and reputation. They are also disruptive to the overall operation of a business, resulting in distractions that harm productivity, growth, and relationships. Disputes often take several months—to several years—to reach a final resolution and can cause irreparable damage to valued business relationships. For these reasons, sound decision-making requires senior business leaders and in-counsel to consider alternatives to the traditional method of litigation. Cost-effective, efficient, and timely alternative dispute resolution mechanisms are available, and when utilized properly, result in more advantageous outcomes. This chapter will discuss two of the most prevalent alternatives: mediation and arbitration; the considerations for in-house counsel when evaluating the use of either mechanism pre- and post-dispute; and the strategic drafting of clauses and best practices when handling a matter internally or working with outside counsel. Given the broad nature of disputes a business might face, counsel should also consult the applicable substantive and procedural law surrounding the nature of the dispute (i.e., employment, commercial, construction, consumer, class actions, etc.) as well as industry standards involving mediation and arbitration, which are beyond the scope of this chapter.

II. OVERVIEW OF MEDIATION

A. What Is Mediation?

Mediation is an informal and collaborative process by which the parties agree contractually in advance, or post-dispute, to select a neutral third party known as the mediator to assist them in identifying and reaching potential solutions to the dispute. In some instances, more than one mediator might be utilized depending on the circumstances of the dispute. Co-mediators often work together if different areas of expertise or skill will be helpful in resolving the dispute. However, the mediator does not make a final or binding decision. Instead, the mediator assists in facilitating discussion that will aid the parties in identifying and agreeing to acceptable solutions. The parties then reduce those agreed-upon solutions to writing in the form of a settlement agreement.

B. The Mediator's Role

The mediator's role is to assist the parties in identifying the disputed issues and their respective needs; ensure that each party gains a better understanding of the other's view; create a comfortable and nonjudgmental environment in which the parties can openly discuss their underlying concerns and challenges; identify creative solutions; and overcome impasse. Mediators utilize different styles to assist the parties in reaching resolution. Depending on what the parties are seeking from the mediator and/or the mediation, some mediators inform the parties of the strengths and weaknesses of their case; these mediators are considered evaluative mediators. Mediators who do not evaluate the strengths and weaknesses of a case but rather facilitate discussion between the parties are known as facilitative mediators. It is common practice for mediators to use a combination of styles. Although there are a variety of other types of mediation styles beyond the scope of this chapter, facilitative and evaluative styles are the most commonly utilized.

C.   The Benefits of Mediation

The benefits of mediation far outweigh litigation. The most commonly cited benefits include over the outcome; cost savings; time savings; preserving valuable business relationships; and confidentiality.

1.   Maintaining Control Over the Final Outcome

Mediation is an opportunity for the parties to control the outcome, avoid uncertainty, create solutions, and find a resolution that is acceptable to all moving forward. The process is informal and flexible, permitting the parties to craft a solution that is agreeable, as opposed to an arbitrator or judge dictating the outcome. Such solutions can be nonmonetary and specifically crafted to meet the parties' needs. Indeed, the parties to a dispute are best suited to craft an outcome that is aligned with their underlying interests, needs, and goals.

2.   Cost Savings

Another benefit of mediation is that it can save the parties a significant amount of money. Fees and costs are substantially less in mediation. Mediators normally charge an hourly or daily rate for their service, which is generally borne equally by the parties. This fee often involves time spent by the mediator to prepare for the mediation; time spent during the in-person mediation; and any post-mediation work. Post-mediation work could involve addressing any remaining issues and/or finalizing the terms of settlement.

Attorney's fees for the parties own attorneys are also significantly less than they would be in litigation. Assuming outside counsel is engaged, billable time involves preparing for the mediation, attending and participating in the mediation, and any follow-up work to finalize the settlement agreement. The attorney's preparation time is generally the costliest part of the process because it requires the attorney to have a full understanding of the case as well as its strengths and weaknesses. This time is necessary and well-spent to assist the parties in getting to a resolution that is acceptable to all during, or shortly after, the in-person mediation session. Additionally, time spent after the mediation may involve more effort on the part of counsel to finalize the terms of the settlement agreement. In-house counsel may decide to handle the matter internally without engaging outside counsel to save money. Nonetheless, there is still a cost to the business because that time could be otherwise spent working on matters that support and enhance the business's goals.

Comparatively speaking, on the whole, mediation fees and costs are substantially lower than litigation. Given that most disputes settle before trial, time and money spent attempting to settle is worthwhile because such preparations will carry over into the arbitration or litigation. Mediation may also result in a narrowing of the issues to be submitted to arbitration or litigation.

Practice Pointer

It is worth noting that court-annexed mediation has become increasingly popular in recent decades. Programs vary widely and, in many instances, state and federal courts require that the parties attempt mediation, often providing mediators that serve pro bono or for a reduced fee.

3. Time Savings

It is well-settled that litigation is a lengthy process and that court dockets are often backlogged. Time spent litigating a dispute to prove who is right or wrong significantly distracts from day-to-day operations, strategic planning, and growth of a business. Litigation also has the potential to reduce the productivity of those involved, negatively impacting the bottom line. Mediation allows the parties to put the dispute behind them quickly and get back to focusing on the goals and objectives of the organization.

4. Preserving Valuable Business Relationships

Much has been written that one of the most powerful benefits of mediation is the ability of the parties to express their views about the dispute and/or vent their frustrations, resulting in an early settlement and a preservation of valuable business relationships. In traditional litigation, the opportunity for parties to personally express their views does not usually present itself until trial when parties are permitted to testify. In addition, such testimony is often controlled and focused in that situation, covering only the relevant points to prove liability. By the time a trial occurs, significant time and money has been spent, and the parties have hardened and become entrenched in their positions to the point where they often can no longer be reasonable. Consequently, settlement is no longer an option, and any hope that the parties might continue their relationship has vanished.

In mediation, there are no restrictions with respect to expressing one's views. Parties are free, and encouraged, to share their views with each other, counsel, and the mediator. The mediation process also allows the attorneys to communicate directly with each other and the mediator about the respective strengths and weaknesses of the case. This process often provides a "reality check" that is helpful in assessing whether it makes financial or legal sense to proceed to arbitration or litigation. Such discussions often elevate the dispute to the attention of a higher level of authority within the company not directly involved in the dispute, allowing for additional assessment.

A good mediator helps the parties work toward resolution while ensuring that each party is listening and understanding the other. Once this occurs, the parties can often find a resolution and, in many instances, continue their relationship and/or part ways less acrimoniously.

5.   Confidentiality

Mediation is a confidential process, whereas litigation dockets are public information. Publicity surrounding the fact a dispute exists, regardless of who is right or wrong, can have far-reaching impact on a business's reputation and bottom line. The mediation process allows the parties to agree to keep the existence of any dispute private as well as the outcome. This benefit is particularly important now, given the proliferation of the internet and social media. The widespread dissemination of information is easier for the average person to come across or locate even when such information is outdated or incorrect, making confidentiality even more valuable.

D. Additional Considerations Surrounding the Use of Mediation

---

Practice Pointer

Although the benefits of a successful mediation far outweigh arbitration or litigation, not all mediations result in settlement. A successful mediation requires that all parties are ready and willing to resolve the dispute. If a party is not ready or willing, settlement is often difficult to achieve, if not impossible. The reasons a party may not be ready or willing to consider settlement vary widely, but often experienced attorneys and mediators are able to identify whether any attempt to mediate is potentially productive. Moreover, a settlement can only be reached if those present and participating in the process have the authority, or access to the person(s) with authority, to sign off on any settlement. The most commonly cited consequences of an unsuccessful mediation involve additional delay and cost; early, free, and insufficient discovery; weakness; and antagonism.

---

1.   Potential Additional Delay and Cost

Mediations can be conducted prior to the formal initiation of an arbitration or lawsuit and concurrently while the dispute is pending. In some instances, the arbitration or lawsuit may be stayed while the parties attempt to mediate. When the mediation is conducted prior to the formal initiation, or conducted during a stay, it has the potential to delay the ultimate resolution of the dispute if the parties' attempt at mediation is unsuccessful. Additionally, one party may use the mediation process as a stall tactic without any real intention of settling. Regardless, the parties will be spending additional time and money attempting to mediate, which could be viewed as wasteful if the parties do not reach resolution. Notwithstanding, as mentioned earlier, not all time and money spent in mediation is wasteful because most cases ultimately end in settlement. At times even some of the issues can be narrowed during an early-stage process, thereby streamlining the dispute and paving the way for a resolution down the road. Therefore, the fruits of any efforts may be realized later. Mediation may also result in narrowing or focusing the issues, which ultimately saves time and money in the long run.

2.   Early, Free, and Potentially Insufficient Discovery

During the mediation process, the parties are not required to engage in any formal discovery. Some will argue that if mediation is conducted too early in the dispute, it is a waste of resources because without discovery, there is not enough information available about the dispute to identify what a reasonable solution would entail or to even guide the parties (and the mediator) in evaluating the strength of their respective positions. In practice, however, parties engage in informal discovery to assist in identifying issues, demonstrating strengths or weaknesses, and/or identifying appropriate settlement terms or solutions.

However, if the mediation is unsuccessful, some contend that an early exchange of discovery could give one party an advantage while putting the other at a disadvantage. Of course, a party could engage in the mediation process for the sole benefit of obtaining such information earlier than normal and/or without having to expend the time, money, or effort to obtain it through the arbitration or litigation process. It is important to realize, however, that any information exchanged during the mediation would be exchanged during an arbitration or litigation; therefore, the fact that it was exchanged earlier should only cause an imbalance in limited circumstances.

3.   Weakness

When a party commences a dispute in arbitration or litigation, they believe they will prevail. The same is true when the party sued files a counterclaim. When these beliefs are extreme, counsel may consider any willingness to explore settlement or mediation a sign of weakness. In recent years, this concern has had less merit because mediation has become a common method of dispute resolution often required by contracts, alternative dispute resolution providers, and court systems. Indeed, dispute resolution providers and courts often raise the subject of mediation independently or have rules requiring mediation be considered and/or attempted. Nevertheless, in some instances a party may feel that a decision from a judicial body is necessary to set a precedent or obtain clarification about a law as applied to a specific business practice and is, therefore, unwilling to mediate.

4.   Potential Antagonism

As referenced earlier, the parties' ability to express their views is one of the benefits of mediation, but it can also be a consequence. Although some disputes, such as partnership, employment, and marital, may involve considerably more emotion, all disputes involve emotion. In addition to money, jobs, and bonuses, reputations can be at stake, impacting the ability of those involved to be rational in their resolution of the dispute. In mediation, the sharing of each party's respective view, if not handled properly, can result in potentially antagonizing the parties and deepening the dispute. An experienced mediator, however, will control the process and ensure that type of antagonism does not occur and that all discussion is conducted professionally, cordially, and respectfully.

E.   Best Advocacy Practices in Mediation

Litigators are highly skilled and well-versed in trial-advocacy skills. These skills are valuable across the board when attempting to resolve a dispute on behalf of a client. However, to increase effectiveness and achieve settlements that advance the client's interests in a cost-effective manner, mediation advocacy requires a different mindset along with a nuanced approach.

1.   Selecting the Mediator

A critical component of any mediation is the selection of the right mediator for your case. Determining who the right mediator is requires consideration of several factors. It is important to first determine what you think you need from the mediator to assist you in reaching your ultimate goal. For instance, a mediator's subject matter and/or industry expertise could be critical if the parties must hear from someone who has handled similar disputes as an advocate, in-house counsel, or mediator. Such a mediator will have greater credibility from the start of the mediation, often increasing the likelihood of success.

Another consideration for counsel is what mediation style will be most effective. Some cases require a mediator whose primary focus is in urging the parties to communicate with each other or shuttling back and forth with messages to facilitate a resolution. This can be particularly helpful where the parties recognize the benefits of settlement but need assistance with communication, whether because of personality issues, a parties' hesitation in making the first move, or the need to save face. A mediator can facilitate such messages in a less adversarial way that is more effective and/or raise considerations him- or herself as an outsider looking in. Other types of cases may require more than facilitation, such as a mediator who will explore and test the parties' strengths and/or weaknesses providing an honest, neutral view of each. Mediation styles are not one-size-fits-all, and most cases require a combination of styles.

Additional considerations when selecting a mediator include an understanding of the mediator's background, experience, and perspective; availability; and fees. It is also important to assess the mediator's reputation by contacting the mediator's references and reaching out to colleagues who have previously worked with the mediator.

2.   Preparing for Mediation

Practice Pointer

Preparation is key to the success of any mediation. Whether handling the matter internally or working with outside counsel, spending the time to prepare in advance will increase productivity during the mediation. First and foremost, all involved must understand how the process works and strategize how best to approach the mediation. Identifying what you hope to accomplish and identifying an outline of how you will get there, while recognizing that flexibility will be necessary, is necessary to ensure everyone is on the same page.

Key considerations include, *inter alia*, an analysis of your best-case, worst-case and likely alternative to a negotiated resolution; what negotiation style and strategy will you use; who is going to take the lead role and/or do most of the speaking; what information will you share—and when—to persuade the other party of the strengths in your arguments. It is imperative that you outline the critical issues as well as the strengths and weaknesses of your case and do the same from the other party's perspective by anticipating the arguments they will make. Such preparations will allow for more rational decision-making. A prepared party is also going to have more credibility with the mediator and be in a better position to convince the mediator their position is reasoned, which will inevitably translate to the other party. Counsel, together with the mediator, may determine that premediation submissions will be helpful.

The preparations above will make preparing the submission much easier. Generally speaking, best practice dictates that counsel provide the key facts and evidentiary support for the claim and those that undermine the opposing party's claim or position. The submission should provide the mediator with sufficient information so that she can objectively understand your client's position. Effective advocacy in mediation requires that counsel focus on information that truly matters but with objectivity. In mediation, counsel must be able to acknowledge the strengths in the opposing party's positions. Anticipating the opposing arguments and facts, and being prepared to explain why those facts are not supported or of little consequence, will lead to a greater chance of resolution.

A few other preparation tips include, *inter alia*, understanding and sharing with the mediator the relationship between counsel; prior and potential future dealings between the parties; and the personalities of all involved because mediation is not strictly about the numbers—it involves emotion as well. It is important to share as much of this information as possible with the mediator in advance of the mediation. Speaking to the mediator privately in advance is encouraged to save time the day of the mediation. Counsel should build rapport with the mediator and be upfront so the mediator can be most effective. It is almost important to determine whether it will be effective to begin in joint session, with mediator's opening remarks followed by opening remarks by counsel and/or the parties. Opening remarks are often an opportunity to persuade and speak directly to the other party without having those remarks filtered by opposing counsel.

Practice Pointer

Remarks should be prepared ahead of time, demonstrate a willingness to listen, and be conciliatory in the spirit of mediation.

III. OVERVIEW OF ARBITRATION

Arbitration is a formal process by which the parties agree contractually in advance, or post-dispute, to submit their dispute to one or more impartial persons, known as an arbitrator, for a final and binding determination. Throughout this chapter, the author refers to arbitrator in the singular; however, in practice, one or three arbitrators generally serve on a particular dispute. In some instances, one or two of the arbitrators may be designated as nonneutral, party-appointed arbitrators. When this occurs, the chair is the only arbitrator that remains impartial. Historically, the origins of arbitration involved particular industries, such as textiles or those involving unionized workforces where quick and efficient alternatives to court were necessary. These matters often had an immediate impact on the business, so they could not wait to be adjudicated by the court system without impacting commerce. Additionally, they often involved nonlawyer arbitrators with industry expertise and knowledge who would apply industry standards and norms to their decisions.

Today, arbitration is widely utilized across all types of industries to resolve various types of disputes, including, but not limited to, real estate, construction, commercial, employment, and intellectual property. Advocates and parties maintain varied views about whether arbitration is a preferred method of dispute resolution. These views are often based on prior experiences, folk lore, and/or an individual's comfort level with the process. When determining whether to arbitrate, careful consideration must be given to the pros and cons of the arbitration process as applied to the parties' specific needs and the nature of the potential disputes.

A. The Arbitrator's Role

Arbitrators have great discretion and broad powers primarily derived from statutory and common-law authority. This requires that arbitrators adhere to the highest standards of ethics and neutrality. Given that there is no automatic right to appeal an arbitrator's decision, many would argue that an arbitrator has more power than a judge. The arbitrator's role is to be an independent, impartial decision maker who provides the parties with a fair hearing on the merits in an economical and efficient manner.

B. The Benefits of Arbitration

1. Efficient and Economical

The goal of arbitration is to provide a more efficient and economical process than litigation. Litigation can often take many years and involve significant motion practice and discovery followed by a trial and appeal. Many court dockets are backlogged, and public resources are limited, resulting in judges unable to devote the time they would like to focus on a particular dispute. The longer and more involved the litigation, the costlier the process becomes as legal fees and other costs associated with the process are incurred. The arbitration process is designed to reduce the amount of time and money spent by streamlining the dispute resolution process.

Many of the traditional litigation tools are limited or discouraged in arbitration, such as discovery and motion practice, respectively. Although document discovery is common in arbitration, it is intended to be focused on the relevant issues that are in dispute and to prevent fishing expeditions, reduce costs, and increase efficiency. Interrogatories are rarely utilized. Depositions are rarely granted unless a showing of good cause is made.

If depositions are permitted, they also are limited and managed to ensure they remain consistent with the expedited nature of the process. Evidentiary hearings are intended to be efficient, and appeals are not automatic. These differences result in a streamlined process that limits both the time and money spent getting to a final award.

2. Expert Neutral

One of the greatest benefits of choosing arbitration is the ability of the parties to identify and select the person that is going to decide the dispute. Litigation does not provide this option, leading to greater uncertainty in the outcome. Worse, many judges do not have specific industry or legal expertise because they are required to adjudicate a wide variety of disputes on a regular basis. This broad experience often requires the parties to spend additional time and effort educating the judge with respect to specific industry standards and substantive legal issues. Arbitration allows, and encourages, the parties to identify the background and qualifications of the arbitrator. In addition to saving time and money educating the arbitrator, this allows for the parties to have greater confidence that the arbitrator's decision will be in line with industry and/or legal standards.

3. Less Formal

In arbitration, the parties can identify the governing procedural and evidentiary rules. Such rules are meant to be relaxed so that the parties can craft a process that best fits their needs. Less formal rules are also meant to increase efficiency and reduce cost. In practice, much of the interaction between counsel and the arbitrator is conducted via phone and e-mail, avoiding numerous, often delayed, time-consuming, and costly court appearances. Evidentiary hearings are generally held in a conference room, providing for a more business-like and comfortable process.

The parties can agree to the procedures and rules in advance of any dispute by outlining them in the predispute arbitration clause contained in the governing agreement and as guided by the arbitrator. They can also agree after the dispute arises. Administering organizations such as the American Arbitration Association (AAA) and JAMS have governing rules for arbitrations involving specific types of disputes. There are several administrative providers domestically and internationally of varying sizes. AAA and JAMS are the most commonly known and utilized administrative organizations for commercial disputes in the United States. If the parties do not agree in advance, or cannot agree once the dispute arises, where an administering organization is identified, the organization's rules will serve as a default.

4. Final and Binding—No Automatic Right of Appeal

Absent party agreement, arbitration awards are not appealable like trial court and appellate decisions. In litigation, there are often various stages and opportunities for a party to appeal, adding significant costs, delays, and uncertainty. Once a final award is issued in arbitration, however, the winning or losing party seeks to confirm or vacate the award, respectively, in a court of law. The grounds upon which an award can be vacated are extremely limited and based in statutory and common law.

Practice Pointer

The lack of an automatic appeal in arbitration provides for a final and binding award that ends the dispute without the added costs, delays, and uncertainties associated with an appeal.

---

5. Interim and Partial Relief Available

Many arbitral institutions now have procedures by which interim and partial relief is available, including on an emergency basis. This allows for additional time and cost-savings by permitting the parties to obtain all the relief they seek in one venue. Historically, such interim relief could only be granted by a court of law absent party agreement. This created a dual venue process, resulting in increased fees, delay, and potentially inconsistent rulings. The ability to select the arbitrator and have input concerning the arbitrator's background and qualifications is an added benefit when it comes to such interim and partial relief. Moreover, having the same decision maker involved throughout the entire case reduces time and cost overall.

6. Confidentiality

Confidentiality in arbitration is another key benefit of the process as court dockets and proceedings are generally open to the public. Publicity surrounding a dispute and its ultimate outcome often negatively impacts reputation and the bottom line. The proliferation of the internet and social media has made such publicity more readily available to the average person. The dissemination of such information is widespread and easy to locate even when outdated. Removing such information is prohibitively expensive for most. Worse, it is nearly impossible to completely remove, and one has little control that such information will not find a way back to the internet or social media.

Most arbitral institutions have rules prohibiting the institution and the arbitrator from disclosing the existence of the arbitration itself and/or the award, but most are silent about the parties' obligations to maintain silence. Of course, disclosure of some or all awards is at times required by law or the governing administrative body. For instance, the Financial Industry Regulatory Authority (FINRA) requires the publication of awards involving customer and industry disputes. Class-action awards administered by the AAA are also made publicly available. However, some organizations provide the arbitrator with the authority to restrict dissemination of confidential information *sua sponte*, or upon a party's request. Absent party agreement or an arbitrator's order, there is generally no prohibition against one or more of the parties disclosing or discussing the existence or substance of a pending arbitration or its award. If the parties are interested in maintaining the highest level of confidentiality, they should craft their arbitration agreement accordingly.

Even when the parties do not disseminate any information, it is important to note that once a final award is issued, the prevailing party might need to have the award confirmed and judgment entered in a court of law if there is not voluntarily and immediate compliance. This requires that the award be filed with the court. Although some courts may permit the filing of such documents under seal, such permission is granted in only rare circumstances. Ultimately, complete confidentiality might not be available because the case will be a matter of public record available for viewing by the press and anyone else that might be interested in the outcome. Confirmation of an award is less likely to receive the attention of the press, but it is a possibility. On-the-other hand, the losing party may seek to vacate the award. Although vacatur grounds are extremely limited and courts give great deference to arbitral awards, if an award is vacated, it is more likely to receive the attention of the press, thereby removing the veil of confidentiality.

C. Additional Considerations Surrounding Arbitration

1. The Potential for Inefficiency and Significant Costs

In recent years, arbitration's reputation for being efficient and economical has weakened. This change in reputation has arisen mainly from anecdotal information, folklore, and individual experiences. Arbitral institutions, arbitration advocates, and arbitrators are aware of this perception and are working hard to ensure efficient and economical dispute resolution. There are many factors that impact the efficiency and economics of the arbitration, including the quality of the arbitration clause and administering organization as well as the experience of the arbitrator(s) and advocates involved in the process.

2. Informality

The informality of the arbitration process is often cited as a positive aspect of arbitration, but some consider it a negative. Litigators are comfortable and accustomed to working with formal, substantive, and procedural rules. Given that arbitration rules and procedures are less formal, they provide the arbitrator with significant discretion. This informality and potential lack of transparency can cause some to choose litigation over arbitration for fear that they will not know what to expect in the process or the outcome.

3. No Automatic Right to Appeal

In litigation, trial court decisions are often appealable as of right. This sometimes adds a level of comfort to counsel and the parties that if the decision maker—whether a judge or jury—makes a decision that a party does believe is correct, there is an opportunity to have that decision reviewed.

Practice Pointer

In arbitration, there is no automatic right of appeal. The parties must agree to participate in an arbitral appellate process.

---

4.   Splitting the Baby

There is a perception that arbitrators "split the baby" by issuing awards that are not in favor of one side or the other. Rather, the belief is that the arbitrator will apportion and split liability and damages almost equally between the parties. When such an award is issued, there could be a rationale reason based on the facts and circumstances of a particular case, but this is not the "norm," as evidenced by a 2007 study conducted by the AAA. Their study found that only seven percent of awards were in the mid-range (41 to 60 percent of their filed claim amount), and 93 percent were outside the mid-range. Earlier AAA research had yielded similar results. A 2001 survey of all domestic and international commercial cases awarded in 2000 found that only nine percent of claims were "split," or divided near the halfway mark.

IV.   STRATEGIC DRAFTING OF DISPUTE RESOLUTION CLAUSES

A.   The Importance of a Well-Drafted Dispute Resolution Clause

A well-drafted dispute resolution clause is the first step in ensuring a successful, streamlined, cost-effective, and efficient arbitration process tailored to meet the needs of the parties. In the event of a breach, this clause will govern the method and process by which disputes are adjudicated. A thoughtfully considered arbitration clause allows the parties to maintain control over the process—a benefit not available in litigation. It also enables the parties to expeditiously address the substantive issues before the arbitrator(s).

On the other hand, a poorly drafted arbitration clause is likely to result in an unwieldy, inefficient, and expensive process. A poorly drafted clause will also result in numerous disagreements over ancillary issues having nothing to do with the result, turning the arbitration process into quasi-litigation. Disputes such as which arbitral forum will administer the matter, the applicable arbitration rules, and the location of the hearing will add unnecessary delay and cost. Indeed, poorly drafted clauses often cause unnecessary delay and require court intervention to be enforced, leading the parties to forfeit control over the dispute.

When drafting and negotiating a contract, the parties' primary focus is finalizing the deal—not what will occur if the terms are breached. For this reason, the arbitration clause is an afterthought. It oftentimes is not until the final hours of negotiation that the parties agree to incorporate an arbitration clause and therefore fail to thoughtfully consider its specific terms. This approach often results in a clause that fails to meet the parties' needs and leads to a frustrated dispute resolution process down the road.

Worse, all too often in haste, counsel mistakenly cut and paste a dispute resolution clause from a different contract. This is a tremendous mistake for numerous reasons. Setting aside that the actual copying and pasting process in and of itself could result in an error, the clause may be outdated or contain provisions that are detrimental to the contract or parties at hand. Caution must be exercised to avoid simply copying a boilerplate arbitration clause from another agreement. For instance, such clauses could reference an administering arbitration organization that no longer exists or rules that are no longer in effect.

Counsel are well-advised to spend the time necessary to carefully consider the needs of the business; the type of contract; the potential nature of the dispute that may eventually arise; which side of the dispute they may be on; and what they hope to accomplish during the dispute resolution process. Although many of these factors may be unknown or difficult to predict at the beginning of the relationship, there are several drafting considerations that apply across the board to many types of disputes. Such considerations are further explored below. This is not to suggest that a well-drafted clause requires each consideration be addressed in all clauses.

Practice Pointer

To the contrary, when drafting a clause, each consideration should be utilized as a guide, and inclusion of any topic should be adapted to the context of the specific transaction. Indeed, too much detail in an arbitration clause will lead to ambiguity.

B. The Standard Arbitration Clause

Tailoring the arbitration clause to fit the business' specific needs is always ideal; however, where counsel has neither the time nor the inclination to negotiate or tailor the dispute resolution clause to the particular deal, it is advisable to utilize a standard arbitration clause. Standard arbitration clauses are simple and short enough to quickly add to a contract without hesitation by any party. Dispute resolution providers such as the AAA and JAMS publish standard arbitration clauses on their websites. The AAA goes one step further and provides an on-line application that allows the parties to build their own clause.[1] These clauses have withstood judicial scrutiny and contain the necessary elements of an enforceable arbitration clause along with a process the parties will follow—namely, identifying the arbitrable disputes; identifying the administrating provider; setting forth the applicable rules; and including language providing that the award may be entered in any court with jurisdiction.

---

1. *See* www.clausebuilder.org. AAA's website is www.adr.org. JAMS' website is www.jamsadr.com.

Beginning with a standard arbitration clause will ensure that the intent to arbitrate is clear and unambiguous. A clear and unambiguous clause allows the parties to proceed to arbitration expeditiously. It also makes clear the parties' intentions enabling the arbitrator, administrative body, or a court to interpret and adhere to those intentions. An ambiguous clause, or a clause that lacks necessary terms, will cause delay and additional expense while the parties determine the intention behind the clause. Absent party agreement, court intervention is almost certain. An example of a standard clause recommended by the AAA follows:

> Any controversy or claim arising out of or relating to this contract, or the breach thereof, shall be settled by arbitration and administered by the American Arbitration Association in accordance with its Commercial Rules [or other], and judgment on the award rendered by the arbitrator(s) may be entered in any court having jurisdiction thereof.[2]

A standard clause such as the one above provides a template from which counsel may begin their drafting and editing as needed.[3] This simple and straightforward clause accomplishes several things. First and foremost, this broad clause sets forth that any "controversy or claim arising out of or relating to this contract, or the breach thereof, shall be settled by arbitration . . . ."[4] This helps minimize any dilatory conduct on the part of a party who attempts to argue that the subject matter of the dispute is not subject to arbitration. If the clause were less broad or ambiguous about the types of disputes to be heard, delay would likely ensue while the parties sought court intervention to stay the matter.

This standard clause also sets forth the applicable rules and the administering body. If the rules or administrative body are not set forth, the parties must agree on each, resulting in additional delay and potential costs because court intervention may also be required. Moreover, incorporating an existing set of rules eliminates the need for counsel to identify dozens of procedural matters and anticipate everything that might occur. The incorporation of a set of rules anticipates almost every scenario encountered in the arbitration, such as service, filing, arbitrator selection, locale, impartiality, and the arbitrator's powers. Finally, this clause provides for enforcement of the award by setting forth the parties' agreement concerning entry of judgment in stating that "judgment on the award rendered by the arbitrator(s) may be entered in any court having jurisdiction thereof."[5]

---

2. AMERICAN ARBITRATION ASSOCIATION, DRAFTING DISPUTE RESOLUTION CLAUSES: A PRACTICAL GUIDE (Oct. 1, 2013) [hereinafter AAA].

3. The AAA and its rules can be substituted for that of another arbitration forum, such as JAMS and its recommended procedures.

4. AMERICAN ARBITRATION ASSOCIATION, *supra* note 2.

5. AMERICAN ARBITRATION ASSOCIATION, *supra* note 2.

Practice Pointer

As suggested earlier, counsel should, where possible, avail themselves of the opportunity to craft a process that meets their particular business needs and limits or expands the powers of the arbitrator accordingly. To effectively accomplish this task, counsel must have a clear and thorough understanding of the selected rules as well as the parties' needs surrounding resolution. Additionally, having an appreciation for the arbitration process and the areas in which delay and additional cost are more likely to occur is critical to avoiding a prolonged and costly arbitration.

C. Key Drafting Considerations

1. Conditions Precedent to Arbitration

Dispute resolution escalation clauses, also known as step clauses, are increasingly popular. They provide for one or more attempts to amicably resolve the dispute prior to commencing arbitration. Mediation is the most common process utilized. Another common method utilized in business disputes involves negotiation or a "sit down" between senior executives involved in the dispute, or executives in the hierarchy above those involved. Either or both processes can be beneficial to successful and early dispute resolution.

An important consideration when drafting such a provision is to specifically identify and outline the process to be utilized (i.e., negotiation or mediation). Counsel should also consider identifying the method and form of notice required to initiate the negotiation process, along with a deadline for initiating the negotiation or mediation once a party is made aware of the dispute. This will avoid delay and ambiguity. Additionally, setting forth the individuals who shall negotiate by title or role will move the process along more quickly. For instance, many agreements explicitly set forth the title of the person likely in charge of the entity or division that would be impacted by the dispute. These people are generally in the chain of command above those involved in the day-to-day dispute or activity, so they come to the table without emotion and focused purely on the business dispute at hand.

Practice Pointer

To avoid dilatory conduct of a party utilizing this clause, an important consideration is to set forth a timeframe in which the negotiation or mediation process is to be completed, as well as a default provision allowing commencement of arbitration if one side fails to comply with the process as set forth.

2.   What Is Arbitrable?

Most standard arbitration clauses provide that all disputes arising from the agreement are arbitrable. Counsel may wish to limit or exclude certain disputes from the arbitration process depending on the nature of the contract. The best way to limit certain disputes is to explicitly outline which disputes the arbitrator is authorized to hear and those that are reserved for the courts. Another common exclusion involves prohibiting the arbitrator from issuing an injunction, whether preliminary or permanent, thereby requiring the parties to seek court intervention for such relief. Many arbitral institutions now have default provisions within their rules concerning interim and injunctive relief, emergency or otherwise.[6]

3.   The Locale of the Arbitration

Identifying in advance the location of the arbitration hearing eliminates any disagreement once the arbitration is commenced. In the event the locale is not set forth in the agreement, the parties will generally be encouraged by the administrative provider to agree on a location. In the event the parties cannot agree, each provider has a method by which to make that determination. Key factors for counsel when selecting the locale consist of the convenience of the parties and witnesses along with the available arbitrator pool. When the selected locale is a remote area and it is anticipated that the available pool of arbitrators is limited, adding language that the arbitrator will be chosen from a broader geographic region would be beneficial to the parties.

4.   Arbitration Rules and Governing Procedural and Substantive Law

All standard clauses set forth the administering organization's rules. Many of these organizations have a variety of rules to choose from depending on the substantive nature of the contract (i.e., commercial, construction, and patent). Additionally, many organizations have rules designed for expedited and large, complex matters.[7] Understanding the differences between these rules is critical to identifying and selecting the most favorable set for your client.

The administering organization's rules primarily govern the arbitration process and often do not address procedural or substantive law. A common mistake made by counsel is to solely identify the substantive law and ignore the procedural law.

Practice Pointer

To avoid confusion and disputes concerning the applicable law, specificity is important. Additionally, many disputes effect interstate commerce and are governed by the Federal Arbitration Act, which may preempt certain state laws. Counsel

---

6.   *See* AAA Commercial Arbitration Rules and Mediation Procedures R-38 (Oct. 1, 2013).

7.   Notably, most providers will administer a differing organization's rules if the clause identifies the administering organization but provides for the application of another organization's rules.

must be familiar with such rules to make informed decisions about procedural and substantive law selections.

5. Case Duration

Consideration should be given to crafting an arbitration clause that requires a specified deadline by which the award must issue following a certain event (i.e., date of filing, completion of discovery, submission of the answer/counterclaim). This will serve to force the parties, the arbitrator, and the administrative forum to stay within this timeframe or subject the award to vacatur. It is imperative to be realistic in setting this deadline to ensure that there is enough time for all involved to prepare for and conduct a full and efficient hearing on the merits. As indicated earlier, if there is concern that this is risky because one never knows what the nature of the dispute will be, it is best to provide the arbitrator the authority to grant a reasonable amount of additional time by setting forth a rigorous standard of review.

6. The Arbitrator—One Versus Three; Area of Expertise; and the Method of Selection

Selecting the right arbitrator is critical to a positive arbitration experience. One of the benefits of arbitration is the ability to choose a decision maker with a specific subject matter expertise related to the dispute. Doing so eliminates the need for educating the decision maker about certain elements of the dispute, allowing the parties to quickly get to the heart of the issues. In addition to subject matter expertise, selecting an arbitrator who is experienced and skilled in the arbitration process will likely increase the efficiency of the process.

7. The Background of the Arbitrator

The well-known arbitration providers such as AAA and JAMS have many experienced and qualified arbitrators on their panels. When a case is filed with an administering organization, the parties often have input into the background and expertise of the arbitrators they are offered. Notwithstanding, the parties may wish to set forth the background and experience they seek in the arbitration clause. For instance, the parties may agree in advance to a litigator who practices in the New York Metropolitan area with experience in commercial contracts.

Practice Pointer

Caution should be exercised, however, to avoid being too specific. If there is not an abundance of arbitrators to select from because the criteria sought is too specific, this could add delay to the process and limit the pool from which to choose.

Moreover, depending on the strengths or weaknesses of the case, counsel may seek an arbitrator with less industry or legal experience in an area.

8. The Number of Arbitrators

Many dispute resolution providers have rules that determine whether one versus three arbitrators will be appointed. The number of arbitrators often is determined by the claim amount. Although the amount in dispute can be one factor to consider when determining how many arbitrators the parties need, it is not the only factor. Other factors to consider include cost, delay, risk, and complexity. Selecting three arbitrators can increase the cost by as much as 73 percent.[8] Identifying available consecutive hearing days that work for all parties, witnesses, and arbitrators in the reasonable future will be more difficult.

Complexity and risk are additional factors to consider. If the issues are complex or there is a significant amount of money at stake, the parties may wish to have three people determining liability and damages, as opposed to one, to make certain that an important issue is not overlooked, and the damage award is reasonable. Additionally, depending on the nature of the agreement and the dispute, various types of backgrounds may be required. For instance, in a complex executive employment contract dispute, it might be helpful to have someone with experience drafting such contracts, a litigator, and/or a benefits/compensation lawyer.

9. The Method of Selection

Many of the administering organizations have a process by which they encourage or require the parties to select the neutral. Generally, each organization provides a list from which to choose. In certain cases, some organizations make their entire list available to the parties. In the case of three arbitrators, each party may prefer to select one arbitrator and have those arbitrators identify and select the third. Such arbitrators may be neutral or nonneutral, and the parties' intent concerning the same should be clearly outlined. If this method is preferred, setting forth a deadline by which each arbitrator will be appointed, along with a default provision for noncompliance, will prevent delay.

10. Discovery

Arbitration is traditionally known to involve limited discovery. In recent years, however, discovery in arbitration has been criticized as becoming akin to that of litigation. Discovery is expensive and time consuming. Although arbitrators are trained to limit discovery and remind the parties that arbitration is meant to be more efficient and less costly than litigation, if both parties agree to extensive discovery, many arbitrators are unlikely to interfere. Although discovery is a necessary part of dispute resolution, in arbitration it should be kept to a minimum for the purposes of efficiency and cost-savings.

---

8. Statistic based on commercial AAA arbitrations awarded in 2013 with claims of $1 million or more.

It is difficult to predict exactly what discovery will be needed when a dispute arises. To control discovery in arbitration, counsel should consider setting forth the permitted and excluded forms of discovery (i.e., each party shall be permitted to take one deposition lasting no more than eight hours each; interrogatories shall not be permitted). All forms of discovery permitted in litigation should not be allowed in arbitration if the goal is a cost-effective and expeditious process. Counsel should also consider setting forth deadlines for the completion of discovery. Additionally, setting forth that the arbitrator will determine all discovery disputes, along with a standard by which the arbitrator shall determine a party has not complied and what consequence should be incurred, would be beneficial. In addition, providing the arbitrator with the authority to provide for more discovery if the explicit standard set forth for doing so is met provides the arbitrator with insight into the parties' objectives.

11. Motion Practice

Motion practice historically had no place in arbitration. This is another litigation tool that has been criticized for becoming more common in arbitration. Motion practice should be considered only when it will streamline the process by limiting or eliminating issues for consideration at the evidentiary hearing. Such types of motions may include jurisdiction/arbitrability challenges; consolidation/joinder requests; interim relief requests; dispositive; and/or discovery motions. Many arbitral instructions now have rules governing motion practice and encourage counsel and the arbitrator to remain mindful about the costs associated with motions. In the event a motion will potentially streamline the process, arbitrators are further encouraged to look for ways to ensure the efficiency of motion practice, such as exploring whether motions can be made orally, limiting page numbers, and condensing the timeframe of submissions.

It is difficult to predict whether such motions will do so in advance of knowing the particular dispute. One way to ensure that motions are used only when helpful is to draft a clause that sets forth a standard by which the arbitrator may consider such motions (i.e., likelihood of success on the motion). Absent doing so, the parties will be subject to their agreement, the arbitrator's broad authority, or the applicable administering organization's rules.

12. Evidentiary Hearing Practices

There are numerous ways to reduce the time spent in the evidentiary hearing, and experienced arbitrators will discuss such ways during the preliminary hearing. However, setting forth time-saving measures in the arbitration clause will guarantee that such methods followed. One example is to require that all direct testimony be submitted via affidavit in advance of the hearing, allowing cross-examination during only the evidentiary hearing. Another example is to require all exhibits be agreed to and marked in advance of the hearing. Both approaches, together or alone, save an extraordinary amount of time during the hearing.

13. Confidentiality

One of the most touted benefits of arbitration is that it is confidential, although this is not entirely true as set forth earlier in this chapter discussing the pros and cons of arbitration. The administering agency and the arbitrator are bound by confidentiality, but the parties are not. To ensure confidentiality, the clause should contain language requiring the parties to keep the existence and substance of the proceedings private, potentially including testimony and documentary evidence as well. A provision should also be added to require that any documents filed with the court, for any reason surrounding the arbitration, will be filed under seal.[9] Finally, adding a liquidated damages clause will ensure compliance with confidentiality or provide compensation in the event one party breaches.

14. Remedies

The parties may wish to add, limit, or exclude remedies available pursuant to the administering organization's rules. Arbitrators have broad powers in granting remedies. Rather than leave it to chance, counsel may desire to specifically set forth the authority of the arbitrator to grant certain remedies. Common additions include interest, including the rate; attorney's fees; costs; and expenses. Consideration should be given to whether a standard should be set forth for the arbitrator in making his or her determination (i.e., prevailing party). Common exclusions include injunctive relief and punitive and consequential damages. Consideration should also be given to whether the arbitrator may order money or goods be held in escrow, liquidated damages, and limiting the total amount of the award.

15. Interim and Injunctive Relief

Practice Pointer

Allowing for interim and injunctive relief through the arbitration forum will reduce cost and delay by avoiding the use of the courts in aid of the arbitration. A motion pending in the courts will often delay the proceedings, given most court's overburdened dockets, not to mention the additional attorney's fees incurred writing and submitting those motions in accordance with court rules. If the arbitrator selected to hear the substantive issues is authorized to also consider interim, injunctive, and emergency relief, it will ultimately save time and money. In addition to keeping the dispute in one forum, the arbitrator will already have knowledge of the parties' respective businesses and the nature of dispute,

---

9.   Many courts will not allow parties to dictate the procedures or protocols of the court, so it is not guaranteed that the court will accept such documents under seal. However, the agreement of the parties puts the court on notice of the parties' desires and increases the likelihood the court will assist the parties in keeping documents confidential where appropriate.

eliminating additional delay educating the judge. The arbitrator may also streamline the process by which any such motions are submitted.

16. The Award: Deadline and Form

To control the timeframe in which the dispute is resolved, the parties may set forth a deadline for issuance of the award that begins to run from the date the arbitration is commenced. Counsel should be careful that any such limitation is, in fact, reasonable. Additionally, as a safeguard, counsel should set forth a standard by which the arbitrator may extend such deadline.

The form of the award is another consideration. In addition to the time to draft and edit the award that will be charged to the parties, the time in which the arbitrator will spend during the hearing taking detailed notes and/or requiring a written record of the proceedings could add significant additional costs to the proceedings. If there are three arbitrators, this cost will be considerable.

There are various forms of awards available in arbitration. A standard award is the simplest in that it generally identifies the prevailing party and the remedy awarded. A reasoned award, as its name suggests, provides the reasons the arbitrator selected the prevailing party, applicable law, and the appropriate remedy. Finally, findings of fact and conclusions of law is another form of award available in arbitration. This award generally is the most detailed and time-consuming to issue.

V. BEST ADVOCACY PRACTICES IN ARBITRATION

Arbitration's reputation for being less costly and more efficient than litigation has been tarnished recently because of the steady stream of full-blown litigation tactics making their way into the arbitration process. Businesses that once utilized arbitration as a primary method of resolving disputes have begun rejecting the process and are returning to traditional litigation. The costs of litigation remain high, however, and not only involve attorney's fees, but considerable staff time producing documents, responding to interrogatories, and preparing for numerous depositions that could be better spent developing the core business. Additionally, given the lengthy appeals process, the lack of finality of a large dispute can often hinder a business' ability to grow, obtain loans, spend money, and make key decisions. Given that businesses cannot afford to waste time litigating, a faster, less costly form of dispute resolution is needed.

Arbitration can once again be the solution if the process is controlled from the beginning. Businesses considering arbitration are looking for ways to reap the benefits of the process as originally promised. In addition to a well-drafted arbitration clause, additional best-practice tips include careful consideration when selecting the arbitrator and counsel, as discussed below.

A. Selecting the Best Arbitrator(s)

In addition to a well-drafted arbitration clause, another critical step in the arbitration process is selecting an arbitrator that is well versed in the subject matter at issue in the dispute as well as highly experienced in managing the arbitration process. Having the subject-matter expertise will reduce the time in which the arbitrator must be educated. It will also increase the likelihood that the award will be equitable. Having significant experience in the arbitration process ensures that the arbitrator is well versed in techniques that streamline the process and will utilize them.

Most arbitral forums have a rigorous application process to be admitted to their panels, but admission to a particular panel is only one consideration. Significant due diligence on the part of the parties prior to selecting an arbitrator is imperative. Understanding the arbitrator's temperament, background, training, experience, expertise, the number of cases the arbitrator has heard as an arbitrator, and the number of cases where the arbitrator has served as an advocate in arbitration are critical.

Additionally, the types of cases, issues presented, whether the arbitrator has chaired cases or only served as a sole arbitrator, as well as the form of the awards issued can also be helpful in identifying the best arbitrator. Depending on the size of the case, some arbitral forums will allow for oral or written questioning of the arbitrator to assist in this process. It is also important to speak to others who know the arbitrator and/or have appeared before him or her. The parties can gain a great deal of insight into that person's style and temperament, which can be extremely helpful when strategizing how best to present the case along with determining whether the arbitrator will be diligent in enforcing an efficient and cost-savings process. Finally, reading articles and viewing presentations given by the arbitrator can be helpful in gaining additional insights.

B. Hiring Counsel Experienced in Arbitration

Hiring counsel familiar and highly experienced in arbitration is another cost-savings measure. Attorneys who handle arbitration matters on a regular basis are more attuned to identifying ways to streamline the process. Having greater knowledge of various arbitral forum rules and their arbitral panels can reduce the overall time spent and billed. Attorneys with more experience in litigation than arbitration may be more comfortable utilizing common litigation practices to advance their position. Specifically, they may be more inclined to require full-blown discovery before they are willing to present the case to the arbitrator and default to motion practice when a dispute arises. Less formal rules of evidence in arbitration may also lead to unnecessary disputes before the arbitrator. Counsel who understands the important differences between litigation and arbitration are extremely valuable when it comes to cost-saving and time-reducing techniques in arbitration.

C. Know the Rules

Most arbitral institutions have a specific set of rules for certain types of disputes. These rules often differ greatly from institution to institution. Indeed, they often differ greatly from the Federal Rules of Civil Procedure and state and local rules.

Practice Pointer

Good arbitration advocacy requires that advocates be familiar with the applicable rules to avoid missing out on opportunities to advance one's position as well as to ensure time and cost savings.

D. Preparation for the Preliminary Hearing

The arbitration process often begins with a preliminary hearing. The preliminary hearing is a critical step in the process because it shapes the entire case. Outside of the pleadings, this is usually the first time counsel has the opportunity to interact with and begin making an impression on the arbitrator. To make the most of this opportunity, counsel should be prepared with a themed elevator speech about the case. Being prepared and efficient will also help build credibility with the arbitrator. To be most effective, counsel should also have a thorough understanding of its position, how long the case will take, what discovery will be needed, what motion practice might lead to greater efficiently, if any, and any other issues that must be raised.

E. Prehearing

After the preliminary hearing, the arbitrator will issue a scheduling order. Counsel should be prepared to follow and adhere to the order because arbitrators are not inclined to adjourn dates unless there is good cause shown for doing so. Arbitrators are always balancing between ensuring the parties have the opportunity for a full and fair hearing while keeping costs down and the process moving efficiently. Discovery requests should be limited to key pieces of information, and if a dispute arises, counsel must be prepared to convince the arbitrator why such discovery is necessary because the arbitrator has broad discretion in limiting discovery. The same applies with respect to motion practice.

F. Hearing

Practice Pointer

Preparation for the hearing should be the same as trial. Witnesses must be prepared, and exhibits must be organized. Counsel must outline the elements of their claim or defense and be readily able to identify what proof supports each. Visual aids can be helpful. Making witness lists available to the arbitrator, including a short description of the testimony, and providing a small notebook with the documents to which the witness will testify is also helpful. During the hearing, do not worry about making every objection, particularly those involving hearsay. Arbitrators are often experienced lawyers who can parse through testimony and give it the appropriate weight. In addition to focusing on liability, do not forget about damages. Damages are often an afterthought, which makes it more difficult on the arbitrator to award them. The same applies with respect to defending against damages.

VI.   CONCLUSION

Mediation and arbitration are practical and efficient alternatives to traditional litigation. Although not appropriate for every case, they are options that should be considered when drafting a commercial lease or facing a leasing dispute. To obtain the benefits and the promise of the process of efficiency and cost-effectiveness, it is critical to have a well-drafted arbitration clause, experienced counsel, and an experienced arbitrator with sophisticated subject matter and case-management experience.

Chapter 5

Cybersecurity and Protecting Data Privacy

By Steven P. Seltzer, John G. Loughnane,
and Susan N. Goodman[1]

Every day the national news includes a story about a company, application, or service that has suffered a data breach. It is a common occurrence, so companies must take steps to protect and respond to these events. Protection begins with understanding those laws and regulations affecting data privacy and developing tools and programs to minimize privacy data security risks. This chapter will educate the reader on data privacy, cybersecurity, breach risk, breach mitigation, and the steps necessary to prepare for and respond to data security incidents and/or breaches.

Electronic transmission and storage of data has become a part of everyday life, both commercially and personally. Most individuals have certainly moved well beyond the mere carrying of a smart phone or swiping of a credit card and now drive vehicles that are full of electronic "syncing" options; track health and fitness information either through an app, a wearable, or both; and pay bills or transfer money through the assistance of an app. Digitization is equally as pervasive in business. Legal counsel

---

1. The authors wish to thank Stephen E. Breidenbach, Esq. of Moritt Hock & Hamroff LLP for his valuable contribution to this chapter. In addition, the authors are grateful for the assistance of the following law clerks: Nicole M. Coulter-Ledbetter of University of Iowa College of Law, Maddy B. Hosey of Drake University Law School, Kaitlyn A. Jenkins of Drake University Law School, and Haley Grissom of Boston College Law School.

representing clients in industries subject to data privacy laws and regulations are required to understand and stay informed on what has become an ever-evolving data privacy landscape. Data compromise has become an equally pervasive theme for many industries. Accordingly, cybersecurity and data breach awareness are clearly a priority issue for counsel, especially in-house counsel. With emphasis on in-house generalists, this chapter provides an overview of how to develop an effective data privacy program, address ongoing risks, and prepare for and mitigate security incidents. Both legal and general media outlets have reported many data breaches in recent years, making it unnecessary to rehash them. No business—whether large or small—is immune from the risk. Although massive breaches like the one reported by Equifax in 2017 gain big headlines, there are many more that escape publicity.

Not surprisingly, data privacy and cybersecurity laws and processes overlap. In fact, what is often thought of and discussed as cybersecurity inherently includes development of data privacy processes to minimize data security breaches. Effective data security programs require engagement and integration throughout various levels of the organization. The best IT/data security team cannot effectively keep any organization's data secure without the engagement of organizational leadership, end-user employees, compliance professionals, vendors, and, ultimately, the board of directors. Organizations often have competent teams covering each of these areas, yet fail to effectively integrate the communication, policies, training, and incident response responsibilities cross-functionally.

Further, although organizations must have robust sanction policies to deal with process-and-procedure violations, overly harsh or punitive approaches to security incidents/breaches may simply cause staff to refrain from reporting incident and/or breaches, fearing immediate termination. In response, some organizations have incorporated specific analytical frameworks for assessment of compliance concerns into organizational handbooks or conduct codes to improve expectation transparency and, hence, compliance engagement at the employee level.

In-house counsel is particularly well-situated to pull together the various aspects necessary for the development and execution of an effective data privacy and cybersecurity program. Rule number one is to acknowledge that data privacy and cybersecurity are not just IT issues. Whether discussing prevention efforts or dealing with a real or suspected breach, the legal department is front and center. Remember, it is not IT that will be talking to regulators or defending against threatened or actual litigation. However, it is still important for you, as in-house counsel, to know your IT partners well. You must meet regularly with your IT department and have at least a working understanding of their security efforts and processes. Your IT department must know you well and feel comfortable calling you as soon as an issue (or even potential issue) arises. If you work inside a smaller company without a significant IT staff, maintaining a solid relationship with the IT vendor who services your computer systems would be helpful, allowing the vendor to come in on short notice without having to learn your business and systems from scratch.

You will also need support and serious buy-in at all levels of your organization—from employees to senior management, all the way up to the CEO. You might enlist support from the CEO by reminding him or her that in the event of a data breach, he or she is likely to be the star witness in any litigation or regulatory investigation (whether or not you have a public-relations spokesperson) and will want to demonstrate the company's robust breach prevention and readiness efforts. If you work in a public company, the board may also have responsibilities to stay informed and ask questions about the company's cybersecurity protection programs. Indeed, regulatory agencies such as the SEC and HHS are taking more interest in companies' cybersecurity risk management and governance, as well as disclosure of cybersecurity preventive programs and actual incidents, making board and C-level awareness imperative.

For example, in 2013 and 2014 an unauthorized third party stole credentials to over one billion Yahoo accounts, but disclosure of those incidents did not occur until December 2016.[2] The outcry that followed was tremendous and included the filing of 43 consumer federal and state class actions, a stockholder class action based on sections 10(b) and 20(a) of the Securities Exchange Act of 1934, four stockholder derivative actions, and investigations by the SEC, FTC, and the U.S. attorney and state attorneys general offices.[3]

Yahoo's 2016 10K noted the resignation of its general counsel as a "management change" adopted in response to the findings of Yahoo's data breach independent committee.[4] The independent committee found "that (i) the 2014 Security Incident was not properly investigated, managed and communicated internally at the time, so that the Company was not adequately advised with respect to the legal and business risks associated with the incident and (ii) the Audit and Finance Committee and the full Board were inadequately informed of the full severity, risks, and potential impacts of the 2014 Security Incident."[5]

Uber experienced a cyberattack in 2014 compromising 50,000 names and driver's licenses of Uber drivers.[6] However, it was the handling of a 2016 breach that resulted in employment ramifications. In November 2017, Uber disclosed that hackers had stolen 57 million driver and rider accounts in the 2016 breach.[7] The disclosure indicated that two company employees, the chief security officer (who reportedly also held the title "deputy general counsel") and the security and law enforcement legal director, had complied with the hackers' ransom, paying $100,000 in exchange for the hackers' promise to delete the compromised data and keep the breach to themselves.[8] Uber did not report the breach in a timely fashion, resulting in adverse legal and media responses.

---

2. Olga V. Mack & Katia Bloom, *Yahoo's 10K: Lessons on What Not to Do in a Breach,* ACC DOCKET, Nov. 27, 2017, http://www.accdocket.com/articles/yahoo-10k-lessons-on-what-not-to-do-in-a-breach.cfm.

3. Yahoo! Inc., Form 10K 2016, *available at* SEC EDGAR, https://www.sec.gov/Archives/edgar/data/1011006/000119312517065791/d293630d10k.htm.

4. *Id.*

5. *Id.*

6. Mike Isaac, Katie Benner & Sheera Frenkel, *Uber Hid 2016 Breach, Paying Hackers to Delete Stolen Data,* N.Y. TIMES, Nov. 21, 2017, https://www.nytimes.com/2017/11/21/technology/uber-hack.html.

7. *Id.*

8. *Id. See also* Eric Newcomer, *Uber Pushed the Limits of the Law. Now Comes the Reckoning,* BLOOMBERG, Oct. 11, 2017, https://www.bloomberg.com/news/features/2017-10-11/uber-pushed-the-limits-of-the-law-now-comes-the-reckoning.

The CSO was subsequently asked to resign, and the director was terminated.[9] These breach incidents make clear that in-house counsel all the way up to the general counsel can and will be held responsible for known data breaches when not investigated and managed properly.

Data breaches in the healthcare sector have also been large and well-publicized. Anthem Blue Cross Blue Shield represented the largest settlement for a breach of protected health information (PHI) under HIPAA with a settlement of $115 million.[10] Anthem was hacked in February 2015, during which the information of approximately 79 million insureds was compromised.[11] Anthem was aware of flaws in its cybersecurity system in 2013 and failed to proactively address them, allowing hackers to access extensive information, including names, birthdates, Social Security numbers, addresses, and e-mail, employment, and income information.[12] As part of the settlement agreement, Anthem agreed to offer each affected person two years of credit monitoring and reimbursement for breach-related expenses.

Regardless of the size of your company, you should have—or may be required to have—an incident response plan ready to go. Notice it is not only a "breach" response plan, given that the company must react when a cyber or data situation occurs even before knowing whether it qualifies as a breach. You need trusted outside counsel on call, preferably someone who knows your business and is generally familiar with your IT department personnel (and/or IT vendor) and systems. You want to avoid the panic of having to find and retain counsel in the heat of a cybersecurity incident. This means investing time and expense to allow your outside counsel to meet with you and your IT colleagues to learn about your company's systems and technology processes, and ensuring your counsel has information security and/or cyber forensic vendors who can be called in quickly.

Now it is time to get into the details. This chapter consists of five parts. Part I provides a summary of various threat sources and attacks that routinely and persistently challenge organizations of all sizes. Part II sets forth a high-level summary of the legal framework governing data privacy and cybersecurity issues in the United States. Part III discusses essential elements of corporate resilience, including the need to foster an internal culture of security, the importance of an interdisciplinary approach, the techniques for managing vendor relationships, the considerations for corporate partnerships and acquisitions, and the importance of securing adequate and appropriate insurance to cover risks. Part IV focuses on designing, testing, and updating an incident response plan as required by various laws and as a matter of essential planning. This section will also address handling an actual breach situation. Finally, Part V presents a summary list of recommendations for in-house counsel to consider when tackling data privacy and cybersecurity issues.

---

9. *Id.*

10. Brendan Pierson, *Anthem to Pay $115 Million to settle U.S. Lawsuits Over Data Breach,* https://www.reuters.com/article/us-anthem-cyber-settlement/anthem-to-pay-record-115-million-to-settle-u-s-lawsuits-over-data-breach-idUSKBN19E2ML (last visited July 12, 2018).

11. *Id.*

12. *Id.*

I. THREAT SOURCES

The most likely source of a data breach comes from within your organization. You may find yourself dealing with an employee who simply made a mistake or fell victim to a scam, not to mention a disgruntled employee or former employee who intends to do harm. Indeed, there are big, bad foreign hackers out there, both state sponsored and part of organized crime, but an internal act is more likely the cause of a problem. One recent example is a purported class action filed against SunTrust Bank in which an employee accessed the personally identifiable information of approximately 1.5 million SunTrust customers with the intent to sell or transfer the information to criminals.[13] In addition to the breach itself, SunTrust allegedly erred in waiting over a month to inform its customers that their personally identifiable information had been compromised.

There are several schemes that hackers use to attack your data. "Spear phishing" is a favored mechanism for fraudulent actors. Basically, the wrongdoer sends an e-mail to certain employees purporting to be from either a senior executive or a known outside vendor asking for a wire transfer. By the time the false identity becomes known, the money is gone, having been wired to an account unaffiliated with the company. The wrongdoer uses publicly available information to figure out the correct e-mail address format and domain name, then develops a realistic-looking e-mail to send to those persons who are most likely have authority in the finance or accounting department to initiate wire transfers. For example, a Michigan-based tool company suffered an $800,000 loss when a fake e-mail pretending to be from a "Chinese supplier" fraudulently requested a wire transfer.[14] Another company suffered a multimillion-dollar loss when an accounts payable employee processed a wire transfer that appeared to come from the company's president.[15] Note that the legal profession is not immune: a New Jersey law firm filed suit against Bank of America for alleged negligence in allowing a fraudulent account to receive funds wrongfully wired after the law firm's accounting department fell victim to an e-mail that appeared to have been sent by the firm's managing partner.[16]

Whether purporting to be from an internal source or an outside vendor, e-mails that appear to be from a known sender can easily cause an unsuspecting employee to wire a payment away from the company. This is especially problematic when a vendor's e-mail system is hacked. Then, the vendor's e-mail would be from a legitimate source but not for a legitimate purpose. A multifactor authorization process for any significant payment is therefore critical for any company, large or small.

"Phishing" is another common scheme to break into corporate electronic systems. Hackers will send blast e-mails into a company's employee roster, hoping that at least one person will click on an attachment disguised as something legitimate, thereby launching a virus and/or other malicious software. In October 2017, Seagate Technology settled a California federal class-action lawsuit filed after an employee fell for a phishing scheme

---

13. Smith v. SunTrust Bank, Inc., No. 1:18-cv-02200-MHC, at 6 (N.D. Ga. 2018).

14. Am. Tooling Ctr., Inc. v. Travelers Cas. & Sur. Co., 2018 U.S. App. LEXIS 19208 (6th Cir. July 13, 2018).

15. Medidata Solutions., Inc. v. Fed. Ins. Co., 2018 U.S. App. LEXIS 18376 (2d Cir. July 6, 2018).

16. Mazie Slater Katz & Freeman LLP v. Bank of Am. NA, No. L-49-18 (N.J. Super. Ct.).

involving a fake e-mail seeking detailed payroll data about company employees. The error was later alleged to have caused fraudulent acts against many of the company's current and former employees.[17]

"Ransomware" is another popular method for hackers. This method is used by criminal hackers to encrypt information, making it unusable without the encryption key. The wrongdoers will then demand "ransom" payments, usually in the form of cryptocurrency, to unlock systems or prevent further virus infection. This type of threat is especially aimed at industries that depend heavily on data. In May 2017, ransomware named WannaCry infected over 200,000 computers in over 150 different countries. The infection spread through an exploit present on unpatched systems. Once WannaCry infected a computer on the victim's network, the ransomware would use a flaw in the software to spread from machine to machine, encrypting the files of each machine to which it gained access. The result was that the companies' machines became inoperable until the ransom of $300 per computer was paid. Of the companies affected, one of the most notable was the U.K. National Health Service, which was forced to turn away ambulances and cancel or delay certain treatments due to the attack. Similar facts led to a class-action complaint alleging that Allscripts Healthcare Solutions, a nationwide medical records software vendor in the United States, allowed a ransomware attack to cause life-threatening delays in medical care.[18]

Ransomware is a serious cyber threat, not only because of the attempts to extort money, but also because it attempts to render confidential trade secrets or other confidential corporate information unusable. It also stops business operations and impacts the revenue stream. Whether to pay a ransom to criminals can be a difficult decision for corporations. Although a modest payment to regain control of company assets is tempting, companies must consider how it will play in the press and the signal it could send to other hackers.

A company that uses consumer credit cards in any aspect of its business is a prime target for hackers. Financial and communications companies are frequent targets, as are retail stores and online businesses. Highly publicized breaches over the past several years have included Home Depot, Neiman-Marcus, Target, and Uber, to name a few. Healthcare companies, including hospitals and insurers, are another favorite target because they have confidential medical information and Social Security numbers on file. However, the important point to keep in mind is that it is not only large national chains and large regional hospitals that fall victim to hackers. Small local businesses and hospitals, which also use and collect credit-card information or patient medical information, are also at risk. This is because it is assumed, usually correctly, that these smaller businesses have less-sophisticated cybersecurity protections (not to mention that these smaller companies often serve as vendors to large companies and may be a gateway to hacking into them). If you think your small business operates under the radar of computer hackers, think again.

---

17. Castillo v. Seagate Tech. LLC, 2017 U.S. Dist. LEXIS 178852 (N.D. Cal. 2017).

18. Surfside Non-Surgical Orthopedics v. Allscripts Healthcare Sols., Inc., No. 1:18-cv-00566, Complaint at 3 (N.D. Ill. 2018).

II. LEGAL FRAMEWORK

The legal framework for cybersecurity in the United States is often described as patchwork in nature. There is no one unifying law applicable to all businesses in all circumstances. Instead, companies are subject to a variety of federal and state laws and regulations depending on their industry and location. For example, certain federal statutes are industry-specific, setting forth obligations and prohibitions for participants in various sectors such as healthcare or the financial sector.

In addition to various federal and state statutes, cybersecurity is regulated through enforcement actions by a myriad of governmental agencies. The Federal Trade Commission (FTC) actively uses its enforcement power to curb "unfair or deceptive trade practices." Other pertinent federal governmental agencies include the Consumer Financial Protection Bureau, the Department of Education, the Department of Health and Human Services, the Federal Communications Commission, and the Securities and Exchange Commission. At the state level, state attorneys general play an active role as a counterpart to the FTC regarding consumer data, especially through the imposition of notification obligations in the event of a data breach impacting consumer data.

The patchwork is also made up of privately negotiated agreements between companies, vendors, and customers, setting forth obligations and responsibilities for cybersecurity issues. Companies are subject to tort-based claims, often in the form of class actions, for alleged violations of duties arising from breaches. Finally, companies in the United States with international operations (including conducting business online intended to reach people outside the United States) must be mindful of applicable foreign laws.

A detailed discussion of all laws applicable to cybersecurity and privacy is beyond the scope of this chapter. Instead, this chapter aims to provide a summary of some of the most critical laws to provide in-house counsel a sense of the legal framework and guiding principles. Set forth below is a discussion of: (1) industry-specific cybersecurity requirements in healthcare and financial services as examples of two, highly regulated industries; (2) a discussion of federal enforcement through the FTC and other agencies as well as state enforcement through state attorneys general; and (3) cross-border issues. Contract issues are discussed in Part III-C, *infra*.

A. Sampling of Industry-Specific Requirements

In-house counsel must have intimate familiarity with industry-specific data privacy and cybersecurity legislation applicable to their own company. Set forth below is a sampling of some of the most important legislation in the highly regulated areas of healthcare and financial services. The purpose of this discussion is to assist in-house counsel with a basic understanding of how such issues are treated in heavily regulated industries, given that these practices serve as examples of how the law has developed to deal with these issues.

The most well-known healthcare privacy law is commonly referenced as HIPAA, which stands for the Health Insurance Portability and Accountability Act of 1996.[19] In fact, much of what makes up the final privacy and security rules were driven by the addition of the HITECH Act, implemented as part of the American Recovery and Reinvestment Act of 2009.[20] HITECH stands for Health Information Technology for Economic and Clinical Health Act. HITECH incentivized the adoption of electronic health record (EHR) technology by providing access to government subsidy dollars to offset the technology capital investment costs associated with the adoption of EHR through a tiered attestation process related to meeting certain adoption milestones. HITECH also legislatively mandated the Office of the National Coordinator for Health Information Technology (ONC).[21]

HIPAA/HITECH (hereinafter HIPAA) applies to health plans, healthcare clearinghouses, and certain healthcare providers that transmit data electronically within the bounds of the Transaction Rule governing the electronic transfer of individually identifiable health-related information .[22] The law also applies to "business associates"—entities providing services to a covered entity involving receipt, creation, transmission, or maintenance of protected health information or PHI.[23] Under HIPAA, covered entities and business associates must request and disclose only the minimum amount of PHI of a patient needed to complete a transaction. Further, covered entities and business associates are responsible for implementing data security procedures, protocols, and policies to safeguard PHI at administrative, technical, physical, and organizational levels.[24] In the event of a breach, HIPAA requires notification to individuals whose PHI has been affected. Larger breaches, defined as involving more than 500 individuals, also require prominent media outlet notification.[25]

HIPAA operates to protect PHI, which is information that relates to an individual's past, present, or future physical or mental health or condition; the provision of healthcare to the individual; and the past, present, or future payment for the provision of healthcare to the individual, as well as information that identifies the individual or that can be reasonably believed to be used to identify the individual.[26]

Two fundamental aspects of HIPAA are known as the Privacy Rule and the Security Rule.[27] The Privacy Rule seeks to protect PHI while allowing for the exchange of

---

19. Pub. L. No. 104-191. The final HIPAA regulations may be found at 45 C.F.R. pt. 160, 164.

20. Pub. L. No. 111-5, 123 Stat. 15.

21. ONC is organizationally situated within the U.S. Department of Health and Human Services and is tasked with coordinating national efforts to implement health information technology in the U.S. health care system. The website for ONC is quite informative, at https://www.healthit.gov.

22. *See* 45 C.F.R. pt. 162 for a complete list of transactions causing HIPAA obligations to flow to a healthcare provider. These transactions generally include activities associated with insurance verification and electronic claim processing.

23. Protected Health Information (PHI) 45 C.F.R. § 160.103.

24. 45 C.F.R. pt. 164(C), §§164.302–164.318.

25. 45 C.F.R. § 164.406.

26. 45 C.F.R. § 160.103; *see generally* definition for "individually identifiable health information."

27. The Privacy and Security Rules are located in 45 C.F.R. pt. 164, with security standards located in sections 300 and 400 and privacy standards in section 500.

information necessary for healthcare. This rule requires covered entities to implement safeguards to protect PHI from inappropriate disclosure and to establish conditions for the use of information without patient authorization. Importantly, the rule establishes the rights of patients to their PHI, such as the right to examine, the right to obtain a copy, and the right to request corrections.

The Security Rule seeks to protect PHI while enabling covered entities to improve patient care. Under the Security Rule, a covered entity must maintain reasonable and appropriate administrative, technical, and physical safeguards for protecting PHI, including ensuring the confidentiality, integrity, and availability of all patient data; protecting against reasonably anticipated security threats and impermissible uses or disclosures; and ensuring workforce compliance.

As the opioid crisis has risen to the headlines in recent months, counsel should be reminded of another important data privacy law relevant to patient information related to substance use disorder, education, prevention, training, treatment, rehabilitation, or research. Records associated with these activities are protected at a higher level than that of HIPAA under 42 C.F.R. pt. 2. (hereinafter Part 2)[28] Organizations subject to these regulations require additional processes to ensure that patient information is not disclosed inappropriately. Part 2 requires a higher level of patient consent for disclosure of information and prohibits free redisclosure of information as is common under HIPAA.

In the financial services industry, the Gramm-Leach-Bliley Act (GLBA), enacted in 1999, applies to financial institutions, including banks, securities firms, insurance companies, and mortgage lenders. The law may also apply to credit counseling services, financial advisors, collection agencies, and credit-card issuing firms, along with other entities that provide or support financial services, as discussed below. GLBA regulates the collection, use, and disclosure by a financial institution of nonpublic personal information from consumers in connection with financial products or services.

As required under GLBA, the FTC issued regulations requiring specified financial institutions to implement measures to secure customer information. The "Safeguards Rule" applies to businesses that are "significantly engaged" in providing financial products or services. This broad definition captures a wide range of businesses. Entities that come into possession of customer information from other financial institutions, such as credit reporting agencies, are also required to comply.

Companies subject to the Safeguards Rule must develop a written information security plan that describes their program to protect customer information. The plan must designate a responsible employee to supervise security, identify and assess risks to customer information, and evaluate the effectiveness of existing safeguards for controlling these risks. The designated employee must also design, implement, monitor, and test a security program, among other steps. Any firm that is subject to GLBA must

---

28. Part 2 regulations have been around since the early 1970s as part of The Comprehensive Alcohol Abuse and Alcoholism Prevention, Treatment, and Rehabilitation Act of 1970, 42 U.S.C.S. § 290dd-3; and the Drug Abuse Office and Treatment Act of 1972, 42 U.S.C.S. § 290ee-3. With the advent of integrated provider networks and health information exchanges, Part 2 requirements were affecting care coordination efforts. Accordingly, the Substance Abuse and Mental Health Services Administration (SAMHSA) updated Part 2 regulations in early 2017, https://www.samhsa.gov/42CFRPart2Final.

have a detailed understanding of how the industry-specific law impacts its business and must develop processes designed to ensure compliance.

Another federal statute relevant to the financial services industry is the Fair Credit Reporting Act (FCRA),[29] which applies to consumer reporting agencies and regulates the use and disclosure of consumer reports and credit card account numbers.

A more recent regulation affecting the financial services industry came from the New York State Department of Financial Services (DFS), which issued cybersecurity regulations that are seen as the new standard for risk control and prescriptive rules in the industry.[30] The DFS regulations set forth detailed requirements that covered companies must follow in terms of establishing cybersecurity policies and programs, risk assessment, testing, data security, incident response plans, and more.

Other federal laws imposing cybersecurity obligations on the use of personal data within certain industries include the Children's Online Privacy Protection Act,[31] the Family Educational Rights and Privacy Act, the Electronic Communications Privacy Act,[32] the Communications Act, and the Computer Fraud and Abuse Act.

B. Enforcement

Every business must be aware of the authority of various governmental entities to exercise enforcement powers to shape standards of corporate behavior in the areas of data security. For example, the Federal Trade Commission Act prohibits unfair or deceptive commercial practices in interstate commerce.[33] The FTC's interpretation of the act allows it to bring enforcement actions against companies for failure to comply with posted privacy policies, changing policies without adequate notice, and/or failing to safeguard personal information. Any dispute about the power of the FTC to act in the area of cybersecurity was resolved by the Third Circuit's decision in *FTC v. Wyndham Worldwide Corp.*,[34] where the court rebuffed a challenge to the FTC's powers. The Eleventh Circuit, however, in a widely anticipated ruling involving the since-defunct company LabMD, threw out an FTC order directing LabMD to overhaul its data security program. The appeals court in *LabMD* found that a lack of specifics on how the cybersecurity changes should be implemented caused the order to fail, but the court deferred to the FTC on the broader question about the scope of its data security authority.[35]

The FTC labels company behavior as "deceptive" when false representations are made to customers through publicly posted policies or announcements. In addition, the FTC considers company behavior to be "unfair" when the company is engaged in practices deemed unreasonable under the circumstances. These labels have been used by the FTC to bring lawsuits against companies for such acts as failing to properly inform

---

29.   15 U.S.C. §§ 1681 *et seq.*
30.   N.Y. COMP. CODES R. & REGS. tit. 23, § 500.00 *et seq.* (West 2017).
31.   Pub. L. No. 105-277 (1998).
32.   18 U.S.C. § 2510, *et seq.*
33.   15 U.S.C. § 45(a)(1).
34.   FTC v. Wyndham, 799 F.3d 236 (3d Cir. 2015).
35.   LabMD, Inc. v. Federal Trade Commission, 891 F.3d 1286 (11th Cir. 2018).

consumers of the types of data the company was collecting, and for using consumer information in a manner that was not previously disclosed.[36] Further, the representations made to consumers at the time of collection continue to exist even when data is acquired as the result of a merger.[37] The typical result of a FTC enforcement action is a negotiated consent agreement.

All companies should be aware of the power of the FTC (and other regulatory bodies) to bring actions to challenge and shape corporate behavior regarding cybersecurity even after the *LabMD* decision. Unfortunately, no concise one-size-fits-all summary allows for easy comfort on this issue. Instead, in-house counsel should generally be aware of the FTC's enforcement actions (and the types of complaints and consent orders previously entered into) as well as the FTC's outreach efforts through the issuance of public guidelines and recommendations (all of which are available on the FTC website at www.ftc.gov).

The SEC has also stepped up its enforcement role through its *Commission Statement and Guidance on Public Company Cybersecurity Disclosures*, issued on February 21, 2018. These enhanced guidelines require public companies to disclose details about board of directors' oversight of cybersecurity, overall corporate risk management, and any risks or incidents that are material. Failure to disclose is a risk for public companies to avoid.

The Office of Civil Rights (OCR) is the organization tasked with investigating and resolving HIPAA violations on behalf of HHS. Over the last three years, settlement figures posted by OCR have ranged from tens of thousands of dollars to tens of millions, as seen in the *Anthem* case. All "large" breaches are posted by HHS on a public breach portal.[38] Counsel should also be aware that other civil monetary penalty obligations could be assessed by HHS consistent with the authority granted under section 1128A of the Social Security Act.

States, of course, enforce their own laws and regulations. State attorneys general have broad enforcement powers, and some are rather activist. State regulators may also have powers to enforce their regulations, such as the New York Superintendent's power to enforce the DFS regulations.

C. Cross-Border Issues

The General Data Protection Regulation (GDPR), promulgated by the European Union and effective as of May 25, 2018, governs the processing and free movement of personal data, recognizing the fundamental rights and freedoms of persons with respect to their personal information. The GDPR applies to data "controllers" and "processors" established in the European Union, regardless of where processing takes place. Importantly, the GDPR also applies to controllers and processors outside the European

---

36. *See* Lesley Fair, *What Vizio was doing behind the TV screen*, FED. TRADE COMM'N, Feb 6, 2017, https://www.ftc.gov/news-events/blogs/business-blog/2017/02/what-vizio-was-doing-behind-tv-screen.

37. *See* Jamie Hine, *Mergers and privacy promises*, FED. TRADE COMM'N, Mar 25, 2015, https://www.ftc.gov/news-events/blogs/business-blog/2015/03/mergers-privacy-promises.

38. *See* https://ocrportal.hhs.gov/ocr/breach/breach_report.jsf.

Union when they are engaged in activities such as offering goods or services in the EU or monitoring a data subject's EU behavior.

The GDPR's reach is broad and may be fairly viewed as stressing privacy more than data protection. The complexity of the regulation has spawned a legal practice specialty in and of itself. Therefore, in order for in-house counsel to determine the extent to which the GDPR (or other foreign laws) impose obligations given the nature of information held or shared by the company, consulting outside counsel with expertise is advisable. Even if determined not to be applicable, in-house counsel will benefit from a working knowledge of the GDPR and other foreign laws, as the thought process behind the enactment of this legislation represents a clear trend for the future.

In certain situations, the GDPR requires a company to undertake a privacy impact assessment, which is an analysis of where data is located and the purpose and context for which it is used. A privacy impact assessment identifies the process by which data is collected, shared, and used, and identifies the risks to such data and the adequacy of measures to guard against such risks. The GDPR also requires (with certain exceptions) companies to designate a data protection officer and imposes many other requirements on those subject to the law.[39]

As further described at Part III-B, *infra*, data security is an interdisciplinary activity. In-house counsel or IT professionals alone will not be positioned to collect, evaluate, and assess the information required by a privacy assessment. It is imperative that in-house counsel involve other relevant members of the organization—both to educate them about the provisions of laws such as the GDPR and, more importantly, to promote a culture of security and compliance. A business operated without regard to such responsibilities is a business operating at a high degree of risk. In addition to the business and public-relations risks, noncompliance with the GDPR imposes the risk of serious economic harm, including penalties of up to four percent of global annual revenue, or €20 million, whichever is greater.

In sum, "patchwork" is indeed the best word to describe the law of cybersecurity (and privacy) in the United States. In-house counsel must be familiar with a host of federal and state laws (including industry-specific laws), the enforcement powers of governmental agencies (such as the FTC), and the reach of foreign laws (such as the GDPR) that can stretch to U.S.-based companies.

---

39. For example, companies are prohibited from transferring information to a country that has not been approved by the European Commission. GDPR art. 46(1). Of note, the United States, as of the date of this publication, has not been approved. However, the European Commission has acknowledged that companies that are compliant with Privacy Shield framework are an exception. *See* https://ec.europa.eu/info/law/law-topic/data-protection/data-transfers-outside-eu/adequacy-protection-personal-data-non-eu-countries_en.

III. BUILDING CORPORATE RESILIENCE

A. Develop, Implement, and Maintain a Culture of Security

The Commonwealth of Massachusetts is generally regarded as a leader in enacting comprehensive standards for the protection of its residents' personal information.[40] The regulation, Standards for the Protection of Personal Information of Residents of the Commonwealth, was promulgated by the Department of Consumer Affairs and Business Regulation in accordance with Massachusetts General Law Chapter 93H. Although many states have enacted data breach legislation that should be reviewed as applicable, it is worthwhile that in-house counsel have working familiarity with the Massachusetts legislation in particular, due to its comprehensive nature.

Under the regulation, businesses holding personal information of Massachusetts residents must comply with minimum security standards. The regulation defines "personal information" as a resident's

> first name and last name or first initial and last name in combination with any one or more of the following data elements that relate to such resident: (a) Social Security number; (b) driver's license number or state-issued identification card number; or (c) financial account number, or credit or debit card number, with or without any required security code, access code, personal identification number or password, that would permit access to a resident's financial account.[41]

Other states have enacted similar laws to protect the personal information of their residents, although the specific definition of the term "personal information" varies among the states' laws.[42] The Massachusetts regulation is noteworthy for its detailed provisions and practically sets forth standards that all companies should consider, whether doing business with Massachusetts residents or not.

A key element of the Massachusetts regulation is the requirement that any business that owns or licenses personal information of a Massachusetts resident must ensure administrative, technical, and physical safeguards for such information through the implementation of a written information security program (WISP).[43] Certain information must be contained in a WISP, including:

- the designation of an employee to maintain the WISP;
- the assessment of risks to the security of records containing personal information and means to mitigate such risks through such action as training sessions for employees and careful monitoring and response to security system failures;

---

40. Its standards appear at 201 CODE MASS. REGS. § 17.00 (West 2018).

41. *Id.* § 17.02.

42. For example, Illinois includes e-mail user name with password and biometric data in its definition of personal information. 815 ILCS 530/5. Further, California and Delaware require companies that collect PII about their residents through the internet to post a privacy policy informing the public about what they collect and how they use that information. *See* CAL. BUS. & PROF. CODE § 22575–22579; DEL. CODE tit. 6 § 205C.

43. 201 CODE MASS. REGS. § 17.03.

- disciplinary measures for violations of the WISP and safeguards for preventing terminated employees from accessing records containing personal information;
- security policies for storing, accessing, and transporting records containing personal information away from business premises;
- reasonable restrictions on physical access to records containing personal information, as well at the appropriate storage of records and data in suitably secure locations;
- regular review of security measures to ensure the security of records containing personal information; and
- documentation of responsive actions to any security breach incidents, as well as post-incident review of events.

Of course, such safeguards must be consistent with any federal or state laws otherwise applicable to the business.

The regulation also requires businesses to limit personal information collected in both scope and duration. Further, the regulation sets forth the requirements for encryption of personal information, as well as minimum standards for secure computing. These items include standards around user identification and authentication, establishing limits to accessing certain information, procedures for patching, and education and general training for employees on the topic of security.[44]

B. Interdisciplinary Approach

Company-wide buy-in is necessary for data privacy and cybersecurity policies to be effective. For in-house counsel to respond effectively to a cybersecurity attack or data breach, extensive planning and relationship-building must have occurred well in advance. Waiting until the moment of need to think through strategic alternatives and assignment of responsibilities is obviously not ideal. This part sets forth some guidelines for in-house counsel to proactively assemble a team and develop relationships. Importantly, counsel must work with others in the organization to ensure that "ownership" of cybersecurity is viewed as a common responsibility—not a problem for only the legal staff or the IT group. In the event of a cyberattack or data breach, all aspects of the organization will be affected. Thus, it makes sense for all stakeholders to be involved in the tasks of prevention and planning.

The first step is identifying with specificity individuals from various company departments who will commit to the cause and work cooperatively to form a response team. Such a group should consist not only of legal and IT personnel, but also C-suite management, risk management, and public-relations employees. A robust compliance function is critical. Sales should also have some involvement, given that cybersecurity is relevant in the buying cycle and that customer satisfaction as part of a response is a critical priority.

---

44. *Id.* § 17.04.

These response team members should then consider which external professionals will complement the team, both for planning purposes and for actual response should the need arise. In the event of an incident, there will be no time for interviewing professionals and negotiating terms of engagement. In-house counsel should work with the internal team to understand which outside professionals might be needed, then make arrangements to finalize the group. In-house counsel must carefully consider the role of outside counsel, and especially the topic of attorney-client privilege, regarding retention of any outside consultants and the scope of legal advice related to a cybersecurity incident.

Once formed, the interdisciplinary group must agree on an incident response plan appropriate to the company that complies with obligations under applicable law. Further, the group must assume ownership of planning for an incident through periodic practice ("table-top") exercises, internal employee training, and a dedicated process for evaluation and improvement of the company's resilience to threats and ability to respond.

C. Vendor/Supplier Due Diligence and Appropriate Contract Terms

Based on legal requirements and risk-management best practices, in-house counsel must ensure that the company's process for engaging vendors vigilantly protects data and serves the cybersecurity needs of the company. Set forth below is a checklist for formalizing a vendor selection process that achieves this objective.

1. Vendor Selection

- Understand the flow of company data to the proposed vendor, the nature of the data to be shared, and the necessary protection needed for such data, including applicable information-security regulations.
- Conduct diligence on the vendor's reputation for compliance and performance.
- Work with your company's information-security personnel to develop appropriate information-security questions (standards-based if applicable) to gauge the potential vendor's sophistication, preparation, and vigilance with data security.
- Require proof of the potential vendor's cyber insurance and assess whether such insurance would be adequate to guard against risks faced by the vendor based on data to be shared.

2. Contracting

- All business stakeholders involved in the vendor selection process must understand the company's need for robust contractual terms on security. Company counsel should develop and maintain a collection of clauses that are generally acceptable. Having others in the business understand this point can help streamline the vendor selection process to avoid providers with terms that are not acceptable.

- Include cybersecurity requirements and procedures that the vendor must maintain.
- Ensure the contract identifies all costs that could stem from a breach and then allocates responsibility for the risk of such costs between the parties.
- Ensure that the contract provides clear guidance on notification procedures in the event of a breach or perhaps even in the event of an incident.
- Understand the vendor's record retention policies and procedures and ensure that such policies are consistent with your own company's requirements.
- Include the right to audit the vendor's cybersecurity procedures and programs.
- Clearly state which party has ownership of data and the circumstances under which data can be transferred (especially if outside the United States).
- Carefully negotiate limitations-of-liability provisions, reflecting the business understanding and allocation of risk regarding data handling.

3. Contract Monitoring

- Once a vendor is selected and final contractual terms have been reached, it is critical to ensure that the vendor's performance under the contract is monitored both for compliance as well as for possible adjustments or amendments.
- Immediately investigate any reports of vendor issues that may surface. Generally, the earlier issues are explored, the greater the range of possible responses.

D. Considerations for Corporate Transactions

Although cybersecurity has always been an extremely important issue in highly regulated industries like healthcare and financial services, concerns arise in the context of virtually every industry. Given that cybersecurity issues can dramatically impact the value of a deal, it is critical that all parties to a potential transaction (including buyers, sellers, investors, board members, and lenders) identify any such potential issues, undertake appropriate diligence, and negotiate tailored agreements. As noted previously, data security issues are not reserved for IT or compliance personnel; the issues demand careful attention from deal makers and decision makers to ensure value is preserved.

Although some deal teams reach for a diligence checklist template from prior deals in preparing for a new transaction, effective diligence requires more critical thinking on data security issues. Before diligence is commenced, the diligence process must first be designed with specific attention to the types of data security issues that ought to be of primary concern given the specific industry, nature of the assets, and contemplated transaction. The process should be designed by a cross-functional team prepared to work together to design a process focused on the highest priority concerns. The team should consider the value of a third-party service provider, preferably one experienced with industry-specific issues, to focus exclusively on cybersecurity concerns.

In using a provider, pay careful attention to the scope of engagement, the terms of retention, and the best practice/industry standards that the provider should bring to the engagement. A few key topics for the provider to examine include whether any prior data disclosures have occurred that may present liability to a new owner; the current data security posture of the company; and the corporate security policy or philosophy/implementation of the entity being acquired.

As with all corporate transactions, critical provisions for agreements with third-party service providers should include representations and warranties, indemnification rights, limitation of liability, and key definitions for terms such as "material adverse change." Contractual rights should be clearly drafted and readily enforceable to protect the expectations of the parties. Due to the unique issues that can arise from inferior data security policies, it is important for parties to understand that even the most brilliant legal language will not fully protect a party from insufficient diligence. Deliberate and thoughtful diligence must go hand-in-hand with tailored documentation, including consideration of other protections, such as suitable insurance.

E. Ensure Cyberinsurance Coverage Is in Place

The cybersecurity insurance market has grown tremendously over the past few years. Traditional liability carriers and new players are entering the field. Such insurance is probably a wise investment, considering the expanding costs and increasing likelihood of a breach. Consider working with a knowledgeable independent risk advisor (not just a broker), and consider the options available, whether a specialized cyber policy or a commercial liability package with some level of cyber coverage. Business interruption is an important type of coverage to consider, as well as coverage for regulatory fines and litigation liabilities. You must evaluate your risk in light of the types of data your company stores and transmits. Personal financial or health data is high risk, whether your business is consumer-facing or not. Specialized cybersecurity policies are new and have not yet been subject to much litigation; however, reviewing a handful of court decisions will allow you to see which provisions may work for special cyber, computer, and commercial general liability (CGL) policies.[45]

---

45. Medidata Solutions., Inc. v. Fed. Ins. Co., 2018 U.S. App. LEXIS (2d Cir. July 6, 2018, *rehearing en banc denied* Aug. 23, 2018) (court held computer fraud provision in crime policy covered losses caused by employee who approved transfer of money based on phony internal e-mails, rejecting argument that policy covered only fraud carried out by third parties); Am. Tooling Ctr., Inc. v. Travelers Cas. & Sur. Co., 2018 U.S. App. LEXIS (6th Cir. July 13, 2018, *rehearing en banc denied* Aug. 28, 2018) (computer fraud provision covered wire transfer executed in response to fake e-mail, reversing lower court and finding a "direct" loss); Aqua Star Corp. v. Travelers Cas. & Sur. Co., No. 16-35614, 2018 U.S. App. LEXIS 9660 (9th Cir. Apr. 17, 2018) (affirming district court decision holding exclusion in computer crime policy barred claim for loss caused by social engineering scam); Posco Daewoo Am. Corp. v. Allnex USA, 2017 U.S. Dist. LEXIS 180069 (D.N.J. Oct. 31, 2017) (travelers wrap and crime policy did not cover loss of money that was a receivable but not owned by insured when supplier's employee fell victim to fraudulent e-mail and wired funds to an improper account); Innovak Int'l Inc. v. Hanover Ins. Co., F. Supp. 3d 1340 (M.D. Fla. 2017) (court ruled that insurer had no duty to defend purported class action, given that the "personal and advertising injury" section of CGL policy did not cover a data breach when the insured did not publish the material); P.F. Chang's China Bistro, Inc. v. Fed. Ins. Co., No. CV-1501322-PHX-SMM, 2016 U.S. Dist. LEXIS 70749 (D. Ariz. May 31, 2016) (breach-related expenses imposed by credit-card processor bank against insured not covered due to exclusion for liability assumed by contract).

To help control premium rates, your company should demonstrate to insurers during the application process that it has a strong cybersecurity program, including a regularly practiced and comprehensive incident response plan informed by knowledgeable counsel, secured vendor relationships, and engaged senior management. It would also help to show mandatory and regular employee training on cybersecurity risks.

IV. PREPARING TO RESPOND TO A BREACH—DEVELOP, TEST, AND UPDATE INCIDENT RESPONSE PLAN

A. Incident Response Plans

A response plan is not just nice to have; it is a must-have. Depending on your line of business and location, you might have a legal requirement to establish and maintain a robust response plan. The plan, manual, or playbook must be taken seriously. Support and input from senior management is critical, including that of executives and perhaps the board. Akin to a disaster recovery plan, the cybersecurity breach plan must be user friendly, comprehensive, and familiar to those who will be expected to implement it. It cannot be tucked away on a shelf; rather, it must be easily accessible and refreshed often. In addition, calling it a "breach" plan can be a misnomer because the plan should also cover situations of a suspected cyber intrusion, even if a "breach" (however defined) did not actually occur.

There are several steps for creating an effective incident response plan. First, you must bring together all necessary stakeholders. As noted earlier in Part III-B, in addition to executive sponsorship, you need colleagues from compliance, public relations, internal audit, human resources, and IT. You especially need colleagues who operate the business in each division, if you have separate divisions, and who know what systems your company uses and how those systems interact with external customers and business partners. If you work in a company that does not have some of these internal functions, then you must engage with outside consultants and vendors who would be called upon in the event of an incident. Depending on your company's size and industry, you may need to engage with media, crisis-management, and forensic IT consultants. A common theme throughout this chapter is the importance of having outside consultants and vendors on standby that could address the breach during a time of panic. These third parties must be lined up and at least preliminarily acquainted with your company, its business, and the various systems in use.

A key outsider you should line up when drafting your incident response plan is, of course, outside counsel. Even a sophisticated in-house legal department with cybersecurity knowledge will benefit from outside counsel's advice and guidance. There is a strong chance that drafting of the plan and internal communications relating to the drafting, when written at the request of counsel to provide legal advice, may be protected by the attorney-client privilege. This protection would give internal stakeholders greater freedom to communicate their concerns and questions regarding cyber risk within the company. Outside counsel should also be fully up to speed on new developments in the law, particularly new cybersecurity legal requirements that might apply to your company. In a sense, outside counsel who is "on call" can provide you some peace of mind.

The incident response plan or playbook is a highly individualized document, unique to your company's line of business, culture, and jurisdictional requirements. Do not expect to take a template and fill in a few blanks; time and thought will be necessary to do this correctly. The following are major points to consider and steps to include in your plan:

- **Reporting.** Map out how suspected cybersecurity incidents will be reported within the company. A large company may have a hotline, whereas smaller companies may need to simply promote calls to IT or the legal department.
- **Confirmation.** Your IT department, or external vendor if needed, must initially investigate the situation and confirm whether some intrusion occurred and whether any data left the company.
- **Escalation.** If a breach, or even meaningful attempted breach, is confirmed, the matter must be raised up to appropriate senior management within the business. You should also inform senior legal department management and other relevant support functions. The legal department, with or without outside counsel, must implement a legal "hold," making sure to freeze IT information and preserve internal communications.
- **Investigation.** Conduct a deeper investigation of facts to determine whether a breach occurred. This should be done under the supervision of counsel (preferably outside counsel) and may require the assistance of outside forensic consultants.
- **Project Manager.** Your company should appoint someone to coordinate and pilot all of the administrative efforts that will begin to ramp up once a breach has been confirmed. This person must be designated in advance and be ready to step up once the alarm sounds. Among other responsibilities, the project manager must carefully document all steps undertaken. This documentation will absolutely be requested by either regulators or plaintiffs' lawyers in the event of a breach.
- **Assessment/Notification.** As facts are developed, determine whether the incident meets the definition of a breach under applicable standards. This step must be headed by legal, which will decide whether any notification requirements have been triggered to customers, regulators, or law enforcement.
- **Mitigation.** The company must act quickly to stop further infiltration or leaking of data, depending on the situation. This is largely the responsibility of IT, but public-relations and marketing colleagues may also be needed to promptly notify customers or business partners to take precautions.
- **De-escalation and Recovery.** The relevant stakeholders, guided by the project manager, will begin to return systems and business to normalcy. Steps to develop long-term improvements are mapped out and implemented.
- **Lessons Learned.** This critical final step includes documenting all remediation actions and preparing applicable reports for senior management and/or the

board (under the direction of counsel). If not already done, this step might include dealing with employees deserving of termination or discipline.

It bears repeating that the above-listed steps are a general outline of points to consider when drafting or refreshing your company's incident response plan. You must customize the plan to fit your company's specific organizational structure and to account for regulatory requirements that may apply.

There are helpful standards that you may want to consult when drafting your cybersecurity incident response plan, even if they don't directly apply. For example, the Massachusetts regulation (described in Part III-A, *supra*) sets out requirements for a WISP. The New York State Department of Financial Services Cybersecurity Requirements for Financial Services Companies[46] mandates that incident response plans also include sections on (1) goals of the incident response plan and (2) roles, responsibilities, and levels of decision-making authority.[47] The National Institute of Standards and Technology (NIST), an agency under the umbrella of the U.S. Department of Commerce, provides a wealth of cybersecurity information online, including its well-known "framework" that one should wisely consult when drafting or refreshing a response plan. Although the framework is neither specific to response plans nor a legal standard per se, it gives excellent context for many points that should be included in your response plan.

There are also other preparatory efforts that may fall outside the corners of the cybersecurity incident response plan document. For example, will your company contact law enforcement if hacked from an outside source? Will your company pay ransom if demanded to unlock critical or confidential data? There are pros and cons either way, and these questions should be considered in advance of a breach, preferably with the advice of experienced outside counsel. Although it's hard to decide for sure until the facts of a real situation present themselves, making it hard to include these topics in your response plan, you are well served to think through questions about law enforcement and ransom payments without the stress of an actual breach at hand. At the very least, you should map out authorizations for decision-making so that the necessary people, including executives, can be pulled in quickly.

Once your incident response plan is polished, you cannot relax. Aside from remembering that the document must be reviewed and updated at least once a year to account for changes in both law and internal staff, you must also remember to practice the plan. This means conducting an all-hands mock breach exercise, or what is often called a "tabletop" exercise. The exercise must be done regularly to keep it in mind and to ensure all employees on the response team are well-versed, especially in light of normal employee turnover. Senior executives should be included. The exercises should be conducted at the request of counsel for the purpose of seeking legal advice about the adequacy of the plan.

---

46. 23 NYCRR Part 500.
47. *Id.* § 500.16.

Post-exercise reports also must be written at the request of counsel so that counsel can provide legal advice about the results of your mock exercise. It is important that participants be open and honest about areas of concern and weaknesses in the plan, knowing that their comments are intended to be held confidential under the attorney-client privilege. It is useful to include IT and public-relations consultants in the exercise if they will be part of the actual breach response team. Consultants should be retained directly by counsel so that steps can be taken to protect their work product. Under *United States v. Kovel*,[48] nonlegal professionals may receive attorney-client privileged materials within the scope of the privilege, and their communications with counsel may be protected, where those professionals are retained by counsel to provide advice and expertise that assists counsel in providing legal advice and/or services to his or her client. Application of the attorney-client privilege is fact-specific in these types of circumstances; therefore, careful guidance by outside counsel is important. As discussed more fully below, if a court finds the materials and communications related to breach preparation efforts were business documents rather than created for a legal purpose, the privilege likely won't apply. In addition, sharing these materials with regulators may waive the privilege and subject them to FOIA requests, but you should consult each state's FOIA rules.

A final point worth noting in connection with breach preparation is the overlap with an old-fashioned disaster recovery plan. Hopefully your company has a disaster recovery plan, which should be consulted as you polish your cybersecurity incident response plan. At a minimum, a robust and up-to-date disaster recovery plan will immediately help in cutting the time needed to recover from a breach and return to normal internet-connected operations. It will also help resist the urge to pay a ransom in the heat of a breach situation.

B. Responding to a Data Incident

There is no difference between responding to a potential breach and an actual breach, at least initially. Thus, in the event of a cybersecurity incident that could evolve into a breach situation, the response plan must be quickly consulted, and all employees must know to contact your legal department right away. In-house or outside counsel should quickly roll out a legal hold, preserving all communications and alerting relevant employees to resist sending internal e-mails discussing the incident and related investigation. You must also quickly contact IT to determine whether any systems must be shut down or frozen (within the confines of carrying on business).

The key players must be contacted and assembled, whether in a room or electronically. Remember that counsel, whether in-house or external, must determine if an actual breach occurred as facts are uncovered. This depends on which federal and state laws apply: on one hand, an unauthorized intrusion into the company's systems may not constitute a breach under some state laws if, for example, the confidential personal information was not actually extracted and shared or was encrypted. On the other hand, other state laws

---

48. United States v. Kovel, 296 F.2d 918 (2d Cir. 1961).

define a mere attempt to access certain personal data as a breach.[49] Even unauthorized disclosure of certain financial account information, without associated names, may be a breach.[50]

Once it is determined that a breach occurred, the project manager must take control, as set out in the response plan. Public-relations colleagues, internal or external, should also be brought in. Notification requirements to both consumers and regulators must be quickly determined by looking at sources such as HIPAA, GLBA, FCC, and various state laws.[51] As counsel, your focus is now on ensuring compliance with notice requirements and preparing for regulatory inquiries and litigation—all while mindful of the attorney-client privilege, including the fact that materials created during the breach investigation may end up disclosed to regulators, state attorneys general, and/or plaintiffs' attorneys. If your internal investigation includes employee interviews, both human resources and the investigating counsel should be present, depending on the situation.

A business should not wait until a breach occurs to determine its notification requirements. Although states' notification laws have many similarities, there are differences that can greatly impact when and how you respond to a data breach. For example, many states require notification only when electronic information is compromised, but some also apply breach notification requirements to disclosure of personal information contained in a tangible form.[52] Some states provide that notification is not required when a business can establish that misuse of the acquired personal information is not reasonably possible, but states such as New York, California, and Texas do not provide such a limitation. Florida's notification law requires that consumers be notified without unreasonable delay and in no event later than 30 days after a business determines, or has reason to believe, a breach occurred, unless the business is notified by the police in writing to hold off.[53] In contrast, New Jersey law can be read to require a business to first report the breach of security to the police prior to notifying consumers, and to delay the notification until after the police confirm that notifying consumers will not compromise the investigation.[54]

Companies and their executives understandably have the urge to keep a breach private until they acquire sufficient information to explain the problem and answer questions. However, some notice requirements will not allow much delay, and regulators and litigants will seize upon delayed notification as another legal liability. In October 2017, Hilton Hotels agreed to pay a large fine and undergo annual assessment of its Payment Card Industry Data Security Standard (PCI DDS) credit card processing procedures after a joint investigation by the New York and Vermont attorney general offices. The regulators alleged that Hilton violated the states' consumer protection and

---

49. *See, e.g.,* the definition of "cybersecurity event" in the New York DFS Regulations, 23 NYCRR 500.01(d).

50. For example, South Dakota: SDCL 22-40 (2018).

51. New York, for example, requires notice to consumers and to the Department of Financial Services via the DFS Web Portal 23 NYCRR 500.17(a); www.dfs.y.gov/about/cybersecurity.

52. *See* ALA. STAT. §§ 45.48.010-45.48.090; MASS. GEN. LAWS ch. 93H; N.C. GEN. STAT. § 75-65.

53. FLA. STAT. § 501.171(4)(a) (West 2014).

54. N.J. STAT. ANN. § 56:8-163 c(1)–(2) (West 2006).

breach notification laws by failing to maintain reasonable data security and by waiting more than nine months after a 2015 breach to notify consumers that their credit card information may have been stolen. In addition, as mentioned early in this chapter, in late 2017 the large-scale data breach announced by Uber resulted in much criticism from consumer groups and regulators, mainly because of the long delay in announcing the breach to the public. These cases demonstrate that company executives and their counsel not only face the pressure of legal problems, but also risk reputational harm to the company upon post-breach scrutiny of response actions.

Unless you are working in a truly local company in which a breach might possibly be handled in a quiet manner, the specter of litigation (most likely class actions) must be front and center. The law in regard to standing to assert a damage claim and the kind of damages that pass muster to maintain a lawsuit remains unsettled. The Supreme Court's holding in *Spokeo, Inc. v. Robins*[55] resulted in an ambiguous new test for standing as applied in cybersecurity breach cases: harm that is intangible, but "concrete" is enough to obtain standing, even if there are no tangible damages. Courts have applied this standard to causes of action in data breach cases based on contract, tort, or statutory violation. There is division among courts on whether standing may be met solely by the increased risk of future identity theft.[56] Parties must be cognizant of the case law in their specific circuit and the patterns of specific judges, given the evident split on what constitutes standing. In a recent development, the Illinois Biometric Information Privacy Act has given potential standing for yet additional causes of action for data breaches involving confidential biometric information.[57]

Not only should you anticipate litigation from consumers affected by the compromise, but your company may also anticipate additional litigation from business partners. If you are a vendor who provides services to other companies and you suffer a breach, you may then face claims pursuant to contractual obligations to your business customers. Take, for example, the lawsuit filed by Chase Bank against Landry's following a data breach. Chase claimed that Landry's failed to comply with credit card industry data security standards and was contractually liable to indemnify Chase.[58]

---

55. Spokeo, Inc. v. Robins, 136 S. Ct. 1540 (2016).

56. *See, e.g.,* Stevens v. Zappos, Inc., 884 F.3d 893 (9th Cir. 2018) (risk of future harm arising from theft of consumer private data is enough for standing); Dieffenbach v. Barnes & Noble, Inc., 887 F.3d 826 (7th Cir. 2018) (appeal court reinstated case finding standing, but cautioned that damages will be hard to prove); Attias v. CareFirst, Inc., 865 F.3d 620 (D.C. Cir. 2017) (grant of motion to dismiss class action reversed based on finding plaintiffs had adequately alleged the data breach exposed them to a substantial risk of identity theft that was "fairly traceable" to CareFirst); In re Supervalu Customer Data Sec. Breach Litig., 870 F.3d 763 (8th Cir. 2017) (court reversed in part lower court's dismissal finding that one of the named plaintiffs had sufficiently alleged actual injury when his credit card was fraudulently charged); Torres v. Wendy's Int'l LLC, 195 F. Supp. 3d 1278 (M.D. Fla. 2017) (plaintiffs seeking class-action status due to stolen credit-card information and alleged lost reward points and cash-back rewards as well as suffering restricted use of their credit cards); In re Banner Health Data Breach Litig., No. 2:16-cv-02696-PHX-SRB (D. Ariz. Apr. 2017) (court dismissed breach-of-contract claims but allowed purported class to proceed with data-breach-related allegations based on unjust enrichment, negligence, and violation of state consumer-fraud law).

57. *See* Wade v. AMB Indus., Inc., No. 18-ch-03855 (Ill. Cir. Ct. Mar. 3, 2018).

58. Paymentech, LLC. v. Landry's Inc., No. 4:2018cv01622, Complaint at 11 (S.D. Tex. May 17, 2018).

As mentioned above, counsel should oversee breach response actions to the extent possible. Although attorney-client privilege will not apply to all of the various steps undertaken, some being purely business functions, the privilege can protect internal strategy and communications if requested by in-house or outside counsel during the course of providing legal advice. Once breach recovery efforts are underway and counsel is providing advice intended to prepare for likely litigation, work-product protection may also apply, but be cautioned that the determination of whether legal privilege will protect internal work product from discovery by regulators or plaintiffs' attorneys is very fact-specific. Courts will examine the specific role of counsel and the context of the work performed to determine whether legal advice and/or anticipation of litigation was actually present or is being created in hindsight merely to oppose disclosure.[59] In addition, if you choose to disclose any conclusions (as opposed to facts) of a privileged forensic investigation, be cautioned that all of the back-up documents created in connection with that investigation may become subject to discovery when you otherwise might have been able to shield them.[60]

As the breach response and recovery winds down, it is extremely important to assemble the team for a "lessons learned" open discussion. Although it may be tempting to skip this step and get back to business as usual, a huge opportunity is lost if time is not taken to review how the situation was handled and what process improvements should be inserted into the next updated version of your response plan. Discussions and communications examining the breach response should be conducted by counsel who is providing legal advice about actions well performed or those needing improvement.

V.   PRACTICE TIPS/RECOMMENDATIONS

A. Threat Sources

- Train employees to minimize internal risks.
- Secure your IT systems and test for penetration.
- Stay current with breach threats so your defenses will be on alert.
- Ensure that vendors have robust cybersecurity protections.

---

59.   *In re* Premera Blue Cross Customer Data, No. 3:15-md-2633-SI, 2017 U.S. Dist. LEXIS 178762 (D. Or. Oct. 27, 2017) (post-breach documents produced merely at request of counsel without legal purpose not privileged, including public-relations documents and forensic vendor's report, but drafts with attorneys' comments embedded may be privileged); *see In re* Experian Data Breach Litig., SACV 15-01592 AG (DFMx), 2017 U.S. Dist. LEXIS 162891 (C.D. Cal. May 18, 2017) (post-breach work product by forensic vendor protected by attorney-client privilege when vendor was specifically hired by outside counsel to assist counsel, and work was separate from pre-breach business function performed by same vendor); *In re* Target Corp. Customer Data Sec. Breach Litig., 2015 U.S. Dist. LEXIS 34554 (D. Minn. Mar. 19, 2015) (dual-track, post-breach investigation served to protect internal communications that had demonstrably legal purpose under either attorney-client privilege or work-product doctrine).

60.   Leibovic v. United Shore Fin. Servs., LLC, No. 15-12639, 2017 BL 301590, (E.D. Mich. Aug. 28, 2017), *mandamus denied*, 2018 U.S. App. Lexis (6th Cir. Jan. 3, 2018).

B. Legal Framework

- Develop and maintain intimate familiarity with industry-specific domestic legislation and regulation.
- Understand and stay informed of governmental enforcement activities applicable to the industry in which your company operates.
- Develop a working knowledge of the principles and requirements of the GDPR and "best practices" even if not directly applicable.
- Commit to involving other relevant members of your organization in promoting a culture of security and compliance.
- Develop and maintain a network of trusted advisors who can help in implementing the above steps on a continuous basis.

C. Building Corporate Resilience

- Develop a culture of security that includes well-functioning relationships at the operations level along with appropriate management and board-level supervision.
- Protect against insider threats through continuous employee training as well as policies and procedures that are implemented and maintained.
- Ensure a robust recovery plan is in place. Practice plan implementation, review for areas of improvement, and repeat on a regular basis.
- Ensure that all aspects of the company's process for engaging and working with vendors vigilantly protect and serve the cybersecurity needs of the company.
- Periodically evaluate sources of potential risk for the company and critically analyze existing insurance coverage and whether additional coverage is needed to help minimize economic harm from risks for which insurance is desired.

D. Preparing to Respond to a Breach

- Understand and inventory your company's data/IT assets.
- Gather a cross-functional team to prepare an incident response plan.
- Outline decision-making procedures and authority in advance.
- Conduct mock exercises, with lessons learned, under the direction of counsel.
- Stay educated in state and federal notice requirements.

E. Resources

- NIST Cybersecurity Framework and Risk Management Framework (National Institute for Standards and Technology, www.nist.gov).
- Your company IT and HR departments (or outside consultants who perform those functions).
- Outside counsel, vetted and educated about your company and its systems.
- International Association of Privacy Professionals, IAPP.org (requires paid membership to access some materials).

- Regulator/law enforcement sources (FBI Internet Crime Complaint Center (IC3); U.S. Computer Emergency Readiness Team; Infragard (membership required); "Order Free Resources" at ftc.gov; www.HealthIT.gov).

Efficient resolution of disputes arising from a data breach should be a top concern for in-house counsel. Disputes that linger pose not only a liability risk, but also a cost concern, given that litigation expenses can quickly escalate. Of course, the key interest of a company affected by a data breach will be responding to and recovering from the breach. Response and recovery will often require interaction with multiple third parties, such as customers, vendors, insurers, regulators, partners, and others. Interests of commercial parties will include confirmation that the specific cause of the breach has been identified and remedied, that the costs of collateral damage created by the breach are covered, and that changes are implemented to reduce the risk of similar breaches in the future.

In situations of widespread harm involving personally identifiable information (PII), it is not uncommon for class-action lawsuits to ensue. In addition to consumers, governmental authorities commonly assert interests in a data breach, seeking compliance with regulatory obligations. Keep in mind that mediation has been used to help parties reach closure on the economic consequences of a breach without having to engage in full-fledged litigation. A successful mediation depends on identifying key interests at stake, as well as options to satisfy those interests. For example, in the fall of 2017, a mediated settlement was preliminarily approved between current and former employees of Seagate Technology LLC and the company arising out of a 2016 data phishing attack that affected approximately 12,000 employees. In the attack, a Seagate employee forwarded PII of fellow employees to attackers who then used the information to file fraudulent tax returns. The settlement provided each current and former employee with two years of credit monitoring and up to $3,500 for out-of-pocket expenses. In sum, when a breach occurs, in-house counsel should consider the possibility of using mediation to help parties identify interests and explore options for satisfying those interests, which can help contain the impact of the breach and avoid collateral consequences.

VI. CONCLUSION

This chapter has provided in-house counsel with a practical overview of major considerations in data privacy and cybersecurity. Although in private practice now, two of the authors have in-house experience at major corporations working directly with business teams on a variety of issues. With that experience in mind, the chapter began with a summary of various threat sources and risks that in-house counsel must understand. The chapter then provided a summary of the legal framework governing cybersecurity issues. Next, the chapter discussed essential corporate resilience steps on which in-house counsel must regularly focus to achieve success in this area. These steps include fostering an internal culture of security, working to develop an interdisciplinary approach, effectively managing vendor relationships, building discipline around corporate partnerships and acquisitions, and ensuring adequate and appropriate insurance is in place to cover risks the company does not want to absorb. The chapter then moved on to considerations in designing, testing, and updating an incident response plan—a core aspect of corporate resilience and a requirement under many laws. The chapter concluded with a summary list of recommendations for in-house counsel to consider, including the recommendation that in-house counsel keep abreast of developments in this area. This area of the law is evolving rapidly and changes often, so you must stay informed. This should be done in close consultation with other leaders of the business, given that ownership of these issues is, and will remain, a responsibility shared across functional lines.

Chapter 6

Requests for Proposal and Alternative Fee Arrangements as an Effective Tool for Evaluating and Selecting Outside Counsel

By Thomas E. Best, Sheila M. Murphy, and Penelope M. Taylor

This chapter is intended to provide an overview of the use of requests for proposals (RFPs) for evaluating, hiring, and consolidating outside counsel, the use of alternative fee arrangements (AFAs), and how to achieve a diverse panel of outside counsel. The goals are to obtain the maximum value and quality of legal services for the best possible price, to ensure that you are selecting the most appropriate counsel for matters, and to keep diversity in the forefront. There are hundreds of law firms that have competent attorneys—many with the expertise that you need—but how do you ensure that you have selected the appropriate counsel at the right price? That is where the RFP process comes into play. We discuss how to evaluate outside counsel as you begin the RFP process and how to evaluate the success of the RFP process. We also weigh in on alternative fee arrangements. We discuss why you might want to use AFAs, various types of AFAs, and best practices. Finally, we discuss the importance of diversity in your selection of firms and how to achieve a diverse panel of attorneys.

I. ADVANTAGES OF RFPs

Why would anyone go through the time and effort to conduct an RFP? Don't you know who the best counsel are? Aren't they the ones who you have worked with for years and already understand you and your business? Well, maybe not if you have not ventured to look at outside counsel other than the same outside counsel your company has been using. You may not know what is out there. In addition, you do not know that you are getting the most competitive rates for the expertise that you need. There are several advantages to using RFPs to select counsel rather than leaving the decision up to individual lawyers in the law department.

A. Level Playing Field

Sending out an RFP that clearly articulates the goals of representation and the factors that are most important to you allows each firm to think about the best representation for that matter and has all firms receiving the same information. Receiving proposals from various legal service providers creates a transparent environment and allows you to clearly compare the benefits and drawbacks of each one on a level playing field. RFPs also allow you to gather similar data from multiple outside counsel, resulting in more of an apples-to-apples comparison. Of course, the more granular the questions for each practice area, the more useful the cross-firm comparison data. It is critical that the questions are not vague. The more open-ended questions you include, the more difficult the comparison process can become. You also want to ensure that you focus on the questions that are most important to you; having lots of boilerplate questions that you do not really care about may muddle the information that you receive and lessen the chance you make the right decision.

B. Better Pricing

Whether an RFP is for a single matter or number of matters, an RFP can help ensure that you are paying the appropriate amount. It is not about selecting the lowest cost provider, but about having a cost structure that is appropriate for the expertise that you need. This includes considering whether an AFA may be appropriate. If you are open to AFAs, then ask for AFAs. You may be able to obtain bulk pricing by using an RFP to cut back on the number of law firms. Firms that will obtain more work are likely to offer better pricing and more efficient billing because the firms will really know and learn your business. During a single-matter RFP process, you can ensure competitive pricing by being able to compare the bids. You also can ask the firms to review their pricing in light of other competitors' bids. We are not suggesting that you disclose the exact bids, but you can tell an outside counsel that they are not competitive—just as you might ask a firm whether they have proposed the best rates for the matter. Remember that although cost is important, you must evaluate various aspects of the responses.

C. Improving Diversity

Diversity refers to any and all characteristics that make one individual different from another. It moves beyond the basic differences of race and gender to encompass differences of all kinds. It works hand-in-hand with inclusion, which focuses on ensuring that your business environment is a place where all feel included, respected, and supported to reach their fullest potential. Diversity and inclusion serve as competitive advantages for those companies and firms that embrace the concepts. When placing diversity and inclusion at the forefront of your overall strategy, you harness the collective background, thought, and experiences of a broader community. Equally as important, you bring to your company a team of lawyers that are reflective of the diverse nature of your company and the community in which your company exists. Placing diversity and inclusion at the forefront will serve as a force multiplier for your entire strategy.

D. Assessment of Available Legal Service Providers

In addition to cost benefits, the RFP allows a company to determine whether there are better or more effective legal services providers for it. The legal landscape is changing radically. No longer do you need a law firm to be just down the block. Depending on the work, you can consider firms and service providers throughout the country and, in some cases, the world. Legal work can be done well by a wide array of law firms. The RFP process may uncover firms of which the company was unaware as well as other pricing approaches. Moreover, lawyers are now more mobile than they have been in the past. As a result, law firm expertise and benches are changing much more frequently.

II.   OUTSIDE COUNSEL EVALUATIONS AS A START

When faced with the dilemma of where to begin, the outside counsel evaluation is the best starting point. Most companies already have a set of lawyers who they have worked with for a number of years. Before embarking on an RFP where you will bring in other firms to bid for the work, it is important to know what you have before you go shopping for someone new. Accordingly, our journey will begin with a discussion of developing a useful outside counsel evaluation template.

With the proliferation of enterprise legal management (ELM)[1] systems and various in-house counsel organizations,[2] the creation of an outside counsel evaluation should not be difficult. However, embarking down a wayward path without planning and foresight

---

1.   "Enterprise Legal Management" is a term that has found its way into the legal vernacular over the past few years. It simply means the technology that law firms and legal departments use to manage their legal business. It includes matter management, document management, and e-billing systems, all which can provide valuable data to measuring the efficiency of the legal profession.

2.   Several leading in-house legal organizations have numerous articles and templates to further your understanding of the importance of the outside counsel evaluation. Such organizations include the Association of Corporate Counsel; CEB Global, a Gartner Company; and the Corporate Legal Operations Consortium (CLOC). All require various fees to join.

will limit the effectiveness of the tool you design. The key to your journey is simple: What do you want to evaluate and how do you want to *measure* what you evaluate?

Faced with pressures from their CEOs and boards, in-house counsel generally answer these questions by focusing primarily on cost. Charged with reining in outside legal costs, in-house counsel will inevitably focus on total cost as the driving force in measuring the success of outside counsel. Effective outside counsel evaluations allow you to ensure that your assessment of outside counsel is multifaceted.

III. ELEMENTS OF AN EFFECTIVE OUTSIDE COUNSEL EVALUATION

An effective outside counsel evaluation should include both objective and subjective measurements, leverage the data you have in your ELM system, weight each measurement you select, and leverage your technology to allow for effective data analysis.

The most difficult aspect when creating an outside counsel evaluation form is deciding what should be evaluated. Given time pressures generally present in each in-house counsel's role, an evaluation form that is too detailed and requires too many data elements will likely result in limited adoption within your legal department. Likewise, an evaluation form that is not sufficiently detailed will not provide a meaningful way to differentiate your outside counsel. The delicate balance needed can be achieved if you segment your outside counsel evaluation. You can consider rating both the law firm and the attorneys (see Appendix A) or you can simply rate the law firm (see Appendix B). In any event, having separate sections of the outside counsel evaluation allows for a great breadth of analysis. We suggest including at least the sections that follow.

A. Financial Results

As a business unit, the legal department must be cognizant of the financial impact of outside counsel fees. The outside counsel evaluation needs an objective way to measure the financial performance of each of the company's law firms. To obtain a full financial picture, the following financial measurements should be tracked.

1. Total Legal Fees/Total Legal Fees by Unit or Type

With the proliferation of e-billing systems, determining the total amount a firm has charged during a given time period should be easy to determine. Proper design and planning should allow such data to be at your fingertips whenever you wish to review it. Although a total cost metric can be skewed by a firm who handles a large volume of matters for you or a significant "bet the company" matter for you, it will provide you with two important insights: (1) it will identify those firms that may be "go to" firms for you, and (2) it will identify an area where you might have tremendous opportunity to cut costs.

In addition to total cost, you should look to segment this metric into subsegments depending on what is meaningful to you and your company. You might consider segmenting the firms that work for you by business unit (e.g., marketing, merchandising, supply chain, etc.) or by the type of work the firm is performing (e.g., litigation, regulatory, commercial transactions, etc.).

2. Average/Median Legal Fee Cost Per Matter

Normalizing the total cost data, in addition to segmenting the data by business unit or type of work, will provide additional helpful data comparisons. Normalizing the data can be accomplished by looking at the average cost per matter or the median cost per matter. Averages can be helpful, but if you have a few matters that are significantly lower or higher than the norm, the average can produce a distorted picture. In situations where outliers may skew your average cost, effective use of medians can provide for a more accurate comparison.

3. Average/Median Settlement Cost Per Matter

Average/median settlement cost per matter is an effective tool to measure firms that are providing you with legal representation in litigation. When comparing this data point with average/median legal fee cost per matter, you will be able to identify firms that may have low legal fees but a high settlement average. A review of these firms may signal an opportunity to increase the legal fees with hopes that the settlement amount will lower.

4. Rate/Fee Time Distribution Mix

During the course of your engagement with your law firms, it is likely that you had discussions about who will be performing your work. Will the work be performed primarily by associates and paralegals, or will the work be performed by junior and senior partners? Is there an ideal mix between the two? The rate/fee time distribution mix will provide this valuable insight.

When setting up the rate/fee time distribution mix, the first step is to segment the levels of experience in a consistent manner across firms. For example, you may choose to segment the experience levels like the following:

- senior partner (20+ years)
- partner (15–19 years)
- junior partner (10–14 years)
- senior associate (5–9 years)
- junior associate (1–4 years)
- paralegals and other staff

After segmenting by levels of experience, you can now utilize the data that you have from your e-billing system to segment the fees paid by each experience segment. A simple spreadsheet provides an excellent example of how this could be organized.

Legal Rate/Fee Analysis

Class of Service or Location	Firm Name	Evaluation Score	Total Approved $	Rate	SP $	% Time	P	% Time	JP	% Time	SA	% Time	JA	% Time	Para	% Time	All Other	% Time	20XX	20XX	20XX
ARIZONA	Firm 1	85.1%	$350,000	Billed/Hr	$ -	0%	$100	5%	$ -	0%	$100	30%	$130	20%	$130	30%	$ 75	15%	0%	8%	0%
	Firm 2	80.9%	$100,000		$ -	0%	$150	40%	$ -	0%	$ -	0%	$ -	0%	$115	40%	$ 65	20%	0%	0%	0%
	Sub-Total		$450,000	Market Rate ($0)		($150-200)		($150-200)		($150-200)		($125-175)		($125-150)		($65-85)					
CALIFORNIA	Firm 3	86.9%	$400,000	Billed/Hr	$ -	0%	$150	20%	$150	10%	$ -	0%	$170	30%	$140	30%	$100	10%	0%	0%	0%
	Firm 4	86.8%	$700,000		$ -	0%	$180	20%	$ -	0%	$ -	0%	$180	40%	$160	20%	$85	20%	0%	9%	0%
	Sub-Total		$1,100,000	Market Rate ($0)		($175-250)		($175-250)		($175-250)		($150-175)		($150-175)		($75-100)					
Virginia	Firm 5	87.6%	$1,200,000	Billed/Hr	$ -	0%	$190	20%	$190	5%	$175	30%	$170	20%	$160	15%	$90	15%	0%	0%	0%
	Firm 6	86.0%	$450,000		$ -	0%	$145	20%	$ -	0%	$ -	0%	$125	40%	$125	20%	$75	20%	0%	7.4%	0%
	Sub-Total		$1,650,000																		
	TOTAL U.S. $'s		$3,200,000	Market Rate ($0)		($150-250)		($150-250)		($150-250)		($125-175)		($125-175)		($65-100)					

FY 20XX — RATE [1] / MIX [2] — Rate Increase [3]

Legend

SP	Senior Partner	->	20+ Yrs
P	Partner	->	15-19 Yrs
JP	Junior Partner	->	10-14 Yrs
SA	Senior Associate	->	5-9 Yrs
JA	Junior Associate	->	1-4 Yrs
NA	Attorney, New	->	0-3 Yrs Experience Attorney

B.   Speed to Resolution

Cost is important, but the old adage "time is money" should not be ignored. If your law firm is able to perform your work cheaply, but they constantly miss deadlines, their work loses all value. Measuring the firm's ability to provide you the finished work product in a timely manner is essential to a full evaluation of outside counsel. There are two possible metrics you may want to use to measure speed: time to resolution and inventory age of matters still open.

1.   Time to Resolution

Time to resolution measures the time between when the law firm receives the assignment and when the assignment is complete. With litigation, the time of commencement will generally follow the serving of the complaint and will end when the litigation is resolved through settlement, dismissal, trial, or appeal. With other practice areas, the time of commencement may begin only when you assign the matter to the law firm and end upon the completion of the assignment. In either situation, measuring the time between the date the assignment commences and the date that the assignment ends will provide for a good comparison between firms that perform substantially similar work for you.

2.   Inventory Age of Matters Still Open

Measuring the speed in which a law firm resolves the work you provide to them should be complemented by measuring the time of the matters that remain open. This data point will demonstrate whether the firm has managed to bring only your less difficult matters to conclusion in a timely manner, and it may show that the firm has a more difficult time handling matters of greater complexity.

C. Accuracy

Law firms that provide you with cheap and timely service are helpful, but only if the service they provide is accurate. In assessing accuracy, you must be willing to place a certain level of subjectivity into your outside counsel evaluation. Accuracy can be measured by assessing the firm's (1) knowledge of the law, (2) quality of work, (3) creativity, and (4) preparation.

1. Knowledge of the Law

You retain law firms and lawyers because you believe that both the firm and the lawyer will provide keen knowledge of the law. It is the lawyer's acumen that separates the lawyer from his or her peers. Objectively measuring acumen across a portfolio of matters can sometime be difficult if not impossible; however, a few key questions will allow you to determine whether the law firm and lawyer know the law.

- Can the lawyer answer basic questions in his or her area of the law without the need to perform additional research?
- Can the lawyer explain the area of the law to you in a manner that is easy for you to understand?
- Does the lawyer have the confidence to inform you when he or she does not know the answer?

2. Quality of Work

Lawyers should be great writers. The work product you receive should be grammatically correct with no typographical errors. With the written word, the lawyer should be able to persuade, be clear and concise, and render the complex simple and the technical easy.

3. Creativity

The essence of being a lawyer is applying the law to a given set of facts or problems. The fascinating part of the law is that much of it is unsettled. An effective lawyer will be creative in his or her thinking. Is the lawyer providing creative solutions to the problem at hand? Is the lawyer synthesizing the law and your business needs to provide you with the best course of action?

4. Preparation

A good amount of an established litigator's time will be spent in preparation for a deposition, trial, motion argument, or appellate argument. A good amount of an established transactional lawyer's time is drafting and reviewing before the negotiation begins. It is not difficult in either instance to identify the well-prepared lawyer in the chaff of the ill-prepared ones.

D. Diversity

Ensuring that your outside counsel have a diverse work force is an incredibly important factor for all leading companies. To be sure, many law firms have also embraced the importance of employing a diverse work force. It is imperative that your outside counsel evaluation contain a section that measures whether your outside counsel and your legal fee spend are in line with your expectations. There are several ways to measure your success, but it will take advanced preparation to ensure that you have the data available to perform a meaningful analysis.

1. Legal Fee Spend Analysis (Total)

A review of the total amount of legal fees you spend annually is a basic building block and an almost requirement to know for every legal department. From this basic building block, tremendous analysis can commence. When setting up your e-billing system, the first step is for you to obtain critical information about the outside lawyers and paralegals performing your work. You typically will obtain the following information: (1) level in firm (e.g., partner, associate, paralegal), (2) years in practice, and (3) billing rate. Additional information will be needed to assist you with measuring whether your firms are providing you with a diverse team. Depending on the level of detail that you seek, you might want to also request the gender and race or ethnicity of those submitting time.

Once you have the necessary data from your law firms, a simple report showing your total overall spend and the total spend with diverse timekeepers is an easy exercise.

2. Legal Fee Spend Analysis (By Level)

When analyzing whether you have met the goals that you have set, review your diverse spend by level as well. By doing so, you will be able to determine whether the diverse legal spend is weighted at the lower-rated timekeepers or the higher-level timekeepers. This information will allow you to have meaningful discussions with your firm about whether the demonstrated cross-section fits within the goals that you have set.

3. Minority-, Women-, and Veteran-Owned Law Firms

As with any lawyer, diverse lawyers practice in large, medium, and small law firms. At times the law firm may be a minority-, women-, or veteran-owned law firm. When determining whether you have the appropriate mix of diverse lawyers that are performing your work, give due consideration to such firms while also seeking diverse timekeepers in law firms that may not fit that criteria.

E. Technical/Administrative

The next element of any outside counsel evaluation is to determine whether the law firms are technically and administratively sound. When analyzing this element, assess whether the firm complies with your outside counsel guidelines, properly provides key documents to you for your record-keeping purposes, and is generally responsive to your requests. You must also verify each firm's data security and privacy safeguards.

IV. CULTURE

The law firms that you select serve as your representative. They are your voice in the courtroom and sometimes in the pressroom. They will interact with your internal business partners, and the selection of the firm is often a reflection of your ability to analyze not only the firm's legal skills, but also whether it represents your culture or your brand in a manner consistent with your company's core values. Their ability to project your culture cannot be underestimated. When assessing a firm's ability to represent your culture, you may simply survey your internal clients to flesh out this aspect.

V. THE RFP PROCESS

A. Who Should Be on the Team?

In-house counsel do not need to undertake the task of running a well-run RFP by themselves. More likely than not, resources exist both inside and outside their companies that can help them with this task.

1. Procurement Professionals

Most, if not all, corporations have a buying or procurement department. Procurement departments and the professionals therein often help different business units in the corporation procure goods and services that the corporation consumes rather than sells. Some corporations may even have a separate procurement department that specializes in the procurement of legal services. There are advantages and disadvantages to having procurement be part of the process. The decision to involve procurement may be determined by corporate policy and how effective they are. Procurement departments may not have the same understanding of the importance of the relationship between inside and outside counsel, the experience of outside counsel, and the quality of outside counsel's services. They also cannot assess legal strategies or approaches. Whether the corporation has a dedicated unit to help with the procurement of legal services or merely a procurement department that helps across multiple departments, procurement professionals are well versed in running RFPs. They can provide immeasurable assistance in preparing for the RFP, conducting the RFP, and negotiating after the selection of the RFP finalists.

2. Legal Operations

The field of legal operations has exploded in recent years. Broadly speaking, legal operations professionals are charged with the business of organizing and running the legal departments. These professionals are often said to perform all tasks in the legal department that do not necessarily require a legal degree.

3.   Outside Consultants

Consultants[3] can always fill the void. As RFPs have proliferated, outside consultants have emerged to help companies with conducting the RFP. Outside consultants can help to augment your internal team and avoid pitfalls that will delay the completion of your RFP. Additionally, outside consultants can help with the sometimes difficult task of sifting through the answers provided by your RFP participants. Of course, with this expertise, there will be a cost—something that you must consider when determining whether the outside consultant provides appropriate value.

B.   Who Should You Invite to Participate in Your RFP?

Although RFPs can be an important vehicle to controlling costs and reducing your overall legal budget, they can also result in failure if you invite the wrong firms to submit bids. How do you determine the right law firms to invite? Part of that will depend on whether your RFP is an "open" invitation—that is, an invitation for any law firm to submit materials for the RFP. An open RFP is generally one that you will see in only one situation: when a public entity is seeking legal services. Private companies will generally have "closed" RFPs where law firms are invited to participate. When conducting a "closed" RFP, selecting the right law firms to participate is critically important to the overall success of the process.

More likely than not, there will be two types of law firms that you will invite to your RFP: firms that have provided legal services to your corporation for years (the incumbents), and firms that have never performed your work, but are keenly interested in doing so (the prospects). Why is it so important to make the right choice on whom to invite? Wouldn't it be easier to simply err on the side of caution and over-invite firms to your RFP? The answer is a resounding "no." As RFPs have proliferated over the years, firms and companies have spent more and more time, and more and more expense, in conducting them. Over-inviting firms will not only increase the work performed in determining who you will select, but will unnecessarily require firms to expend time and capital to respond to an RFP where they have little, if any, legitimate chance to prevail.

1.   The Incumbency Bias

Inertia is a powerful force. An object in motion will remain in motion, and an object at rest will remain at rest. Inertia can result in an incumbent having an advantage in the RFP. The incumbent has been performing legal services for you for years. They know

---

3.   With the growth of RFPs in the legal space, there has been a corresponding growth in outside consultants who will assist with the running of an RFP. Two such outside consultants include Argopoint and BanyanRFP.

your business better than the prospects. They know how you like to respond to discovery; they know your outside counsel guidelines; they know your forms and how you like reports to be written. Armed with this knowledge, it should be easy for the incumbents to win. There is one simple fact that can help to overcome this bias: if the incumbents are so wonderful and have been providing legal services for so many years, why are you conducting the RFP? The mere fact that you are conducting the RFP can be a powerful counterweight to the incumbency bias, but it may not be enough. In order to conduct an RFP that lessens the incumbency bias even further, you must affirmatively make every attempt to level the playing field. How can you level the playing field?

Inviting all incumbents to the RFP is a simple solution to a difficult problem, and the natural tendency is to invite them. In a way, it is easier to do so. As stated previously, the incumbents have been with you for years. Failing to invite them to the RFP can be difficult. The incumbent that is not invited will certainly exert whatever favor or pressure it can exert to be invited. Questions will be asked, and tough and difficult answers are not always easily given. Nevertheless, the answer is obvious: incumbents should not be included solely as a result of their incumbency status. Prior to launching your RFP, you should spend considerable time pouring over your outside counsel evaluation as well as any metrics data you have to determine the minimum score that an incumbent must have before inviting the firm to the RFP. Being disciplined in your efforts here will pay off later when you are scoring the final round of the RFP.

2. Expose Your Data

When you create your RFP, know the data and metrics that are important to you. Are you simply focused on reduction in overall cost? Are you more focused on cycle time, or how long it takes for firms to take your matters to a final resolution? Are you focused on the cost of legal fees, or are you focused on indemnity costs—that is, the cost of the settlement? It does not really matter where your focus lay; what matters is what you will share with the prospects.

If you are creating an RFP where you are preparing to award a large portfolio of business to firms, you are surely seeking firms that will provide an improvement to your current stable of law firms. The law firms who will prevail will be making every effort to provide you with what you want, but without exposing your data to the law firms, they will be shooting in the dark. If you are seeking firms that will help you control costs, you should consider providing a few year's cost data to your firms. Break the cost data for the firms down by geographic region, if appropriate, or type of case. If your RFP is based off of a volume calculation, provide the volume of matters you have had over the past few years.

With this data provided to everyone, you can level the playing field. Although the incumbents have been with you for years and know your company and your expectations, the most powerful information you have is your data. With the right approach and analytics, prospects can eliminate the incumbency bias and provide a competitive response.

There may be a certain amount of fear with providing sensitive data to firms that may never perform your work. How can you ensure that the data is not used in a way that can harm you? When creating your RFP and when inviting the law firms to participate, you should make it clear that participation in the RFP is contingent upon two things: (1) signing a nondisclosure agreement (NDA), and (2) acknowledging that the receipt of the information creates an attorney-client relationship with the firm, even if the firm does not prevail.

3.   Other Prospective Firms

Selecting the prospects to participate in your RFP can be tricky; without foresight and planning, it can be a little like finding a needle in a haystack. Recent statistics show that although over 70 percent of all lawyers ply their trade in private practice, only 14 percent of those lawyers work for firms that have greater than 100 lawyers.[4] There are some techniques that can help you find prospects, but none are fool proof.

Industry-compiled lists of firms.[5] Industry lists are a good place to begin, but simply relying on industry lists will exclude high-quality, and often lower-cost, small and boutique law firms. One of the most famous of the industry lists, the Am Law 200, focuses on firm revenue and profits per partner, both of which can be indicative of a successful and stable firm. *U.S. News and World Report* publishes its "Best" Law Firms List on an annual basis. Its list is based off surveys from lawyers and in-house counsel, and it boasts that its results are derived from over one million law firm assessments and input from over 7,500 clients. To be sure, cross-referencing these industry lists will confirm that you will have a strong list of prospects from which to choose. It will be strong, but it will be incomplete.

Referrals from in-house counsel from other companies. More likely than not, you have met and work with in-house counsel from other companies both within your industry and outside your industry. A referral from a trusted resource with another company can help to further refine your prospect list. Before acting on the referral, however, it is important that you identify the type of firm or lawyer that you are seeking before seeking out the referral. Armed with this knowledge, you can ask pointed questions of your trusted resource to determine whether the referral will be a good fit.

Do you have the right mix of firms and attorneys? Before wrapping up your thoughts on those firms and attorneys that you will invite, you should look critically at the list that you have created. Is it a diverse list? Is it an inclusive list? If not, you have more work to do. Although you can potentially defer the determination of whether the lawyers are diverse to the evaluation of the RFP submissions, you cannot pass this step without reviewing the list of firms you are inviting. Have you given due consideration

---

4.   Margaret Grisdela, Overview of the U.S. Legal Market: Information and Strategies to Promote Your Law Firm Online (Nov. 30, 2010), *available at* www.hg.org/marketing-us-market.html.

5.   Some examples of lists of potential law firms include the AmLaw200, Martindale-Hubbell, U.S. News Best LawFirm, and Avvo.com. Although these lists are helpful to supplement your overall knowledge of the industry, full reliance without your own due diligence is not recommended.

to adding minority- and women-owned firms?[6] Have you included both large firms and small firms? If not, you must expand your list.

VI. CONDUCTING THE RFP

With your team in place, and the participating law firms selected, you can turn your attention to the structure of the RFP document itself. A well-structured RFP will be true to your business requirements, provide participants with all they need to submit a meaningful and competitive bid, and provide you with an output that you can easily digest and extract data. The RFP structure itself should be easy to follow for all the firms. An easy to follow RFP will reduce or eliminate any procedural questions the firms may have on the mechanics of submitting the RFP. In general, a well-prepared RFP will have the following sections in some shape or form.

A. Introduction

In the introduction of your RFP, you should set the stage. Tell the law firms the purpose of the RFP—that is, what is it your company needs? You should also provide general background information about your company and, if desired, information about the legal department and how it connects to the business. Although you will want to have separate sections in the body of the RFP to discuss the pricing structure you desire (fixed fee, hourly, retainer) and the deadline for submission and notification, a brief mention at the front of the RFP puts the most critically important information about the timing and expectations at the front where it will not be overlooked. Don't forget to include your company's requirements regarding data security and information privacy.

B. Overview of Law Firm and Description of Lawyers and Staff

Having a general understanding of the structure and makeup of the firms can be meaningful data for you. Letting the firms know how you want this formatted is important. Many firms employ internal marketing resources, whereas others employ outside resources, to help with marketing pitches. These resources have the capability to produce high-quality brochures and portfolios. You may find those helpful, but if you are not careful, you will receive more than you can handle. If you want only electronic submissions, for example, the glossy brochures will only inundate your office with excess paper. Having the firms produce the same information in an electronic format of your own choosing will allow for easier comparison of all submissions.

When describing what you desire in this section, you should let the law firms know the importance of diversity and inclusion to your legal department and your corporation.

---

6. The National Association of Minority and Women Owned Law Firms (NAMWOLF) is an excellent resource for finding excellent lawyers who practice at minority- and women-owned law firms.

When telling the firms that you will want to know who will be performing the work if the firm is selected, you can clearly convey your expectations.

C. References

Successful firms with long-serving relationships with clients will have a large number of clients that can serve as client references. Request the names and contact information of these references and, importantly, contact the references as part of your due diligence prior to your final selection. Firms will select only those clients they believe will provide the best references. To obtain a balanced view of the capabilities of the firm and those that may perform your work, consider also asking for the name and contact information for a client that recently stopped using the firm.

D. Communication Expectations

For the firm to properly provide competitive pricing, it is important that the law firms know your expectations for communication with you once work is underway. Will you be requiring an update every 30 days or 90 days? Will the firm be required to use forms that you will require for reporting purposes? If so, including those forms in an appendix of the RFP will be helpful.

E. Pricing

Although you mentioned it in your introduction, having a separate section that focuses on pricing ensures that the firms clearly understand your expectations. Many companies have moved to various AFAs, including flat-fee or retainer-based models. The more complicated your pricing model, the more time you must spend explaining how it works to the firms.

F. Timeline

It is critical to determine a deadline by which the company must make a decision and then to work backwards in determining a timeline for each step of the process. As part of creating a timeline, determine whether this will be a one- or two-step process, and if two steps, whether the evaluation process will entail telephone or in-person interviews. Place the dates in a separate section. Some dates and deadlines to consider include: (1) a deadline for submitting questions about the RFP; (2) a deadline for submitting materials for RFP consideration; (3) a deadline for your submission; (4) dates for interviews; and (5) a date for the awarding of the business.

RFPs often have tight timeframes. It is important be clear as to the reasons for your timeframe and whether the company is willing to grant any extensions. Your timeframe may drive the timeline, but try to be fair and give the firms as much time as you can. You will get higher-quality responses and begin the relationship off on the right foot. For example, in a complex litigation context, giving more time allows the firm to do their homework and develop what they would propose for a strategy going forward.

In addition, giving more time may allow a firm to navigate their internal politics and perhaps offer a deeper discount or an alternative fee arrangement. Ask the firm to look for any conflicts, including issue conflicts. More often than expected, a firm discovers there is a conflict after it has been hired and can put the company in an awkward position.

G. Questions to and from RFP Participants

You also should have a procedure in place for participants to ask questions and for the company to pose follow-up questions to the participants. You should decide whether questions can be posed via direct contact, or whether the company will permit questions only via a website or e-mail. If the company provides clarification or additional information to the requesting firm, that information should be shared with all of the RFP participants if generic in nature. However, where the firm's specific questions arise because the firm is thinking about a certain strategic approach or a different type of AFA, you should think about whether sharing with the other law firms is appropriate. You want to have a level playing field, but you should also reward strategic thinking and intellectual capital

VII. RFP SUBMISSIONS AND EVALUATION PROCESS

Once the law firms have submitted their responses to the RFP, the real fun can begin. Provided you have set up your RFP correctly, it is now time to mine the data that the firms have provided. Are you able to quickly organize your data to determine which initial response from the firms is closest to your business requirements? Are you able to see which firms have "mailed it in" and have not thought much of their response? Can you spot the outliers that show that the firms either did not understand the RFP or are simply trying to underbid their competitors? Although the impulse may be to rashly accept the lowest bid, caution should dictate a more measured response. Did the firm underbid to win the business? Although this may provide you with a short-term gain, the old adage, "You get what you pay for" is always lurking in the background. The low bid must be scrutinized to verify that the firm has properly understood the RFP and that its plan will not impact the overall viability of the firm.

You should form an evaluation committee to evaluate the proposals for larger RFPs. For smaller RFPs, you may be able to have a more limited evaluation mechanism, but the same principles should apply. You should decide on the key criteria and the weight to be given to each criterion. It is useful to have a rating sheet to be completed by each member of the evaluation committee for each RFP participant. The criteria might include:

- reputation and expertise of firm
- geographical reach of firm
- diversity of firm overall
- diversity of proposed team
- reputation and expertise of proposed staffing

- proposed fees/costs
- alternative/creative fee arrangements
- past experience with firm (this could be a bonus points item)
- industry experience
- understanding of your business
- for litigation, past experience with the court and/or plaintiff's counsel
- e-discovery expertise
- creativity of RFP response

The committee should decide whether to rate the firms prior to discussing them or afterwards. Either way, after you rate the firms, you should have further discussion to ensure that you are comfortable with the ratings. For example, if the same firm has a wide variance in how they are being viewed, you may want to take some time to ensure everyone understands how each rater approached the assessment. Listening to others may impact how a rater views a firm. As part of this process, you may discover that you have some questions for some or all of the firms. You should decide whether they are best handled through an e-mail or an interview process. This is one reason to ensure you include extra time your schedule. Despite your best planning, issues may arise. You should decide whether there is a need for a second written round and whether telephone or in-person interviews will be part of the process.

As mentioned earlier, this is an opportunity to signal to the firm where they may fall short of their peers. For example, you could advise a law firm that although they are in the next round, their strategic focus or cost structure were not as strong as some of the other participants. You can decide whether you want the law firm to supplement prior to the interview or during the process. Remember, the goals are to be fair and to achieve appropriate representation for the company.

VIII. INTERVIEWS OF FINALISTS

Most companies decide to include an interview phase. Interviews allow you to determine whether there is a good fit beyond the numbers. This will allow you to evaluate whether the firm really knows your business and the legal subject matters relevant to your business. You also can see how the firm lawyers react to unexpected situations. For example, when interviewing potential trial counsel, a law firm was discussing a possible strategy. When the company explained that the court had disallowed that strategy, lawyers from one firm froze and could not recover and suggest another recommendation. That made the company question how effective that lawyer would be during trial if there was an adverse ruling. In addition, if you need someone who can explain things in plain English to your business people, the firm's ability to do that is best assessed during the interview process. If you have told the firms that diversity is important to your organization, it allows you to see how it is staffed and whether diverse individuals will be actively engaged in the representation.

You should decide how each interview will last and prepare a list of open-ended questions. The list of questions should include questions that you will ask every firm (and you may want to decide if you want to spend time evaluating how they did on those questions against their peers) and questions specific to their proposal. You also should decide who will take the lead regarding certain questions/topics. You can also use these questions as a way of telegraphing your philosophy or expectations regarding the topics. For example, you can discuss the review time you need, how communications and updates should be handled, and the decisions of which you should be a part. The following are some suggested questions:

- Tell us about a little about yourself and your firm and why you are interested in this work.
- What do you believe will be the most important issues facing our industry over the next decade?
- Please tell us your prior experience in handling _____ matters.
- Would your firm consider a flat rate for any types of matters?
- What is your proposed staffing? Are you open to less or more junior people? (if appropriate)
- How will your firm ensure that our matters are staffed with diverse candidates? Are you open to partnering with a MWBE firm on this case?
- Consider your partner rates; how will you control legal fees?
- Do you expect there may be changes to any proposed budget?
- Your billing rates are significantly higher than the other finalist. Is there any room for negotiation in these prices?
- How, if at all, does your firm use technology to reduce costs?
- How would you keep us apprised of legal trends?
- Do you have any questions for us?

IX. THE DECISION-MAKING PROCESS

Once the interview process is over, it is time to start making decisions. As part of this process, it is important not to lose site of the data analytics and how each firm scored. Qualitative assessments of the firms should be backed up by the numbers. Your RFP committee should use a matrix to score the firms and to note any key evaluation considerations. If possible, try to meet together in person to discuss, review, and reach a decision. If further negotiations are needed, this is where procurement can add value. They can engage in tough negotiations without impacting the long-term relationship.

Once you have made your final selection, notify the responding firms. If certain factors tipped the scale in favor of a winning firm(s), advise the responders of those factors. Feedback will ensure that firms will fine-tune their responses the next time they have an opportunity to respond to your RFP. You also can advise some of the firms that were not selected that there may be opportunities where the prevailing firm has a conflict of interest or cannot provide coverage for some other reason.

X. PUT IT IN WRITING

Once outside counsel is selected, the company and the firm should enter into a written agreement regarding the terms of the representation. This may be as simple as having a cover letter that references outside counsel guidelines and discusses the specifics of the particular matter regarding staffing and rates. You may want to lock in rates for a particular time period and/or address the following items in your engagement letter:

- Conflicts
- Confidentiality and Preservation of Privilege
- Document Management
- Public Comment
- Diversity
- Attorney Assignment/Reassignment
- Billing Guidelines and Procedures
- Communication
- Budgeting
- Firm Evaluation Criteria and Process
- Privacy and Security of Company Information
- Governing Law
- Termination of Representation
- Malpractice Insurance

You should specify in detail prohibited fees and expenses. Following are examples of services and expenses you may not want to pay:

- Time spent "getting up to speed" for a legal professional due to staff turnover or vacation
- Time spent preparing invoices, discussing or resolving billing inquiries or disputes, utilizing the electronic invoice system, and budgeting tasks
- Time spent responding to audit letters
- Proofreading
- Professional development time
- Graphics and desktop publishing
- Drafting or reviewing interoffice memoranda
- Participating in interoffice conferences, unless such conferences involve substantive discussions of case strategy and handling
- Routine administrative tasks incidental to an engagement
- Legal research over three hours (except as approved by the company)
- More than one attendee at appearances, meetings, depositions, trials, and other events without preapproval
- Document translation that has not been requested or preapproved
- File creation, organization, and maintenance (including file storage)
- Time spent or costs associated with preparing, transferring, closing, or destroying files, research, memoranda, pleadings, communications, records, drafts, and other related material, including electronic copies of documents

- Communication charges including phone, video, word processing, and fax
- Postage and courier fees (including overnight mail), unless preapproved
- Publications, subscriptions, librarian services, and online databases, such as Lexis and Westlaw, whether cost or time
- Document scanning, unless preapproved
- Copying (color or otherwise), whether cost or time
- Any items of overhead expenses (e.g., staff overtime, meals, local transportation, conference rooms, calendaring, rental fees, etc.)
- Unauthorized third-party fees
- Administrative, clerical, and secretarial staff work; word processing, proofreading, and any other nonprofessional services or service providers, such as administrators and document clerks
- Preparing invoices, submitting appeals, or resolving billing questions
- Indexing pleadings
- Closing files
- Calendar maintenance
- Transcribing
- Copying
- Data entry
- Scanning
- Filing of documents, electronic or otherwise
- Routine scheduling of or confirming depositions, client conferences, court conferences, etc.
- Enclosure or transmittal letters
- File organization
- Bate-stamping or stamping documents
- Database maintenance
- Making travel arrangements
- Word or document processing
- Running conflicts checks
- Requesting checks and paying for third-party vendor invoices
- Sorting and routing correspondence
- Time spent by attorneys performing paralegal work
- Preparing letters of representation/acknowledgement
- Travel
- All charges for air travel must be at economy or coach rates
- Hotel rates no more than $____ per night
- Meals no more than $___ per person per day
- Mini-bar charges, personal telephone calls, movie rentals, dry cleaning, or similar personal items

XI. ONGOING EVALUATION

Once counsel is engaged, the company should evaluate each firm's performance and provide feedback on an ongoing basis. Common reasons for terminating the relationship with a firm or taking a specific attorney off of the firm team include:

- Representing adverse parties without requesting a waiver
- Lack of responsiveness
- Poor communication
- Bad results
- Poor work product, analysis, or writing
- Lack of understanding of the industry
- Overbilling
- Unwillingness to respond to constructive criticism
- Unwillingness to partner with in-house counsel

The in-house relationship partner should review the outside counsel evaluation forms and conduct a firm performance review. If there are areas that require improvement, the in-house relationship partner should ask the firm for a plan to improve the problems.

Although the RFP process may be time-consuming, companies that invest the time to properly launch and manage the process will derive significant benefits, including costs savings and higher-quality outside counsel.

XII. ALTERNATIVE FEE ARRANGEMENTS

Whether as part of an RFP process or individual negotiations, you should consider AFAs. AFAs are arrangements in which the law firm is compensated based on something other than an hourly billing rate. In-house legal departments are realizing that hourly billing does not necessarily result in better value or better solutions.

A. Reasons for AFAs

There are two main reasons why legal departments use AFAs. The first is predictability of legal costs. Your legal department has a greater chance of meeting its legal spend budget by regularly using AFAs. The second reason for using AFAs is alignment of objectives between your company and the law firm. Given that AFAs force law firms to have more "skin in the game," AFAs tend to result in more efficient and effective representation. The relationship tends to be more focused on results and requires less monitoring. Providing bonuses for successful outcomes further aligns the law firm with your company's metrics of success.

B. Guidelines for AFAs

One guideline in crafting an AFA is to focus on paying fair value for the legal services. Attempting to have the corporation "win big" likely will not result in a sustainable long-term arrangement. Establishing and building trust with open, ongoing communications and transparency is key to making AFAs work. The AFA also should promote getting results more quickly and efficiently.

C. Types of AFAs

There are several types of AFAs to consider, each with its advantages and disadvantages.

1. Fixed Fees

A fixed-fee AFA is where the firm agrees to handle all or part of a transaction for a fixed fee. A fixed fee has the advantage of providing you with predictability and avoids fee disputes. It is important to discuss how expenses will be treated and to advise the firm to be clear if anything is excluded from the flat fee. In other words, the firm should know that if it is not excluded, your company assumes it is included. A fixed fee is easier to implement in connection with a corporate transaction than for litigation. However, there are ways to limit risk.

For litigation involving a high volume of matters, any swings up or down can be offset due to the large number of matters. Safeguards such as caps and collars also can be put in place to prevent unfair wins. A capped fee sets a ceiling as to what your company will pay the law firm for a particular service or matter. Pursuant to this arrangement, if the law firm's fees end up being less than the ceiling, the company gets the added bonus of paying less. However, a ceiling does not give the law firm the incentive to keep its fees below the cap. If the right ceiling is set using comparative assessments, however, this approach is more advantageous than uncapped hourly rates.

The fixed fee also can be broken down by task or phases of the litigation (e.g., motion to dismiss, discovery, trial, etc.). If it is a more complex task, such as discovery in a large matter or trial, it is best to build in clear assumptions about the days of trial, the number of depositions, the number of discovery motions, and the amount of third-party discovery.

For example, a fixed fee for a phase of litigation might read:

> Your firm will analyze the legal and factual issues presented by the complaint (including preliminary witness interviews), prepare a memorandum of law in support of a motion to dismiss, analyze ABC's opposition brief, prepare a reply brief, and prepare for and argue the motion for $20,000, including costs and fees.

2. Volume, Blended, and Discount Fees

Another option is to agree to an arrangement involving a volume discount, discounted hourly rate, or blended hourly rate. Although discounts can be helpful, discounts do not incentivize speed and efficiency because there is no cap on hours.

A blended rate is one negotiated hourly rate that is less than the partner rate but more than the typical associate rate. If a particular project is going to require a significant amount of partner time, then this arrangement can result in lower costs; however, the engagement must be closely monitored to ensure that the partner does a significant and meaningful percentage of the work.

If you shift your work to a firm that provides bigger discounts, you also should compare the fees paid to the new firm with the fees paid to the more expensive firm. You might see that your bills go up because the more expensive firm used smarter, more experienced, and more efficient lawyers.

3. Contingency Fees

If your company is attempting to recover money, you may enter into an arrangement where the firm will be paid a percentage of the recovery. The percentage also can be on a sliding scale depending on the amount of the recovery, and the percentage can vary depending on whether the recovery is pre-litigation or post-litigation. For example, a corporation might engage counsel to handle real estate tax appeals and agree to pay a contingent fee of 25 percent of all savings for each year under appeal. If no tax reduction is obtained, the firm would receive no legal fee.

Your company also can propose a reverse contingency fee, which fee is set as a percentage of the difference between the company's estimated exposure and the amount, if any, the client ultimately pays in damages or settlement, plus avoided legal costs.

Regardless of the contingency fee arrangement, it is important to itemize what costs the company and/or law firm are paying.

4. Success Fees

Any fee arrangement also can have built-in success fees or bonuses. Your company and the law firm must first define what result constitutes "success" and how bonuses will be paid for those successes. Successes may include settlement below a certain amount, winning a dispositive motion, or limiting discovery. For example, your company can agree that the law firm will receive a success fee of a certain amount if the fees are less than a certain amount and the law firm wins a motion to dismiss. The company can agree to different success fees if the win occurs at the summary judgment stage. You also can agree that the firm will receive a bonus if the matter is concluded and the fees are less than a certain amount. For example:

> Bonus fee: (a) if case is resolved and total hourly fee billings are less than $500,000, the firm receives a bonus amounting to 20 percent of fees actually billed; (b) if case is resolved and total hourly fee billings are less than $750,000, the firm receives a bonus amounting to 10 percent of fees actually billed; (c) if case is resolved and total hourly fee billings are less than $1,000,000, the firm receives a bonus amounting to five percent of fees actually billed.

5. Retainer Fee

Another type of AFA is a retainer fee. This is where the company pays a fixed, recurring fee over a period of time for specific work. When the period expires, the arrangement is reviewed and adjusted. It provides predictable costs.

D. AFA Best Practices

Below are some best practices to consider when entering into and designing AFAs:

- Understand the metrics in terms of what you have paid for this work before so that you can be sure the arrangement will result in cost savings.
- Define what would be a success and measure against it.
- Communicate with the law firm regarding what is and is not working, and encourage the firm to do the same.
- Use technology to maximize value.
- Be creative and consider building in fee bonuses and success metrics.
- Seek advice from other in-house law departments regarding what has worked and what has not worked.

Appendix A:
Outside Counsel Evaluation of Attorneys and Law Firms

INSTRUCTIONS: Complete one Outside Counsel Evaluation form for each office of each law firm that serves your practice group. On this form, you will rate up to three attorneys (main partner contacts) and the firm overall. Type the requested information in the blanks highlighted in yellow. All categories will be rated on a scale of 1 (low) to 10 (high). The items listed under each category heading are factors to be considered when determining the rating. Once the Evaluation Form is completed, click on the "Score" tab at the bottom of the screen to view a scoring summary and the firm's overall score.

Name of Evaluator:	
Date of Evaluation:	
Practice Group:	
Name of Law Firm:	
Number of Attys. Evaluated:	

INDIVIDUAL ATTORNEY RATING

Criteria	Attorney Name (please type below):	Attorney Name (please type below):	Attorney Name (please type below):
	Rating	Rating	Rating
1. Experience			
Track record with HD			
Knowledge of HD business			
Relevant experience with other retailers			
Relevant experience with other large companies			
Number of years in practice			
Number of trials (if applicable)			
Experience with environmental matters/remediations (if applicable)			
Experience with crisis management and/or "high profile" matters			
Enter Rating (1-10):			
2. Quality of Service			
Provides high-quality work product and representation			
Consistently provides reliable evaluations of matter			
Recommendations are practical			
Exercises good judgment			
Internal client satisfaction			
Enter Rating (1-10):			
3. Effective Advocacy and Negotiation Skills			
Resolves matters favorably (i.e., for litigation, wins or favorable settlements)			
Negotiates effectively			
Ability to vigorously represent HD without fostering antagonism			
Enter Rating (1-10):			
4. Ease to Work With			
Is willing and able to assign work down to the appropriate level and to provide adequate and competent supervision			
Accessibility to attorney or "go to" person(s)			
Chemistry between members of HD Legal Dept. (including paralegals) and attorney			
Compliance with outside counsel and department specific guidelines			
Enter Rating (1-10):			
5. Communication			
Keeps us advised of critical developments			
Keeps us appropriately informed (do they call us about every little issue; alternatively, do they do things without telling us)			
Promptly returns telephone calls			
Copies us on correspondence, etc. as appropriate			
Capable of providing immediate, "on the phone" response in an emergency and /or other situation in which instant guidance is required			
Enter Rating (1-10):			

6. Partnering Skills
Partners/consults with us when necessary
Timeliness (prepares documents sufficiently in advance of due date allowing us adequate time to review
Responsiveness (responds to our inquiries/requests in a timely and efficient manner
Enter Rating (1-10):

7. Processing Abilities
Advances matters rather than delays them
Exploits every opportunity to settle or resolve matter
Enter Rating (1-10):

8. Honesty, Integrity and Loyalty
Does the right thing
Thinks about HD and how to improve service
Enter Rating (1-10):

9. Billing Practices
Adheres to HD billing guidelines
Meets budgets
Performs work in a cost-effective manner without compromising quality
Enter Rating (1-10):

10. Expertise in Applicable Subject Matter
Practice devoted primarily to applicable specialty
Nationally recognized expert in field
History in handling similar matters
Enter Rating (1-10):

LAW FIRM RATING

Criteria	Rating
1. Quality & Management of Firm	
Recruits and retains high quality attorneys and staff	
"Band width" or "depth" (is the level of <u>talent</u> sufficient to handle tough matters)	
Impeccable reputation	
Frequency of turnover of attorneys on file	
Enter Rating (1-10):	
2. Cost Effectiveness	
Reasonable billing rates for location	
Ability and willingness to staff projects and perform work in cost-effective manner	
Enter Rating (1-10):	
3. Size of Firm/Geography	
Sufficient staffing to handle HD matters efficiently	
Sufficient staffing to handle a large volume of matters	
Cross pollination (does the firm have other practice areas we can call on if needed, I.e., tax, employee benefits, land use, bankruptcy)	
Proximity to court or division to be serviced and/or willingness to travel at no charge to HD	
Importance of hiring local firm (is jurisdiction known for favoring "home town" attorneys?)	
Enter Rating (1-10):	
4. Technology/Systems in Place	
Ability to transmit important documents electronically	
Willingness to communicate via email if desired by HD staff	
Willingness to share key document database	
Commitment to investing in additional technological innovations	
Effective use of e-billing	
Enter Rating (1-10):	
5. Diversity	
Diverse staff assigned to HD cases (gender, race/national origin, age)	
Minority-owned firm, where appropriate	
Enter Rating (1-10):	

Appendix B:
Outside Counsel Evaluation
of the Law Firm

INSTRUCTIONS: Complete one Outside Counsel Evaluation form for each office of each law firm that serves your practice group. On this form, you will rate up to three attorneys (main partner contacts) and the firm overall. Type the requested information in the blanks highlighted in yellow. All categories will be rated on a scale of 1 (low) to 10 (high). The items listed under each category heading are factors to be considered when determining the rating. Once the Evaluation Form is completed, click on the "Score" tab at the bottom of the screen to view a scoring summary and the firm's overall score.

Name of Evaluator:	
Date of Evaluation:	
Practice Group:	
Name of Law Firm:	

LAW FIRM RATING

Criteria	Rating
1.Financial Results/Cost Effectiveness Total Legal Fees in Line with Expectations Average/Median Fees in Line with Expectation Average/Median Settlements in Line with Expectation Rate and Mix of Work Distributed Appropriately Enter Rating (1-10):	
2.Speed to Resolution Time to Resolve Matter Assigned Inventory Age of Matters Still Open Enter Rating (1-10):	
3.Accuracy Knowledge of the Law in Line with Expectations Quality of Work in Line with Expectations Creativity in Line with Expectations Preparation in Line with Expectations Enter Rating (1-10):	

4.Diversity
   Fee Spend Analysis (Total)—Diverse Timekeepers appropriately assigned
   Fee Spend Analysis (By Level)—Diverse Timekeepers at all levels of assignment
   Minority- or Woman-Owned Law Firm
 	
                                  Enter Rating (1-10):	

5.Technical/Administrative Expertise **6.Culture** Firm understands the Company's culture Enter Rating (1-10):	

Chapter 7

Managing Regional and National Litigation

By Charles F. Smith, Amy Van Gelder,
and Alexandra Morgan

This chapter is intended to provide a roadmap for the management of regional and national litigation at all stages of a case, from complaint intake through settlement or trial. In particular, this chapter supplies in-house counsel with key considerations and practice pointers for the efficient and effective administration of large-scale litigation, including multiple related cases and multidistrict litigation.

I.   INTRODUCTION

This chapter provides an overview of key issues that in-house counsel should consider when coordinating large-scale regional and national litigation. In particular, this chapter provides practice pointers for early case management, assessment of jurisdiction, venue, claims and defenses, and management of discovery, as well as considerations affecting summary judgment, trial, and settlement. Although the issues addressed herein are broadly applicable to any litigation, where appropriate the authors draw attention to tips for the simultaneous, coordinated management of multiple related matters. Effective management of multiple related cases at once is essential to ensuring—to the extent possible—favorable litigation results and reducing costs and inefficiencies.

II.   EARLY CASE MANAGEMENT

A.   Complaint Intake and Assessment

All litigation begins with a complaint—the central pleading that guides the litigation. One of the first decisions in-house counsel may face is whether to waive formal service of a complaint. Under the Federal Rules of Civil Procedure and many state rules, waiver of service extends the deadline for a response.[1] Especially in cases where large-scale litigation was unanticipated, extra time for response may alleviate unnecessary timing pressures. Counsel should also consider accepting service of a complaint on behalf of any employees who are named as co-defendants; the presence of process servers on company grounds may be distracting and embarrassing to employees.

Once the complaint is in hand, in-house counsel should undertake a careful review of the pleading to become familiar with the parties and allegations. As discussed further below, counsel should consider threshold questions such as venue and jurisdiction immediately upon receiving a complaint.

When assessing the parties, counsel should determine whether the company has potential indemnification obligations to any co-defendants, including current and former employees. Counsel should gather and assess any relevant contracts and policies to determine its position on indemnification and, if relevant, assumption of the defense. Counsel should also assess the complaint's factual allegations and make note of (1) potentially relevant employees, departments, and business lines; (2) any contracts or other key documentary evidence; and (3) any third-party witnesses.

Once counsel has a basic understanding of the nature of the action, counsel should identify next steps in the litigation and calendar key deadlines. This includes identifying and calendaring responsive pleadings, deadlines for removal, and any interim measures, such as deadlines for preliminary injunction, attachments, and initial court conferences. Answer dates often come quickly; it is important not to let a complaint languish in the inbox for a week or more.

B.   Determine the Availability of Insurance Coverage

Companies regularly insure against certain liability risks. When assessing a new complaint, counsel should consider whether all or some of the claims at issue may be covered by the company's insurance program and consult with internal insurance specialists and external brokers regarding the potential for coverage. If insurance policies are implicated, promptly notifying insurance carriers of the litigation in accordance with the terms and conditions of the policies will be a top priority.

---

1.   Fed. R. Civ. P. 4(d)(3).

Practice Pointer

Counsel should also review the policies for other key provisions, such as cooperation requirements, whether the policies provide for assumption of the defense or payment of defense costs and fees, and whether any applicable insurance exclusions may apply. Insurers often will identify panel counsel whom the carriers find have relevant expertise for specialized matters, such as claims against directors and officers or brought under a statute like the Employee Retirement Income Security Act. Especially in complex or potentially high-stakes matters where coverage may be contested, in-house counsel is well-advised to retain outside insurance counsel to assess the availability of coverage, ensure compliance with all policy requirements so as not to void coverage, and pursue coverage, if necessary, through a declaratory judgment action at an appropriate juncture.

C. Retention of Outside Counsel

Especially in cases of regional and national prominence, retention of outside counsel is a task that warrants immediate attention. For any litigation, in-house counsel must consider many factors when deciding to engage outside counsel, including experience, strength of relationships, pre-existing knowledge of the business, fees, and whether counsel is on an insurer's approved defense counsel panel.

Practice Pointer

When facing large-scale litigation and the potential need for coordination of multiple matters, in-house counsel should also pay particular attention to:

- the depth of outside counsel's bench (will the firm be able to allocate sufficient resources to all potential work-streams; does the firm have a presence or relationships in various jurisdictions where litigation may arise; can (and should) the firm advise on issues tangential to the litigation, e.g., regulatory, corporate, and insurance matters?);
- outside counsel's experience with complex matters, including complicated electronic discovery (does the firm have a proven track record of successfully managing regional and national litigation; does the firm have experience leveraging electronic discovery tools and coordinating discovery across multiple matters?); and
- outside counsel's ability and willingness to work with other advisors (will outside counsel work cooperatively with local counsel, joint defense counsel, and other outside counsel and advisors?).

Once lead outside counsel is selected, in-house counsel must also consider whether it is necessary to retain local counsel in the jurisdiction(s) where the litigation is pending. If so, in-house counsel should clearly define the respective roles and responsibilities of lead and local counsel at the outset of the engagement. This is critical to ensure appropriate coordination among counsel and avoid paying for unnecessary duplication of effort. Lead counsel oftentimes can assist with the selection and retention of local counsel. It is a mistake to consider local counsel as just a mail drop: the best local counsel have a deep understanding of local judges and local practices and procedures that may not appear in written rules. Additionally, local counsel may be able to provide insight as to the skill and depth of expertise of opposing counsel.

In consultation with outside counsel, in-house counsel should also consider whether it is necessary to retain separate counsel for any current or former employees who are individually named in the suit. Although many times these individuals may be represented by lead counsel pursuant to a joint client arrangement, conflicts may prevent joint representation, or there may be other reasons to maintain separateness. To the extent separate counsel is retained, entering into a joint defense agreement is usually advisable.

D. Immediately Institute a Broad Litigation Hold

To ensure that all relevant documents and evidence are preserved, counsel should issue a broad litigation hold notice as soon as the company is aware of impending or existing litigation. Certain basic information must be ascertained in order to properly implement the hold: which employees may have relevant information or were involved in the issue at hand; the relevant time period for which documents should be preserved; and the potential data types and sources that must be preserved.

The litigation hold notice should be in writing and clearly inform employees of their obligation to preserve information that may be relevant to the litigation. See Appendix A, Sample Litigation Hold Notice. The notice should include a description of the subject matter so employees can easily determine whether they possess relevant materials. The notice should also contain express instructions not to modify or destroy any documents, including a reminder that relevant documents may exist in various sources such as e-mail, office and personal computers, shared and personal directories, cell phones, tablets, flash and USB drives, voicemail systems, and in hard copy. Finally, the hold notice should include an explanation to the recipients that the duty to preserve is continuing, and that the recipients should continue to preserve information until told otherwise.

Practice Pointer

Once the hold notice has been issued, counsel should require each recipient to acknowledge the litigation hold and keep a record of who received the hold and when. As litigation continues, counsel should periodically assess the need to update the litigation hold to reflect new information or add additional hold recipients. A common mistake is to put a hold in place and neglect to revisit it as the matter changes in scope.

In addition to sending a hold notice to employees who may possess relevant information, in-house counsel should also notify internal departments with data-management responsibility of the litigation hold. Which departments are implicated will often depend on the subject matter of the litigation, and counsel should carefully consider what data, e.g., purchasing systems, customer databases, payroll systems, internet archives, etc., may be relevant to the issues at stake. Regardless of the type of litigation, two departments should always be notified of litigation holds: information technology and human resources. In-house counsel should work closely with the IT department to preserve electronic data on the back-end, including through suspension of auto-deletion policies, disabling individual users' ability to delete e-mails, and taking snapshots of potentially relevant data. IT should also be instructed to alert in-house counsel before engaging in routine data-management activities that could result in the unintentional spoliation or alteration of data, such as data transfers, database decommissioning, updating websites or systems, or wiping and reassigning company computers and devices. Likewise, HR should be notified of all litigation holds. HR can help monitor and assure the preservation of data when relevant employees separate from the company, including conducting exit interviews to determine where the employee's electronic and hardcopy data is stored, collecting and preserving company devices used by the employee, and alerting in-house counsel of the need to preserve employee files.

E. Developing a Public-Relations Strategy

With large-scale litigation comes the risk of negative media attention and increased scrutiny by regulators, customers, shareholders, and even employees. Quickly developing and executing a coordinated public-relations strategy is critical to eliminating, or at least reducing, backlash collateral to litigation.

Although there is no finite list of litigation that should trigger a public-relations response, in deciding whether an immediate action plan is necessary, in-house counsel should weigh the following questions:

- Has the company been accused of bad corporate citizenship, e.g., engaging in fraud, conspiracy, pollution, or other corporate crime or mass tort?
- Is a key product of the company alleged to be unsafe or to have caused serious injury or death to a consumer?
- Has the company experienced a cyber breach, or is it alleged to have otherwise wrongfully disclosed private data about its customers?
- Has a key executive, member of the management team, or other public face of the company been accused of a crime or sexual harassment?

If the answer to any of these questions is "yes," or the litigation otherwise calls into question the integrity of the operations or management of the company, counsel immediately should take steps to develop an appropriate business and public-relations response.

First, in-house counsel should notify key internal stakeholders, including the board of directors, relevant executive and management teams, and government relations and internal brand-management personnel of the issues at stake in the litigation. As soon as possible thereafter, an appropriate team should be assembled to develop a coordinated response and determine how to respond to inquiries from media, customers, or the public with one, centralized voice. For matters expected to draw especially harsh criticism, retention of a third-party public relations/crisis management firm may be advisable. Note that costs associated with such an engagement may be covered by general liability or other insurance policies; counsel should ascertain any available coverage, limits, and restrictions before hiring an external firm.

Counsel should be aware that a public-relations crisis could set in motion PR and business plans that overshadow or even work in opposition to the litigation defense strategy. In order to avoid compromising defenses and potentially increasing the risk of liability, in-house and outside counsel should stay involved in these work-streams to provide advice, appropriately adjust defense strategy, and preserve privilege to the extent possible. For example:

- Public relations professionals often will weigh various strategic responses and consider multiple draft statements and press releases that could be discoverable in litigation. To the extent practicable, attorneys should be involved in this process and provide final sign-off on any statements released so that the company can maintain privilege over draft statements and internal strategy discussions.
- The company may desire to publicly disclose favorable facts learned through privileged internal investigations in order to answer public scrutiny. Counsel should carefully consider this strategy and proceed with caution: disclosure of favorable facts while attempting to shield unfavorable facts could result in wholesale waiver of the privilege.[2]
- The relevant business lines may determine that evaluation and remediation of a risk is required. Counsel should never discourage these good business practices; however, counsel should advise on appropriate steps to maintain any applicable privileges, such as the attorney-client privilege or, potentially, the self-evaluative privilege.[3]

As the litigation moves forward, it is imperative that in-house and outside counsel do not lose sight of the company's ongoing public-relations strategy. Counsel should stay abreast of relevant media and public disclosures, and should consider creating an e-mail distribution list for dissemination of key press and public statements as well as any important internal updates. In addition, counsel should notify public-relations personnel prior to any important case filings so that they are prepared to respond to any resultant media inquiries.

---

2. *See, e.g.*, Doe 1 v. Baylor Univ., 320 F.R.D. 430, 434, 437–40 (W.D. Tex. 2017); Banneker Ventures, LLC v. Graham, 253 F. Supp. 3d 64, 73–74 (D.D.C. 2017); Pensacola Firefighters' Relief Pension Fund Bd. of Trs. v. Merrill Lynch Pierce Fenner & Smith, Inc., No. 3:09cv53/MCR/MD, 2010 WL 11520021, at *1–*4 (N.D. Fla. July 28, 2010); *In re* Kidder Peabody Sec. Litig., 168 F.R.D. 459, 461–62, 467–70 (S.D.N.Y. 1996).

3. "Most federal courts have declined to apply the self-critical analysis privilege, although many have been ambiguous as to whether or not they recognize it." Dorato v. Smith, 163 F. Supp. 3d 837, 892 (D.N.M. 2015). For a comprehensive summary of the self-critical analysis privilege in each circuit, *see* Lund v. City of Rockford, No. 17 CV 50035, 2017 WL 5891186, at *8–*13 (N.D. Ill. Nov. 29, 2017).

F.   Should You Expect Copycat or Related Cases?

Some types of litigation are particularly susceptible to copycat or multiple related cases. For example, multiple similar or related securities actions may arise out of like allegations. The financial crisis provides a prime example of this: as a result of the crisis, Wall Street banks faced numerous investor suits in multiple jurisdictions, including class actions and individual actions, arising out of the sale of residential mortgage-backed securities (RMBS). Banks also faced suits based on the same conduct filed by monoline insurers, RMBS trustees, and governmental entities and regulators. Other examples of litigation that may be replicated by multiple plaintiffs across more than one jurisdiction include antitrust claims, consumer fraud actions, and mass personal injury claims arising from the same conduct or occurrence. In-house counsel should stay apprised of litigation trends and continually assess whether the company faces incremental litigation and regulatory exposure. Outside counsel can help with this analysis, as well as monitor court dockets and media so that the litigation team is immediately alerted to copycat or related case filings.

G.   Accounting Matters

With litigation comes the potential for financial losses, i.e., settlement payouts or adverse judgments. Under prevailing accounting standards, companies are required to disclose certain litigation loss contingencies and create a litigation reserve. In coordination with the accounting and financial departments and outside counsel, in-house counsel should quickly determine at the outset of litigation whether disclosure and the establishment of a reserve are required. Counsel and accounting professionals should revisit this decision during each financial reporting cycle as the state of litigation play changes. The failure to properly report loss contingencies is a serious matter that could result in the need for a financial restatement, which in turn could lead to shareholder litigation or regulatory enforcement actions.

Under the Financial Accounting Standards Board's Accounting Standards Codification Topic 450 (ASC 450) (formerly, Financial Accounting Standards No. 5), a defendant-company must create a litigation loss reserve if the loss is both (1) probable, and (2) material and reasonably estimable. If a litigation loss is merely reasonably possible or not reasonably estimable, a reserve need not be established; however, the company still must disclose sufficient information regarding the litigation such that its financial statements are not misleading. This might include, for example, the nature of the claims and the damages sought, or a range of possible damages. Although a comprehensive discussion of accounting standards for loss contingencies is beyond the scope of this chapter, it suffices to say that any company that has been sued must carefully weigh all available information to determine what is required from an accounting perspective.

In-house counsel should also expect that the company's auditors will evaluate the reasonableness of its litigation disclosure and reserve decisions. In so doing, auditors may seek information concerning the litigation, including attorney analyses of likely exposure. In responding to these requests, in-house counsel should resist auditors' attempts to gain access to attorney-client privileged materials; sharing attorney-client privileged information with auditors generally will result in waiver of the privilege, opening the door for litigation adversaries to gain access to the information.[4] Courts generally hold, however, that attorney work product shared with auditors may continue to be protected from discovery by litigation adversaries so long as the materials are kept confidential.[5]

Practice Pointer

Thus, prior to making disclosures to auditors, in-house counsel should carefully assess whether the materials to be supplied constitute attorney-client privileged materials or attorney work product (or both). When making this determination, it is important that counsel consider the circumstances under which the materials were created (whether the materials were created in anticipation of litigation) as well as the governing law (how the courts in the relevant jurisdiction define attorney work product). Only materials that comfortably fit the controlling definition of attorney work product—and not attorney-client privilege—should be shared. Additionally, to further guard against any risk of waiver, counsel should also confirm with the auditor in writing the expectation that the confidentiality of the materials will be maintained.

III. CONDUCTING INTERNAL INVESTIGATIONS

A. Internal Versus Independent Investigations

At the outset of every litigation, it is important to conduct an internal investigation to develop and gain an understanding of the facts and evidence. What form this investigation takes, especially in matters of regional or national prominence, may be the subject of internal debate. In-house and outside defense counsel undoubtedly must conduct a review of the facts and interview witnesses. This purely internal investigation is standard and, if

---

4. *See, e.g.*, First Horizon Nat'l Corp. v. Houston Cas. Co., No. 2:15-cv-2235-SHL-dkv, 2016 WL 5867268, at *10 (W.D. Tenn. Oct. 5, 2016) (finding disclosure of attorney-client privileged information to outside auditors waived privilege); Westernbank Puerto Rico v. Kachkar, No. CIV. 07-1606 ADC/BJM, 2009 WL 530131, at *3 (D.P.R. Feb. 9, 2009) ("Disclosure to outside auditors generally waives the attorney-client privilege.").

5. *See* United States v. Deloitte LLP, 610 F.3d 129, 139 (D.C. Cir. 2010) ("While voluntary disclosure waives the attorney-client privilege, it does not necessarily waive work-product protection."); *see also, e.g.*, Lawrence E. Jaffe Pension Plan v. Household Int'l, Inc., 237 F.R.D. 176, 183 (N.D. Ill. 2006) (finding that disclosure to external auditor did not result in a waiver of work-product doctrine protection); SEC v. Berry, No. C07-04431 RMW HRL, 2011 WL 825742, at *6–*8 (N.D. Cal. Mar. 7, 2011) (same); Merrill Lynch & Co. v. Allegheny Energy, Inc., 229 F.R.D. 441, 449 (S.D.N.Y. 2004) (same). *But see, e.g.*, Medinol, Ltd. v. Boston Sci. Corp., 214 F.R.D. 113, 115–17 (S.D.N.Y. 2002) (finding disclosure to independent auditors waived attorney work-product protection).

conducted properly, the attorney-client privilege and attorney work-product protections will shield counsel's assessments and analysis, as well as confidential communications between employees and counsel during interviews.[6]

In extraordinary circumstances, in-house counsel may consider whether an outside, independent investigation is also required. Such investigations are not controlled by in-house or defense counsel and usually will result in an independent, written report that could reach conclusions unfavorable to the company. The report could be received confidentially—as opposed to being made public—but may not be protected by privilege, and could thus be discoverable in litigation.[7] Investigations of this sort may be necessary to restore confidence where the integrity of internal personnel is called into question such that they, in connection with outside counsel, cannot be trusted to reasonably and objectively assess the facts.

B. Internal Investigation in Aide of Litigation

Even where an independent investigation is commissioned, in-house and outside counsel must review facts and interview witnesses in order to assess the strengths and weaknesses of pending litigation. The sooner in-house and outside lawyers learn the facts—both good and bad—the sooner they will be able to provide meaningful advice on strategy and tactics. The opposite is equally true: sheltering counsel from the facts, whether by intent or in an effort to save money up front, often leads the lawyers to make decisions that they would not have made with a more complete view of the chess board.

Counsel must determine, as a preliminary matter, which individuals are likely to have relevant information. Counsel should then develop a plan for conducting interviews, likely in consultation with, or at the direction of, outside counsel. The goals of these interviews are to develop an understanding of the key facts underlying the claims and defenses at issue, as well as to ascertain an individual's role in, and personal knowledge of, the events at issue. Counsel should not overlook individuals who may not have personal knowledge of the facts at issue, but who can provide an overview of relevant corporate practices and processes, as well as identify additional fact witness who may possess relevant information.

During these interviews, it is important to provide an *Upjohn* warning to employees.[8] See Appendix B, Sample *Upjohn* Warning. Counsel should clearly explain that it represents the company, not the employee individually. Counsel should further

---

6. Note that "the privilege exists to protect not only the giving of professional advice to those who can act on it but also the giving of information to the lawyer to enable him to give sound and informed advice." Upjohn Co. v. United States, 449 U.S. 383, 390 (1981).

7. Whether an attorney's investigative work and report will be protected by privilege turns on the nature of the attorney-client relationship and the conduct of the attorney and client. *Compare* Sandra T.E. v. South Berwyn School District 100, 600 F.3d 612, 620–22 (7th Cir. 2010), *with* Doe v. Phillips Exeter Acad., No. 16-cv-396-JL, 2016 WL 5947263, at *1–*5 (D.N.H. Oct. 13, 2016), *and* Wartell v. Purdue Univ., No. 1:13-CV-99 RLM-APR, 2014 WL 4261205, at *1–*2, *7–*8 (N.D. Ind. Aug. 28, 2014).

8. *See* Upjohn, 449 U.S. at 386–87.

explain that any communications between the employee and counsel are protected by the attorney-client privilege, and that the privilege that protects these communications belongs to the company and not the individual employee.

Another important aspect of the fact investigation is gathering and preserving key documents. Although an in-depth review of potentially relevant documents will occur at a later stage, counsel should gather key documents as early as possible. This includes the electronic and hard-copy documents of the key individuals involved in the dispute. Through initial interviews with key witnesses, counsel should attempt to ascertain additional locations where potentially relevant documents may be housed. Key questions related to document storage include:

- What e-mail addresses do you use for business purposes? Do you use your personal e-mail for business purposes?
- Do you use your cell phone for business purposes? Do you text co-workers about business-related matters?
- Do you save documents to the hard drive of your desktop or laptop computer? Do you have a personal computer that you use for work matters?
- Do you work in any network shared drive or intranet site (such as SharePoint)?
- Do you use instant messaging for business purposes?
- Do you have any other devices—such as an iPad or tablet—that you use for business purposes?
- Do you keep paper records? Do you or your department have any paper records related to the issues in this matter stored outside your office (e.g., archives, off-site storage, home)?

Practice Pointer

Counsel should keep detailed records of all witness interviews and document collection efforts. Especially in complex matters, tracking these efforts in detail is important to ensure counsel can intelligently discuss document collection efforts during discovery conferences and efficiently formulate answers to complaints and interrogatory responses and prepare for depositions.

C. Related Issue: Personnel Actions

Oftentimes litigation calls into question the propriety of certain employee conduct. In-house counsel may be called upon to advise the company on whether adverse personnel actions are necessary or appropriate in light of pending allegations against the company. In-house counsel may be able to leverage the internal review process to gather information relevant to these questions. In addition to the necessary factual review, when considering personnel issues, in-house counsel should work with HR to review employee files and any logs of customer complaints, whistleblower hotlines, or similar resources. Although internal employment policies control employment decisions, in-house and outside counsel should consider how to manage litigation risk that may be created by adverse personnel actions, such as formulating a separation agreement that ensures ongoing cooperation in the litigation, and avoiding communications regarding the personnel action that could be later used as admissions against interest.

IV. INITIAL CONSIDERATIONS IN RESPONDING TO THE COMPLAINT

A. Assessing Personal Jurisdiction

An important initial consideration in responding to a complaint is assessing whether the company is subject to jurisdiction by the court where it has been sued. If a defendant determines that there are facts that would support a personal jurisdiction challenge, counsel should still consider the time and expense of a jurisdictional defense, including that the plaintiff may be allowed to take jurisdictional discovery.

Counsel should be aware that an objection based on personal jurisdiction can be waived—filing an appearance and responsive pleading without moving to dismiss for lack of personal jurisdiction will constitute a waiver. Thus, the defendant must challenge jurisdiction in the motion to dismiss or the answer.[9] When asserting a lack of personal jurisdiction in state court, it is imperative to assess proper local procedure for bringing the challenge (e.g., filing a motion to quash versus entering a special appearance to contest personal jurisdiction). Counsel should also consider whether substantive defenses can be asserted simultaneously with the jurisdictional challenge without resulting in a waiver.

Given the risk of waiver, an early assessment of whether facts exist that would support a personal-jurisdiction challenge is important. Under the Due Process Clause, an out-of-state defendant may not be bound by a judgment rendered in a forum in which it has no meaningful contact or ties. To determine whether the assertion of jurisdiction is appropriate, a court will assess the defendant's contacts with the forum state. As an initial step, counsel should compile facts reflecting lack of contacts with the forum state and the unreasonableness of an exercise of jurisdiction.

Whether a defendant's contacts with the state are adequate to render it amenable to jurisdiction will depend on whether the plaintiff is seeking to establish general or specific jurisdiction. When a court has general jurisdiction over a defendant, it has jurisdiction over *all* claims against that defendant, regardless of whether the suit arises out of the defendant's contacts with that state. General jurisdiction is a high bar to meet—it is only proper where the defendant has purposefully established continuous and systematic contact with the forum state. The Supreme Court's 2014 decision in *Daimler AG v. Bauman*[10] limited the scope of general jurisdiction over corporate defendants and thus

---

9.   *See* FED. R. CIV. P. 12(g)(2), (h)(1).
10.   Daimler AG v. Bauman, 571 U.S. 117 (2014).

had significant implications for the amenability of corporate defendants to general jurisdiction. The Court held that a defendant may be subject to general jurisdiction only where it is "at home" in the state, and indicated that a corporate defendant is likely to be "at home," and thus subject to general jurisdiction, only where it is incorporated or has its principal place of business.[11]

If no general jurisdiction exists, a court may still have specific jurisdiction over the defendant when the lawsuit arises out of, or is related to, the defendant's contacts with the forum state. Specific jurisdiction depends on how closely tied the cause of action is to the defendant's contact with the forum state. The Supreme Court recently analyzed this issue in *Bristol-Myers Squibb Co. v. Superior Court of California*,[12] a case in which a group of individual plaintiffs filed product liability claims in California state court alleging that the defendant company's medication caused them personal injuries. The majority of the individual plaintiffs were not California residents and did not purchase or ingest the medication in California. The defendant, which was incorporated and had its principal place of business elsewhere, moved to dismiss the nonresidents' claims based on lack of personal jurisdiction. The Court held that although the defendant had contacts with California (such as conducting research unrelated to the medication there), none of these contacts had a connection to the nonresident plaintiffs' claims; therefore, personal jurisdiction was lacking.[13] In other words, where the plaintiffs' claims would have been exactly the same even if the defendant had no forum state contacts, there is no basis for specific jurisdiction. In the wake of the *Bristol-Meyers Squibb* decision, a defendant is more likely to win dismissal of cases filed in jurisdictions where the defendant did not have contacts specifically related to the litigation.

B. Is Removal to Federal Court an Option?

When facing a lawsuit in state court, counsel should consider whether a transfer to federal court is advisable. A case filed in state court is removable to federal court if the federal court would have had original jurisdiction over the action.[14] Federal courts have original jurisdiction where diversity jurisdiction exists or over matters that constitute a federal question.[15]

Once it is determined that the case is removable, the tactical decision of whether to remove will turn on a multitude of factors, including the general differences between federal and state courts and how those differences may prove detrimental or beneficial to the specific case at hand. Although the specifics of a given case will dictate what factors are important to consider in deciding whether to remove a case, factors favoring removing to federal court include:

---

11. *Id.* at 137–39.
12. Bristol-Myers Squibb Co. v. Superior Court of Calif., 137 S. Ct. 1773 (2017).
13. *Id.* at 1781–82.
14. 28 U.S.C. § 1441(a).
15. 28 U.S.C §§ 1331, 1332.

- federal judges may be better equipped to handle large complex cases;
- it may be possible to move the case to another federal district court through a motion to transfer venue or a transfer to a multidistrict litigation court;
- federal judges may be more likely to dismiss a pleading on summary judgment or other pretrial dispositions;
- application of the Federal Rules of Civil Procedure may provide a tactical advantage in comparison to state procedural rules; and
- juries in federal cases are typically chosen from a larger geographic area than juries in state court cases (which are drawn from the county in which the court sits); this may be desirable to a defendant sued in an unfavorable county.

In contrast, state courts may be more knowledgeable when the controlling issue is one of state law, and the state procedural rules may prove beneficial in certain scenarios.

The required removal procedures are set forth at 28 U.S.C. § 1446. A defendant seeking removal is required to file a timely notice of removal in the appropriate federal district court, setting forth the grounds for removal. The 30-day time limit for filing the notice of removal in district court is triggered in one of two ways: by the initial pleading providing notice that the case is removable, or by an amended pleading or other paper that indicates the case is or has become removable.[16]

Where the action is removable based on the initial pleading, the defendant must file the notice of removal within 30 days from the earlier of (1) the date the defendant receives a copy of the initial pleading, or (2) the date the defendant is served with a summons if the initial pleading is filed in court and is not required to be served on the defendant.[17] Actual notice is insufficient to trigger the running of this time period; rather, the formal state rules governing service must be followed.[18] For example, if a defendant receives a draft copy of the complaint, such receipt does not start the clock on the defendant's time to remove. Where the case stated by the initial pleading is not removable, the defendant has 30 days from the date of receipt of an amended pleading or other paper from which it may be first ascertained that the case is one that is or has become removable to federal court.[19] Additionally, cases in which federal jurisdiction would be based on diversity of citizenship cannot be removed more than one year after the action commences, regardless of when the case becomes removable.[20] Counsel should be aware that limited statutory exceptions to these time limits exist. Notably, the one-year time limit applying to diversity actions does not apply to class actions.[21]

---

16. 28 U.S.C. § 1446(b).
17. 28 U.S.C. § 1446(b)(1).
18. Murphy Bros., Inc. v. Michetti Pipe Stringing, Inc., 526 U.S. 344, 347–48 (1999).
19. 28 U.S.C. § 1446(b)(3).
20. 28 U.S.C. § 1446(c)(1).
21. 28 U.S.C. § 1453(b).

Practice Pointer

In multidefendant cases, all properly served defendants in the state action must join in the petition for removal except in certain limited circumstances.[22] Given this "rule of unanimity"—and the strictly enforced 30-day time limit for removal—counsel should consider early coordination with co-defendants regarding removal.

An issue that sometimes arises in multidefendant cases is how to calculate the running of the 30-day time limit in situations where the defendants are served at different times. In multidefendant cases, *each* defendant is permitted 30 days from the date of service to seek removal.[23] Thus, a later-served defendant is not bound by an earlier-served defendant's decision not to remove. Rather, an earlier-served defendant that did not remove a case within its 30-day window has the ability to join in or consent to a later-served defendant's removal petition.[24]

C. Assessing Venue

1. Improper Venue, Inconvenient Forum, and Motion to Transfer

When facing a lawsuit in federal court, an important consideration is whether the plaintiff has selected a proper forum for the action and, if not, whether there is any basis to challenge venue. If there is a basis for challenging venue, counsel must assess whether challenging venue makes sense from a strategic perspective. Although this involves many considerations, the key consideration is whether the selection of a particular district will affect the outcome of the litigation in a material way. In actions arising under a federal statute, this will involve an analysis of how a particular district construes the statute in question. In the context of diversity cases, counsel should assess the differences in state law that might be applied. Counsel should also bear in mind how a venue motion may affect what law governs the action. Generally, where a diversity action is transferred for convenience alone, the law of the transferor forum will be applied.[25] Where the transfer is made because of improper venue, however, the law of the transferee forum will apply.[26]

Besides assessing how the district varies in its application of substantive law, counsel should also consider the frequency with which a particular action is brought in a particular district and the consistency of outcomes in that district. This includes an analysis of whether the judge is likely to be familiar with the issues to be litigated or

---

22. 28 U.S.C. § 1446(b)(2)(A).

23. 28 U.S.C. § 1446(b)(2)(B).

24. 28 U.S.C. § 1446(b)(2)(C).

25. *See* Van Dusen v. Barrack, 376 U.S. 612, 639 (1964); *see also* 15 CHARLES ALAN WRIGHT ET AL., FEDERAL PRACTICE AND PROCEDURE § 3846 (4th ed. 2013).

26. Muldoon v. Tropitone Furniture Co., 1 F.3d 964, 967 (9th Cir. 1993); Manley v. Engram, 755 F.2d 1463, 1467 (11th Cir. 1985).

whether the case would likely present unfamiliar issues. Variations in procedural rules should also be considered—counsel should consult with outside counsel that is familiar with a particular district to determine how local rules and standing orders may affect the course of the action. (As indicated earlier, this is one benefit of hiring experienced local counsel.)

Generally, there are two bases on which to challenge venue: improper venue or inconvenient venue. Venue is proper in a district where any defendant resides if all defendants reside in the same state, or where all or a substantial part of the events or omissions giving rise to the claim occurred, or a substantial part of the property that is subject to the action is situated.[27] If no district is available under either of those bases, venue is proper in a district "in which any defendant is subject to the court's personal jurisdiction."[28]

If none of those bases are met, a challenge based on improper venue should be considered. Upon a motion to dismiss for improper venue, a court may either dismiss the action or transfer it to any district in which it originally could have been brought.[29] Generally, courts will transfer, rather than dismiss, the action.

Alternatively, venue can be challenged "[f]or the convenience of parties and witnesses, in the interest of justice."[30] This is a case-by-case inquiry, and courts consider a range of factors, including: judicial familiarity with governing laws; relative ease and practicality of trying the case in an alternative forum; convenience of the parties and the witnesses; the availability of compulsory process for getting unwilling witnesses to attend; the location of the relevant sources of proof; and public interest factors, such as the relative congestion of court dockets and the relation to the community to the occurrences that give rise to the litigation.[31]

2.   Arbitration Requirements

At the outset of an action, counsel should also consider any arbitration requirements that may apply to the case. When litigation is commenced contrary to the terms of an arbitration agreement, a party may seek a court order to compel arbitration proceedings. If there is a valid arbitration agreement between the parties, and the agreement covers the dispute at issue, a court will generally grant a request to compel arbitration.[32]

---

27.   28 U.S.C. § 1391(b)(1), (2).
28.   28 U.S.C. § 1391(b)(3).
29.   28 U.S.C. § 1406(a).
30.   28 U.S.C. § 1404(a).
31.   *See* Van Dusen v. Barrack, 376 U.S. 612, 644–46 (1964); Research Automation, Inc. v. Schrader-Bridgeport Int'l, Inc., 626 F.3d 973, 978 (7th Cir. 2010); D.H. Blair & Co. v. Gottdiener, 462 F.3d 95, 106–07 (2d Cir. 2006).
32.   *See, e.g.*, Parm v. Bluestem Brands, Inc., 898 F.3d 869, 877–78 (8th Cir. 2018); Willacy v. Marotta, 683 F. App'x 468, 471–72 (6th Cir. 2017); United Steel, Paper & Forestry, Rubber, Mfg., Energy, Allied Indus. & Serv. Workers Int'l Union v. Phillips 66 Co., 839 F.3d 1198, 1206–07 (10th Cir. 2016); U.S. Nutraceuticals, LLC v. Cyanotech Corp., 769 F.3d 1308, 1312 (11th Cir. 2014); AT&T Techs., Inc. v. Commc'ns Workers of Am., 475 U.S. 643, 650 (1986).

In addition to moving to compel arbitration, counsel should consider moving to stay the litigation pending arbitration.

D. Assessment of Claims and Defenses

Outside of the various procedural issues that counsel must consider when a case first arises, it is important to quickly gain an understanding of the relevant legal landscape governing the action. Outside counsel should assess governing law to develop a strategy for responding to the complaint. This includes understanding the elements of, and affirmative defenses to, each claim, including any statute of limitations defense. This early research is important in finding potential grounds on which a defendant can file dispositive motions, and this initial groundwork will guide the strategy going forward.

Unless the defendant moves to dismiss the complaint, it must prepare an answer admitting or denying the plaintiff's allegations. Preparing an answer is generally a fact-intensive exercise, and counsel should be prepared to devote company resources to assist with the answer, especially if the information requires verification from company employees. Besides responding to the plaintiff's allegations, the answer also pleads the defendant's defenses. As discussed above, outside counsel should develop a clear understanding of the governing law and any affirmative defenses early on, given that the defendant must include in its answer any affirmative defense that it wants to raise.[33]

Additionally, failure to join a necessary party can also be raised in an answer or motion to dismiss, although this argument is not waived even if first raised at trial.[34]

Preparing the answer also involves assessing whether the defendant will assert any counterclaims that must be raised in the pleadings. The Federal Rules of Civil Procedure divide counterclaims into two types: compulsory and permissive.[35] Compulsory counterclaims are any claims that (1) arise out of the transaction or occurrence that is the subject matter of the opposing party's claim, and (2) do not require adding another party over whom the court cannot acquire jurisdiction.[36] In determining whether a claim arises out of the same transaction or occurrence—and therefore is a compulsory counterclaim—courts generally consider whether the issues of fact and law raised by the claim and the counterclaim are largely the same; whether substantially the same evidence will support or refute the claim and counterclaim; and whether there is any logical relationship between the claim and the counterclaim.[37] If a counterclaim is compulsory, a defendant must plead it in its answer or abandon the claim altogether. In other words, a defendant cannot assert an unpled compulsory counterclaim in a later action.[38]

---

33. FED. R. CIV. P. 8(c)(1).

34. FED. R. CIV. P. 12(h)(2)(A)–(C).

35. FED. R. CIV. P. 13(a), (b).

36. FED. R. CIV. P. 13(a)(1).

37. *See, e.g.*, Underwriters at Interest on Cover Note JHB92M10582079 v. Nautronix, Ltd., 79 F.3d 480, 483 n.2 (5th Cir. 1996).

38. *See e.g.*, Kane v. Magna Mixer Co., 71 F.3d 555, 562–63 (6th Cir. 1995).

In contrast, a permissive counterclaim is any other claim, and the rules provide that a pleading *may* state as a counterclaim any claim that is not compulsory.[39] However, failing to plead a permissive counterclaim does not preclude the defendant from asserting it in a later action. The timing of when a claim arose is important in determining whether a claim is compulsory or permissive—only a claim that the defendant could have asserted when it answered can be deemed compulsory.[40] Although a defendant may move to file a supplemental answer asserting a newly arisen counterclaim, the defendant need not assert that claim in the action.

At this stage, counsel should also consider whether the claims may be heard by a jury. Generally, the plaintiff selects whether to request a jury by including a jury demand in the complaint. If the plaintiff has not made a jury demand, however, defense counsel should consider whether requesting a jury may be advantageous. A jury demand may be made in the answer or in a separate document.

V. MULTIDISTRICT LITIGATION AND COORDINATION WITHIN A SINGLE JURISDICTION

Counsel faced with potential nationwide litigation arising out of a common or related set of events should be aware of the procedural devices available that may aid in the coordination of widespread litigation.

A. Consolidation of Federal Cases

1. Multidistrict Litigation

Counsel facing litigation in multiple federal districts may want to consider using the federal multidistrict litigation (MDL) procedure available under 28 U.S.C. § 1407. The threshold requirement for seeking coordination is that at least two cases involving one or more common questions of fact are pending in two different federal courts.[41] The purpose of the MDL process is to provide a mechanism for cases involving common issues of fact to be transferred to a single district court for coordinated pretrial proceedings. The MDL process may allow counsel to avoid duplicative discovery and conflicting decisions among the district courts. The advantages of an MDL proceeding include the reduction in litigation costs and efficiency realized through consolidation; the elimination of problems created by inconsistent pretrial rulings among jurisdictions; and the increased possibility of global resolution, either through dispositive motions or settlement. Counsel should be aware of the disadvantages of an MDL proceeding, however, including that an MDL proceeding multiplies the risk of an adverse decision and renders multiple cases dependent on the decision of one judge; an MDL proceeding

---

39. FED. R. CIV. P. 13(b).
40. FED. R. CIV. P. 13(a)(1).
41. *See* 28 U.S.C. § 1407(a).

may remove the opportunity for early dispositive motions in cases having favorable facts, and high-profile MDL proceedings may spur the filing of additional litigation or trigger regulatory action.

An MDL process may be initiated by a party to any action or by the Judicial Panel on Multidistrict Litigation upon its own initiative.[42] The principal way to initiate the MDL process is through a motion to transfer—any party in an action in which transfer is appropriate under section 1407 may file a motion to transfer with the Judicial Panel on Multidistrict Litigation.[43] Under the panel's rules, the moving party must file a supporting brief along with its motion to transfer, as well as information regarding each action involved.[44] The moving party bears the burden to demonstrate the three statutory prerequisites to transfer: (1) there are multiple actions pending in different districts involving one or more common questions of fact; (2) transfer will be for the convenience of parties and witnesses; and (3) transfer will promote the just and efficient conduct of such actions.[45]

If the panel decides that transfer is appropriate, the panel selects the transferee district and the judge who will handle the matter.[46] The panel may select any district court; it need not be one of the transferor districts. Factors that the panel may consider in determining the transferee court include: the parties' residences and principal place of business, the location of relevant evidence and witnesses, the district with the largest number of cases already pending, and the location of related proceedings, including related state court cases.[47] This is a significant decision that counsel should carefully consider and be prepared to address in front of the panel.

2. Single Jurisdiction Consolidation

For cases filed within the same jurisdiction, the multidistrict litigation procedure is not necessary. Rather, counsel may want to consider seeking consolidation of the cases for purposes of discovery, motions, settlement, and/or trial. Whether consolidation is favorable is a strategic decision that will depend upon a host of factors, including the extent to which the cases present a number of common issues of law and fact, whether consolidation might lead to limitations or efficiencies in discovery, and the potential impact of consolidation on settlement. Generally, but not always, cases will be consolidated before the judge who received the first-filed case. Counsel's perspective on that judge may influence the decision whether to consolidate.

Even without formal consolidation, once a significant number of cases are filed within a jurisdiction, the court may act on its own—either pursuant to a local rule or

---

42. *See* 28 U.S.C. § 1407(c).
43. *See id.*
44. J.P.M.L. R.P. 6.1(b).
45. 28 U.S.C. § 1407(a).
46. 28 U.S.C. § 1407(a), (b).
47. *See, e.g., In re* Online DVD Rental Antitrust Litig., 609 F. Supp. 2d 1376, 1377 (J.P.M.L. 2009) (taking into account the defendants' headquarters, the location of relevant documents and witnesses, and the district where the majority of actions were already pending).

otherwise—to assign all of the cases to the same judge. Alternatively, the court may order coordination of discovery or motion practice in cases that otherwise remain pending before separate judges.

B. Coordination of Related State Actions

Counsel facing parallel litigation in federal court and one or more state courts lack a formal mechanism by which to consolidate the state and federal litigation. However, even without express authority for the coordination of related state and federal actions, coordination—often through informal mechanisms—is common. Additionally, the Judicial Panel on Multidistrict Litigation has recognized the need to coordinate with parallel state litigation and may consider the location of related state court litigation as a factor in the selection of the transferee court.[48]

Coordination of related cases can be initiated by the state or federal judge as well as by counsel. The most common form of coordination is coordination of the various aspects of discovery, likely because of the considerable efficiencies to be gained through coordination. This may include coordinated or joint scheduling to allow discovery to proceed on parallel tracks, and the adoption of coordinated discovery plans. A joint discovery plan should address document production and depositions, and set tentative deadlines for those events, as well as for the open and close of discovery. If a joint discovery plan is established, counsel should consider whether the appointment of a special master to resolve discovery disputes is appropriate. Additionally, joint discovery plans may provide for master discovery requests and common document depositories. Common document depositories provide a central location where parties can produce documents, copy productions, and cross-reference documents.

Although coordination is most common during the discovery phase, counsel should consider whether coordination after discovery would serve its interests. Post-discovery coordination may include joint hearings, joint trial scheduling, and joint mediation or settlement.

C. Management of Related Regulatory Actions

A key challenge that counsel facing multiple nationwide lawsuits will likely encounter is the management and coordination of parallel regulatory proceedings. In defending parallel proceedings, counsel must continually consider how an action taken in one proceeding—including resolution or settlement—may affect the company's interest in the remaining proceedings. Parallel government proceedings also raise important privilege issues in that counsel must weigh the benefits of cooperating with regulators against the risk that disclosures to government agencies will be discoverable by civil litigants.

---

48. *See, e.g.*, *In re* Zicam Cold Remedy Mktg. & Sales Practices Litig., 655 F. Supp. 2d 1371, 1373 (J.P.M.L. 2009).

VI. MANAGEMENT AND COORDINATION OF DISCOVERY

A. Protecting Confidential Information

At the outset of discovery, counsel should consider the type of information that will be exchanged and whether such information should be the subject of a protective order. The initial step is to gain an understanding of what sensitive information the entity possesses that the other party may request in discovery. In particular, trade secrets, confidential commercial information, and certain personally identifying information of employees or customers may warrant protection under a protective order.[49] Although protective orders are common in commercial litigation, counsel should keep in mind that the order must balance the entity's need to protect sensitive information against the general principle that the public should have access to judicial proceedings. Thus, while drafting and negotiating the protective order, counsel should ensure it protects the entity's privacy interests without being so restrictive that the court will not approve it.

While drafting the protective order, there are certain provisions that warrant closer attention. First, the protective order should contain a provision that protects a party against inadvertent disclosure of privileged or confidential documents. In cases with large electronic document productions, a "clawback" provision protecting the parties from wavier in the event of inadvertent disclosure of privileged or confidential is critical. Although the Federal Rules provide a clawback procedure for retracting inadvertently produced information, an overt clawback provision in a protective agreement is advisable because parties can agree to broader protection for inadvertently produced materials, thus reducing the risk of waiver. It is important that the agreement establishes a clear procedure to invoking the clawback, responding to the clawback, and resolving disagreements regarding the information intended to be clawed back.

Second, provisions that set the protocol for filing documents under seal warrant close attention. Some courts consider protective orders authorizing parties to seal any documents considered confidential under seal as overbroad.[50] A protective order should specify that the party seeking to file confidential documents under seal must also file a motion to seal the confidential information prior to the filing of the substantive motion that implicates the confidential document. This should apply when either party wants to submit confidential information before the court, even if that party was not the party who designated the information confidential.

Third, counsel should consider whether a provision allowing certain highly confidential materials to be limited to "attorneys' eyes only" is advisable. This will likely be the case where allowing the opposing party to view confidential materials is problematic, which is often the case with trade secrets or proprietary business information, for example. The opposing party may complain that such a provision is overly restrictive

---

49. *See, e.g.*, Wedgewood Ltd. P'ship I v. Twp. of Liberty, No. 2:04-CV-1069, 2007 WL 1796089, at *3 (S.D. Ohio June 21, 2007).

50. *See* Shane Grp., Inc. v. Blue Cross Blue Shield of Mich., 825 F.3d 299, 305 (6th Cir. 2016); Citizens First Nat'l Bank of Princeton v. Cincinnati Ins. Co., 178 F.3d 943, 944–45 (7th Cir. 1999).

because it does not allow for the discussion of important information and facts between the attorney and client. If an attorneys'-eyes-only provision is necessary to properly protect the entity's information, its counsel should exercise restraint in designating documents as such to avoid scrutiny by opposing counsel and the court.

Finally, a protective order should include a third-party endorsement that requires any party who receives confidential information to sign an acknowledgment agreeing that the protective order binds it.

B. Establishing a Realistic Discovery Schedule

At the outset of discovery, it is important to establish a realistic discovery schedule. This includes coordinating with opposing counsel as required by Federal Rule of Civil Procedure 16. Prior to this conference, counsel should evaluate its case and what discovery it anticipates having to turn over, as well as what discovery it anticipates requesting from the other side. Counsel should also consider what orders it needs from the court, including protective orders, to accomplish its contemplated discovery.

The schedule should address the timing of key discovery milestones, including initial disclosures, fact discovery, and fact witness depositions, as well as expert discovery and expert witness depositions. Setting a realistic fact discovery deadline includes anticipating how long it will take to collect the relevant data, process that data, review that data, and produce any responsive documents. Counsel should address this issue with outside counsel early in the litigation. The process may include retaining a vendor to aid in data collection, processing, review, and production. This inquiry should include working with the vendor and outside counsel to analyze the data provisionally identified as relevant to better understand the size of the population that must be reviewed and ultimately produced, and the types of documents involved. Additionally, counsel should consider whether the documents relevant to the litigation will implicate any unique privilege or confidentiality concerns that would increase the time required to review and produce those materials.

C. Managing Discovery of Electronically Stored Information

The importance of proper and efficient management of electronic discovery in large, regional, or national litigation cannot be understated. Developing and executing on a coordinated discovery plan will save time and money, systematically alert all counsel to key pieces of evidence, and help ensure uniform discovery responses across related matters.

1. Hiring an Electronic Discovery Vendor Versus Relying on Internal IT

When the time comes to collect, process, review, and produce electronically stored information (ESI), in-house counsel's first decision will be whether to rely on internal IT resources or hire an outside e-discovery expert (or both). Many companies have enhanced internal capabilities to collect and process ESI, or have obtained an internal document management and review database. The presence of these capabilities and systems does not necessarily mean that reliance on internal IT is appropriate, especially in large-scale litigation.

Practice Pointer

In-house counsel should weigh the following considerations:

- Can internal IT dedicate adequate resources to litigation efforts? Although collecting data and instituting back-end litigation holds may be part and parcel of the IT department's daily workload, other litigation requirements may quickly constrain internal resources. Litigation counsel often requires full-time, dedicated support when electronic discovery is at its peak.
- Does internal IT have sufficient capabilities for the collection and processing of relevant data? Although basic collection and processing of e-mail and electronic documents may be well within internal expertise, an outside expert may be better equipped to handle more complicated collections, such as forensic restoration of data and text message, recorded voice, and instant message collections.
- Is internal IT adept at documenting chain of custody and collection processes? If data spoliation occurs, are they willing and able to serve as litigation witnesses? Many internal IT employees would prefer to shift these risks and responsibilities to outside experts.
- To the extent the company prefers to host data on an internal document management and review database, will outside counsel and any document review teams be able to adequately access it? Oftentimes law firm and company data-security requirements provide that internal systems will not be freely accessible to or by outside entities. Reduced access to document databases could severely hamper litigation counsel.
- If something goes wrong with the production (as often is the case in large productions), is the client better off having a third-party vendor testify to the issue and its remediation, rather than in-house IT personnel who may be viewed as biased or at least with suspicion by the opposing party and the court?

Especially in large-scale matters, in-house counsel should err on the side of caution and retain appropriate e-discovery experts. Regardless, in-house counsel should work closely with outside counsel to answer the above questions, and hire third parties to assist with discovery as appropriate.

2. Efficient Storage, Review, and Production of ESI Across Multiple Matters

Although a full discussion of e-discovery management and best practices is beyond the scope of this chapter, suffice to say that in-house counsel should assure the leveraging of e-discovery collections, processing, and review across multiple matters. Unless in-house counsel is particularly adept at managing e-discovery, experienced outside counsel will be a critical asset in this process to assure that: (1) relevant data is collected and processed only once; (2) the database environment takes into account the needs of various litigation and regulatory teams who may need to access it; and (3) data is adequately coded during the review process such that the work product, especially identification of key documents, privilege logging, and redaction work, can be utilized in future related matters.

Practice Pointer

To the extent multiple related cases are anticipated across multiple jurisdictions and will be led by various outside counsel, in-house counsel should consider appointing one firm as national discovery coordination counsel, with responsibility to oversee a data repository accessible by all counsel and to manage document reviews and productions across multiple matters.

D. Managing Depositions

Counsel should work closely with outside counsel in the preparation of witnesses for depositions. Prior to the beginning of depositions, this includes meeting with employees who may have relevant knowledge of the events in order to gain an understanding of which witnesses will have important information. Preparing witnesses to be deposed will include confirming the witnesses' knowledge of the relevant facts and explaining the legal principles at issue in the case. Counsel should also ensure that witnesses have an understanding of the opposing party's case, including explaining how opposing counsel is likely to try to use the deposition to further their theory of the case. Prior to a deposition, counsel should ensure that the witness has practiced mock questions, most likely with outside counsel, including questioning using specific documents that may be used in the deposition.

For key fact witnesses, depositions play the role of preserving testimony for trial. This becomes imperative if the witness later becomes unavailable to testify at trial, in which case the deposition testimony may be relied upon.[51] Counsel should consider whether there are employees whose testimony will be critical at trial and, if so, whether they should be deposed in case these witnesses ultimately become unavailable. This is an important consideration for former employees, especially those who may have moved.

Where multiple related matters are pending simultaneously, consider whether it is prudent to coordinate deposition testimony across matters, especially for key former employees who may have reduced availability. Even if coordination is not possible or advisable, keep in mind that plaintiffs' counsel is likely to request the production of

---

51. *See* FED. R. CIV. P. 32(a)(4).

deposition transcripts from other related matters. Outside counsel should be made aware of all prior relevant testimony, and when preparing witnesses, caution should be taken to assure testimony is consistent.

E. Managing Expert Discovery

The work of litigation experts can also be leveraged across litigation and regulatory matters. If multiple related cases are pending or anticipated, all of which will require similar, complex expert analysis, in-house counsel should consider engaging a strong consulting expert firm with the capability to support testifying experts as necessary. This allows counsel to develop trusted relationships with the consulting experts, who in turn will have adequate time to become familiar with the client and learn the intricacies of the matters at issue. Although specific expert studies or analysis may ultimately vary from matter to matter, consulting experts should be able to develop efficiencies that will result in reduced expert support costs over time.

In addition, before selecting testifying experts in multicase matters, in-house counsel should coordinate with various outside counsel defense teams. Selection of a testifying expert is a somewhat subjective process. Although the expert's experience is of paramount importance, defense counsel will also want to consider the expert's demeanor and presence, communication skills, and personality traits. An expert who is perfect before a New York jury may be less desirable to present in Texas. In addition, expert availability in relation to the case schedules will affect the selection process. In-house counsel should coordinate this process to assure that the most critical matters are prioritized and the defense teams are each fully apprised of expert capabilities and opinions across all cases.

VII. SUMMARY JUDGMENT AND TRIAL

Counsel should constantly, objectively assess the merits of any case at all stages. As litigation approaches summary judgment and trial, however, an unbiased evaluation is even more important; the case is approaching the point where claims may be decided and dismissed or liability imposed. Where multiple related matters are pending, whether consolidated or not, merits decisions could have effects beyond just one case, which in-house counsel must consider.

In consolidated or coordinated proceedings, a decision on a particular claim, defense, or issue of fact will bind all parties to the proceedings, preventing relitigation of the issue.[52] Even if related matters are proceeding in separate jurisdictions, a legal

---

52. *See, e.g.*, Parungao v. Cmty. Health Sys., Inc., 858 F.3d 452, 457–58 (7th Cir. 2017) (affirming the district court's finding that the plaintiff's claim was barred by the doctrine of res judicata); A.H. *ex rel.* Hubbard v. Midwest Bus Sales, Inc., 823 F.3d 448, 453–54 (8th Cir. 2016) (affirming the district court's dismissal on the basis of issue preclusion); Padmanabhan v. Hulka, 308 F. Supp. 3d 484, 495–96 (D. Mass. 2018) (dismissing claims *sua sponte* as barred by claim preclusion), *appeal filed*, No. 18-1301 (1st Cir. Apr.

decision in one case can be cited as persuasive authority in another. If the decision is positive for the client, this could have multiplying advantageous effects in all related matters. On the other hand, a negative decision could have the opposite effect and raise the price of settlements across all matters. In the same vein, if the client takes a position on the interpretation of facts or law in one case, it could be judicially estopped from taking a contrary position in later litigation.[53] For these reasons, in-house counsel managing multiple related matters should carefully coordinate to ensure outside counsel are asserting consistent positions on behalf of the client. In addition, counsel should consider which case may be the best bellwether for summary judgment and trial issues so that other pending matters are not adversely affected. If a poorly situated case is approaching merits decisions on a faster timetable than other, stronger matters, it may be time to consider settlement.

VIII. SETTLEMENT DISCUSSIONS AND SETTLEMENT

In-house counsel and key business stakeholders, including potentially the board of directors, should assess and reassess whether settlement is advisable throughout the course of a case. Outside counsel usually have more frequent communication with opposing counsel and can help gauge whether they may be amenable to settlement discussions at any particular point in the proceedings. Oftentimes early settlement discussions—either before or shortly after responding to the complaint—will prove valuable to understanding what the plaintiff hopes to gain from the case. Defendants should strongly consider early settlement when the early case assessment has indicated that legal defenses are weak or the facts are particularly poor. Plaintiffs may be willing to provide steeper discounts at a point in the proceeding where they and their counsel have expended fewer resources to prosecute the case. Defendants may also consider early settlement in opposite circumstances: where legal defenses are particularly strong or the facts are good, but nevertheless early dismissal of the proceedings is unlikely. In such circumstances, defendants can use the settlement negotiation process, whether through mediation or otherwise, to apprise the plaintiff of the weaknesses in the case and potentially extract a nuisance value settlement and release.

Even if early settlement discussions are not possible or are unsuccessful, counsel should keep an open mind about the possibility of settlement throughout litigation. At key points in the case, e.g., after hearings or opinions on dispositive motions, when critical facts are learned in discovery, or prior to trial, counsel should re-evaluate the settlement position and strategy. Remember that litigation is a distraction for most

---

11, 2018); Casares v. Wells Fargo Bank, N.A., 268 F. Supp. 3d 248, 253–55 (D.D.C. 2017) (granting the motion to dismiss on res judicata grounds).

53. *See, e.g.*, Am. Transp. Grp. LLC v. Cal. Cartage Co., 168 F. Supp. 3d 1074, 1081–82 (N.D. Ill. 2016) (granting the motion for summary judgment on the basis of judicial estoppel); Grochocinski v. Mayer Brown Rowe & Maw, LLP, 719 F.3d 785, 795–97 (7th Cir. 2013) (affirming the district court's determination of judicial estoppel).

company employees; if settlement can be achieved on reasonable terms, it is worth considering.

Practice Pointer

When approaching settlement discussions, counsel should consider at least several questions:

- Will the parties negotiate directly or engage a third-party mediator? Especially in complex or multiparty litigation, a mediator is advisable to help manage the negotiation process and facilitate discussion among the parties.
- Should the company's insurers attend any mediation? Do insurance policies give carriers the right to consent to settlements or offers to settle? Counsel must proceed cautiously to ensure compliance with applicable policies. Carriers generally will want input into timing, settlement authority, and the selection of a particular mediator.
- Will any settlement set a precedent for pending related matters? Where counsel is juggling multiple related matters, settlement in one case— especially if not confidential—could set a floor for settlement with plaintiffs in other cases.

If the parties are able to agree on a settlement amount, counsel must also carefully consider other key settlement provisions. First and foremost, any settlement should contain broad (usually mutual) releases. Settlements also must include a requirement that the plaintiff dismiss the litigation with prejudice. Additionally, defendants should insist on a no-admissions clause, which provides that the defendant does not admit liability. Other terms counsel should consider may include a covenant not to sue,[54] confidentiality provisions or limitations on publicity, representations and warranties, and venue or arbitration requirements for future disputes arising out of the agreement.

---

54. Although narrowly construed, covenants not to sue as between the settling parties are generally enforceable and deprive courts of jurisdiction over subsequent litigation. *See, e.g.*, Skilstaf, Inc. v. CVS Caremark Corp., 669 F.3d 1005, 1017 (9th Cir. 2012); Nike, Inc. v. Already, LLC, 663 F.3d 89, 96–97 (2d Cir. 2011), *aff'd*, 568 U.S. 85 (2013); CIC Prop. Owners v. Marsh USA Inc., 460 F.3d 670, 672 (5th Cir. 2006). However, counsel should be aware that contractual provisions forbidding a plaintiff law firm from instituting similar actions against the defendant on behalf of different, nonsettling clients raise ethical concerns and are typically void. *See* Tradewinds Airlines, Inc. v. Soros, No. 08 Civ. 5901(JFK), 2009 WL 1321695, at *9 (S.D.N.Y. May 12, 2009); *see* MODEL RULES OF PROF'L CONDUCT R. 5.6(b) (1983) (prohibiting a lawyer from making an agreement that restricts another lawyer's right to practice as part as a settlement); ABA Comm'n on Ethics and Prof'l Responsibility, Formal Op. 00-417 (2000); N.Y.C. Bar Ass'n, Formal Op. 1999-03 (1999).

IX. CONCLUSION

Managing regional and national litigation, especially multiple related matters, is no easy task; however, if in-house and outside counsel develop a coordinated approach, they will be able to maximize efficiencies, eliminate redundancies, and produce high-quality results for the client.

Appendix A:
Sample Document Preservation Notice

ATTORNEY-CLIENT PRIVILEGED
CONTAINS ATTORNEY WORK PRODUCT

The purpose of this memorandum is to advise you of [describe the current or anticipated litigation, investigation, or audit]. As a result of this [litigation/investigation/audit], the Company has a legal obligation to preserve all paper documents, physical items, and electronic documents and data in Company records that may be relevant in the [litigation/investigation/audit].

Please read this memorandum carefully because the failure to preserve relevant documents can result in severe sanctions. You may be required to give testimony about your document and data preservation efforts.

It is essential that until further notice from the Legal Department, you do not alter, destroy, throw away, electronically erase, or otherwise dispose of any of the following categories of information: [List all potentially relevant categories of documents.]

For purposes of this memorandum, the term "document" is to be construed broadly and includes all information concerning the subject matters listed above, whether in final or draft form, and whether in paper documents, notes, electronically stored information (ESI), or any other form. ESI includes e-mail, text messages, voicemail, audio and visual recordings, word processing documents, spreadsheets, databases, calendars, networks, computer systems, servers, archives, backup and disaster-recovery systems, tapes, disks, drives, cartridges, other storage media, laptops, internet records, web pages, personal computers, and other information storage devices.

You are responsible for determining whether any documents in your custody, possession, or control are subject to the preservation obligations and for taking appropriate steps to preserve such information. To satisfy your preservation obligations, please follow all of the below instructions.

1. Maintain all documents in your possession, custody, or control. This includes documents in your office; on your Company or personal computer, portable hard drives, memory cards, "thumb drives," personal digital assistants, mobile telephones, tablets, iPads, iPods, and smart phones; in shared Company storage locations, including but not limited to filing cabinets, closets, shared electronic drives, and Company databases; in off-site storage locations; or at your home.
2. Maintain all documents in their current, unaltered form. Do not remove staples, clips, or post-it notes. Do not make any changes or additions to documents. Do not copy electronic documents to another location or external drive. If you need to work in a document subject to the preservation obligations, contact [name].

3. Do not discard any documents. This instruction applies to documents now in your possession, as well as those you create or receive after the date of this memorandum.

4. Suspend any practices regarding the retention or destruction of ESI, including programs or processes that automatically delete ESI at the conclusion of a set period of time.

5. Any significant hardware/software upgrade, repair, or replacement that might impact the identification and preservation of ESI must be deferred. If a computer, laptop, mobile telephone, or tablet that contains relevant documents must be replaced, please contact [name] before taking any steps to replace it.

6. Your only obligation at this time is to identify and preserve relevant documents. Please do not sort, categorize, index, or summarize any documents—including ESI—that may be responsive to this memorandum; rather, merely identify and preserve them intact in the way that they were collected or created and filed in the ordinary course of business. The Legal Department will collect the documents in way that will ensure the integrity of the data.

7. Provide all employees under your management who many have relevant information, including your assistants, with a copy of this memorandum and ensure that they follow the preservation obligations set forth herein.

8. If you become aware of any individual within the Company who is likely to have or to create relevant information, but who has not received a copy of this memorandum, please contact the Legal Department.

9. **If you are not sure whether a particular document is subject to the preservation obligations, err on the side of preservation.**

If you have any questions about this memorandum or your preservation obligations, please contact [name]. If you have a large volume of information that you believe is or may be subject to the preservation obligations, and/or you have concerns about your ability to preserve information, please contact [name] for assistance.

Please sign, date, and return the attached acknowledgement to confirm that you received this Document Preservation Notice and that you will comply with its instructions. Thank you for your cooperation and assistance with this process.

Sincerely,

_____

Name:

Title:

Sample Document Preservation Notice Acknowledgement

I acknowledge receipt of this Document Preservation Notice, and I understand that I am obligated to comply with the directions it sets forth.

_____

Employee Name (Print):

Title:

Date:

Appendix B:
Sample *Upjohn* Warning Statement

We are attorneys for the Company. We are gathering facts related to [brief description of subject matter of action] for the purpose of providing legal advice to the Company.

Although you are an employee of the Company, we do not represent you personally. This means that we cannot give you legal advice.

Nonetheless, your conversation with us is protected by the attorney-client privilege because you are an employee of the Company. This means that our conversation is confidential. Given that the Company is our client, however, the attorney-client privilege belongs solely to the Company. The privilege does not belong to you. That means that the Company—in its sole discretion and without notifying you—may elect to waive the privilege and reveal your conversation with us to third parties, including but not limited to law enforcement and regulatory agencies.

In order for our conversation to be privileged, the conversation must be kept confidential. This means that you may not disclose the substance of this conversation to anyone else. Exceptions include your own personal attorney and/or disclosure of facts to law enforcement or regulators.

Your candor and honestly are critical to our ability to conduct the investigation effectively.

Do you have any questions?

May we continue?

Chapter 8

The Impact of the Automatic Stay

By Megan M. Adeyemo, Shelby A. Poteet,
Leslie A. Berkoff, and Krista L. Kulp

Bankruptcy can be an overwhelming and far-reaching construct that impacts many aspects of day-to-day businesses. To cover every aspect of a business that can be touched by a bankruptcy filing is beyond the scope of this chapter. Rather, the goal of this chapter is to provide in-house counsel with an understanding of the initial impact of a bankruptcy filing on ongoing collection efforts and litigation and some guidelines on how to maneuver through the minefield of immediate issues and concerns.

One of the main reasons that debtors file for bankruptcy is for the protections afforded to debtors by section 362 of the Bankruptcy Code. Section 362 is known as the automatic stay. This chapter focuses on practical tips for corporate counsel in addressing the automatic stay.

I. FILING BANKRUPTCY INVOKES THE AUTOMATIC STAY

Immediately upon filing a bankruptcy petition, the automatic stay provisions of section 362 go into effect,[1] regardless of whether the filing is voluntary or involuntary, under any chapter of the Bankruptcy Code. The automatic stay acts similarly to an injunction and stays various acts.

II. SCOPE OF THE AUTOMATIC STAY

If you find out that a customer (a debtor) filed for bankruptcy, one of the first things you should know is the scope of the automatic stay. It is broad and applies to almost every formal and informal action against a debtor, including actions against the debtor's property.[2] For example, creditors may no longer conduct any collection efforts against a debtor, including sending demand letters or making telephone calls. All collection efforts or other actions that may violate the stay should be ceased immediately upon receipt of either formal or informal notice of the bankruptcy filing, which is typically given by the bankruptcy court or debtor's counsel.[3]

Section 362(a) of the Bankruptcy Code lists all acts that are stayed upon the filing of a petition.[4] Particularly, section 362(a)(1) stays "the commencement or continuation, including the issuance or employment of process, of a judicial, administrative, or other action or proceeding against the debtor that was or could have been commenced before the commencement of the case . . . or to recover a claim against the debtor that arose before the commencement of the case."[5] Therefore, this section provides for a broad stay of litigation against the debtor that could have been or was commenced against the debtor prior to the commencement of the bankruptcy case. Additionally,

---

1. The automatic stay is effective upon the filing of a bankruptcy petition. *In re* Delta Res., Inc., 54 F.3d 722 (11th Cir. 1995), *cert. denied sub nom.,* Orix Credit Alliances, Inc. v. Delta Res., Inc., 516 U.S. 980, 116 S. Ct. 488, 133 L. Ed. 2d 415 (1995).

2. The reach of the automatic stay is intended to be broad because it is designed to shield debtors from financial pressure. *In re* Stringer, 847 F.2d 549 (9th Cir. 1988). Thus, any exceptions to the automatic stay should be read narrowly to secure the broad grant of relief. *Id.; accord In re* Shamblin, 878 F.2d 324 (9th Cir. 1989) ("any equitable exception . . . should be narrow and applied only in extreme circumstances").

3. *See In re* Henley, 480 B.R. 708, 718 (Bankr. S.D. Tex. 2012) ("[T]he Court issues this opinion to highlight the need for debtor's counsel to give notice of the bankruptcy filing—both oral and written—to any known creditors' counsel as soon as the petition is filed. Failure to give immediate notice can result in harsh consequences to debtors whose creditors are willing to aggressively seek and collect the debts owed to them.").

4. 11 U.S.C. § 326(a); Pennsylvania Dep't of Public Welfare v. Davenport, 495 U.S. 552, 110 S. Ct. 2126, 109 L. Ed. 2d 588 (1990) (the automatic stay protects a debtor from efforts to collect money over a specified time period, but it does not extinguish or discharge any debt). The automatic stay creates no greater rights for a debtor than those it has outside of bankruptcy. *In re* Synergy Dev. Corp., 140 B.R. 958 (Bankr. S.D.N.Y. 1992).

5. 11 U.S.C. § 362 (a)(1).

section 362(a)(3) stays all actions, whether judicial or private, that seek to obtain possession of property of the estate or control over property of the estate.[6]

Generally, causes of actions that arise after the filing date are not stayed, although enforcement of a judgment on such claim typically would be.[7]

Practice Pointer

The best practice, however, is to seek an order granting relief from the automatic stay, as discussed later in this chapter, before pursuing any claims against the debtor.

Additionally, at times the filing may occur after you, as the creditor, have possession of collateral that was in the debtor's possession, but the debtor's interest in the same has not yet been terminated. The courts (Second, Seventh, Eighth, Ninth and Eleventh Circuits) hold generally that the creditor must turn over the repossessed property immediately or face a contempt citation. However, some courts (the minority) have held that it is permissible to hold onto that asset passively until such time as the parties' rights to the property are determined. This is a developing area of the law.[8]

It is important to note that the imposition of the stay does not impact or destroy creditors' claims, but rather merely suspends their rights to enforce such claims outside the bankruptcy forum.[9]

A. Litigation Involving the Debtor

The stay precludes the commencement or continuation of judicial and administrative actions and/or proceedings against a debtor for claims that existed prior to the bankruptcy filing.

Thus, if you have a case against a debtor, when a bankruptcy case is commenced, you are obligated to notify the court in which the matter is pending of the bankruptcy filing.[10] Once this notice is filed, the court overseeing the pending action will normally

---

6. *Id.* § 362 (a)(3).

7. *See* 11 U.S.C. §§ 362(a)(4)-(a)(5); *See* Avellino & Bienes v. M. Frenville Co., Inc., 744 F.2d 332, 335 (3d Cir. 1984) (holding automatic stay inapplicable to debtor when plaintiff filed action against debtor after debtor filed for bankruptcy); *see also* Bellini Imports, Ltd. v. Mason & Dixon Lines, Inc., 944 F.2d 199, 201 (4th Cir. 1991) (breach of contract action against freight company debtor not stayed when damages arose post-petition); *In re* Gull Air, Inc., 890 F.2d 1255, 1263 (1st Cir. 1989); Bellini Imports, Ltd. v. Mason & Dixon Lines, Inc., 944 F.2d 199, 201 (4th Cir. 1991).

8. *See* WD Equip. v. Cowen (*In re* Cowen), 849 F.3d 943 (10th Cir. 2017); Davis v. Tyson Prepared Foods Inc. (*In re* Garcia), 17-5006, 2017 BL 234622 (Bankr. D. Kan. July 7, 2017).

9. *See In re* Astroturf, No. 16-41504, 2017 Bankr. LEXIS 2515, at *44 (Bankr. N.D. Ga. Sept. 5, 2017) (explaining "[t]he automatic stay suspends the exercise by creditors of their collection and other remedies to avoid 'races to the courthouse' and the piecemeal liquidation of assets in distressed sales as a result of foreclosure, repossession, or judicial levy.")

10. *See In re* Perez, No. 12-03808, 2014 Bankr. LEXIS 3219, at *14 (Bankr. D.P.R. July 28, 2014).

impose an administrative stay of the case.[11] If there are multiple parties involved in the litigation, the automatic stay applies only to the debtor; thus, the administrative stay will not necessarily stay the action against the other nondebtor parties to the litigation.[12] A bankruptcy court may extend the stay to co-defendants if the continuation of the action could substantially interfere with a debtor's reorganization.[13]

If the debtor is not a party to the litigation, the commencement of the bankruptcy will not stay the action or other matters that do not directly affect the debtor, such as pending discovery against a nonparty even if the information obtained from discovery could be used against the debtor at a later date.[14]

However, if the debtor has commenced prepetition litigation against your client, then the *debtor* is free to continue the prepetition litigation despite the stay.[15] Your client, however, is barred by the automatic stay from litigating its counterclaims. Your client is allowed to take actions to defend against the debtor's claim, but your client is barred from taking any offensive type of action, such as filing a counterclaim or initiating a separate new action. Instead, you must obtain relief from the stay to litigate counterclaims or take nondefensive action.

Practice Pointer

The best practice is to seek relief from stay in order to ensure that your actions are not construed as offensive and thus in violation of the stay. Such relief is routinely granted.[16]

If the parties both agree to continue with the litigation, often the debtor and nondebtor can present a consent order to the bankruptcy court to permit the litigation to continue.

The stay also applies to appellate proceedings; therefore, it is prudent to obtain an order granting relief from the stay for the nondebtor to appeal or continue an appeal against a debtor so as not to violate the automatic stay.

---

11. *See, e.g.*, *In re* Voslite, Inc., No. 07-10217, 2008 Bankr. LEXIS 294, at *8-*9 (Bankr. D. Kan. Jan. 28, 2008).

12. GAF Corp. v. Johns-Manville Corp. (*In re* Johns-Manville Corp.), 26 B.R. 405 (Bankr. S.D.N.Y. 1983) (declining to extend automatic stay to nondebtor co-defendants); A.H. Robins Co. v. Piccinin, 788 F.2d 994 (4th Cir. 1986) (extending automatic stay to nondebtor co-defendants).

13. McHale v. Alvarez (*In re* The 1031 Tax Grp., LLC), 397 B.R. 670, 684 (Bankr. S.D.N.Y. 2008); *In re* Residential Capital, LLC, 480 B.R. 529 (Bankr. S.D.N.Y. 2012).

14. *See In re* Miller, 262 B.R. 499 (B.A.P. 9th Cir. 2001); *see also* Tel. Sci. Corp. v. Pizzo, No. CV 15-1702 (LDW) (AYS), 2016 U.S. Dist. LEXIS 54956, *16-*17 (E.D.N.Y. Apr. 22, 2016); Le Metier Beauty Inv. Partners LLC v. Metier Tribeca, LLC, 2014 U.S. Dist. LEXIS 136152, at *11 (S.D.N.Y. Sept. 25, 2014).

15. Groner v. Miller (*In re* Miller), 262 B.R. 499 (B.A.P. 9th Cir. 2001).

16. *See, e.g.*, *In re* Countryside Manor Inc., 188 B.R. 489, 491 (Bankr. D. Conn. 1995); *In re* Jenkins, No. 03-60548, 2004 Bankr. LEXIS 1035, at *12-*15 (Bankr. S.D. Ga. Mar. 30, 2004); *In re* Barry P. Parker's, Inc., 33 B.R. 115, 118 (Bankr. M.D. Tenn. 1983).

B. Actions Against Property of the Estate

The automatic stay also prohibits creditors from enforcing their rights against property of the bankruptcy estate.

1. What Constitutes Property of the Estate?

What is property of the estate? The bankruptcy estate is formed upon the filing of the petition and is comprised of all legal or equitable interests of the debtor in property as of the commencement of the case.[17] Generally, the debtor's estate includes: any interest in property held by the debtor when the bankruptcy case was commenced; community property interests of the debtor or the debtor's spouse if the debtor controls and manages those interests, or if the property is subject to claims against the debtor under state law; property recovered by the trustee pursuant to its avoidance powers; property interests preserved for the benefit of the estate pursuant to sections 510(c) and 551 of the Bankruptcy Code; certain property acquired by the debtor within the 180 period after the filing of the bankruptcy petition, including inheritance, divorce settlements, proceeds of life insurance policies; and proceeds, offspring, and profit from any of the foregoing.[18] It is important to note that property of the estate also includes rents and profits generated by property of the estate and, in certain circumstances, property acquired by the estate after the bankruptcy filing.[19] It also is important to note that even though the Bankruptcy Code defines what property of the estate is, "[t]he property rights of a Debtor must be determined by reference to [] State law."[20]

For example, a lease or executory contract is considered property of the estate and is therefore protected by the automatic stay.[21] However, the lease or executory contract may not be considered property of the estate based upon state law. For example, the Second Circuit found under New York law that "while the issuance of a warrant of eviction cancels any existing lease and seemingly terminates the landlord-tenant relationship, the tenant, in fact, retains a residual interest in the lease until the execution of the warrant. Prior to such execution, the state court may vacate the warrant of eviction for good cause

---

17. *See* 11 U.S.C. § 541; *In re* 48th St. Steakhouse, 835 F.2d. 427, 430 (2d. Cir.1987).

18. *See* 11 U.S.C. § 541(a).

19. *Id.* § 541(a).

20. *In re* Liggett, 118 B.R. 213, 216 (Bankr. S.D.N.Y. 1990) (internal citations omitted); *see also In re* Contractors Equip. Supply Co., 861 F.2d. 241, 244 (9th Cir. 1988); COLLIER ON BANKRUPTCY 541.03 ("Even though Section 541 provides the framework for determining the scope of the debtor's estate and what property will be included in the estate, it does not provide any rules for determining whether the debtor has an interest in property in the first place. That gap is filled most of the time by nonbankruptcy law.").

21. *In re* Lucre, Inc., 339 B.R. 648, 653 (W.D. Mich. 2006) ("It is well settled that a debtor's interest as a lessee in an unexpired lease (i.e., a leasehold interest) is property of the estate."); MMM Healthcare, Inc. v. Santiago (*In re* Santiago), 563 B.R. 457, 474 (Bankr. D.P.R. 2017) ("The court thus finds that the debtor's provider agreement is an executory contract, and therefore considered property of the estate. As such, the unilateral termination of an executory contract may constitute a violation of the automatic stay.").

and thereby reinstate the lease."[22] In New York, if a lease is terminated prepetition, the only legal interest remaining with the debtor is merely the right to redemption.[23]

Conversely, under New Jersey law, "judgment for possession terminates [a] nonresidential lease, not the issuance of the warrant for removal."[24] However, under the New Jersey Anti-Eviction Act, a tenant may cure a default by making the rent payments "at any time on or before the entry of a final judgment."[25]

Practice Pointer

Thus, it is important to assess the rights your client may have based upon state law.

"[A] mere possessory interest in real property, without any accompanying legal interest, is sufficient to trigger the protection of the automatic stay."[26] For example, the right to redeem the property is part of the debtor's estate. "It is well settled that the owner of the equity of redemption has a right to redeem [the property] at any time before an actual sale under a judgment of foreclosure."[27] Other states permit the owner of the equity to redeem the property even after the foreclosure sale.[28]

2. What Constitutes Actions Against Property of the Estate?

What are actions against property of the estate? Section 362(a)(2) of the Bankruptcy Code stays the enforcement against the debtor or against property of the estate of a judgment that was entered prepetition, including levy and execution, restraining orders, or other

---

22. Super Nova 330 LLC v. Gazes, 693 F.3d 138, 142 (2d Cir. 2012) (citing *In re* Sweet N Sour 7th Ave. Corp., 431 B.R. 63, 70 (Bankr. S.D.N.Y. 2010)).

23. *See* Ridge Realty LLC v. Goldman, 263 A.D.2d. 22, 25-26, 701 N.Y.S.2d. 69, 72 (2d Dep't 1999) (citing Polish Nat'l Alliance v. White Eagle Hall Co., 98 A.D.2d. 400, 404, 406, 470 N.Y.S.2d. 642, 646-47 (2d Dep't 1983)); Bruce J. Bergman, Bergman on New York Mortgage Foreclosures § 32.04 [2].

24. *In re* Seven Hills, 403 B.R. 327, 331 (Bankr. D.N.J. 2009).

25. N.J. Stat. § 2A:18–55.

26. *In re* 48th St. Steakhouse, 835 F.2d. 427, 428 (citing *In re* Onio's Italian Rest. Corp., 42 B.R. 319, 320-21 (Bankr. S.D.N.Y. 1984); *Matter of* GSVC Rest. Corp., 3 B.R. 491, 494 (Bankr. S.D.N.Y.), *aff'd,* 10 B.R. 300 (S.D.N.Y. 1980)).

27. Wells Fargo Bank Minn., N.A. v. Ray, 23 Misc. 3d 931, 935, 880 N.Y.S.2d. 454, 457 (N.Y. Sup. Ct. Kings Cnty., 2009) (citing NYCTL 1996-1 Trust v. LFJ Realty Corp., 307 A.D.2d. 957, 958, 763 N.Y.S.2d. 836 (2003), *overruled in part on other grounds by* 13 N.Y.3d 573, 578 (2009)). Other states that permit redemption before any foreclosure sale include: Colorado, Connecticut, Delaware, Georgia, Hawaii, Idaho, Indiana, Louisiana, Maryland, Massachusetts, Mississippi, Nebraska, Nevada, New Hampshire, New York, Ohio, Oklahoma, Oregon, Pennsylvania, South Carolina, Texas, Utah, Vermont, Virginia, West Virginia, and Wisconsin.

28. *See, e.g.,* Alabama, Florida, Illinois, Iowa, Kansas, Kentucky, Massachusetts, Minnesota, Missouri, New Mexico, North Dakota, and Tennessee.

post-judgment remedies.[29] The stay also prohibits any supplementary proceeding, such as the examination of the debtor to discover assets.[30]

An administrative freeze on a debtor's bank account is not deemed to constitute a violation of the automatic stay only if, immediately after such action is taken, the bank promptly seeks relief from the automatic stay for such action.[31] The stay precludes the setoff of prepetition mutual debts and credits after the commencement of the case.[32] Any actions to repossess or foreclose on any property of the estate are considered to be an action in violation of the stay.[33] In addition, the retention of property of the estate may also be an action against the estate if demand is made for turnover.[34] In addition, section 362(a)(3) of the Bankruptcy Code stays any actions whereby creditors seek possession of property of estate or property in the possession of the estate.[35]

C. Co-Debtor Stay

Usually the automatic stay applies only to actions involving the debtor or the estate. The stay typically does not affect a creditor's rights to proceed against co-obligors, co-signers, or guarantors.[36] The rule is different in Chapter 12 and 13 cases, however, which impose a limited stay for certain co-debtors. In order for the co-debtor stay to apply, the debt must be a consumer debt, and the co-debtor must be an individual.[37]

Practice Pointer

Pay close attention to these key points because the provisions of this section are often misunderstood and/or misused by debtors in an over-reaching attempt to invoke the protections of the co-debtor stay.

---

29.   11 U.S.C. § 362(a)(2).

30.   *See, e.g.,* Romagosa v. Bankr. Estate of Dr. Gail Van Diepen, P.A. (*In re* Dr. Gail Van Diepen, P.A.), No. 6:07-cv-1835-Orl-19, 2008 U.S. Dist. LEXIS 107506 (M.D. Fla. Sep. 30, 2008).

31.   Citizens Bank of Maryland v. Strumpf, 516 U.S. 16, 19, 116 S. Ct. 286, 289, 133 L. Ed.2d 258, 263, 33 C.B.C.2d 869, 872.

32.   *See In re* Mealy, 16 B.R. 800, 801 (Bankr. E.D. Pa. 1982) ("Although § 553 of the Bankruptcy Code allows the setoff of mutual debts, such action is expressly subject to the automatic stay of § 362. Section 362(a)(7) stays the exercise of any pre-petition setoff.")

33.   *See In re* Johnson, 335 B.R. 805, 807 (Bankr. W.D. Tenn. 2006).

34.   *See* Williams v. GMAC (*In re* Williams), 316 B.R. 534, 544 (E.D. Ark. 2004) ("Creditors in possession of collateral constituting estate property violate the automatic stay if they retain possession of that collateral postpetition following a debtor's demand for turnover.").

35.   *See, e.g.,* *In re* Burg, 295 B.R. 698, 701 (Bankr. W.D.N.Y. 2003) (granting the debtor's motion to preliminarily enjoin the creditor's eviction proceeding in state court due to the automatic stay and creditor's acknowledgment of the debtor's possession of the property).

36.   *In re* LOG, L.L.C., No. 10-80378, 2010 Bankr. LEXIS 3976, at *6 (Bankr. M.D.N.C. Nov. 9, 2010).

37.   The co-debtor cannot be an entity such as a corporation, limited liability company, partnership, or professional surety.

For example assume a husband and wife sign a note and mortgage securing their home. The wife files for Chapter 13 bankruptcy. The husband is protected by the co-debtor stay. Thus, if the creditor seeks to foreclose against the home, the creditor must seek relief from the automatic stay as well as from the co-debtor stay under section 1301 of the Bankruptcy Code. However, if the nature of the debt is not consumer-based, and it is instead for a business obligation, the co-debtor stay will not apply.

III. STATUTORY EXCEPTIONS TO THE AUTOMATIC STAY

The Bankruptcy Code identifies certain statutory exceptions to the automatic stay. Such exceptions allow certain creditors to take certain actions despite the automatic stay. Some common exceptions include:

- criminal proceedings against the debtor;[38]
- proceedings relating to child or spousal support, or establishment of paternity, including the enforcement of domestic support obligations;[39]
- perfecting, maintaining, or continuing to perfect security interests;[40]
  - if a creditor perfects its interest in the property during the grace period granted under nonbankruptcy law, then the perfection is deemed to have occurred prior to the bankruptcy filing and is not a violation of the automatic stay;[41] or
  - a creditor may file a continuation statement despite the automatic stay;
- government proceedings to enforce its police or regulatory powers;[42]
- setoffs by commodities brokers and securities, including financial institutions;[43]
- acts to obtain possession of nonresidential real property when lease has terminated;[44]
- withholding income under a debtor's agreement for the payment of a loan based on a retirement account;[45] and
- ministerial acts.[46]

---

38. 11 U.S.C. § 362(b)(1).

39. *Id.* § 362(b)(2).

40. *Id.* § 362(b)(3).

41. For example, the "Uniform Commercial Code" gives a creditor a 20-day grace period to perfect a purchase money security interest. If the debtor files for bankruptcy in this period, and the creditor perfects in this period, the perfection does not violate the automatic stay. U.C.C. § 9-317(e).

42. 11 U.S.C. § 362(b)(4).

43. *Id.* § 362(b)(6).

44. *See id.* § 362(b)(10).

45. *Id.* § 362(b)(19).

46. Ministerial acts of the state court are not stayed. *In re* Papatones, 143 F.3d 623 (1st Cir. 1998); Rexnord Holdings, Inc. v. Bidermann, 21 F.3d 522 (2nd Cir. 1994); *In re* Taylor, 216 B.R. 366 (Bankr. S.D.N.Y. 1998), *rev'd on other grounds*, 233 B.R. 639 (S.D.N.Y. 1999); *In re* Aultman, 223 B.R. 481 (Bankr. W.D. Pa. 1998). Moreover, a decision of a state court judge on the record prior to a filing may be signed after the

There are a total of 28 enumerated exceptions to the automatic stay.[47] Some exceptions pertain to certain creditors, whereas others pertain to certain types of actions. Regardless, there are many that do not apply to the standard unsecured creditor. Even those exceptions that appear to provide a creditor reprieve from the automatic stay may have strict requirements. If an exception does not clearly apply to your claim, the best practice is to seek relief from stay.

A. The Automatic Stay and Lessors

Section 362(b) of the Bankruptcy Code contains two, narrowly tailored exceptions to the automatic stay that apply to lessors. First, subsection 10 provides that the automatic stay does not apply to a lessor's efforts to retake possession of nonresidential real property when the lease terminated prior to the bankruptcy filing.[48] Section 541(b) of the Bankruptcy Code provides that the interest of the debtor under a lease does not become property of the estate if the stated term expired prior to the commencement of the case and ceased to be property of the estate upon expiration of the stated term after the commencement of the case.[49] This automatic stay exception applies only to leases where the stated term expired prepetition, but not to leases where the term expired for other reasons, such as default.[50]

The second exception is outlined in subsection 22 and states that a lessor who obtained a judgment for possession prior to the bankruptcy filing may continue with any "eviction, unlawful detainer action, or similar proceeding."[51] Lessors outside of these two exceptions are subject to the automatic stay.

B. Exception for Restitution under Section 362(b)(1) of the Bankruptcy Code

Within the strict constructs of section 362(b)(1) of the Bankruptcy Code, some courts have held that restitution falls within the scope of the criminal proceedings exception. There are now three circuits (the Second, Sixth, and Ninth Circuit) that permit collection of criminal restitution despite the automatic stay.[52] The Ninth Circuit joined the Sixth and Second Circuit with its holding in *In re Partida*, a 2017 decision. More specifically, the Ninth Circuit Bankruptcy Appellate Panel found no stay violation where the government garnished the debtor's wages to collect a restitution fine.[53] The court held that the

---

filing without there being a stay violation if the order on the record is sufficiently being detailed. *Taylor*, 216 B.R. 366. For example, the clerk can enter judgment after a bankruptcy filing if the state court judge signed the order prior to the filing.

47. *See* 11 U.S.C. § 362(b) (listing the statutory exceptions).

48. *See id.* § 362(b)(10); *see also In re* Truong, 557 B.R. 326 (Bankr. D. N.J. 2016).

49. 11 U.S.C. § 362(b)(10).

50. *Id.*

51. *Id.* § 523(b)(22).

52. *See In re* Robinson, 764 F.3d 554 (6th Cir. 2014); United States v. Colasuonno, 697 F.3d 164 (2nd Cir. 2012); *In re* Partida, No. 15-60045, 862 F.3d 909 (9th Cir. 2017).

53. Partida v. United States DOJ (*In re* Partida), 862 F.3d 909, 913 (9th Cir. 2017).

Mandatory Victims Restitution Act expressly intends to preserve the government's post-judgment ability to collect restitution.[54] The Second, Sixth, and Ninth Circuits have expanded the criminal proceedings exception such that it accounts for other federal laws. Despite this expanded interpretation, courts often provide strict limits regarding the interpretation of exceptions to the automatic stay.

C. Scope of the Police Power under Section 362(b)(4) of the Bankruptcy Code

The Ninth Circuit recently clarified the extent of the aforementioned police-power exception.[55] In *Porter*, the court held that the police-power exception does not apply when an individual acts as a private attorney general.[56] There, the plaintiff sought to recover against his employer for the violation of a California state labor law.[57] The state regulators did not participate in the suit; accordingly, the employee proceeded under California's Private Attorney General Act.[58] After the suit was initially dismissed and while the appeal was pending, the employer filed a Notice of Suggestion of Bankruptcy, which indicated that the debtor filed a voluntary petition seeking bankruptcy protection under Chapter 11.[59] The petitioner attempted to invoke the police-power exception, arguing that a private party could invoke the governmental unit exception when it acts as an agent of the government so long as the private party sought to protect the public health and safety.[60] The court rejected the petitioner's argument, reasoning that the phrase "by a governmental unit" in section 362(b)(4) of the Bankruptcy Code was inapplicable, in part because automatic stays generally apply to *qui tam*[61] actions and, relatedly, the petitioner, as an individual, retained complete control over the suit, and the state did not intervene.[62]

Each exception to the automatic stay outlines specific requirements. In addition to the strict constructs of the Bankruptcy Code, courts often interpret the Bankruptcy Code and implement further requirements with respect to each exception.

Practice Pointer

Accordingly, it is important to consult local counsel about each jurisdiction's interpretation of the statutory exceptions to the automatic stay. Again, when in doubt, request relief from the automatic stay.

---

54. *Id.*
55. 11 U.S.C. § 523(b)(4).
56. Porter v. Nabors Drilling USA, L.P., 854 F.3d 1057 (9th Cir. 2017).
57. *Id.* at 1059.
58. *Id.*
59. *Id.* at 1060.
60. *Id.* at 1062.
61. A *qui tam* action is an action in which a private citizen is authorized to sue on behalf of the government.
62. *Porter*, 854 F.3d at 1062.

IV. DURATION OF THE AUTOMATIC STAY

Section 362(c) of the Bankruptcy Code governs the duration of the automatic stay. Unless relief is granted sooner by the court, the stay of an act against property of the estate expires when the property is no longer property of the estate.[63] For example, when the property is sold, abandoned, or returned to the debtor as exempt property, or a plan is confirmed, the automatic stay expires.[64] The automatic stay against all acts other than against property of the estate expires at the earlier of the time the case is closed, the case is dismissed, or the debtor receives a discharge.[65]

Practice Pointer

It is important to be aware that a discharge injunction that similarly limits collection efforts may be in effect when the automatic stay expires, thereby precluding ongoing collection efforts.

V. LIMITATIONS ON THE AUTOMATIC STAY FOR REPEAT FILERS AND SINGLE-ASSET REAL ESTATE CASES

The 2005 amendments to the Bankruptcy Code (BAPCPA) added specific provisions to section 362 to address the termination of the automatic stay in cases of repeat filers.

Section 362(c)(3) limits the duration of the automatic stay in a case filed by a debtor who has had a prior case dismissed within a year.[66] If a single or joint case is filed by or against an individual debtor under chapter 7, 11, or 13, and the debtor has had a prior single or joint case pending within the preceding one-year period and was dismissed, then the automatic stay with respect to any action taken in relation to a debt or property securing such debt, or to any lease, expires with respect to the debtor on the 30th day after the filing of the later case. The stay terminates only "with respect to the debtor." It does not prevent application of a co-debtor stay in a chapter 13 case; therefore, the co-debtor stay under section 1301 of the Bankruptcy Code applies as against any actions taken against a co-debtor on a consumer debt. However, the stay limitation under section 362(c)(3) does not apply in a chapter 11 or 13 case following the dismissal of a prior chapter 7 case.

Further, where a debtor has had two or more prior cases dismissed within one year, then section 362(c)(4) provides that the automatic stay does not take effect in the

---

63. 11 U.S.C. § 362(c).
64. *Id.*
65. *Id.* § 362(c)(2).
66. *Id.* § 362(c)(3).

case.[67] This limitation only applies where a single or joint case is filed by or against an individual debtor under any chapter, and the debtor had two or more single or joint prior cases pending within the preceding one-year period that were dismissed.[68] However, upon motion of a party in interest filed within 30 days after the filing of the case, and showing that the case was filed in good faith, the court can order the stay to take effect as to any or all creditors.[69]

VI. MODIFICATION AND TERMINATION OF THE AUTOMATIC STAY

Creditors may ask the court to modify or terminate the automatic stay with respect to its claim. Section 362(d)(1) of the Bankruptcy Code provides that the stay may be modified for cause, including lack of adequate protection.[70]

A. Relief under Section 362(d)(1) of the Bankruptcy Code

Section 362(d)(1) allows the bankruptcy court to grant relief from stay for cause.[71] Cause is not defined by the Bankruptcy Code. Bankruptcy courts will look at all of the circumstances surrounding the case, including the actions of the parties, whether good- or bad-faith exists, and the parties' motives.[72]

Some courts have developed 12 factors used to determine whether "cause" exists to lift the stay. These factors are: (1) whether the relief will result in a partial or complete resolution of the issues; (2) the lack of any connection with or interference with the bankruptcy case; (3) whether the foreign proceeding involves the debtor as a fiduciary; (4) whether a specialized tribunal has been established to hear the particular cause of action, and that tribunal has the expertise to hear such cases; (5) whether the debtor's insurance carrier has assumed full financial responsibility for defending the litigation; (6) whether the action essentially involves third parties, and the debtor functions only as a bailee or conduit for the goods or proceeds in question; (7) whether litigation in another forum would prejudice the interests of other creditors, the creditors' committee, and other interested parties; (8) whether the judgment claim arising from the foreign action is subject to equitable subordination under section 510(c) of the Bankruptcy Code; and

---

67. *Id.* § 362(c)(4).

68. *See* Miley v. Thornbug Mortg. Home Loans, No. 1:14-CV-2819-CC, 2014 U.S. Dist. LEXIS 186980, at *2 (N.D. Ga. Nov. 24, 2014) (holding that no automatic stay went into effect and thus could not be violated where plaintiff had filed two bankruptcy cases that were dismissed less than a year before the instant filing).

69. 11 U.S.C. § 362(c)(4)(ii)(B).

70. "On request of a party in interest and after notice and a hearing, the court shall grant relief from the stay provided under subsection (a) of this section, such as by terminating, annulling, modifying, or conditioning such stay for cause, including the lack of adequate protection of an interest in property of such party in interest." 11 U.S.C. § 362(d).

71. *Id.* § 362(d)(1).

72. J E Livestock, Inc. v. Wells Fargo Bank, N.A. (*In re* J E Livestock, Inc.), 375 B.R. 892, 897 (B.A.P. 10th Cir. 2007).

(9) whether the movant's success in a foreign proceeding would result in a judicial lien avoidance by the debtor under section 522(f) of the Bankruptcy Code.[73]

Courts also consider factors such as lack of equity, status of insurance,[74] and any past due amounts.

In addition, section 1112(b) of the Bankruptcy Code, which governs conversion or dismissal of the case, provides a nonexhaustive list of examples of what may constitute cause.[75] Many of the factors courts have held are indicative of a debtor's bad faith in the context of a motion to dismiss a case under section 1112(b) are relevant to a court's analysis of whether cause exists for relief from the automatic stay.[76] Such factors include, but are not limited to:

- the debtor has only one asset;
- the debtor has few unsecured creditors whose claims are small in relation to those of the secured creditors;
- the debtor's one asset is the subject of a foreclosure action as a result of arrearages or default on the debt;
- the debtor's financial condition is, in essence, a two-party dispute between the debtor and secured creditors, which can be resolved in the pending state foreclosure action;
- the timing of the debtor's filing evidences an intent to delay or frustrate the legitimate efforts of the debtor's secured creditors to enforce their rights;
- the debtor has little or no cash flow;
- the debtor can't meet current expenses, including the payment of personal property and real estate taxes; and
- the debtor has no employees.[77]

For example, cause exists to grant a bank relief from the stay because the debtor's filing was merely a continued ploy of legal maneuvers to avoid an inevitable foreclosure.[78]

In determining whether there is sufficient cause, courts will also consider whether a creditor is adequately protected. Section 362(d)(1) of the Bankruptcy Code specifically includes a lack of "adequate protection" as cause to lift the stay. Some courts have held

---

73. *In re* Mazzeo, 167 F.3d 139, 143 (2d Cir. 1999) (citing *In re* Sonnax Indus., Inc., 970 F.2d at 1286.)); *In re* Curtis, 40 B.R. 795 (Bankr. D. Utah 1984).

74. *See In re* McCullough, 495 B.R. 692, 696 (W.D.N.C. 2013) (holding that the bankruptcy court correctly decided to grant relief on the basis that the debtor's property interest was not adequately protected where debtor did not have insurance on its property).

75. ALAN N. RESNICK ET. AL., COLLIER ON BANKRUPTCY 1112.04[6] (16 ed. 2016). ("Courts that have analyzed 1112(b)(4) almost unanimously conclude that the list of the items that constitute cause is not exclusive."); *see generally* C-TC 9th Ave. P'ship v. Norton Co. (*In re* C-TC 9th Ave. P'ship), 113 F.3d 1304, 1310-11 (2d. Cir. 1997) (noting that the list of factors under section 1112(b) is not exhaustive; *see also* 11 U.S.C. § 102(3) ("'includes' and 'including' are not limiting").

76. *See, e.g., In re* 68 W. 127 St., LLC, 285 B.R. 838, 843 (Bankr. S.D.N.Y. 2002); *see In re* Eclair Bakery, Ltd., 255 B.R. 121, 137-41 (Bankr. S.D.N.Y. 2000); *In re* 234-6 W. 22nd St. Corp., 214 B.R. 751, 755-61 (Bankr. S.D.N.Y. 1997); *see also* COLLIER ON BANKRUPTCY, *supra* note 75, at 362.07.

77. *See C-TC 9th Ave. P'Ship*, 113 F. 3d at 1311 (emphasis added).

78. *In re* Pacific Rim Inv., LLP, 243 B.R. 768, 772 (Bankr. D. Colo. 2000).

that a creditor is adequately protected when the value of the collateral equals or exceeds the amount of the creditor's claim.[79] To the extent the collateral is worth less than the creditor's claim, the creditor is not adequately protected, and a court will likely grant relief from the automatic stay.[80]

Rather than modify the automatic stay, courts may order the debtor and the creditor to arrange for, and enter into, an adequate protection agreement. Section 361 of the Bankruptcy Code provides that when adequate protection is required under section 362, "adequate protection may be provided by (1) requiring the trustee to make a cash payment or periodic cash payments to such entity, to the extent that the say under section 362 . . . results in a decrease in the value of such entity's interest in such property; (2) providing to such entity an additional or replacement lien to the extent such stay . . . results in a decrease in the value of such entity's interest in such property; or (3) granting such other relief, other than entitling such entity to compensation allowable under section 503(b)(1) of this title as an administrative expense, and will result in the realization by such entity of the indubitable equivalent of such entity's interest in such property."[81] As a result, courts have granted adequate protection to creditors through both periodic payments to compensate for any decrease in the value of the property and additional or replacement liens.[82]

B. Relief under Section 362(d)(2) of the Bankruptcy Code

Relief from the automatic stay may also be obtained with respect to property if the debtor does not have equity in such property, and the property is not necessary to an effective reorganization.[83] Thus, if the debtor has no equity in the property and filed a chapter 7 case, then courts will normally lift the stay with respect to that property.[84] A debtor has no equity in property when the debts secured by liens on the property exceed the value of the property.[85]

With respect to the second prong, there are two determinations that courts must make: (1) whether the debtor can effectively reorganize, and (2) whether the property at issue is necessary for that reorganization.[86] The debtor may not be able to effectively reorganize because the reorganization is not feasible, dissent by certain creditors

---

79.   *In re* Ledis, 259 B.R. 472, 476 (Bankr. D. Mass. 2001); *In re* 354 East 66th St. Reality Corp., 177 B.R. 776 (Bankr. E.D.N.Y 1995) (purpose is to keep value of creditor's interest in its collateral constant).

80.   *Id.*

81.   11 U.S.C. § 361.

82.   *Id.*

83.   *Id.* § 362(d)(2).

84.   *See In re* Evans, No. CO-10-031, 2011 Bankr. LEXIS 273, at *7-*8 (B.A.P. 10th Cir. Jan. 4, 2011) (affirming trial court's decision to grant relief from stay); *In re* Sanbria, 317 B.R. 59, 61 (B.A.P. 8th Cir. 2004) (same); *In re* Suggs, 355 B.R. 525, 529 (M.D.N.C. 2006) (granting debtor's motion for relief from stay in a chapter 7 case where there was no equity in the property).

85.   *See, e.g., In re* Bowman, 253 B.R. 233, 238 (B.A.P. 8th Cir. 2000) (affirming lower court's decision that the debtor had no equity in the property, regardless of whether the property was worth $700,000 or $1.4 million, because the liens on the property exceeded $4 million dollars).

86.   *In re* Timbers of Inwood Forrest Assocs. Ltd., 484 U.S. 365, 375-77 (1988) (must be a reasonable possibility of a successful reorganization within a reasonable amount of time).

makes reorganization unlikely, or the proposed plan contains unsupported or incredible assumptions and projections.[87]

C. Relief under Section 362(d)(3) of the Bankruptcy Code

BAPCPA provided certain limitations for single asset real estate cases. Single asset real estate (SARE) cases involve real property consisting of a single property or project, other than residential real property, with fewer than four units, which generates substantially all of the gross income of a debtor, on which no business is operated other than operating the real property.[88]

Section 362(d)(3) of the Bankruptcy Code provides that relief from the automatic stay for acts against "single asset real estate" *must* be granted unless: (1) the debtor files a reorganization plan that has a reasonable possibility of being confirmed within a reasonable time, or (2) the debtor has commenced monthly payments equal to interest at the then-applicable, nondefault contract rate of interest on the value of a consensual lienholders' interest in the property within the latest of either (a) 90 days after the order for relief; (b) such longer period as the court determines during the initial 90-day period; or (c) 30 days after the court determines that the debtor is subject to the single asset real estate provisions.[89]

The purpose of this section is to address abuses by debtors of the bankruptcy system who file bankruptcy solely in order to prevent mortgage foreclosure. It allows the court to condition, modify, or lift the stay when the debtor cannot propose a viable plan or make payments to the secured creditor.

D. Relief under Section 362(d)(4) of the Bankruptcy Code

This section of the Bankruptcy Code, which works in tandem with section 362(b)(20), provides that an *in rem* order entered in a prior bankruptcy case will exclude real estate from the protection of the automatic stay in a subsequent case. This section is intended to protect secured creditors with a lien in real property (not rentals) in the case of serial filers.[90]

Practice Pointer

There is a heavy burden for a secured creditor to obtain relief from the stay on these grounds, and proof that the debtor intended to hinder or delay or defraud creditors by these repeat filing is required.[91]

---

87. *In re* Pegasus Agency, Inc., 101 F.3d 882 (2d Cir. 1996).
88. 11 U.S.C. § 101 (51B).
89. *Id.* § 362(d)(3).
90. *In re* McCray, 342 B.R. 668 (Bankr. D.D.C 2006).
91. *In re* Muhaimin, 343 B.R. 159 (Bankr. D. Md. 2006).

VII. STAY STIPULATIONS IN LIEU OF LITIGATION

Frequently, debtors may be amenable to entering into stipulation relative to relief from stay rather than incur the costs and risks of a motion for relief from stay. Such stipulations can be attractive for the creditor because they can contain provisions that are beneficial to the creditor. Typically, stipulations provide for monthly adequate protection payments in exchange for the use of the lender's collateral. Importantly, these stipulations typically include a "drop dead clause." A drop-dead clause grants the creditor relief from stay without further action or order of the court in the event of default. In addition, the stipulation can provide for other important terms, such as (1) an obligation to maintain insurance, (2) allow the creditor to inspect the collateral, (3) value the collateral, and (4) stipulate to lien priority on the collateral.

Before approving a stipulation, the court will look at competing interests and considerations. The court will want to ensure that the debtor has a fresh start and is given the time necessary to propose and effectuate a viable reorganization, along with the creditor's interest in payment, its collateral, and ability to exercise state law remedies.

For example, assume that debtor is in the business of renting and operating certain construction machinery and equipment. Lender has properly perfected first-priority liens on, or security interests in, such machinery and equipment (and proceeds thereof). Collateral has no current or good market for resale. Debtor needs additional time to find a lessee(s) for collateral. Rents from collateral will enable debtor to reorganize and pay creditors. Lender agrees to accept reduced payments until collateral is operating, and debtor agrees to make increased payments to lender once collateral begins generating revenue. Automatic stay is deemed lifted upon any payment default by debtor.

An additional type of stay relief stipulation is an insurance-only stipulation pursuant to which a creditor (typically a personal injury claimant) is granted relief from the automatic stay to proceed with litigation and collection of its prepetition claim, but only to the extent of available insurance.

Practice Pointer

Be aware that bankruptcy courts may decline or hesitate to approve a stipulation where the debtor is responsible for payment of a deductible.[92] Some bankruptcy courts have held that the insurance company is obligated to provide a defense regardless of payment of the deductible by the debtor.[93]

---

92. *See, e.g., In re* The Great Atlantic & Pacific Tea Co., Inc. *et al.* 10-24549-rdd, Dkt. Nos. 893, 1589 (Bankr. S.D.N.Y.) (In response to personal injury claimant's lift stay motions, debtors argued that stay should not be modified because the deductible must be satisfied by property of the estate prior to any insurance proceeds being paid; therefore, the debtors' estate is directly impacted by any stay relief).

93. *In re* Eli Witt Co., 213 B.R. 396, 397-98 (Bankr. M.D. Fla. 1997); Zurich Am. Ins. Co. v. Int'l Fibercom, Inc. (*In re* Int'l Fibercom, Inc.), 311 B.R. 862 (Bankr. D. Ariz. 2004) (finding that a deductible for a claim arising from a prepetition injury is a general unsecured claim) (confirmed by Zurich Am. Ins. Co. v. Int'l Fibercom, Inc. (*In re* Int'l Fibercom, Inc.), 503 F.3d 933 (9th Cir. 2007)).

VIII. VIOLATIONS OF THE AUTOMATIC STAY HAVE SERIOUS CONSEQUENCES

The automatic stay is intended to provide debtors breathing room while their bankruptcy case is pending. To the extent a creditor continues its collection efforts or fails to stay pending litigation, that creditor is in violation of the automatic stay and may be subject to sanctions by the court and liable for the debtor's damages.

Section 362(k) of the Bankruptcy Code provides for damages to the debtor for any violation of the automatic stay. The severity of the damages will depend on the creditor's knowledge of the bankruptcy filing, the creditor's actions, and the jurisdiction.

A. Willful Violations of the Automatic Stay

A willful violation of the stay does not require a specific intent to violate the stay. A creditor willfully violates the stay if the creditor knew the automatic stay was in place and intended the actions that violate the automatic stay.[94] There are many ways in which a creditor can violate the automatic stay, whether it is taking some action to further litigation against the debtor or accidently sending a collection letter. For example, the Ninth Circuit held that a creditor committed a willful violation of the stay by filing a motion for contempt in a pending state court case against the debtor.[95] Another example of a willful violation includes a creditor who sent a collection letter to a debtor that included the amount due and that the debtor should send payments to cure her default.[96] In both instances, the courts found the creditors willfully violated the automatic stay.

Practice Pointer

To avoid a willful violation of the stay, it is important to implement a procedure to notate a bankruptcy filing to ensure that anyone reviewing an account or customer is made aware of the filing.

B. Actions Violating the Automatic Stay May Be Void

Circuits are split over the issue of whether actions taken in violation of the automatic stay are void or merely voidable.[97]

---

94. *In re* Bloom, 875 F.2d 224, 227 (9th Cir. 1989) (citing INSLAW, INC. v. United States (*In re* INSLAW, Inc.), 83 Bankr. 89, 165 (Bankr. D.D.C. 1988)).

95. *Id.* at 227.

96. *In re* Law, 497 B.R. 843, 845 (Bankr. N.D. Tex. 2013).

97. *Compare* Jones v. Garcia (*In re* Jones), 63 F.3d 411, 412 (5th Cir. 1995), *cert. denied,* 517 U.S. 1167 (1996); *with In re* 48th St. Steakhouse, Inc., 835 F.2d. at 431 (finding that actions taken in violation of the automatic stay are void).

The Sixth Circuit has recognized that "[t]he Fifth Circuit is alone in explicitly holding that actions taken during the pendency of the stay are voidable."[98] However, the Sixth Circuit then went on to hold that "actions taken in violation of the stay are invalid and voidable and shall be voided absent limited equitable circumstances."[99]

One of the "limited equitable circumstances" identified in the *Easley* opinion in which the protections provided by section 362(a) of the Bankruptcy Code should be unavailable concerned instances "where the debtor is attempting to use the stay unfairly to avoid an unfavorable result . . ."[100]

Depending on the jurisdiction, any action taken by a creditor in violation of the automatic stay is likely void. This treatment of a creditor's actions makes it that much more important to ensure any action taken is done with permission from the bankruptcy court via relief from the automatic stay.

Practice Pointer

If you inadvertently violated the automatic stay, it is important to consult counsel to determine the best course of action to mitigate damages and determine whether such actions are void or voidable.

C. Damages for Violations of the Automatic Stay

Section 362(k)(1) of the Bankruptcy Code provides for the recovery of costs and attorney's fees for violations of the automatic stay. The Bankruptcy Code even goes so far as to allow for punitive damages in certain instances.[101]

A growing number of circuits even allow damages for emotional distress that result from a willful violation of the automatic stay under section 362(k)(1).[102] The circuit split[103] stems from the ambiguous language of section 362(k)(1), which provides that

---

98. Easley v. Pettibone Mich. Corp., 990 F.2d. 905, 909 (6th Cir. 1993).

99. *Id.* at 911 (emphasis added).

100. *Id.*; *see also* Roseman v. Roseman, No. 93-5099, 1993 U.S. App. LEXIS 32307, at *5-*11, *15 (6th Cir. Dec. 9, 1993) (affirming the application of an equitable exception to the automatic stay when a debtor uses the stay as a litigation tactic unfairly).

101. *See, e.g., In re* Gaston, No. 09-00249, 2011 Bankr. LEXIS 1433, at *4 (Bankr. D. Haw. Apr. 14, 2011) ("For an award of punitive damages, the conduct must be malicious, wanton or oppressive, or the violator engaged in egregious, intentional misconduct.").

102. The First, Third, Ninth, and Eleventh Circuits permit emotional distress damages for willful stay violations. *See* Fleet Mortg. Grp., Inc. v. Kaneb, 196 F.3d 265, 269 (1st Cir. 1999); *In re* Lansaw, 853 F.3d 657 (3d Cir. 2017); *In re* Dawson, 390 F.3d 1139, 1148 (9th Cir. 2004); Lodge v. Kondaur Capital Corp., 750 F.3d 1263, 1271 (11th Cir. 2014).

103. There are four circuits that have expressly concluded that emotional distress damages are available. *See supra* note 102. The Fifth Circuit and the Seventh Circuit have left open the possibility that these damages may be available in some circumstances. *See In re* Repine, 536 F.3d 512, 522 (5th Cir. 2008); Aiello v. Providian Fin. Corp., 239 F.3d 876, 880 (7th Cir. 2001). A district court in Ohio explicitly rejected the idea that damages for emotional distress are available as "actual damages" under section 362(k)(1). *See* United States v. Harchar, 331 B.R. 720, 732 (N.D. Ohio 2005).

"an individual injured by any willful violation of [the automatic stay] shall recover actual damages, including costs and attorney's fees, and, in appropriate circumstances, may recover punitive damages."[104] The Third Circuit is the most recent circuit to consider damages from emotional distress to constitute "actual damages."[105]

In *Zokaites*, the Third Circuit awarded $7,500 for emotional distress where the individual debtors' landlord locked them out of the premises where they operated a daycare business and threatened to sue the debtors' new landlord unless the debtors terminated their lease and renewed a lease with the landlord.[106] The Court declined to decide whether financial injury was a predicate for emotional distress damages,[107] but the decision seems to stand for the proposition that emotional distress damages will be available where the stay violation is egregious.

Practice Pointer

The amount of damages will depend upon the severity of the violation. As soon as you realize you have violated the stay, it is important to cease any and all actions and consult bankruptcy counsel to determine how to correct any violation.

D. Damages under Section 362(k) of the Bankruptcy Code Are Available Only to Individual Debtors

The language contained in section 362(k) of the Bankruptcy Code is intended to address damages sustained by individuals when a creditor violates the automatic stay. "Individual" is not defined by the Bankruptcy Code, and several courts have declined to extend section 363(k) to entities other than natural persons, e.g., partnership and corporations.[108] Courts have opted to limit the recovery of damages for violations of the automatic stay to individuals only. Despite the limited interpretation, a creditor should adhere to the automatic stay regardless of the type of debtor.

Given the potential for sanctions, including punitive damages, it is best practice to obtain relief from the automatic stay prior to taking any action against the debtor.

E. Lack of Notice and Violations of the Automatic Stay

Section 342(g)(2) of the Bankruptcy Code, added by BAPCPA, states that a "monetary penalty" cannot be imposed on a creditor under section 362(k) if the creditor did not

---

104. 11 U.S.C. § 362(k)(1).
105. *Lansaw*, 853 F.3d at 667.
106. *Id.* at 670.
107. *Id.* at 668.
108. *See, e.g., In re* Chateaugay Corp., 920 F.2d 183, 184-87 (2d Cir. 1993).

receive notice of the stay.[109] Therefore, if effective notice has not been given to the creditor, monetary sanctions are not appropriate under section 362(k).[110]

Prior to taking any collections action, a creditor should conduct due diligence by researching whether a debtor has filed a bankruptcy case. Doing so could avoid costly consequences.

IX. CONCLUSION

The scope and effect of the automatic stay can be a nuanced issue. The consequences of violating the stay are substantial. Thus, it is always best to proceed with caution after a client has filed bankruptcy.

---

109.   11 U.S.C. § 342(g)(2).
110.   *Id.*

Chapter 9

Managing Class Actions

By Daniella Quitt and Chet B. Waldman

This chapter is intended to provide an overview of several of the most prominent issues of which class-action litigators should be aware, including the elements a plaintiff must meet in order to obtain class certification; ways to manage a class action before it begins (arbitration clauses and class-action waivers); ways to protect potential class-action defendants from diminishing their personal assets (i.e., relevant insurance coverage issues); potentially mooting class actions by making the named plaintiff whole; how to deal with multiple class actions in different courts arising from the same set of facts; and relevant issues concerning settlements of class actions.

I. WHAT IS A CLASS ACTION? OVERVIEW OF CLASS ACTIONS

In a class action, one or more persons or entities sue on behalf of a larger group in a representative capacity. In every class action, the issues in dispute are common to all members of the class, and the persons affected are so numerous to make it impractical to bring individual claims before a court. Class actions are brought on behalf of, among others, consumers who purchased a defective product or were deceived by false advertising or manipulative business practices; investors who lost money due to securities fraud in a publicly traded company or seek to contest a proposed transaction, such as a merger or management buy-out; employees subjected to a pattern of racial, age, or gender discrimination by their employer or for violations of the Employee Retirement Income Security Act of 1974 (ERISA); consumers or business owners who paid an inflated price as a result of a conspiracy to fix prices; and violations of various federal and state statutes, including, for example, the Telephone Consumer Protection Act.

Class actions have been criticized over the years because of the potential *in terrorem* effect these suits can have on defendant companies. In some cases, if the defendant-corporation loses a class action, even if the likelihood of losing is small, the company could face devastating financial consequences, even bankruptcy. This can force companies who did not violate the law to nevertheless settle claims. Another criticism of class actions is that, in some cases, it is the successful plaintiffs' attorneys and defense counsel, who are paid regardless of the outcome of the litigation, and who are seen to gain the most from these actions as opposed to the class members on whose behalf the actions are brought.

On the other hand, class actions have their positive attributes. For example, where a company has taken advantage of a group of consumers or customers who do not individually have the wherewithal or financial incentive to remedy the wrongdoing (e.g., unlawfully overbilling every customer by $20), a class action is likely the only way to provide relief to these individuals and deter future wrongdoing. In addition, instead of a defendant company facing death by a thousand cuts, class actions can be an effective means to ensure consistent results without the cost and delay of dozens of individual lawsuits. Generally, the resolution of a class action lawsuit binds all members of the certified class and provides closure to defendants whether they settle the case or win it outright.

II.   CAN A COMPANY FORCE ITS CUSTOMERS TO GIVE UP THE RIGHT TO BRING A CLASS ACTION? ARBITRATION CLAUSES AND CLASS ACTION WAIVERS

One of the key considerations in filing or defending class actions is the availability and enforceability of arbitration clauses and/or class action waivers in written contracts or agreements between companies and potential class members. These provisions are designed to eliminate the possibility of a class action and appear in banking, loan, and brokerage agreements; telephone contracts; insurance policies; and on websites. Arbitration clauses gained momentum after the U.S. Supreme Court's opinion in *AT&T Mobility LLC v. Concepcion,*[1] which held the Federal Arbitration Act of 1925 (FAA) preempts states' laws that prohibit contracts from disallowing class-wide arbitration.

The Ninth Circuit Court of Appeals recently held that forcing AT&T Wireless customers to arbitrate their claims concerning misrepresentations about AT&T's "unlimited" data plan does not violate the FAA.[2] However, *Concepcion* left open the possibility that courts could find a particular clause unconscionable on other grounds,

---

1.   563 U.S. 333 (2011).
2.   Roberts v. AT&T Mobility LLC, 877 F.3d 833 (9th Cir. 2017).

provided it does not conflict with the FAA. At least one state, California, has enacted legislation that precludes forced arbitration where an account has been created by fraudulent or other illegal activity.[3]

In *Meyer v. Kalanick*,[4] the trial court issued a ruling barring Uber from enforcing against a customer its mandatory arbitration provision because the provision had been buried in Uber's terms of service on its website, and the customer had not been provided adequate notice that he was agreeing to arbitration when he signed up to use Uber's service. On August 27, 2017, the Second Circuit Court of Appeals vacated and remanded the lower court decision, ruling that Uber's arbitration provision was enforceable because when the customer registered for an Uber account on his smartphone, the screen clearly informed him that by proceeding he was agreeing to abide by Uber's terms of service, which included the mandatory arbitration provision.[5] Distinguishing circumstances in other cases, which invalidated arbitration clauses, the Second Circuit noted that the Uber agreement screen containing the hyperlink to the terms of service was "uncluttered," and that the button to manifest consent was spatially and temporally coupled with the hyperlink.[6] In addition, the mere facts that the terms of service were available only by hyperlink and that the arbitration provision was contained near the bottom of the lengthy terms of service did not preclude a determination of reasonable notice.[7]

In July 2017, the Consumer Financial Protection Bureau (CFPB) adopted a rule banning mandatory arbitration agreements in the consumer financial products sector, i.e., products issued by banks and credit-card companies. However, on October 24, 2017, Congress voted to scrap the rule by the narrow margin of 51 to 50 votes, with Vice President Mike Pence breaking a 50-50 tie. This action by Congress not only killed the new CFPB rule, but also prohibits the CFPB from attempting to enact any similar rule in the future.

Although it seems that there is considerable momentum behind the enforceability of arbitration clauses and class action waivers, it is important to keep in mind that arbitrators' rulings are much harder to appeal than a court decision and may not always be the preferred forum for a defendant corporation.

III. WHAT IS NEEDED FOR A LITIGATION TO BECOME AN OFFICIAL CLASS ACTION? THE ELEMENTS OF FEDERAL RULE 23

In federal courts, the rules governing class actions are found in Federal Rule of Civil Procedure 23. There are similar statutes under each state's laws, which have slight

---

3. Cal. S.B. 33.
4. 199 F. Supp. 3d 752, 755 (S.D.N.Y. 2016).
5. Meyer v. Uber Techs., Inc., 868 F.3d 66, 78 (2d Cir. 2017).
6. *Id.* at 78.
7. *Id.* at 79.

variances.[8] The enactment of the Securities Litigation Uniform Standards Act of 1998 (SLUSA) and the Class Action Fairness Act (CAFA), however, forced many actions traditionally brought in state courts into federal court.[9] SLUSA amended the securities laws to preempt certain class actions that alleged fraud under state law. CAFA grants federal courts original jurisdiction over any action in which the proposed class has at least 100 members, minimal diversity, and an amount in controversy exceeding $5 million.[10] There are exceptions to CAFA, including where one- to two-thirds of the class are citizens of the same state as the defendants. It is a removing defendant's obligation to establish federal jurisdiction based on CAFA. A party can also remove a state court case to federal court if plaintiff's underlying case is "founded on a claim or right arising under" federal law.[11]

The basic requirements of establishing a class action in federal court include:

1. **Numerosity.** Rule 23(a)(1) requires that a plaintiff show that "the class is so numerous that joinder of all members is impracticable . . . ." Some courts have found that numerosity is established when there are at least 40 class members.[12] Other courts have held that there is no fixed number of class members and that you must consider the size and nature of the claims and the geographic location of the class members.[13]

2. **Commonality.** Rule 23(a)(2) requires that the plaintiff show that "there are questions of law or fact common to the class." The Supreme Court's decision in *Wal-Mart Stores, Inc. v. Dukes*[14] clarified the analysis of plaintiff's allegations of common questions. The claims "must depend upon a common contention . . . of such a nature that it is capable of class-wide resolution—which means that determination of its truth or falsity will resolve an issue that is central to the validity of each of the claims in one stroke."

3. **Typicality.** Rule 23(a)(3) requires the plaintiff to show that "the claims or defenses of the representative parties are typical of the claims or defenses of the class . . . ." Courts consider whether the named plaintiff's claims are generally the same as those of the other class members with respect to the factual and legal allegations—that is, whether they arise from the same event or practice and are based on the same legal theory. Courts also consider whether the named plaintiff is subject to any unique defenses that could become a distraction in the litigation.

4. **Adequacy.** Rule 23(a)(4) requires that a plaintiff demonstrate that "the representative parties will fairly and adequately protect the interests of the class." This requirement seeks to ensure that the named plaintiff's interests

---

8. *See, e.g.,* Cal. Code of Civ. P. § 382; N.Y. C.P.L.R. § 901, *et seq.*
9. 28 U.S.C. § 1332(d).
10. 28 U.S.C. § 1332(d)(2)(A)–(C).
11. 28 U.S.C. § 1441(b).
12. *See, e.g.,* Marcus v. BMW of N. Am., LLC, 687 F.3d 583, 595-97 (3d Cir. 2012).
13. *See, e.g., In re* TWL Corp., 712 F.3d 886, 894 (5th Cir. 2013).
14. 564 U.S. 338 (2011).

are aligned, and not in conflict, with those of the other members of the class. For instance, if a plaintiff's wife is an executive of the defendant company, the plaintiff would have a conflict with other class members (in that he may not fight the company that aggressively and jeopardize his wife's job) and would, therefore, not be an adequate representative. Courts sometimes also consider the adequacy of class counsel when determining the adequacy of the plaintiff.[15]

5. **Risk of Inconsistent Dispositive Adjudications.** Rule 23(b)(1) applies when "prosecuting separate actions by or against individual class members would create a risk of: (A) inconsistent or varying adjudications with respect to individual class members that would establish incompatible standards of conduct for the party opposing the class; or (B) adjudications with respect to individual class members that, as a practical matter, would be dispositive of the interests of the other members not parties to the individual adjudications or would substantially impair or impede their ability to protect their interests." Thus, if two separate individual cases before different courts allege that a common defendant's practice is unlawful, and if one court says the practice is unlawful and another says it is lawful, these "inconsistent adjudications" put the defendant between the proverbial "rock and a hard place." If a suit is brought on an individual basis seeking to enjoin a merger, and if the court finds for the plaintiff, that ruling "would be dispositive of the other [stockholders], not parties" to that case. Classes certified under 23(b)(1) are not entitled to notice or the right to opt out of the class.

6. **Declaratory or Injunctive Relief.** Rule 23(b)(2) applies when class members seek declaratory or injunctive relief and do not assert individualized claims for damages. Under this rule, "the party opposing the class has acted or refused to act on grounds that apply generally to the class, so that final injunctive relief or corresponding declaratory relief is appropriate respecting the class as a whole." Notice and the right to opt out are at the discretion of the court.

7. **Predominance and Superiority.** Rule 23(b)(3) requires a determination by the court that "questions of law or fact common to class members predominate over any questions affecting only individual members." In a 23(b)(3) class, damages can be awarded and class members are entitled to notice and the right to opt out. The existence of individualized damages does not automatically preclude class certification. If class-wide damages can be awarded based on a common formula, common damages issues would predominate over individual ones.[16] For example, in a case claiming that a merger price received by a class of shareholders was unfair due to breaches of directors' fiduciary duties, damages would be subject to a common formula if, based on expert testimony and other proof, it was determined that a fair price would have been a specific dollar price per share more than the merger price, notwithstanding each class member has a different number of shares and, therefore, a different damages amount.

---

15. Belfiore v. P&G, 311 F.R.D. 29, 64 (E.D.N.Y. 2015).
16. Comcast Corp. v. Behrend, 569 U.S. 27, 30 (2013).

However, if consumers of a product all got food poisoning from it, any claim for damages stemming from consumers' medical bills or pain and suffering would be unique to each individual and not susceptible to calculation by a common formula. In such a case, individual issues of damages would predominate over common ones. If the poisoned consumers simply asked for their money back for buying the product, however, those claims could be brought on a class-wide basis because a formula (what each class member paid for the product) would be common and susceptible to proof.

8. **Finding of Superiority.** Rule 23(b)(3) also requires a determination that "a class action is superior to other available methods for fairly and efficiently adjudicating the controversy. The matters pertinent to these findings include: (A) the class members' interests in individually controlling the prosecution or defense of separate actions; (B) the extent and nature of any litigation concerning the controversy already begun by or against class members; (C) the desirability or undesirability of concentrating the litigation of the claims in the particular forum; and (D) the likely difficulties in managing a class action." A large number of individualized issues could preclude a finding of superiority.

    Usually, the "superiority" element is easily satisfied by plaintiffs. However, an example of a case where superiority might be a real issue would be a train derailment caused by the negligence of a railroad company where most passengers had cuts and bruises or no serious injury, but a few passengers died, had heart attacks, or sustained other serious injuries and consequently could potentially recover large, individual damages awards. Those train passengers with potentially large damages would likely have interests in "individually controlling the prosecution" of their own individual actions, whereas those with nonserious injuries would not. Some courts may find individual actions to be superior to a class action in those circumstances, whereas other courts might find that the right of individuals with serious injuries to "opt-out" of the class (allowing them to bring their own individual actions) is sufficient protection to permit a class action to proceed for those with smaller but legitimate claims who would not have the incentive or financial means to bring individual actions.

Practice Pointer

One practical consideration is that there can be strict page limitations on class certification briefing. Consequently, it often makes sense for the parties to agree that certain of the class certification elements have been satisfied and then focus the court on the issues that are genuinely in dispute in their briefs. This should be something that is considered before a class certification motion is filed so that discovery and briefing can focus on the disputed issues and put them before the court as soon as possible.

IV. ASCERTAINABILITY

Ascertainability is not technically one of the requirements of Rule 23; however, courts generally agree that a class can be certified only if it is defined by reference to objective criteria.[17] However, courts have differed as to whether the plaintiff must go the further step of proving the existence of some "administratively feasible" method of determining class membership. Some jurisdictions have required a plaintiff to demonstrate at the class certification stage that it is feasible to identify the members of the class. Courts that require the ascertainability of class members do so to protect the due-process rights of defendants to challenge the alleged membership of individuals in a class.[18] Although the Third Circuit Court of Appeals has been the most vocal on this requirement in the past, it appears from recent decisions that this position has softened since the court has allowed the use of plaintiff affidavits to demonstrate ascertainability.[19] The Second, Sixth, Seventh, Eighth, and Ninth Circuits have found that administrative feasibility is not a requirement for class certification.[20] Although most circuits have not adopted this requirement, the proposed Fairness in Class Action Litigation Act of 2017,[21] which passed the House and is still pending in the Senate, would make changes to the class-action requirements, including the requirement that plaintiffs demonstrate a reasonable method of notice distribution prior to certification.

V. WHAT HAPPENS WHEN MULTIPLE CLASS ACTIONS ARE FILED IN DIFFERENT COURTS STEMMING FROM THE SAME FACTS?

There often may exist overlapping class actions in multiple federal or state courts arising from the same alleged misconduct. These could include cases that assert nationwide classes in multiple jurisdictions or overlapping state and federal actions raising the same issues and involving the same parties. The timing of the filing of the multiple actions will dictate whether to pursue a multidistrict litigation (MDL) proceeding, or whether

---

17. Brecher v. Republic of Argentina, 806 F.3d 22 (2d Cir. 2015).

18. *See, e.g.,* Carrera v. Bayer Corp., 727 F.3d 300, 307 (3d Cir. 2013). The Fourth and Eleventh Circuits, in addition to the Third Circuit, require a showing of "administrative feasibility" for class certification. *See* EQT Prod. Co. v. Adair, 764 F.3d 347, 358 (4th Cir. 2014); Karhu v. Vital Pharmaceuticals Inc., 621 F. App'x 945, 947-48 (11th Cir. 2015). *But see In re* Nexium Antitrust Litig., 777 F.3d 9, 22-23 (1st Cir. 2015) (plaintiffs must establish feasibility during the liability phase of the case rather than the class certification phase).

19. City Select Auto Sales, Inc. v. BMW Bank of N. Am., Inc. 867 F.3d 434, 441-42 (3d Cir. 2017).

20. Briseno v. ConAgra Foods, Inc., 844 F.3d 1121, 1124-25 (9th Cir. 2017); Rikos v. Procter & Gamble Co., 799 F.3d 497, 525 (6th Cir. 2015); Mullins v. Direct Digital, LLC, 795 F.3d 654, 661-62 (7th Cir. 2015); Sandusky Wellness Ctr. LLC v. Medtox Sci., Inc., 821 F.3d 992, 995-96 (8th Cir. 2016); *In re* Petrobras Sec., 862 F.3d 250, 264-69 (2d Cir. 2017) (wherein the court "clarified" that a previous Second Circuit case, *Brecher v. Republic of Argentina*, 806 F.3d 22, 24-25 (2d Cir. 2015), did not create an "administrative feasibility" requirement).

21. Fairness in Class Action Litigation Act of 2017, H.R. 985, 115th Cong. (1st Sess. 2017).

to seek to stay one or more of the actions pending the resolution of an earlier filed or broader action.

The purpose of an MDL is to ensure the just, efficient, and consistent conduct and adjudication of actions pending in multiple jurisdictions by providing for the centralized management of pretrial proceedings under a single court's supervision.[22] Upon a motion to transfer, the MDL panel (a panel of judges who determine whether similar actions should be coordinated or consolidated in one joint litigation and, if so, the forum in which that litigation should proceed) "analyzes each group of cases in light of the statutory criteria and the primary purpose of the MDL process to determine whether transfer is appropriate."[23] The MDL panel assesses whether centralization will: (1) avoid the possibility of inconsistent or conflicting rulings; (2) "eliminate [or reduce] duplicative discovery"; and (3) "conserve the [efforts and] resources of the parties, their counsel[, witnesses,] and the judiciary."[24]

> Transfer under Section 1407 has the salutary effect of placing all actions in this docket before a single judge who can formulate a pretrial program that: (1) allows discovery with respect to any non-common issues to proceed concurrently with discovery on common issues, *In re Joseph F. Smith Patent Litig.*, 407 F. Supp. 1403, 1401 (J.P.M.L. 1976); and (2) ensures that pretrial proceedings will be conducted in a streamlined manner leading to the just and expeditious resolution of all actions to the overall benefit of the parties and the judiciary.[25]

This is often a useful tool for managing multiple class actions.

In some instances, staying one action in favor of another may be appropriate, particularly where there is both state and federal jurisdiction. "[T]he power to stay proceedings is incidental to the power inherent in every court to control the disposition of the causes on its docket with economy of time and effort for itself, for counsel, and for the litigants."[26] The burden is on the movant to "show that there is pressing need for delay, and that neither the other party nor the public will suffer harm from entry of the order."[27] Courts use various rationales in deciding whether to stay a case in favor of another forum. Those considerations include comity and judicial efficiency as well as the first-filed rule and *forum non conveniens* analysis. Although New York and Texas, for example, generally follow the first-filed rule, the Delaware Court of Chancery does not.[28] Rather, Delaware courts consider actions filed within a relatively short timeframe

---

22. *See* 28 U.S.C. § 1407(a).

23. *In re* Phenylpropanolamine Prods. Liab. Litig., 460 F.3d 1217, 1230 (9th Cir. 2006).

24. *In re* Imagitas, Inc., 486 F. Supp. 2d 1371, 1372 (J.P.M.L. 2007).

25. *In re* Vonage Mktg. & Sales Practices Litig., 505 F. Supp. 2d 1375, 1376-77 (J.P.M.L. 2007).

26. Landis v. N. Am. Co., 299 U.S. 248, 254 (1936).

27. Ohio Envtl. Council v. U.S. Dist. Ct., S.D., 565 F.2d 393, 393 (6th Cir. 1977).

28. *In re* NYSE Euronext Shareholders/ICE Litig., 39 Misc. 3d 619, 625 (Sup. Ct. N.Y. County 2013); *In re* AutoNation, Inc., 228 S.W.3d 663, 670 (Tex. 2007) ("When a matter is first filed in another state, the general rule is that Texas courts stay the later-filed proceeding pending adjudication of the first suit."); VE Corp. v. Ernst & Young, 860 S.W.2d 83, 84 (Tex. 1993) (where there are identical suits in different states, comity requires deference to the first-filed action).

to be simultaneously filed and undertake a *forum non conveniens* analysis that considers the state's interest in "the behavior of fiduciaries for its [corporations] . . . ."[29] Under principles of comity, California courts have stayed first-filed litigation in favor of parallel Delaware litigation.[30] In determining whether to stay a federal action in favor of parallel state proceedings, courts apply what is known as the Colorado River Doctrine, which provides a list of factors similar to a *forum non coveniens* analysis.[31]

In the area of merger litigation, some defendants file what is known as a one-forum motion, wherein they request that the courts in the multiple jurisdictions confer to determine the most appropriate forum for the litigation so that the movant is not placed in the position of telling a judge that they do not want to litigate in their forum.[32] These motions have mixed reactions from judges, and there have been instances where neither jurisdiction stood down.[33]

Recently, the Supreme Court limited personal jurisdiction over nonresident plaintiffs whose claims were unrelated to Bristol-Myers' contacts with California.[34] Although *Bristol-Myers* involved a mass action, not a class action, it could impact plaintiff's ability to select a forum in which to bring a litigation.[35]

VI. PRACTICAL CONSIDERATIONS IN MANAGING A CLASS ACTION

There are many issues that must be addressed by a company faced with defending a class action. At the onset of the litigation, it is necessary to understand the subject matter underlying the claim, the potential size of the class, the potential damages, and the possible effect of the class action on the overall financial condition of the company and the possible reputational damage to the company. Thereafter, one of the first issues that must be considered is the availability of insurance to cover the damages in the event of a settlement or judgment in plaintiff's favor. Second, in the case of multiple defendants, is there a need for a cooperation agreement amongst the defendants? This latter consideration may be impacted by the first consideration. Specifically, if there are multiple defendants, a defendant must consider the impact of one defendant agreeing to an early settlement to avoid the expense of litigation or the participation in discovery.

---

29. Dias v. Purches, 2012 Del. Ch. LEXIS 42, at *4 n.5 (Mar. 5, 2012).

30. *In re* Quest Software S'holder Litig., Case No. 30-2012-0052957 (Cal. Sup. Ct. Orange County Mar. 12, 2012).

31. Colo. River Water Conservation Dist. v. United States, 424 U.S. 800, 817 (1976).

32. *See* Randall S. Thomas & Robert B. Thompson, *A Theory of Representative Shareholder Suits and Its Application to Multijurisdictional Litigation*, 106 Nw. U. L. Rev. 1753, 1804 n.270 (2012).

33. *In re* Topps Co. S'holders Litig., 924 A.2d 951, 953 (Del. Ch. 2007); *In re* Topps Co. S'holders Litig., 859 N.Y.S.2d 907, 907 (Sup. Ct. N.Y. County June 2007).

34. Bristol-Myer Squibb Co. v. Superior Court, 137 S. Ct. 1773 (2017).

35. *Compare* Fitzhenry-Russell v. Dr. Pepper Snapple Group, Inc., 2017 WL 4224723, at *4-*5 (N.D. Cal. Sept. 22, 2017) (court declined to extend *Bristol* to class actions) *with In re* Dental Supplies Antitrust Litig., 2017 WL 4217115, at *9 (E.D.N.Y. Sept. 20, 2017) (*Bristol* helpful in determination of personal jurisdiction).

A third important consideration is the probable success of a motion to dismiss for failure to state a claim even before the issue of class certification is reached, and how much information should be disclosed in that motion. Courts are sensitive to the *in terrorem* effect of class actions, and on proper showing may be inclined to dismiss the action at the onset of the litigation if a strong showing can be made that plaintiff has not adequately pled a cause of action.

Another issue to consider is the timing of the class certification motion. Rule 23(c)(1)(A) provides that the court shall determine whether the action should proceed as a class action "at an early practical time." Although it is the plaintiff that brings a class certification motion, usually at the initial Rule 26(f) conference, which is held prior to the commencement of discovery in federal court, the court determines the schedule that will act as a guideline for the litigation. In an appropriate case, the defendant can press the court to schedule briefing on class certification at an early stage of the litigation so that it can attempt to get the court to deny or limit the scope of certification, which, if successful, dramatically changes the dynamic of the litigation.

VII. STANDING OF THE NAMED PLAINTIFF

A. Article III's Injury-in-Fact Requirement

One of the issues that can been addressed at the pleading stage is the standing of the named plaintiff to bring the suit. In recent cases, courts have considered at the pleading stage whether the plaintiff has suffered an injury-in-fact or whether plaintiff's injury is consistent with the class-wide allegations.[36] In *Spokeo, Inc. v. Robins*,[37] the Supreme Court held that the plaintiff could not allege a bare-bones procedural violation of the Fair Credit Reporting Act (FCRA) without demonstrating the injury-in-fact requirement of Article III of the U.S. Constitution. Specifically, the Court ruled that "Article III standing requires a concrete injury even in the context of a statutory violation." Therefore, a violation of a statutory right alone does not automatically give rise to standing.[38]

Since the *Spokeo* decision, standing-based challenges in class actions have become routine. Despite seemingly contradicting rulings by federal district courts, some clear trends have appeared. For example, most district courts have found that plaintiffs in Fair Debt Collection Practices Act and in Telephone Consumer Protection Act cases satisfied the standing requirement. In cases involving the FCRA, the statute involved in *Spokeo*, district courts have found plaintiffs satisfied the standing requirement approximately

---

36.   Mahon v. Ticor Title Ins. Co., 683 F.3d 59, 62-63 (2d Cir. 2012); *In re* Toyota Motor Corp. Hybrid Brake Mktg., 915 F. Supp. 2d 1151, 1157 (C.D. Cal. 2013).

37.   136 S. Ct. 1540, 1549 (2016).

38.   *Id.* After the Supreme Court sent the case back to the Ninth Circuit to apply its new standard, that court found that the plaintiff had sufficiently alleged a concrete injury to support standing. Robins v. Spokeo, Inc., 867 F.3d 1108 (9th Cir. 2017).

half the time. In addition to rulings at the pleading stage, courts are also weighing the impact of *Spokeo* at the class certification stage.[39]

For several years, courts have been split on whether a plaintiff who asserts a false advertising claim has standing to seek an injunction, given that the plaintiff, by virtue of filing a lawsuit, has admitted it is aware of the deception and not likely to be misled again.[40] The Ninth Circuit recently held in *Davidson v. Kimberly-Clark Corp.*[41] that where the plaintiff stated that she might want to purchase wipes that the company had falsely claimed were "flushable" again in the future, the plaintiff's inability to rely on the company's future representations about the wipes constituted a threat of injury sufficient for standing purposes. The court noted that, as a matter of public policy, a contrary holding would "effectively gut[]" California's consumer protection laws.[42]

B. Does a Plaintiff Have Standing to Sue for Consumer Products or Securities the Plaintiff Did Not Purchase?

Another issue that is sometimes raised at the pleading stage is whether to require separate plaintiff representatives for each product or security upon which a state cause of action is asserted, or whether a plaintiff can assert claims for a variant of a product or security type that he did not purchase.[43] For example, in *Michael v. Honest Company, Inc.*, the district court explained that "[t]here is no controlling authority [within the 9th Circuit] on whether Plaintiffs have standing for products they did not purchase," but that "[t]he majority of the courts that have carefully analyzed the question hold that a plaintiff may have standing to assert claims for unnamed class members based on products he or she did not purchase so long as the products and alleged misrepresentations are substantially similar."[44] "In considering whether unpurchased products are sufficiently similar to purchased products to satisfy Article III, the Court considers factors that include whether the challenged products are the same kind, whether they are comprised of largely the same ingredients, and whether each of the challenged products bears the same alleged mislabeling."[45] Applying these principles, the *Michael* court found that the

---

39. *See, e.g.,* Sandoval v. Pharmacare US Inc., 2016 WL 3554919, at *8 (S.D. Cal. June 10, 2016).

40. *See, e.g.,* McNair v. Synapse Group, Inc., 672 F.3d 213, 224-26 (3d Cir. 2012) (holding that because the named plaintiffs did not allege that they were likely to purchase the defendant's services in the future, they lacked standing for injunctive relief); Nicosia v. Amazon.com, Inc., 834 F.3d 220, 239 (2d Cir. 2016) (plaintiff's "injuries are only cognizable where the plaintiff alleges actual future exposure" to harm from purchasing the misleadingly labeled product, but that was impossible in this case because defendant ceased selling the product warranting dismissal of the case); *but see* Kurtz v. Kimberly-Clark Corp., 2017 U.S. Dist. LEXIS 44576 (E.D.N.Y. Mar. 27, 2017) (certifying injunctive class in case where the defendant continued selling the misleading labeled product; therefore, "consumers are still at risk of [being harmed by] purchasing a mislabeled product").

41. 873 F.3d 1103, 1109 (9th Cir. 2017).

42. *Id.* at 1116.

43. *See* NECA-IBEW Health & Welfare Fund v. Goldman Sachs & Co., 693 F.3d 145, 160 (2d Cir. 2012); *In re* HSBC Bank, USA NA, Debit Overdraft Fee Litig., 1 F. Supp. 3d 34, 49 (E.D.N.Y. 2014).

44. 2016 WL 8902574, at *7-*8 (C.D. Cal. Dec. 6, 2016) (internal quotation marks and citations omitted).

45. *Id.* at *9 (quoting Romero v. Flowers Bakeries, LLC, 2015 WL 2125004, at *5 (N.D. Cal. May 6, 2015)).

named plaintiffs, who purchased the defendant's sunscreen, hand soap, and dish soap products, also had standing to bring claims on behalf of purchasers of the defendant's diapers and multisurface cleaner, which the named plaintiffs had not purchased. As the court explained, although the products were different in kind and contained different ingredients, it was dispositive that the defendant had uniformly advertised them as "natural," and that the plaintiffs had alleged that they all contained synthetic ingredients, which allegedly caused all consumers to experience the same harm by paying a price premium for a falsely advertised "natural" product.[46]

VIII. SETTLEMENT OF CLASS ACTIONS

The decision as to whether and when to settle a class action turns on many considerations, including nonfinancial considerations. Participating in an early mediation often is a useful tool for learning the positions of the other side if the likelihood of a settlement is minimal. It is often advisable to consider mediation even prior to filing a knee-jerk motion to dismiss where the distraction of litigation will have more effect than the cost of resolving the litigation.

A. Can a Defendant Simply Pay the Plaintiff to Eliminate the Possibility of a Case Proceeding as a Class Action? Mooting a Class Action Through Offers of Settlement

In *Campbell-Ewald Co. v. Gomez*,[47] the Supreme Court held that prior to certification of a class, an unaccepted offer of judgment of the named plaintiff's claims does not automatically moot the entire case. However, the court left open the possibility that the result may be different where a defendant deposits the full amount of the plaintiff's individual claim in an account payable to the plaintiff, and the district court then enters judgment for the plaintiff in that amount. Notwithstanding this opening, since *Campbell-Ewald*, defendants have largely failed in their efforts to moot claims by depositing funds into an escrow account in the name of the plaintiff.[48] Sometimes, such efforts have been rejected because the payment did not afford the plaintiff with the complete relief they sought—injunctive relief, attorney's fees, and litigation costs.[49] Whether a different result would be achieved if the defendant offered the plaintiff complete relief for its claims, attorney's fees, and litigation costs remains to be seen.

---

46. *Id.* at *11.
47. 136 S. Ct. 663, 671 (2016).
48. *See* Chen v. Allstate Ins. Co., 819 F.3d 1136 (9th Cir. 2016); Fulton Dental LLC v. Bisco, Inc., 860 F.3d 541 (7th Cir. 2017); Stromberg v. Ocwen Loan Servicing, LLC, 2017 WL 2686540, at *8 (N.D. Cal. June 22, 2017); Luman v. NAC Mktg. Co., 2017 WL 3394117, at *3 (E.D. Cal. Aug. 8, 2017).
49. *Luman*, 2017 WL 3394117, at *3.

B. If a Defendant Wishes to Settle, Should Mediation Be Considered?

Litigation is costly. Litigation distracts and takes time away from board members, executives, and some rank-and-file employees doing their real jobs for a company. Litigation is notoriously unpredictable. The consequences to a company of losing a class-action litigation may be devastating both financially and reputationally. Consequently, if a complaint survives a motion to dismiss or otherwise clearly states a claim, the concept of a settlement of a class action should be considered. Settling a case for something you can live with may beat, by a country mile, losing the case. However, in considering the prospect of a settlement, many important issues must be addressed: When should settlement discussions commence? Should settlement negotiations be conducted among the parties alone or should a third-party neutral (i.e., a mediator) be used? If a mediator is used, who should be used? These and other factors, such as what insurance is available to a company and its directors and officers (see Part IX, *infra*), must be carefully weighed, even if the idea of reaching a settlement is perceived as beneficial to a defendant.

There are advantages to trying to negotiate a settlement with and without a mediator. The key advantage of conducting negotiations party-to-party is cost. Mediation[50] has associated costs, such as the mediator's fee (either an hourly rate or a day rate that increases exponentially the more reputable the mediator), travel to the mediator's location (if not all parties and their counsel are within close proximity), and paying for attorneys to prepare mediation statements (briefs of around 10–20 pages laying out the case and key points of contention with legal and/or factual authority), which most mediators require. In addition, timing is not as easy to control when a mediator is involved. Parties may have to wait three to six months to secure a mediation date with a highly sought-after mediator. Sometimes, the mediator, acting as a go-between with less knowledge about the evidence and law than the parties and their counsel, is just not as effective as face-to-face direct communications between the parties. Many a litigator and corporate counsel have felt their time wasted sitting in a conference room for a day or days when nothing seems to be getting accomplished.

On the other hand, mediation brings many advantages over direct negotiations between parties and their counsel. First, if a litigation has been long and contentious, sometimes a real dislike between the parties and/or their counsel arises and can interfere with the goal of an amicable resolution. Mediation neutralizes personal animosity. Second, after a long litigation, it is common for parties and counsel to fall in love with their own litigation positions. Similarly, a lawyer who has been telling a client how they will surely prevail in the long run may be reluctant to inform the client, when faced with an adverse ruling or factual development, that the ultimate outcome does not look good anymore. Having a nonbiased mediator listen to both sides and provide an evaluation of the respective positions provides a sobering reality check. Third, good mediators know how to bring sides together, know how to get top dollar from insurance carriers (a hugely difficult task), and oftentimes bring expertise on a subject and knowledge of how similar

---

50. A more detailed discussion on mediation can be found in Chapter 4.

cases have resolved that they utilize to facilitate a settlement. Fourth, even if you are pessimistic about the prospects for settlement, the process of mediation, especially early on in a litigation, might allow you to learn more about your adversary's case, both its strengths and weaknesses. It also allows your side to put doubt in the other side's mind about their ultimate likelihood of prevailing and/or the realistic size of any recovery they may obtain through settlement or trial. Moreover, you will have a better view of what it will take to resolve the lawsuit by settlement.

IX. INSURANCE COVERAGE ISSUES RELATED TO CLASS ACTIONS

Every corporate officer or director knows that they face the risk of personal liability for corporate wrongdoing and responsibility for the costs of litigation. The risk becomes exponentially increased when their company faces the possibility or reality of a class-action lawsuit. To protect themselves against these risks, board members and officers need at least two things: (1) provisions in their company's articles and by-laws that allow for litigation fees and expenses to be advanced, as well as indemnification against obligations stemming from settlement or litigation to the maximum extent permitted by the law of their states of incorporation; and (2) effective directors' and officers' liability insurance coverage (D&O Policy).

The insurance coverage provided by a D&O Policy in return for the payment of premiums to the insurance carrier is intended to protect directors and officers from having to personally pay damages and litigation costs in a lawsuit (i.e., protect their personal assets), as well as reimburse the company for payments made to indemnify its directors and officers. Whether directors and officers receive the insurance coverage they thought they were buying usually comes down to the precise language of the particular D&O Policy they purchased. Often it seems that insurance carriers collect premiums for as much and as long as possible, and then rescind or drastically narrow coverage if a claim on the D&O Policy is ever made.

A. Types of Coverage

D&O Policies usually contain three distinct types of coverage: (1) *liability coverage* insuring directors and officers for the attorney's fees and litigation costs they incur defending themselves as defendants in lawsuits, and for any judgments entered against them resulting from such claims; (2) *corporate reimbursement coverage* for the company's responsibility to indemnify its directors or officers; and (3) *entity coverage*, which insures the company for any judgment entered against it on claims against itself, as well as defense costs and attorney's fees, even if no individual or officer is also named as a defendant. Most D&O Policies cover certain "claims" and expenses, for the "named insureds" only, for claims made within the policy period (usually one year, but can be longer), within the express limits of liability (the specified amount of the insurance, e.g., $10 million), which is usually inclusive of expenses and is only paid after the insured satisfies the amount of the deductible stated in the D&O Policy.

To combat situations where certain defendants or the corporation "waste" the D&O Policy on defense costs, attorney's fees, and potentially on partial settlements, or in the event the insurer goes bankrupt,[51] companies can purchase "Side-A" or "last resort" policies, which are designed to protect "innocent" individual directors and officers. Side-A coverage is only activated when the corporation cannot, or does not, indemnify the directors and officers because, for example, the corporation goes bankrupt or defendants willfully breach their fiduciary duties or breach a duty of loyalty. Because Side-A coverage very rarely comes into play, it is usually much cheaper than a normal D&O Policy.

B. Coverage Layers

For companies seeking substantial insurance for their directors and officers, they typically purchase several D&O Policies from different insurance carriers structured on layers of coverage called "towers." Within the base of the tower structure contains the first, or "primary," D&O Policy that pays the first dollar (after the deductible has been satisfied) up to the policy limits (e.g., $20 million). Another insurance carrier covering losses (and/or fees and costs) beyond the limits of the primary policy (e.g., from between $20–$30 million), followed by another company providing coverage for amounts in excess of the second D&O Policy (e.g., from $30–$40 million), would constitute secondary towers. The layers of coverage above the primary D&O Policy are known as excess policies, and those policies are generally cheaper than the primary D&O Policy. Although obtaining a tower of coverage has the benefit of acquiring substantial insurance generally at a lower total cost, with a hedge against an insurer going bankrupt (among other reasons), it also can present problems, especially when attempting to settle a case. For instance, D&O insurers generally have little incentive to settle any claim unless they can do so for less than the full amount of the Policy; otherwise, they may as well fight to the bitter end and hope to win before the policy limits are exhausted. However, a settlement of a D&O Policy at a lower layer of the tower (e.g., the primary policy) for less than the policy limits may mean that all higher layers on the tower can no longer be triggered because they do not kick in until the lower layer of coverage is exhausted.[52]

C. Five Key Coverage Issues

1. Rescission

Generally, an insurance carrier can seek to rescind a D&O Policy based on alleged misrepresentations or omissions in the application for the policy. A D&O Policy usually expressly states that the insurer relied on the application in issuing the policy. In cases where a company issues a restatement of its financial statements, and the financial statements were incorporated by reference in the application, for example, the carrier

---

51. *In re* Reliance Group Holdings, Inc. Sec. Litig., Master File No. 00-CV-4653 (AGS) (S.D.N.Y. July 16, 2001).

52. *See, e.g.*, J.P. Morgan Chase & Co. v. Indian Harbor Ins. Co., 98 A.D.3d 18, 24-25 (1st Dep't 2012).

can claim it was fraudulently induced to enter into the policy. If proved, rescinding the policy is the carrier's remedy, which, if granted, means zero coverage even for innocent directors and officers who had nothing to do with the application for insurance.[53] Nonrescindable coverages may be available at additional cost.

2. Limits of Coverage

Some of the most common types of class actions are brought under the federal securities laws alleging fraud or dishonest acts, or arise out of mergers, or are brought derivatively, claiming that directors or controlling stockholders breached their fiduciary duties of loyalty to a company and/or its stockholders or otherwise acted in bad faith. However, D&O Policies usually exclude coverage for such acts, indeed any acts of willful or knowing wrongdoing by a director or officer. Many, but not all, D&O Policies limit coverage only if a judgment is entered against an insured finding that the insured acted with wrongful intent, as opposed to negligence or carelessness.

3. Insured Versus Insured Exclusion

Another typical limit on coverage is for claims made by one insured against another. The purpose of these "insured versus insured exclusions" is to protect the carrier against collusive lawsuits among insureds to get at the D&O Policy proceeds. If a D&O Policy is not clear, a derivative action in which the corporation as nominally represented by a stockholder is suing a director for breach of fiduciary duty to the corporation, may run afoul of the insured-versus-insured exclusion. Consequently, corporate counsel should ensure that the D&O Policy clearly provides that this exclusion does not cover derivative actions; actions by or on behalf of a bankruptcy trustee, creditors committee, and the like should the company go into bankruptcy; or claims by whistleblowers.

4. The Insurer's Refusal to Settle: Bad Faith

Can an insurer simply refuse to settle even if a company believes settling is in its best interests? The answer is, "it depends." The language of D&O Policies usually requires the prior written consent of the insurer, and vice versa, for any settlement of a claim to happen. A carrier does not want to settle a case unless it can restrict its payout to less than the D&O Policy limits. Thus, an insurer that receives a settlement offer that is well below the policy limit will be much more willing to settle than a settlement offer for the remainder on the policy limit. However, if a plaintiff makes a settlement demand for less than the then-current policy limit, and the carrier refuses the settlement demand, the carrier may be put into what is called a bad-faith position. The consequence? If the plaintiff ultimately prevails on its claims and is awarded more than the policy limit, the carrier is on the hook for the entire damages award. Thus, a demand of $9 million of a $10 million policy, for example, may result in the insurer paying $50 million if a jury

---

53. *See, e.g.*, Fed. Ins. Co. v. Homestore, Inc., 144 F. App'x 641, 647-48 (9th Cir. 2005).

awards that much in damages if the carrier refused to settle for the $9 million.[54] Certain courts have held that insurers have an affirmative duty to attempt to settle cases within policy limits once liability becomes reasonably clear, even without a settlement offer by the plaintiff.[55]

5. The Bankruptcy of an Insurer

Excess layers in a tower of insurance coverage with multiple insurers usually provide coverage at the point that lower-level carriers have exhausted the limits of their policies. However, if a lower-level carrier in the tower were to declare bankruptcy before its policy was exhausted, the excess carriers would not have to pay out on any claims, leaving the company and its directors and officers without any coverage unless there is express language in the excess policies to the contrary. As remote as it is, the possibility of an insurer bankruptcy, and the potential dire consequences that might present, should cause a corporation to ensure that any excess D&O Policy has a provision that provides that the upper-level coverage "drops down" and attaches in the event a lower-level carrier fails.

X. CONCLUSION

Managing a class action is often a complex undertaking involving many complicated legal issues and practical considerations. As a start, it is important to conduct a careful analysis of the issues discussed in this chapter when faced with the prospect of bringing or defending a class action.

---

54. *See, e.g.,* Nat'l Union Fire Ins. Co. v. Continental Illinois Corp., 673 F. Supp. 267, 273 (N.D. Ill 1987).

55. *See, e.g.,* Yan Fang Du v. Allstate Ins. Co., 697 F.3d 753, 757-58 (9th Cir. 2012).

Chapter 10

Electronic Discovery in Civil Litigation

By Kelly M. Warner, Martin T. Tully,
Lauren E. Jaffe, and Lauren H. Cooper

The goals of this chapter are to familiarize the reader at a high level with various key aspects of electronic discovery (e-discovery) that often arise in civil litigation matters; to identify e-discovery issues that frequently call for deeper strategic analysis, depending on the nature and scope of the litigation and electronic data involved; and to note and briefly describe some common best practices to potentially consider in handling e-discovery, with references to more comprehensive and detailed sources of guidance.

Electronic discovery (e-discovery) is often thought of as a spectrum of activities that track the life cycle of a typical civil litigation matter.[1] It includes identification, preservation, collection, processing, review, analysis, production, and presentation, with information governance intersecting and influencing that spectrum from the creation of

---

1. E-Discovery has been defined as "the process of identifying, preserving, collecting, preparing, analyzing, reviewing, and producing electronically stored information ('ESI') relevant to pending or anticipated litigation, or requested in government inquiries. E-discovery includes gathering ESI from numerous sources, reviewing and analyzing its relevance and the applicability of any privileges or protections from disclosure, and then producing it to an outside party." *The Sedona Conference Commentary on Information Governance*, 15 Sedona Conf. J. 125, 130 (2014).

electronically stored information (ESI)[2] to its ultimate disposition.[3] This chapter takes a high-level look at some of the key aspects of the e-discovery spectrum, identifying the issues that sometimes call for deeper strategic analysis, depending on the nature and scope of the litigation and ESI involved.

Of course, it is critical to identify and understand at the outset whether the court in which the matter is pending has any local rules or standing orders that bear upon the manner in which e-discovery is to be handled in a particular case. Some courts and judges have implemented model e-discovery orders and template "ESI protocols" (which will be discussed later in this chapter) that parties are required to utilize and that address many aspects of e-discovery. For example, a number of judges in the U.S. District Court for the Northern District of Illinois have adopted model standing orders and Principles Relating to the Discovery of ESI (the Principles) that were developed by the 7th Circuit Council on eDiscovery and Digital Information.[4] The Principles contain innovative recommendations, such as the mandatory use of e-discovery liaisons, to assist parties in efficiently managing e-discovery, particularly discovery involving complex ESI. The U.S. District Court for the Northern District of California has developed a similar set of ESI guidelines, checklists, and model stipulated orders.[5] Other courts have even issued proposed procedural rules on the use of e-discovery tools, such as technology-assisted review.[6] Understanding whether and how such provisions may apply to a given case is an essential first step in the process. This chapter reviews the subsequent steps in that process.

Practice Pointer

Always check first to see what local standing orders, rules, guidelines, or forms a particular forum may have available or require regarding the conduct of e-discovery.

---

2. EDRM-Duke Law defines "electronically stored information" as "information that is stored electronically on enumerable types of media regardless of the original format in which it was created."

3. *See, e.g.*, the Electronic Discovery Reference Model (EDRM) diagram, https://www.edrm.net/frameworks-and-standards/edrm-model/. The EDRM diagram "represents a conceptual view of the e-discovery process, not a literal, linear or waterfall model. One may engage in some but not all of the steps outlined in the diagram, or one may elect to carry out the steps in a different order than shown here." *Id.*

4. *See* https://www.discoverypilot.com/sites/default/files/StandingOrde8_10.pdf.

5. *See* https://www.cand.uscourts.gov/eDiscoveryGuidelines.

6. *See* Commercial Division Advisory Council, New York Commercial Division, Proposal for a Rule Concerning the Use of Technology-Assisted Review in Discovery, *available at* https://images.law.com/contrib/content/uploads/documents/389/37989/TAR-CDAC-memorandu1.pdf.

I. IDENTIFICATION OF RELEVANT ESI: FINDING WHAT MATTERS

A. Investigating and Identifying Potential Sources of Electronic Evidence

Like sand at the beach, data can find its way into inconvenient places. Parties and their counsel should therefore be mindful of the ever-evolving number and variety of data-generating technologies and repositories of ESI. Sources of relevant ESI may include: local and network computers, laptop and desktop computers, servers, smartphones, tablets, and other mobile devices, photocopiers, portable storage devices, database systems, document management systems, business intelligence platforms, network attached storage, cloud-based storage and information-sharing systems and services, archives, backup systems, voice-mail systems, and video monitoring systems. Indeed, there are countless systems and devices that individual users within an organization can employ to utilize, store, and access data. There also may be legacy data to contend with, such as a database that still exists, but the application used to access the data is obsolete and unusable. Social media content (e.g., Facebook, Instagram, and LinkedIn), ephemeral content (e.g., SnapChat), and the "Internet of Things" (which involves data that resides on devices such as fitness bracelets, Apple watches, baby monitors, cars, and home monitoring systems) constitute more recent sources of ESI that contribute more and more potentially relevant and challenging data to litigation matters. What's more, these data sources can be scattered across the country or even overseas as a result of the growth of the global economy and multinational companies generating ESI that is stored in multiple places.

Beyond location, different types or categories of information may be stored in different formats within an organization's repositories. For example, data can exist as structured data (e.g., a SQL database) or unstructured data (e.g., .pst files residing on a Microsoft Exchange e-mail server). The data can include any electronic files an organization might possess, including e-mails, instant messages, word-processing files, spreadsheets, presentations, voicemails, videos, social networking content, and files stored in collaboration systems or third-party applications. Depending on the case, potentially relevant ESI may also include nonobvious data such as source code, cached data, call logs, audio recordings, image and video files, databases, backup tapes, and archived materials.

The identification of potentially relevant information is a necessary initial step prior to undertaking the remaining tasks associated with e-discovery. Therefore, even before a litigation matter commences, it is important for an organization to know what ESI it has, how and why it is created, where and how it is kept, how and by whom it is accessed and used, and who has ownership of or responsibility for it. Given that the answers to these questions may be reflected in a data map or in the records retention policies and schedules for the organization, they are usually a good starting point for identifying potential sources of ESI evidence.[7] Although some lawsuits may involve facts and claims so simple that in-house counsel is already aware of all necessary sources of evidence, additional inquiry is typically required in order to thoroughly identify the information that is potentially relevant to a lawsuit.

Practice Pointer

Ideally, counsel should familiarize themselves in advance with the types, locations, and key custodians of organizational data that is most likely to be involved in potential disputes.

B. Custodian Questionnaires and Interviews

Most organizations provide an employee with access to a computer, e-mail account, user-specific storage location (i.e., repositories that can only be accessed by the individual user), and one or more shared storage locations (i.e., repositories that are accessible by more than one employee). An employee also may have access to multiple databases or applications maintained or licensed by the organization, including sales, inventory, accounting, human resources, customer relationship management, payroll, and financial systems. The specific portfolio of data associated with a particular employee will likely vary based on the individual's function and the environment in which he or she works. These functions are also increasingly outsourced to third-party cloud-based providers instead of hosted by on-premises applications.

Therefore, once a litigation matter has commenced, it is essential to interview the individuals who are likely to have knowledge of the facts relevant to the dispute as well as the individuals who are most familiar with the sources and locations of ESI in an organization to determine what might be relevant to the dispute. This is often true even if the environment is well-documented (e.g., by a document retention policy or through a data map) because there may be instances where practice has diverged from historical policy or procedure. Such an inquiry typically can be accomplished through the use of written questionnaires issued to the relevant custodians, a brief conversation with the information technology professionals who are familiar with and responsible for the use of the tools and applicable retention periods, or both. Follow-up interviews with the key custodians may be helpful to ensure there is no miscommunication regarding identification of potentially relevant repositories and to verify whether practice has followed policy and procedure regarding the creation and retention of electronic data. (A sample custodian questionnaire is attached as Appendix A.)

---

7. For a list of common data sources for companies and individuals, *see* The Sedona Conference Jumpstart Outline, Questions to Ask Your Client & Your Adversary to Prepare for Preservation, Rule 26 Obligations, Court Conferences & Requests for Production (Mar. 2016), at 8-13, *available at* https://thesedonaconference.org/publication/The%20Sedona%20Conference%C2%AE%20%22Jumpstart%20Outline%22.

Ideally, custodian interviews should be conducted by legal counsel who is knowledgeable of the facts and issues involved in the litigation and familiar with e-discovery principles generally. If feasible, interviews should be conducted in person where the custodian typically works, or via screen sharing in a web meeting in order to facilitate counsel's understanding of the particular data repositories at issue. All information learned during these discussions and inquiry should be tracked and well-documented. From these conversations, counsel can develop a collection plan that identifies the most relevant information about the case.

Practice Pointer

If needed, counsel familiar with the facts and issues in dispute should collaborate with internal or outside e-discovery resources to ensure sufficient understanding and appreciation of the technical issues involved.

II. PRESERVATION OF ESI AND AVOIDING CLAIMS OF SPOLIATION OF ELECTRONIC EVIDENCE

A. The Duty to Preserve

The common law has long provided for a duty to preserve potentially relevant evidence, including ESI.[8] Generally speaking, the duty to preserve exists "when the party has notice that the evidence is relevant to litigation or when a party should have known that the evidence may be relevant to future litigation."[9] In other words, the duty to preserve records may exist before a lawsuit or investigation commences. Thus, the common-law duty to preserve is triggered where a lawsuit, government investigation, or audit has been *threatened*, initiated, or when a party knows or should know litigation or an investigation is anticipated.

Precisely when the duty to preserve arises requires careful analysis of the specific facts and circumstances; however, the following are some examples of circumstances upon which a legal hold is commonly issued:

- the receipt of a complaint or notice of filing a lawsuit;
- a court order requiring preservation;
- a party's well-developed plans to initiate a lawsuit;

---

8. *See* FED. R. CIV. P. 37(f) advisory committee note to 2006 amendment ("A preservation obligation may arise from many sources, including common law, statutes, regulations, or a court order in the case."). *See also* Kronisch v. United States, 150 F. 3d 112, 126-27 (2d Cir. 1998).

9. *Convolve, Inc. v. Compaq Computer Corp.*, 223 F.R.D. 162, 175 (S.D.N.Y. 2004) (quoting *Fujitsu Ltd. v. Federal Express Corp.*, 247 F.3d 423, 436 (2d Cir. 2001)). *See also In re Kmart Corp.*, 371 B.R. 823, 844 (Bankr. N.D. Ill. 2007) ("[T]he 'trigger date' should represent the date by which a party is on notice of the potential relevance of documents to pending or impending litigation.").

- receipt of a grand jury subpoena or notification of an imminent law enforcement investigation; and
- notice that an employee has filed a discrimination claim with the EEOC.

Given that not all these examples include a legal proceeding filed in court, it can be helpful for an organization that experiences frequent preservation triggers to have policies and procedures in place to help it determine when and how to impose a legal hold and other preservation procedures that will appear reasonable in hindsight. In addition to having a written policy in place regarding the consideration and implementation of legal holds, organizations may also train employees to communicate with counsel whenever they *reasonably believe* litigation appears likely so that timely decisions regarding the issuance of a legal hold can be made by appropriate persons.

B. Legal Holds

A legal hold should clearly communicate to recipients the need to preserve information relevant to the particular lawsuit or inquiry, which is typically done through a clear and conspicuous statement of the purpose behind the request (e.g., "the company has been sued," or "the company has received a request from law enforcement"). The request to preserve information should be distributed to all those with knowledge or possession of information within the scope of the legal hold. Although a legal hold need not necessarily be in writing and may be communicated verbally under appropriate circumstances, a written legal hold provides clarity and consistency, and assists with defensibility as well.

The content of the legal hold often includes a brief description of the pending lawsuit, anticipated litigation, or investigation; sets forth the issues involved; and contains guidelines regarding what kinds of materials should be maintained. It is often prepared and sent by legal counsel. Note that although a legal hold notice is typically held to be protected by the attorney-client privilege, it is prudent to draft it as though it will be required to be disclosed to a third party.

It is important that the legal hold notice make clear that the preservation obligation extends to materials within the organization's possession, custody, or control, which would include not only information held in company-owned or licensed repositories, but also information held by third parties retained by the organization, such as attorneys and accountants. In the event the information to be preserved includes more complicated categories of data, such as instant messages, social media content, or collaborative tools (e.g., SharePoint), special consideration should be given to ensure the effective and efficient preservation of data.

It is essential that the legal hold notice sets forth the importance of preserving materials and the potential ramifications of failing to comply, as well as describe the actual steps that a recipient must take to verify preservation of materials. Finally, the legal hold should contain the name and contact details of the person overseeing the litigation or investigation about which the legal hold is being issued, and request that the recipient inform the designated contact person if he or she has any questions or is aware of any other person who may have materials covered by the legal hold. (A sample legal hold notice is attached as Appendix B.)

Distribution of legal hold notices should be done by whatever means will be most likely effective, considering confidentiality concerns that may be relevant to particular circumstances such as law enforcement investigations. Legal holds are most commonly distributed by e-mail. If the organization is aware that any of the intended recipients do not have an e-mail address, those individuals should receive the hold by an alternative method, including by attending and participating in a discussion covering the topics discussed above. If a recipient does not receive a written legal hold, the content of instruction provided to that recipient should be memorialized and retained (e.g., in a memo to file by the individual who had the conversation). Regardless of how the hold is distributed, it should be clearly labeled and dated. Once the legal hold is distributed, it is important to track the receipt of the hold. Under certain circumstances, the organization may wish to require an acknowledgement of receipt or to track which recipients have opened the e-mail or attachment thereto.[10] It is also important to verify that the legal hold has been sent to all necessary individuals, that these individuals understand the hold's meaning and importance, and agree to comply with its directives.

An organization may also consider monitoring and auditing compliance with the legal hold notice. In this regard, it is not advisable to merely "send it, and forget it." Courts have stressed the importance of issuing legal holds and the need to regularly reiterate the obligation to preserve relevant information and to continually monitor compliance. Consequently, having follow-up procedures is important, given that courts expect a legal hold to be done properly and effectively and may not be forgiving of poorly conceived and implemented legal hold practices.[11]

Practice Pointer

Take reasonable steps to follow up on legal hold notices to ensure receipt, understanding, and compliance by the recipient custodians. Periodically revisit legal holds and adjust their scope as needed.

Even those matters that do not last for years will encounter the challenge of employees arriving and departing from an organization that has a preservation obligation as part of a large, complex litigation matter. Departing employees should be identified, tracked, and

---

10. *See e.g., In re Prudential Ins. Co. of Am. Sales Practices Litig.*, 169 F.R.D. 598, 604 (D.N.J. 1997) (finding fault with implementation of legal hold where not all employees received the notice, and others who did receive it ignored it).

11. *See, e.g., id.* at 615 ("When senior management fails to establish and distribute a comprehensive document retention policy, it cannot shield itself from responsibility because of field office actions."); *Danis v. USN Commc'ns*, No. 98 C 7482, 2000 WL 1694325, at *32 (N.D. Ill. Oct. 23, 2000) (attorney did nothing to ensure that the directives were followed, and some documents were destroyed in accordance with prelitigation practices. The *Danis* court blamed the corporate executive team for the failure, stating that "when senior management fails to establish and distribute a comprehensive document retention policy, it cannot shield itself from responsibility because of field office actions.") (quoting *In re Prudential*, 169 F.R.D. at 615).

accounted for before they leave in order to ensure that their company data and devices, if subject to a legal hold, are not lost. Conversely, a mechanism should be put into place to identify new hires, who might come to the legal hold from outside the organization and become part of an ongoing duty to preserve. Tracking the comings and goings of employees within an organization and accounting for their relevant ESI subject to a preservation obligation can be a challenge within organizations that have adopted a bring-your-own-device (BYOD) policy that permits employees to do company business on personally owned devices.[12]

Finally, there are also instances in which a legal hold's content should be modified or renewed depending on the progress and scope of the litigation or investigation. Updates to notices should be distributed if issues in an investigation or litigation change such that relevant materials are not likely to be covered under the original notices. The list of individuals who receive legal hold notices should be updated if the scope of the litigation or investigation expands.[13]

C. Documenting Preservation Efforts

As the foregoing suggests, the absence of reasonable preservation procedures or the inability to demonstrate that reasonable and proportional steps have been taken to preserve relevant ESI can be problematic. Therefore, it is important to keep reasonably thorough records of any steps taken to implement the legal hold, which can assist in the event the party is required to defend against later spoliation charges. In particular, "[r]esponding parties and their counsel should consider what documentation of their discovery process (i.e., preservation, collection, review, and production) is appropriate to the needs of the particular case. Such documentation may include a description of what is being preserved; the processes and validation procedures employed to preserve, collect, and prepare the materials for production; and the steps taken to ensure the integrity of the information throughout the process."[14]

Whether counsel delegates all or a portion of the preservation process to an outside vendor or to the client's own personnel, he or she must be cognizant of the certification requirements of Federal Rule of Civil Procedure 26(g) and be reasonably knowledgeable and confident that steps taken to preserve ESI are consistent with what has been represented to the court in discovery disclosures, requests, responses, and objections. This is another reason why documenting every step in the preservation and collection process is critical.

---

12. For a further discussion of this topic, *see* The Sedona Conference Commentary on BYOD: Principles and Guidance for Developing Policies and Meeting Discovery Obligations, Public Comment Version, Jan. 2018, *available for free at* https://thesedonaconference.org/.

13. For a further discussion of best practices regarding legal holds, *see The Sedona Conference® Commentary On Legal Holds: The Trigger & The Process*, 11 Sedona Conf. J. 265 (2010).

14. *The Sedona Principles, Third Edition: Best Practices, Recommendations & Principles For Addressing Electronic Document Production*, 19 Sedona Conf. J. 1, 126-27 (2018).

III. RESPONDING AND OBJECTING TO WRITTEN DISCOVERY FOR ESI

The changes to the Federal Rules of Civil Procedure (the Rules) that became effective December 1, 2015 (the 2015 amendments), were intended to address systemic problems in how discovery requests and responses were handled.[15] Yet, "[d]espite the clarity of the no-longer-new 2015 Amendments," courts are still seeing "too many non-compliant Rule 34 responses" as well as noncompliant requests.[16] Many practitioners improperly continue to rely on their prior practices, templates, boilerplate[17] requests, instructions, definitions, objections, and forms. The courts have become increasingly intolerant of these old habits.[18]

The 2015 amendments to Rule 34 (b)(2) require the following:

- Responding parties must respond to Rule 34 Requests for Production (RFPs) within 30 days of service or, if the request was delivered prior to the Rule 26(f) conference, within 30 days after the parties' first Rule 26(f) conference.
- Objections to RFPs must be stated with specificity.
- Responses must state whether responsive materials are being withheld on the basis of objections. Advisory Committee Note to Rule 34 states that describing the search to be conducted can satisfy the specificity requirement.
- Responses to RFPs may state that the responding party "will produce documents" but must do so within 30 days "or another reasonable time specified in the response."

The 2015 amendments also allow for delivery of Rule 34 requests 21 days after service of the complaint.[19] According to the 2015 Advisory Committee Notes, "[t]his relaxation of the discovery moratorium is designed to facilitate focused discussion during the Rule 26(f) conference."[20]

In drafting responses to RFPs, counsel for responding parties should meet with their clients as early as possible to determine what documents exist, what requested documents are going to be withheld and for what reasons, and what requested documents are going to be produced and when that production can be completed. This will allow the

---

15. *See* Report of the Advisory Committee on Federal Rules of Civil Procedure (June 14, 2014); 2015 Year-End Report on the Federal Judiciary.

16. *Fischer v. Forrest*, Case No. 1:14-cv-01307, 2017 WL 773694, at *3 (S.D.N.Y. Feb. 28, 2017).

17. "Boilerplate" language includes "[r]eady made or all-purpose language that will fit in a variety of documents." *United States v. Needham*, 718 F.3d 1190, 1199 (9th Cir. 2013) (quoting Black's Law Dictionary (9th ed. 2009)).

18. *See, e.g., Fischer*, 2017 WL 773694, at *3 (any discovery response that does not comply with Rule 34's requirement to state objections with specificity (and to clearly indicate whether responsive material is being withheld on the basis of objection) will be deemed a waiver of all objections (except as to privilege)); *Liguria Foods, Inc. v. Griffith Labs, Inc.*, 320 F.R.D. 168, 192 (N.D. IA 2017) (using "boilerplate" objections to discovery in any case places counsel and their clients at risk for substantial sanctions).

19. Fed. R. Civ. P. 26(d)(2).

20. Fed. R. Civ. P. 26 advisory committee's note to 2015 amendment.

responding party to avoid using general objections and boilerplate responses that state only "responsive nonprivileged documents will be produced."

Practice Pointer

Boilerplate objections that simply state rote objections and do not specify what categories of documents will or will not be produced are no longer permissible under Rule 34.

Amended Rule 34 requires that objections: (1) be stated with specificity, including the reasons for the objections; and (2) state whether any responsive materials are being withheld on the basis of each objection.[21] Given these requirements, courts have held that general objections should be limited. General objections should be used only if the objections apply to all the document requests. It can be helpful to expressly incorporate general objections by reference in the sub-set of requests to which they are being asserted to avoid repeating the objection. General objections as to form of production, time-period/date range, or other global-scope objections may be listed as a general objection, but the reason for these objections still must be specified in order to facilitate a meaningful discovery conference.[22] Other than the limited exceptions described above, objections are generally provided in an individual response. Either way, the objection should explain the reason behind it.

Rule 34 and the 2015 Advisory Committee Notes require a responding party to identify the documents withheld pursuant to objection or, alternatively, to describe the scope of the production the party is willing to make. The Committee Notes further clarify that the withholding party is not required to specifically identify or log withheld documents and may comply with this requirement by stating the scope of what it will produce. When stating what is being withheld, the intention is to "alert the other parties to the fact that documents have been withheld and thereby facilitate an informed discussion of the objection."[23]

When a responding party intends to produce a more limited scope of documents than requested, it can meet Rule 34's requirements by describing the scope of what it is willing to produce, which may include the parameters of a search for documents, such as custodians, sources, date ranges, and search terms (or search methodology). Regarding the timing of document productions, a general response that "documents responsive to this request will be produced" is insufficient. Production either must be completed by the time specified in the request or another reasonable time specified in the response.[24]

---

21. *See* FED. R. CIV. P. 34(b)(2)(B)–(C).

22. *See The Sedona Conference, Federal Rule of Civil Procedure 34(b)(2) Primer*, 19 SEDONA CONF. J. 447 (Mar. 2018).

23. FED. R. CIV. P. 34 advisory committee's note to 2015 amendment.

24. FED. R. CIV. P. 34(b)(1)(B).

The responding party should include enough detail as necessary to support the objection, and keep in mind that its objection may have to be justified to the court. An objection on the grounds that a request is vague or ambiguous should explain why this is the case, and should be based on a logical interpretation of what is requested.

Responding parties should also be mindful that the certification requirement of Rule 26(g) applies to all responses and objections to document requests. Rule 26(g) requires that the requesting and responding attorneys certify that their requests, responses, and objections are consistent with the Rules and are "not interposed for any improper purpose, such as to harass, cause unnecessary delay, or needlessly increase the cost of litigation," and are "neither unreasonable nor unduly burdensome or expensive, considering the needs of the case, prior discovery in the case, the amount in controversy, and the importance of the issues at stake in the action."

IV. NEGOTIATING ESI DISCOVERY REQUESTS AND RESPONSES: THE MEET AND CONFER

We have reviewed a number of topics that involve inside and outside counsel making critical decisions regarding data that may be collected, reviewed, or produced in litigation. These decisions and conversations typically occur without involvement or consultation from the opposing party's counsel. As a party crafts written discovery responses and considers what evidence will be important to establishing claims or defenses, communications with opposing counsel become much more frequent. Those communications are expected to involve negotiation—and, importantly, cooperation—between the parties. Of course, counsel should be guided by any standing orders or local rules that govern the meet-and-confer process.

The concepts of negotiation and cooperation are embedded in the Rules and their Advisory Committee Notes and are emphasized by court-sponsored and industry organizations.[25] The 2015 amendments to the Rules make this clear from the start with Rule 1, which was amended to include obligations on both courts and litigants "to secure the just, speedy, and inexpensive determination of every action and proceeding." The Advisory Committee Note to Rule 1 explicitly refers to an expectation of cooperation among the parties. Chief Justice Roberts addressed the 2015 amendments in his Year-End Report on the Judiciary, emphasizing that the revision to Rule 1 "highlights the point that lawyers—though representing adverse parties—have an affirmative duty to work together, and with the court, to achieve prompt and efficient resolutions of disputes." The parties' obligation to cooperate is typically carried out through the negotiation

---

25. *See* Sedona Conference Cooperation Proclamation, Seventh Circuit Pilot Program on Electronic Discovery Principle 1.02 ("An attorney's zealous representation of a client is not compromised by conducting discovery in a cooperative manner. The failure of counsel or the parties to litigation to cooperate in facilitating and reasonably limiting discovery requests and responses raises litigation costs and contributes to the risk of sanctions.")

of a number of documents that have significant strategic and cost implications for a particular matter.

A. Discovery Plan

Rule 26(f) requires the parties to work together to create a discovery plan, including a proposed schedule for discovery, the subjects of discovery, any issues that may arise about ESI disclosure or preservation, privilege issues, and a Federal Rule of Evidence 502 (FRE 502) agreement, if applicable.[26] The scope of and timing for discovery set forth in the discovery plan will dictate the resources a party must dedicate to completing discovery as set forth therein.

B. Culling Methods

Given the volume of ESI retained by individuals and corporations, the use of culling methods to narrow the scope of potentially responsive information is increasingly important. Different culling methods—including technology-assisted review, search terms, and limitations on sources—are discussed in greater detail below.[27] The important take-away for purposes of this negotiation section is that these discussions occur and that the culling methodologies are hashed out in great detail by the parties early in the process.

C. ESI Protocol

Parties increasingly enter an "ESI protocol" in a particular case, which sets forth agreements between the parties and a roadmap for the production of ESI (and paper) in a matter. By creating an ESI protocol, the parties work through a number of decision points on document production in a matter, often including identification of the custodians, search terms, and date ranges to be used; which metadata fields will be produced; the manner of duplication of data to be applied; whether documents will be redacted or e-mail/attachment relationships will be modified for nonresponsive or protected information; the way in which withheld documents will be logged for privilege; and the technological format of production. The negotiation of an ESI protocol can take significant resources, but often the decisions underlying the ESI protocol have significant cost implications. Parties should consider whether an ESI protocol should merely be an agreement between the parties, or whether it should be entered by the court, given that doing so will increase the repercussions for noncompliance with the protocol. A number of court-sponsored organizations offer template ESI protocols or orders that provide a blueprint for the

---

26. Several good references and checklists exist for preparing for a Rule 26(f) meet & confer. *See, e.g.,* The Sedona Conference Jumpstart Outline, *supra* note 6; The LTPI Meet and Confer Instructional Guide, https://www.legaltechpi.org/resources/Pictures/Meet%20and%20Confer%20-%20v1.0.pdf.

27. For an excellent summary of pre-search culling and search methodologies, *see In re Broiler Chicken Antitrust Litigation Order Regarding Search Methodology for Electronically Stored Information,* Case No. 1:16-cv-08637 (N.D. Ill. Jan 3, 2018).

issues the parties can address in their negotiations and a suggested strategy for such issues, depending on the resources of the parties and the amount in controversy in the matter.[28] (A sample ESI protocol is attached as Appendix C.)

Practice Pointer

Negotiating and entering into stipulated ESI protocols early in a litigation can reduce disputes, headaches, costs, and motion practice.

D. Protective Orders

Parties often negotiate the existence and provisions of a protective order. Pursuant to Rule 26, the court "may, for good cause, issue an order to protect a party or person from annoyance, embarrassment, oppression, or undue burden or expense." Arguably, documents and information provided in discovery do not give the receiving party any greater rights to the materials beyond using them in prosecuting or defending its case. That said, documents and other information produced by one side to the other in litigation are not explicitly accorded any presumption of confidentiality or protection.

Particular judges and courts often have standing orders including sample provisions for or regarding the entry of protective orders (sometimes disfavoring their use).[29] The precise substance of what is to be protected, and the steps undertaken in order to designate and treat information as protected, often involves detailed negotiations. In addition to identifying information that is to be protected from disclosure in public filings, or limited from view of particular witnesses or parties, protective orders may also govern how information is to be transmitted or stored to ensure appropriate protection. In addition, protective orders may also include provisions related to the intentional or inadvertent production of information that is protected by the attorney-client privilege or work-product doctrine. (A sample protective order is attached as Appendix D.)

E. FRE 502(d) Orders

Parties also often negotiate the provisions of orders to be entered by the court pursuant to FRE 502, which was enacted in 2008 (and mirrored by an increasing number of state rules of procedure) to "resolve[] some longstanding disputes in the courts about the effect of certain disclosures of communications or information protected by the attorney-client privilege or as work product—specifically those disputes involving

---

28. *See, e.g.,* Seventh Circuit Electronic Discovery Pilot Program Model Discovery Plan, https://www. discoverypilot.com/content/model-discovery-plan-and-privilege-order.

29. *See, e.g., In re Roman Catholic Archbishop of Portland in Or. v. Various Tort Claimants,* 661 F.3d 417, 424 (9th Cir. 2011) ("[A]s a general rule, the general public is permitted access to litigation documents and information produced during discovery.").

inadvertent disclosure and subject matter waiver."[30] Parties should consider the utility of a FRE 502(d) order, which allows a party to intentionally produce protected information without resulting in a waiver of any of the protections for that information. A number of judges and industry organizations advocate for the entry of an FRE 502(d) order in every matter. Indeed, former U.S. Magistrate Judge Andrew Peck has gone so far as to equate the failure to obtain an FRE 502(d) order to malpractice.[31] (A sample Rule 502 order is attached as Appendix E.)

V. COLLECTION OF ESI

At some point in the data investigation process, it will be time to collect the data in order to review and prepare it for production to the opposing party. A party may collect data early in the process—before even initiating negotiations with opposing counsel— in order to better understand the impact and burdens associated with the requested discovery as it negotiates the scope of discovery with opposing counsel, or in order to meet early discovery requirements. A party may also choose to collect data later in the process, after the scope of discovery has been determined by agreement or court order.

The Rules do not specify the manner in which data must be collected, but the courts have weighed in on various strategies. The touchstone of data collection established by the courts is that the manner be *defensible*, given the particular facts and circumstances of the case. What is reasonable and defensible in a particular matter may not be so in a different matter. For example, it may be reasonable and defensible for an individual to collect his or her tax documentation from a folder on his or her personal computer in a $25,000 employment discrimination case, but it may not be reasonable or defensible for a large company to rely on its employees to search their own e-mail accounts to collect data responsive to a broad range of trade-secret allegations.

Documenting the manner of collection—whatever manner is chosen—can be helpful if a party is called on to defend the process at some later point in time. Having a contemporaneous record of the manner of collection, why it was chosen, and why it was deemed to be appropriate can assist a party to remember the rationale if this choice is later called into question.

Note also that the manner of collection may have consequences for the format of production. For example, if a party relies on a collection of e-mails from a journaling tool, it will not be able to report particular metadata fields. Thus, counsel should consider holistically the method of collection, the ESI protocol, and the format of production.

There are different collection strategies for different types of data. Generally, these differences apply to (1) devices; (2) e-mails stored on an organization's e-mail server or within a custodian's mailbox; and (3) files stored on a network, shared, or cloud-hosted

---

30. *See* Fed. R. Evid. 502 Explanatory Note ("The rule seeks to provide a predictable, uniform set of standards under which parties can determine the consequences of a disclosure of a communication or information covered by the attorney-client privilege or work-product protection.").

31. https://www.brighttalk.com/webcast/15737/288641/is-it-malpractice-not-to-get-a-fre-502-d-order.

repository. A party may choose to use several different manners of collection in a particular case, depending upon the data collected.

For devices (e.g., mobile phone, thumb drive, laptop computer), the primary methods of collection include the following:

- **Forensic collection.** The most complete (and often most expensive) manner of data collection is the use of forensic collection tools by a certified forensic examiner. A forensic collection provides for the copying of every byte of data on a particular device, including both active and deleted content. A forensic collection will provide details on when files were accessed and deleted, and the different drives that accessed the device, such as the number of different thumb drives that were plugged into the computer, and which files were copied over to them. Conducting the collection with forensic collection tools is often important in cases where there is a question about inappropriate access to or deletion of particular files. When a forensic collection is used, the producing party typically relies on some further manner of culling the data before production, including search terms and technology-assisted review. Some corporations with a more significant litigation profile have their own in-house forensic specialist who can conduct this collection, whereas other parties do so through a third-party service provider.

- **Active collection.** An active collection copies all "active" (i.e., nondeleted) content on the device. An active collection will not allow for the identification of deleted data, including files that simply were deleted a long time ago or files that were deleted as part of inappropriate conduct or a nefarious motive. When a complete collection of active data is used, the producing party typically relies on some further manner of culling the data before production, including search terms and technology-assisted review. An active collection can be conducted by a third-party service provider or by an in-house resource.

- **Targeted collection.** A targeted collection focuses on copying files only on the device that will have potentially responsive data, e.g., copying over particular folders on a custodian's computer or thumb drive that potentially relate to the case. A targeted collection may be conducted by a third-party service provider or by an in-house resource.

- **Search-term-based collection.** A party may apply search terms using a device's searching capabilities. This strategy is intended to collect less data from the source, which will save a party from the costs of processing more data. A party should consider the searching capabilities of the device when choosing this strategy, including ensuring that the search syntax used is recognized by the tool. A search-term-based collection may be conducted by an internal resource, such as a representative from the IT department or a third-party service provider. Consistent with the suggestion above to retain a contemporaneous documentation of the particular strategy used, be sure to retain a record of the particular search terms used.

- **Custodian identification.** A party may ask an employee with knowledge of the particular claims and defenses at issue in the case (a "custodian") to review his or her device in order to identify potentially responsive files. Although custodian self-identification has been criticized by some courts,[32] a custodian who is well-educated about the facts of the case and the boundaries of discovery can be a valuable part of the collection process. The party should retain the instructions provided to the custodian regarding how to identify potentially relevant files.

For e-mails stored in an organization's e-mail systems, the primary methods of collection differ somewhat. E-mails have unique characteristics that provide for different options:

- **Active collection.** A party may collect all of the e-mails contained within a particular custodian's mailbox. Such a collection may be conducted on an e-mail account provided by a corporate employer or on an e-mail account an individual may have created with a publicly available resource such as Gmail or Yahoo. When an active collection of e-mail is used, the producing party typically relies on some further manner of culling the data before production, including search terms and technology-assisted review, which may be applied with the assistance of a service provider.

- **Search-term-based collection.** A party may apply search terms using the e-mail system's searching capabilities. The same comments noted above for a search-term based collection of a device apply, including ensuring that the syntax of the search terms is recognized by the particular system. Some corporations have implemented an e-mail journaling system, where one copy of all e-mails in or out of the domain is retained for a particular period of time. Such a system can be a good resource for e-mail collection because the e-mails are already de-duplicated (i.e., only one version of the e-mail exists, which avoids over-collection of data) and are retained regardless of whether the custodian has deleted the e-mail from his or her individual mailbox. A party should consider whether the tool used for the application of search terms is limited. For example, if the tool used to apply search terms does not render attachments to e-mails text searchable, particular files may be missed by the search-term application process.

- **Custodian identification.** A party may ask an employee with knowledge of the particular claims and defenses at issue in the case to review his or her e-mails to identify potentially responsive files. The same comments noted above for custodian identification above apply, including ensuring that the custodian has been well-educated on the issues involved and the scope of discovery in the particular case.

---

32. *See, e.g., Jones v. Bremen High School Dist.* 228, 2010 WL 2106640 (N.D. Ill. May 25, 2010) ("It is unreasonable to allow a party's interested employees to make the decision about the relevance of such documents, especially when those same employees have the ability to permanently delete unfavorable e-mail from a party's system.").

For files stored on an organization's on-site servers or in a cloud-hosted repository, the primary methods of collection include the use of search terms and targeted collection of a particular repository. Forensic collection is typically not available for a server or cloud-hosted repository because the resources continue to be in active use and constantly updated.

Databases such as accounting and customer relations management databases can also be a source of potentially relevant information for a case. Information can be exported from a database using a predefined report available in the database or by conducting a query to create a custom report.

An organization may also have unique file types, such as audio files, video files, design files, and files associated with proprietary software, that are relevant to a particular matter. The discovery plan and ESI protocol negotiated by the parties may address the manner in which such information is to be collected and produced, including making a system available on which the opposing party may view the information. Parties often raise the issue of unique file types early in the process in order to provide additional time to determine the most efficient and effective way of collecting and producing such information.

VI. LEVERAGING ASSISTANCE FROM IT/SERVICE PROVIDERS/FORENSIC EXAMINERS

Companies sometimes dispatch the task of ESI collection to staff whose role is not to collect data for litigation or even directly to custodians. Either of those scenarios can suffer from the same challenges—a lack of appropriate knowledge of the necessary process to ensure defensibility, repeatability, and integrity of the data. Failure to follow defensible collection processes can lead to charges of spoliation, or even sanctions. Further, many organizations would prefer to avoid having one of their employees called to testify about how data was identified and collected, and the appropriateness of the methods for doing so. Therefore, in order to defensibly gather and search preserved information for litigation purposes, companies may engage an independent outside e-discovery vendor with the proper software tools capable of processing this information and culling and searching it for relevant evidence.

As Comment 6.e of *The Sedona Principles, Third Edition: Best Practices, Recommendations & Principles for Addressing Electronic Document Production* notes, "[d]iscovery counsel, consultants, and vendors offer a variety of software and services to assist with the electronic discovery process and a party's evaluation of software and services should include the defensibility of the process in the litigation context, the cost, and the experience of the discovery counsel, consultant or vendor, including its project management and process controls."[33] Engaging a litigation support vendor to assist with the processing, culling, search, and analysis of collected ESI in a large case can be indispensable, but it is important to first understand the services provided and tools

---

33. *The Sedona Principles, supra* note 13.

employed by the vendor before signing a service agreement. The process of determining whether and which vendor to engage includes at least the following steps:

- Defining the need for the vendor and the scope the project. For example, does it include data preservation/collection? Data recovery/forensics? Data processing/hosting/production? Document search/culling/review?
- Gathering information about potential vendors, their capabilities, tools, software solutions, workflows, and cost structures. This can most often be done by preparing and sending out a request for proposal (RFP) that allows responding vendors to be evaluated on an apples-to-apples basis.
- Evaluating the potential vendors using the same criteria for all providers within the same categories.
- Developing and implementing the process for onboarding the vendor, once selected, to the client organization.
- Ensuring there are processes in place to monitor, control, and close out the vendor engagement.

For a more detailed discussion of things to consider when selecting and engaging an outside e-discovery vendor, see *The Sedona Conference, Guidance for the Selection of Electronic Discovery Providers*, 18 SEDONA CONF. J. 55 (2017).

VII. REVIEW: HOW BEST TO ASSESS WHAT POTENTIALLY RELEVANT ESI YOU HAVE

After data has been collected, files are often reviewed prior to production to the opposing party. Although the costs of document review generally dwarf all other costs of litigation, there are a number of ways to streamline and economize the review process.

A. Culling

Prior to review, the data collected is often culled by a number of technological processes in order to identify potentially responsive documents for review. Parties want their attorneys to spend time reviewing only the most likely responsive materials, not spam e-mails or multiple copies of the same file. As with the collection strategies discussed above, a party should consider maintaining a contemporaneous record of the culling methods applied. The culling methodology in a particular case can include one or more of the following techniques:

- **De-duplication.** When the data is processed to be loaded into a document review database, it can be "de-duplicated," resulting in only one version of each unique document to be presented for review. De-duplication can be done (1) "globally," meaning all of the data in the particular review set is compared and only one instance of a unique document will appear, or (2) on a "custodian-level," meaning the data collected for a particular individual is compared only to the other data collected for that individual.

- **File type exclusion.** A party may choose to focus on files with a particular file extension (e.g., .doc, .pdf) as relevant to a particular case. For example, a party may choose to ignore video files in a straightforward breach-of-contract case where there is no allegation that any particular conduct is relevant. A party may focus on particular file types by either excluding or including a particular list of file types.
- **Date range.** A party may consider setting out a date range within which the potentially relevant files are likely to have been accessed or created or e-mails sent or received. When a date range is used, it is important to ensure that the parties agree with respect to what particular data field will be used. For example, the parties should have clarity (and may address in the ESI protocol) regarding whether the date range applies to the "date created," "date modified," "date last accessed," or some other date field.
- **Keywords.** A party may choose to apply particular keywords to the data collected in order to refine the pool of documents to be reviewed. A party should keep in mind that there is more to search terms than single words—most tools are capable of using sophisticated search phrases that include phrases, proximity operators, and inclusive and exclusive phrases. When keywords are used, parties will often negotiate over the selection of those terms. A party may test the terms suggested by opposing counsel to determine the expense and burden associated with a particular set of terms. A party may also choose to apply additional iterations of keywords for additional purposes. For example, a party may create a list of "presumptively privileged" terms that are used to highlight potentially protected communications and files and that would include names of counsel and phrases like "attorney client privilege."
- **Technology-assisted review.** A party may choose to use technology-assisted review (TAR) to assist with the document review process. When a party uses TAR, a subject matter expert with extensive knowledge of the claims and defenses at issue in the case reviews a "seed set" of documents to identify those clearly relevant documents that can be analyzed and used by computer software to identify other documents in a data set that are most likely to also be relevant to the claims and defenses at issue in the matter. Other forms of TAR do not utilize seed sets, but randomly selected samples of documents within a data set that are then tagged by subject matter experts as relevant or not relevant, allowing the computer to continuously learn from the tagging process and predict the likelihood that other documents are similarly relevant.[34]

B. Document Review

A party may consider producing documents without review following the application of one or more of the culling criteria mentioned above (i.e., if it is not protected by

---

34. For a more detailed discussion of TAR, *see* THE SEDONA CONFERENCE TAR CASE LAW PRIMER (Jan. 2017), *available at* https://thesedonaconference.org/publication/TAR%20Case%20Law%20Primer.

a privilege, if it is an appropriate file type for production, within the date range, and contains one or more of the search terms identified by the parties). This approach may be appropriate in particular matters or for particular sets of data related to a matter, such as communications sent to or from a former employee who is the plaintiff in the case, or all e-mails sent to a customer-support e-mail address related to a particular product.

More frequently, however, a party determines that the culled information should be reviewed by an attorney in order to make a final decision as to whether a particular file is appropriate for production (i.e., responsive to the requests for production, as limited by the producing party's objections, the parties' agreements, and the court's orders, and not protected from production by the attorney-client privilege, attorney work-product doctrine, or some other protection). A party will often use a combination of technological tools and attorney resources to conduct review prior to production. In addition, a party may consider implementing a "quality control" or "validation protocol" where a particular percentage of documents are randomly sampled to ensure the reviewing attorney made the appropriate determination with respect to a particular document. Frequent communication and meetings are helpful with consistency of decisions and efficiency of review when teams of attorneys are conducting document review on large data sets. Such communications can also facilitate the flow of information from the reviewing attorneys back to the primary outside counsel for the matter.

1. Technological Tools for Document Review

When a party determines that document review is to be conducted, there are a number of technological tools that can be employed by the producing party to make the review more efficient and economical.[35] In-house counsel may want to collaborate with outside counsel on whether such tools are appropriate for the particular matter. Some of the more commonly used tools include:

- **E-mail threading.** E-mail threading is an analytical tool that groups e-mail strings together so that only the most complete e-mail strings are reviewed for production.
- **Smart and efficient batching.** Care can be given to the manner in which files are "batched" or allocated for review, with a particular reviewer focusing on a particular custodian's files or substantive area.
- **Clustering.** A variant of smart batching is the application of analytics to a particular data set to identify clusters of data that relate to a particular subject matter, and to assign such files for review with this common characteristic in mind.
- **Near-duplicate identification.** In addition to identifying exact duplicate files (and suppressing these from review so as not to duplicate efforts or create

---

35. For a better understanding of the terminology associated with various ESI tools, please refer to THE SEDONA CONFERENCE GLOSSARY: E-DISCOVERY & DIGITAL INFORMATION MANAGEMENT (Fourth Edition, April 2014), *available at* https://thesedonaconference.org/publication/The_Sedona_Conference_Glossary.

inconsistent decisions), it is possible to identify "near duplicates," which are files that are nearly identical, and can be batched together for review.

- **Tag and privilege log layouts.** Most document review tools used by attorneys to review large quantities of files are easily customizable. A party should consider creating a layout for substantive tags from which a reviewing attorney may quickly select when reviewing documents. Similarly, a party can create a privilege log layout that provides the reviewing attorney with a range of privilege categories from which to select in order to provide more detailed information regarding the reason why a particular file was withheld.

2. Using Contract Attorneys to Assist with Document Review

A party may choose to retain attorneys for the limited purpose of assisting with document review in a matter (contract attorneys). Contract attorneys are a flexible and valuable resource that allows a party to quickly scale up to review documents prior to production. If contract attorneys are retained, outside counsel often creates a "review manual" that provides the contract attorneys with critical facts about the case, custodians, confidentiality, and documents subject to review. A party may choose to differentiate the review, allowing contract attorneys to review only those documents that are less sensitive or unlikely to be protected. In addition, as noted above, a second level of review is often used in order to provide a quality check on contract attorneys' review.

3. Privilege Review and Logging

It has been estimated that 70 percent of the costs of e-discovery are devoted to review, and a large portion of that is devoted to review for privilege. The rules require that if you are going to assert that a document is privileged, you must make the claim specifically, claiming the privilege in a way that permits the court and opposing counsel to know why the document is privileged without disclosing its contents. The rule is often honored in its breach; too many privilege logs fail to meet this criterion, leading to expensive litigation. Judges are not happy with this process, especially when it results in their having to review many documents in camera. However, there is an alternative to the tedium and expense of logging every document: divide the data by separating it into categories, agreeing with opposing counsel, for example, that certain categories are so unlikely to have privileged information that they need not be logged, or use other categories, such as date range or authors, to eliminate documents that need logging. The New York Commercial Court has accepted such categorical privilege logging and encourages it. It is well worth consideration and discussion with opposing counsel.[36]

---

36. For a more detailed discussion of categorical privilege logging, *see* Hon. John M. Facciola & Jonathan M. Redgrave, *Asserting and Challenging Privilege Claims in Modern Litigation: The Facciola-Redgrave Framework*, 4 Fed. Cts. L. Rev. 1 (2009).

Practice Pointer

The time and expense of traditional privilege logging can be potentially reduced or eliminated by exploring the use of categorical logging with the requesting party. Some courts have already accepted such categorical privilege logging, and it is well worth consideration and discussion with opposing counsel.

VIII. FORM OF PRODUCTION

Rule 34(b)(2)(E) provides, in part, that unless otherwise stipulated or ordered by the court, "[i]f a request does not specify a form for producing electronically stored information, a party must produce it in a form or forms in which it is ordinarily maintained or in a reasonably usable form or forms," and that a party need not produce the same ESI in more than one form. Sedona Principle 12 advises that a "reasonably usable form" should take into account the need to produce reasonably accessible metadata that will enable the receiving party to have a reasonable ability to access, search, and display the information where appropriate or necessary in light of the nature of the information and the proportional needs of the case.[37] What is "reasonably usable" may be, but is not necessarily, informed by the ability of the producing party to use the information. In this regard, ESI need not be produced in its "native format" in order to be reasonably usable in most instances, where TIFF+ productions are typically sufficient. In any event, parties should understand and consider the pros and cons of native production, and that responding parties may be subject to repeat productions and added costs if they unilaterally choose a form of production later found to be not reasonably usable.

Practice Pointer

The form or forms of production for ESI should be discussed and agreed upon early in a case, and parties generally should not demand forms of production for which they have no practical need.

IX. SPOLIATION AND SANCTIONS

Sanctions due to discovery violations are often a sideshow that no lawsuit needs. (They are also something that judges hate). The early identification and preservation efforts parties exhaustively undertake ensure relevant information will be available for litigation, but also that a party will not be adversely affected in the litigation due to

---

37. *See The Sedona Principles*, *supra* note 13, at cmt. 12.b.i, 174-76 (2018).

discovery conduct. Courts and parties want litigation to be decided on the merits, not due to a discovery failure. These concerns often led parties to "over-preserve," or retain far more electronic information than was likely to be deemed relevant and produced in a particular action. Such a strategy could result in significant costs and create vulnerability for privacy and protection of the data.

As part of the 2015 amendments to the Rules, Rule 37—the rule addressing the penalties available for a failure to properly preserve ESI—was modified to address "significantly different standards for imposing sanctions or curative measures on parties who fail to preserve electronically stored information." The modifications were intended to address parties' over-preservation. The revisions were thought to bring a more reasonable standard to the inquiry of whether a party should be penalized for issues with preservation of ESI.

Under amended Rule 37(e), for a court to consider imposing sanctions for the loss of ESI, it must find that:

- the ESI "should have been preserved" because of anticipated or current litigation;
- the ESI must have been lost because a party failed to take "reasonable steps" to preserve it; and
- the lost ESI must not be able to be restored or replaced through additional discovery.

In addition, sanctions may only be awarded upon a finding of prejudice to another party or a finding that the party that lost the information had the intent to deprive another party of the information's use in the litigation. Upon a finding of prejudice, the court may award sanctions that are "no greater than necessary to cure the prejudice." A finding of intent to deprive allows the court to presume (or instruct a jury to presume) that the lost information was unfavorable to the party that lost it, dismiss the case, or enter a default judgment.

In assessing whether sanctions are appropriate, courts may consider a variety of factors:

- whether the party was on notice that litigation was likely and that the ESI would be discoverable;
- whether the party received a request to preserve ESI, the clarity and reasonableness of the request, and whether the requestor and recipient engaged in good-faith consultation regarding the scope of preservation;
- the "reasonableness" of the party's efforts to preserve the ESI, including the implementation of a litigation hold and the scope of the preservation efforts;
- the proportionality of the preservation efforts to an anticipated or ongoing litigation;
- good-faith adherence to neutral policies and procedures;
- whether the information not retained reasonably appeared to be cumulative or duplicative;
- the party's resources and sophistication, including whether the party "has a realistic ability to control or preserve some ESI";

- factors outside the party's control, like acts of God or cloud computing disasters;
- adherence to best practices standards and guidelines (e.g., the *Sedona Conference Commentary on Legal Holds: The Trigger and the Process* (2010));
- the steps a party took to acknowledge and remedy a problem once it arose;
- if possible, whether the party sought timely guidance from the court regarding any preservation dispute.

A party can demonstrate the absence of intent to deprive by documenting what information it chooses to preserve and why, and by issuing, tracking, and periodically updating effective legal holds. If a loss of ESI occurs, a party may consider whether any measures can be taken to remedy the problem and avoid prejudice to other parties seeking to use the information, including stopping the loss, determining its scope, seeking alternative sources of lost information, and seeking timely court guidance, if necessary.

Appendix A:
Sample Custodian Questionnaire

Questionnaire Identifying Location of
Custodial and Noncustodial Data

Custodial Data	**Custodial Data** is information potentially relevant to a litigation matter that is in the possession, custody, or control of a custodian. It includes, but is not limited to, e-mail, text messages, instant messages, voicemails, electronic documents, and printed documents, regardless of where they are physically located (i.e., the custodian's smart phone, tablet, laptop, personal computer, or even personal e-mail account).
Noncustodial Data	**Noncustodial Data** includes, but is not limited to, enterprise and/or business unit information, whether electronically stored in shared drives, databases, file share sites, global enterprise systems (e.g., SAP) etc., or in other media. It also includes hard-copy documents and/or tapes sent to storage (either on site or off site).

A. Basic Information
1. Name:
2. E-mail Address/Phone Number:
3. Position/Title:

B. Primary Locations of Custodial and Noncustodial Data
1. Where, primarily, do you work (e.g., which company location(s), at home)?

2. What technology do you primarily use for work (e.g., desktop computer, laptop computer)?

3. Where do you primarily store work product or custodial and noncustodial data you receive (e.g., servers, drives, external media)?

C. Potential Additional Locations of Custodial and Noncustodial Data
1. How many **laptop** computers (both company-owned and personally owned) have you used or are currently using?

    a. How many of these **laptop** computers currently contain custodial and Noncustodial data (including e-mails)? Please list the applicable **laptop** computers and their locations.

2. How many **desktop** computers (both company-owned and personally owned) have you used or are currently using?

   a. How many of these **desktop** computers currently contain any custodial and noncustodial data (including e-mails)?

   b. Where specifically are these **desktop computers** physically located? Please provide location (including actual street address, as the information collection team may need to go to the **desktop** computer itself and download any relevant information).

   c. Where on the computer do you store files containing custodial and noncustodial data (e.g., c:\drive, network drives, shared drives, desktop, My Documents)?

   d. On which servers and in which specific databases or collaboration sites (such as Office365, SharePoint, Google Vault, internal wikis) have you stored custodial and noncustodial data in?

3. Have you used any form of web-enabled mobile devices (either company-owned or personally owned or both) for work-related purposes (e.g., Blackberry, cell phone, iPhone, Android, Treo, etc.) for accessing, storing, and/or creating custodial and noncustodial data?

   a. What specific devices have you used to access, create, or store custodial and noncustodial data? Please list all types of devices used and how many of each.

   b. Where are each of these devices physically located?

4. Have you used external media to store custodial and noncustodial data (e.g., USB flash drives, zip drives, external hard drives, CDs, etc.)?

   a. What types of media have you used?

   b. Where are each of these media/devices located?

5. Have you used internet/intranet sites to access, store, or create custodial and noncustodial data (e.g., any and all portals, public e-mail accounts such as Yahoo mail, Hotmail, Gmail, etc., or Google Docs)?

   a. What e-mail accounts have you kept, both personally and professionally, that contains custodial and noncustodial data? Please list each applicable account.

b. Other than e-mail, what internet sites have you used to store, create, or view custodial and noncustodial data? Please list each applicable site.

6. Do you have any paper copies of information and/or work product (e.g., documents, charts, notes, written correspondence, etc.)?

a. Describe the type(s) of nonelectronic custodial and noncustodial data and work product in your possession, custody, or control.

b. Where is this custodial and noncustodial data physically located? Please list the volume of information, to the extent ascertainable, at each location.

7. Are there any other sources, not noted above, that may contain custodial and noncustodial data (including e-mails) that you have in your possession, custody, or control, such as those located on custodial- and noncustodial-data-owned computers or devices? Please list the type of source (e.g., laptop, desktop, e-mail, etc.) and where it can physically be found.

Appendix B:
Sample Written Legal Hold Notice

Memorandum

TO: Distribution List for Legal Hold Notice

FROM: [Legal Counsel or Legal Department]

DATE: [Issue Date]

RE: **WRITTEN NOTICE OF LEGAL HOLD re:**

[Title of Action or Reference to Dispute]

YOUR ATTENTION PLEASE: This Legal Hold Notice (Notice) contains important legal information regarding the need to save and preserve certain documents and information in response to a [lawsuit/subpoena/investigation] that has been [served/ filed/commenced/threatened] against [name of entity]. **All employees have a duty to ensure that [name of entity] is preserving all appropriate corporate records and information relating to the subject of this [lawsuit/subpoena/investigation].** Please understand that document preservation is both a company and individual responsibility, and we require your full attention and cooperation in this matter. Any failure to follow these procedures may result in severe penalties against [name of entity] and could form the basis of legal claims for destroying evidence. Therefore, please review this memorandum carefully and adhere to the mandatory document retention policy outlined below.

OBLIGATION TO PRESERVE: It is imperative that you immediately take every reasonable step necessary to preserve, and to not lose, alter, or destroy any Potentially Relevant Documents (as defined below). This means that, unless specifically directed otherwise, you must save and preserve every piece of paper and electronic document or data now in existence or that may be created in the future that is related in any way to the subject of this dispute. In addition, you must also ensure that you have stopped any routine or automatic purging, deletion, or destruction of any paper records or electronically stored information that may constitute or contain any Potentially Relevant Documents. This directive, which is sometimes referred to as a "litigation hold," overrides any record retention policy or document or data destruction practice or procedure of [name of entity]. **To reiterate, it is crucial that you make absolutely certain no potentially relevant documents, information, or data are altered, lost, or destroyed.**

The obligation to preserve and retain documents also extends to all other members of your organization. If you are aware of anyone else (whether or not they are currently an employee) who may possess documents concerning this matter who does not appear on the attached distribution list, please let me know immediately. Please do not forward this memorandum to anyone without first advising me and then copying me on the message.

SUBJECT OF THE [LITIGATION/DISPUTE/SUBPOENA]: [Insert brief description of subject matter of lawsuit/dispute/subpoena; 1 to 2 paragraphs at most, written in language a business person will be able to understand easily]. [Name of entity] denies Plaintiffs' allegations and intends to vigorously defend the lawsuit.

POTENTIALLY RELEVANT DOCUMENTS: All documents in your possession or under your control, whether in paper or electronic form, and whether located on your computer, in your office or elsewhere, that concern or relate to any of the following subjects or the subject of the [litigation/ dispute/subpoena/investigation], must be saved and preserved because they may be potentially relevant to this matter:

- [Insert bullet-point list of subject matter areas covered by the legal hold, including description of potentially relevant materials].

PERIOD COVERED BY LEGAL HOLD: You must save and preserve any Potentially Relevant Documents that were created or received from [time period covered by the Hold]. [If applicable, state that the obligation to preserve is a continuing obligation with respect to documents created or received on an ongoing basis.]

DEFINITION OF DOCUMENTS: Please note that "Documents" are more than just paper records. The term "Documents" is used herein in its broadest possible context and covers all computer files and written, recorded, or graphic materials of every kind. It means all documents and **all forms of communication** of any type, and all other preserved data, regardless of the storage media. In particular, the term "Documents" includes, but is not limited to:

- All forms of communication, information, or data recorded, stored, created, or conveyed through physical or electronic means;
- All written documents, of any kind (such as memoranda, letters, handwritten notes, date books, desk calendars, message slips, and files inherited from former employees), including drafts, copies of documents that are not identical duplicates of originals, handwritten notes, calendar entries, and the like, and also including paper copies of electronically stored information and copies of printed documents that include handwritten notes;
- All electronic data or files maintained electronically (e.g., on laptops, PCs, or home computers; cell phones, smart phones, Palm Pilots, Blackberries, or other PDAs; hard drives, portable drives, flash drives, ZIP drives, jump drives, or other removable storage drives; CDs, DVDs, disks, or magnetic tapes; and on e-mail or network servers or databases), including e-mail, presentations, spreadsheets, images, audio files, and other such data, regardless of whether a paper version also exists.

- You should also save any voicemails and or instant messages (IM) related to this matter.
- If your paper or electronic files contain duplicate copies of documents, all must be preserved. Please note that the existence of any back-up tapes or archives does not relieve you of your obligation to retain electronic data.
- All Potentially Relevant Documents must be preserved, including any "personal" copies you have saved separately from any "official" or "company" file.

PRESERVATION IN-PLACE AND IN CURRENT FORM: [Name of entity] has a legal obligation to preserve all paper and electronic documents in the form in which they were created and maintained in the normal course of business.

- For example, if the document is paper-clipped, leave the paper clip on it. If the document has post-it notes on it, leave the post-it notes on it. Documents should be filed and kept as you normally maintain them. If you have a need to discuss or handle a Potentially Relevant Document in the ordinary course of business, that is fine so long as you do not alter or lose it. Do not reorganize documents in response to this memorandum or the [lawsuit/dispute/subpoena].
- Do not copy electronic files and delete the originals, and do not change the format of electronic files (e.g., from MS Word to .pdf). In addition, do not attempt to collect or preserve electronic files yourself. Legal counsel and/or IT staff will advise how potentially relevant electronic files will be preserved and collected in a forensically sound manner that will not inadvertently result in their alteration or deletion.

All files where responsive documents may be found must be retained, including any files that have been sent to storage or to other individuals, or any files kept by you or your assistant. If you have any doubt about whether a document falls within a category listed above, please retain it. For any potentially relevant documents, you should preserve the original and all nonidentical copies and drafts of the same documents. You should preserve the documents in the files in which they would be normally stored and should not segregate or collect them together in response to this memorandum.

You need not create any records that do not currently exist to respond to this request. You must simply preserve all Potentially Relevant Documents described above that have already been created or that are created in the future as part of your normal business activities.

NO UNNECESSARY DISCUSSION: In addition to your preservation obligations, we ask that you avoid unnecessary discussions about any aspect of the [lawsuit/dispute/subpoena]. Your conversations with nonlawyers may be required to be repeated in some legal proceeding later.

Unless otherwise specifically directed by _____ General Counsel's office or outside counsel, you should not create documents or written messages (including e-mails) regarding the [lawsuit/dispute/subpoena] or the parties involved.

If you are directed to or must create such documents, you must preserve those newly created documents pursuant to this notice.

CONTINUING OBLIGATION TO PRESERVE DOCUMENTS: You may be contacted by a representative of _____'s General Counsel's office or outside counsel to discuss the collection of responsive documents in your possession, including electronically stored documents. Even after your responsive documents have been collected, you must continue to preserve them until instructed otherwise by _____'s General Counsel's office or outside counsel. Your preservation obligations are ongoing requirements. Any Potentially Relevant Documents you receive or create after your documents have been collected also must be preserved.

IF YOU HAVE ANY QUESTIONS OR NEED HELP: Please call if you have questions concerning this litigation hold or preserving Potentially Relevant Documents. Your discussions about the matter should be directed solely to _____, one of our outside counsel, or in the event of an emergency where _____ cannot be reached, to _____, _____'s General Counsel. Thank you in advance for your cooperation and assistance.

bcc Distribution List for Written Notice of Legal Hold
(Remove Distribution List Before Distributing Memorandum)

Appendix C:
Sample Stipulated ESI Protocol

UNITED STATES DISTRICT COURT
SOUTHERN DISTRICT OF NEW YORK

ABC GROUP LLC,	Civil Action No. 00-cv-00000
Plaintiffs,	**STIPULATION AND [PROPOSED]**
	ORDER CONCERNING PROTOCOL
vs.	**FOR DISCOVERY OF**
	ELECTRONICALLY STORED
XYZ HOLDINGS, INC.,	**INFORMATION**
Defendant.	

WHEREAS, in accordance with Federal Rule of Civil Procedure 26(f), counsel for Plaintiffs ABC Group LLC ("ABC") and counsel for Defendant XYZ Holdings, Inc. ("XYZ") (collectively, the "Parties," and each, a "Party") have met and conferred regarding application of the discovery process set forth in the Federal Rules of Civil Procedure and the Local Rules of the Southern District of New York, to this case;

WHEREAS, the Parties have reached agreement on certain of the issues discussed regarding such discovery;

WHEREAS, the Parties have entered into this Stipulation and Order Concerning Protocol for Discovery of Electronically Stored Information ("Stipulation and Order") to facilitate the just, speedy, and inexpensive conduct of discovery involving electronically stored information ("ESI") and to promote, to the fullest extent possible, the resolution of disputes regarding the discovery of ESI without Court intervention;

IT IS HEREBY ORDERED that:

1. Scope.

    a. This Stipulation and Order shall govern the discovery of documents and ESI, as described in Fed. R. Civ. P. 26, 33, and 34;

    b. Nothing in this Stipulation and Order shall be construed to supersede or alter any provision of any Federal or Local Rule; and

    c. All Parties are bound by and subject to the terms of this Stipulation and Order.

2. Cooperation. The Parties and counsel are expected to work cooperatively during all aspects of discovery to ensure that the costs of discovery are proportional to what is at issue in the case. The failure of a Party or counsel to cooperate will be relevant in

resolving any discovery disputes and determining who shall bear the costs of discovery. Whether a Party or counsel has cooperated during discovery also will be relevant in determining whether the Court should impose sanctions in resolving discovery motions.

3. <u>Proportionality</u>. The proportionality standard set forth in FED. R. CIV. P. 26(b)(2)(C) shall be applied in all matters related to discovery of ESI, including without limitation the preservation, collection, and production of such information. To further the application of the proportionality standard, requests for production of ESI, including e-mail production requests, and related responses, shall be reasonably targeted, clear, and as specific as practicable.

4. <u>Discovery Motions.</u>

a. No discovery-related motion may be filed unless the moving party attempted in good faith, but without success, to resolve the dispute and has requested a pre-motion conference with the Court to discuss the dispute and to attempt to resolve it informally. If the Court does not grant the request for a conference, or if the conference fails to resolve the dispute, then upon approval of the Court, a motion may be filed.

d. Unless otherwise permitted by the Court, discovery-related motions and responses thereto will be filed in letter format and may not exceed five, single-spaced pages, in twelve-point font. Replies will not be filed unless requested by the Court following review of the motion and response.

5. <u>E-Discovery Liaisons.</u>

a. Each party has identified an e-discovery liaison who is and will be knowledgeable about and responsible for discussing matters related to its ESI.

b. Each e-discovery liaison will be, or have access to those who are, knowledgeable about the technical aspects of e-discovery, including the location, nature, accessibility, format, collection, search methodologies, and production of ESI in this matter.

c. The Parties will rely on the e-discovery liaisons, as needed, to meet and confer about matters involving ESI and to help resolve disputes without court intervention. The Parties agree to work in good faith to schedule conferences concerning discovery of ESI when their e-discovery liaisons are available.

d. The e-discovery liaison for ABC shall be _____. The e-discovery liaison for XYZ shall be _____.

6. <u>Search Methodology</u>.

a. The Parties expect to employ one or more search methodologies, including possibly but without limitation the use of advanced search and retrieval technologies, to identify potentially relevant ESI, including e-mail. The Parties will meet and confer and attempt in good faith to reach agreement regarding:

     i.   methods of searching and, if applicable, the words, terms, and phrases to be searched; and

     ii.   custodians and other sources from which ESI will be collected and searched.

    b.   Once a final search protocol has been agreed to and executed, a requesting Party may, in good faith, seek to expand the scope of the search subject to the limitations set forth in the Federal Rules of Civil Procedure and the Local Rules of the Southern District of New York. Where such a request is made, the Parties will meet and confer and attempt in good faith to reach agreement as to the timing and conditions of such expansion, including whether and to what extent cost-sharing is appropriate. If the Parties cannot reach agreement, any dispute shall be presented to the Court.

    c.   All meet and confer sessions under this paragraph [6] will involve the Parties' respective e-discovery liaisons and will give appropriate consideration to minimizing expense.

   7.   <u>Prioritized Searching</u>.

    a.   <u>Data Sources That Are Reasonably Accessible</u>. The Parties agree that any search for potentially relevant documents and ESI shall initially involve searching for such documents in data sources within which such documents and ESI are likely to be most readily accessible.

    b.   <u>Data Sources That Are Not Reasonably Accessible</u>. Data sources that are not reasonably accessible because of undue burden or cost shall not be considered for search until the search(es) described in the preceding subparagraph have been completed. Requests for information expected to be found in data sources identified as not reasonably accessible because of undue burden or cost must be narrowly focused with factual bases supporting them. Where such requests are made, the Parties will meet and confer and attempt in good faith to reach agreement as to the conditions of any such search, including whether and to what extent cost-sharing is appropriate. If such data sources are determined to be unreasonably accessible, the Parties are not required to use extraordinary efforts to obtain the data.

   8.   <u>Deduplication</u>.

    a.   A Party is only required to produce a single copy of a responsive document. Parties may deduplicate stand-alone documents or entire document families vertically within each custodian or horizontally (also referred to as globally) across custodians. Documents are exact duplicates if they have matching MD5 or SHA-1 hash values.

    b.   Parties also may deduplicate stand-alone documents or entire document families using near-duplicate identification technology, provided, however, that only documents identified by such technology as 100-percent near-duplicates shall be deduplicated. For purposes of this paragraph [8], 100-percent near-duplicates are documents that have identical text content, embedded files, and attachments. 100-percent near-duplicates may have different MD5 or SHA-1 hash values.

    c.   When comparing document families, if a parent document is an exact duplicate or 100-percent near-duplicate, but one or more attachments or embedded files are not exact duplicates or 100-percent near-duplicates, neither the attachments or embedded files, nor the parent document, will be deduplicated.

d. Attachments to e-mails shall not be eliminated from their parent e-mails. Where a stand-alone document is an exact duplicate or 100-percent near-duplicate of an e-mail attachment, the e-mail attachment must be produced and the stand-alone document may be deduplicated.

9. Known Software Files. Known software files identified in the National Software Reference Library database maintained by the National Institute of Standards and Technology need not be collected or produced.

10. E-mail Threads. Where multiple e-mail messages are part of a single "thread," a Party is only required to produce the most inclusive message and need not produce earlier, less inclusive e-mail messages that are fully contained, including attachments, within the most inclusive e-mail message. For the avoidance of doubt, only e-mail messages for which the parent document and all attachments are contained in the more inclusive e-mail message will be considered less inclusive e-mail messages that need not be produced; if the later message contains different text (such as where the later message adds in-line comments to the body of the earlier message), or does not include an attachment that was part of the earlier message, the earlier message must be produced. Where an e-mail thread is withheld from production under a claim of privilege, the Party's privilege log should reflect only the most inclusive message.

11. Production Format for ESI.

a. General Provisions. Except as provided in subparagraph (b), below, documents originally collected as electronic files will be converted to *.tiff image format with extracted or OCR text in accordance with the specifications set forth on Attachment A. After such production in image file format is complete, a Party must demonstrate a particularized need for production of ESI in any other format.

b. Spreadsheets, Desktop Databases, and Multimedia Files. Spreadsheet files including Microsoft Excel (*.xls, *.xlsx), desktop database files including Microsoft Access (*.mdb), and multimedia files including audio and video will be produced in native format. For each file produced in native format, the designation and original file name will be included in a standard delimited load file. For each native file produced, the production will include a *.tiff image slipsheet indicating the production number of the native file and the confidentiality designation, and stating "Produced in Native Format."

c. Enterprise Databases. To the extent that any Party requests information that is stored in an enterprise database or database management system (e.g., Oracle, SQL Server, DB2), the Parties will make reasonable efforts to agree upon production of data from such sources in existing report formats, or report formats that can be developed without undue burden.

d. Time Zone. Unless otherwise agreed, all dynamic date and time fields, where such fields are processed to contain a value, and all metadata pertaining to dates and times will be standardized to Universal Coordinated Time (UTC). The Parties understand

and acknowledge that such standardization affects only dynamic fields and metadata values and does not affect, among other things, dates and times that are hard-coded text within a file. Dates and times that are hard-coded text within a file (for example, in an e-mail thread, dates and times of earlier messages that were converted to body text when subsequently replied to or forwarded; and in any file type, dates and times that are typed as such by users) will be produced as part of the document text in accordance with subparagraph (b), above.

12. <u>Production Format for Hard-Copy Documents</u>. Documents that exist in hard copy will be produced in accordance with FED. R. CIV. P. 34. Documents in hard copy that are identified for production, either by the producing Party or by the requesting Party upon inspection pursuant to FED. R. CIV. P. 34(a), will be scanned to *.tiff image format and produced in accordance with the specifications set forth on Attachment A. Reasonable costs of such scanning will be paid one-half by the requesting Party and one-half by the producing Party.

13. <u>Data and Image Load Files</u>. Unless otherwise agreed, each production of ESI, including *.tiff images of hard-copy documents scanned pursuant to paragraph **[12]**, above, will include a data load file and an image load file in accordance with the specifications set forth on Attachment A. Each Party reserves the right to request data and/or image load files in other formats, and such requests will not be unreasonably denied.

14. <u>Text Searchability</u>. ESI and hard-copy documents that are not text-searchable need not be made text-searchable. To the extent that a Party contemplates or requests Optical Character Recognition (OCR) or other upgrades of ESI and hard-copy documents that are not text-searchable, the Parties will discuss cost sharing for such OCR or upgrades. If a producing Party is requested, and agrees, to apply OCR or other upgrades to paper documents or nontext-searchable electronic images that it produces, then reasonable costs of such OCR or other upgrades will be paid one-half by the requesting Party and one-half by the producing Party. To the extent that, at the time that ESI or hard-copy documents that are not text-searchable are initially processed or scanned, a producing Party makes such ESI or hard-copy documents text-searchable for its own purposes, then it shall produce such resulting OCR or other searchable text at no additional cost to the receiving Party.

15. <u>Use of ESI Produced in Native Format</u>. The Parties agree that prior to using any document produced in native format (including without limitation at any hearing or deposition), the Party seeking to make such will provide the Bates number and MD5 or SHA-1 hash value to the producing Party, sufficiently in advance of such use that the producing Party can confirm that the file to be used is the same as the file produced. Should any document produced in native format be printed to *.tiff image or hard copy, the unique production number and any applicable confidentiality designation shall be placed on each page of such *.tiff image or hard copy. Both the unique production number for the *.tiff image or hard copy and the MD5 or SHA-1 hash value of the native file from which the *.tiff image or hard copy was generated will also be placed on the first page of the *.tiff image or hard copy for identification purposes.

16. <u>Authenticity and Admissibility</u>. Nothing in this protocol shall be construed to affect the authenticity or admissibility of any document or ESI. All objections to the authenticity or admissibility of any document or ESI are preserved and may be asserted at any time.

17. <u>Confidential Information</u>. The Parties incorporate the provisions of any protective order(s) concerning protection of confidential or otherwise sensitive information that may be entered by the Court in these proceedings. For the avoidance of doubt, nothing in this Stipulation and Order shall supersede or alter any provision of the protective order(s) concerning confidential or otherwise sensitive information that may be entered by the Court in these proceedings.

18. <u>Reimbursement of Costs</u>. Except as specifically addressed herein, this Stipulation and Order shall have no effect on any producing Party's right to seek reimbursement for costs associated with collection, review, or production of documents or ESI.

19. <u>Reservation of Rights</u>. Nothing in this Stipulation and Order shall be interpreted to require disclosure of irrelevant information or relevant information protected by the attorney-client privilege, work-product doctrine, or any other applicable privilege or immunity. The Parties do not waive any objections as to the production, discoverability, admissibility, or confidentiality of documents and ESI. Nothing in this Stipulation and Order is intended or should be interpreted as narrowing, expanding, or otherwise affecting the rights of the Parties or third parties to object to a subpoena.

Dated: _____

SO ORDERED:

_____

United States District Court Judge

ATTACHMENT A
TECHNICAL SPECIFICATIONS

A.1.   Image Files. Documents produced in *.tiff image format will be single-page, monochrome, Group IV *.tiff image files at 300 dpi or greater. Original document orientation will be maintained (i.e., portrait to portrait and landscape to landscape). Each *.tiff file will be assigned a unique name matching the production number of the corresponding page. Such files will be grouped in folders of no more than 1,000 *.tiff files each unless necessary to prevent a document from splitting across folders. Documents will not be split across folders, and separate folders will not be created for each document.

A.2.   Document Text. Except where ESI contains text that has been redacted under assertion of privilege or other protection from disclosure, full extracted text will be provided in the format of a single *.txt file for each document (i.e., not one *.txt file per *.tiff image). Where ESI contains text that has been redacted under assertion of privilege or other protection from disclosure, the redacted *.tiff image will be OCR'd, and OCR text will be provided in lieu of extracted text.

A.3.   Word Processing Files. Word processing files, including without limitation Microsoft Word files (*.doc and *.docx), will be produced without tracked changes and/or comments showing. The requesting Party may request that particular word processing files be produced with tracked changes and/or comments showing, and such particularized requests will not be unreasonably denied.

A.4.   Presentation Files. Presentation files, including without limitation Microsoft PowerPoint files (*.ppt and *.pptx), will be produced with comments, hidden slides, speakers' notes, and similar data showing.

A.5.   Parent-Child Relationships. Parent-child relationships (e.g., the associations between e-mails and attachments) will be preserved. E-mail attachments will be produced as independent documents immediately following the parent e-mail record. Parent-child relationships will be identified in the data load file pursuant to paragraph **[A.9]**, below.

A.6.   Dynamic Fields. Documents containing dynamic fields such as file names, dates, and times will be produced showing the field code (e.g., "[FILENAME]" or "[AUTODATE]"), rather than the values for such fields existing at the time the file is processed.

A.7.   Scanned Documents.

a.   In scanning hard-copy documents, distinct documents should not be merged into a single record, and single documents should not be split into multiple records (i.e., hard-copy documents should be logically unitized).

b. If a production includes OCR text for scanned images of hard-copy documents, OCR should be performed on a document level and provided in document-level *.txt files named to match the production number of the first page of the document to which the OCR text corresponds. OCR text should not be delivered in the data load file or any other delimited text file.

A.8.   <u>Production Numbering</u>. Each *.tiff image file will be named according to the production number of the page it contains. Production numbers will:

a.   be consistent across the production;

b.   contain no special characters; and

c.   be numerically sequential within a given document.

Attachments to documents will be assigned production numbers that directly follow the production numbers on the documents to which they were attached. If a production number or set of production numbers is skipped, the skipped number or set of numbers will be noted. In addition, wherever possible, each *.tiff image will have its assigned production number electronically "burned" onto the image.

A.9.   <u>Data and Image Load Files</u>.

a.   <u>Load Files Required</u>. Unless otherwise agreed, each production will include a data load file in Concordance (*.dat) format and an image load file in Opticon (*.opt) format.

b.   <u>Load File Formats</u>.

i.   Load file names should contain the volume name of the production media. Additional descriptive information may be provided after the volume name. For example, both ABC001.dat or ABC001_metadata. txt would be acceptable.

ii.   Unless other delimiters are specified, any fielded data provided in a text file should use Concordance default delimiters, or pipe (|) as field separator and caret (^) as quote character. Semicolon (;) should be used as multi-entry separator.

iii.   Any delimited text file containing fielded data should contain in the first line a list of the fields provided in the order in which they are organized in the file.

c.   <u>Fields to Be Included in Data Load File</u>. For all documents produced, the following metadata fields will be provided in the data load file pursuant to subparagraph (a), above, for each document to the extent that such information is available at the time of collection and processing, except to the extent that a document has been produced with redactions. The term "Scanned Docs" refers to documents that are in hard-copy form at the time of collection and have been scanned into *.tiff images. The term "E-mail and E-docs" refers to documents that are in electronic form at the time of their collection.

Field	Sample Data	Scanned Docs	E-mail and E-docs	Comment
BegBates [Key Value]	ABC 000001	Yes	Yes	Beginning production number
EndBates	ABC 000008	Yes	Yes	Ending production number
BegAttach	ABC 000009	Yes	Yes	Beginning production number of first document in an attachment range
EndAttach	ABC 000015	Yes	Yes	Ending production number of last document in an attachment range
ParentBates	ABC 000001	Yes	Yes	Beginning production number of parent document, if applicable
ChildBates	ABC 000009, ABC 000012, ABC 000018	Yes	Yes	Beginning production number of each document in attachment range; one production number for each attachment
Custodian	Beech, John	Yes	Yes	Name of custodian of file produced (last name, first name)
GlobalCustodian	Beech, John; Maple, Frank; Birch, Janice	N/A	Yes	Where global deduplication has been applied, names of all custodians having duplicate copies of file produced (last name, first name)
FileName	Document1.doc	N/A	Yes	Name of original electronic file as collected
EmailSubject	Changes to Access Database	N/A	Yes	"Subject" field extracted from e-mail message
From	John Beech	N/A	Yes	"From" field extracted from e-mail message
To	Janice Birch	N/A	Yes	"To" field extracted from e-mail message
Cc	Frank Maple	N/A	Yes	"Cc" or "carbon copy" field extracted from e-mail message
Bcc	John Oakwood	N/A	Yes	"Bcc" or "blind carbon copy" field extracted from e-mail message
DateRcvd	10/10/2005	N/A	Yes	Received date of e-mail message (mm/dd/yyyy format)
DateSent	10/10/2005	N/A	Yes	Sent date of e-mail message (mm/dd/yyyy format)
DateCreated	10/08/2005	N/A	Yes	Date that file was created as extracted from file system metadata

Field	Sample Data	Scanned Docs	E-mail and E-docs	Comment
DateModified	10/09/2005	N/A	Yes	Date that file was modified as extracted from file system metadata
FileExten	DOC	N/A	Yes	File extension for e-mail or e-doc
TextPath	Text\001\001\ABC000001.txt	Yes	Yes	Path to *.txt file containing extracted or OCR text
NativeLink	Natives\001\001\ABC 000001.xls	N/A	Yes	Path and file name for native file on production media
Redacted	Yes	N/A	Yes	"Yes" for redacted documents; otherwise, blank
Confidential	Confidential	Yes	Yes	"Confidential" or "Highly Confidential" as designated under Protective Order

A.10. <u>Production Media</u>. Unless otherwise agreed, documents and ESI will be produced on optical media (CD/DVD) or external hard drive. Such media should have an alphanumeric volume name; if a hard drive contains multiple volumes, each volume should be contained in an appropriately named folder at the root of the drive. Volumes should be numbered consecutively (ABC001, ABC002, etc.). Deliverable media should be labeled with the name of this action, the identity of the producing Party, and the following information: volume name, production range(s), and date of delivery. A *.txt file containing the beginning and ending production number of each document should be provided on each production media.

A.11. <u>Encryption</u>. To maximize the security of information in transit, any media on which documents are produced may be encrypted by the producing Party. In such cases, the producing Party shall transmit the encryption key or password to the requesting Party, under separate cover, contemporaneously with sending the encrypted media.

Appendix D:
Sample Stipulated Protective Order

UNITED STATES DISTRICT COURT
SOUTHERN DISTRICT OF NEW YORK

ABC GROUP LLC,	
Plaintiffs,	Civil Action No. 00-cv-00000
vs.	
XYZ HOLDINGS, INC.,	**STIPULATED PROTECTIVE**
Defendant.	**ORDER**

During the course of the above-captioned lawsuit ("Lawsuit"), the parties or nonparties may be required to produce confidential records and information containing trade secrets or other confidential research, development, or commercial information. The parties also may be required to produce documents and information that contain personal identifiers that should not become part of the public record; the redaction of those identifiers may, however, hamper rather than facilitate discovery. The parties agree that such confidential records must be protected from further disclosure. Pursuant to Rule 26(c) of the Federal Rules of Civil Procedure ("Rule"), the Court finds good cause for entry of this Stipulated Protective Order ("Protective Order") to provide such protection. To expedite the flow of discovery material, facilitate prompt resolution of disputes over confidentiality, and adequately protect material entitled to be kept confidential, it is, by agreement of the parties, STIPULATED and ORDERED that:

1. This Protective Order shall apply to all documents, electronically stored information ("ESI") materials, and information, including without limitation, documents produced, answers to interrogatories, responses to requests for admission, deposition testimony, and other information disclosed pursuant to the disclosure or discovery duties created by the Federal Rules of Civil Procedure, that are designated as "Confidential" by the producing party under the terms of this Protective Order.

2. As used in this Protective Order, "document" is defined as provided in Rule 34(a). A draft or nonidentical copy is a separate document within the meaning of this term.

3. Whenever any party or third party in this case (the "Producing Person") is called upon to produce or make available to any other party (the "Receiving Party") information or material whether oral, written, or demonstrative, including any documents, interrogatory answers, admissions, things, deposition testimony, or other information,

the Producing Person or any party may designate that information, whether in the form of documents, interrogatory answers, admissions, things, deposition transcripts, or otherwise, as "Confidential." All tangible items designated "Confidential" shall be conspicuously stamped or written upon each page or separate item by the Producing Person as "Confidential." ESI may be designated by either conspicuous stamping on the medium holding the information (e.g., the CD), or by express written notice to the Receiving Party sufficiently detailed to identify the particular electronic files that are being designated as Confidential.

4. Any party may designate information as "Confidential" upon a reasonable and good-faith determination that such information is confidential and concerns trade secrets, proprietary information, sensitive third-party information, medical records, or other business, personal, or financial information that is not publicly available, or is otherwise protected from disclosure by statute, common law, or by Rule 26(c)(1)(G). "Confidential" information shall not be used or disclosed for any purpose except the preparation and trial of this case.

5. Confidential documents, ESI materials, and/or information (collectively, "Confidential Information") shall not, without consent of the Producing Person or further Order of the Court, be disclosed *except that* such information may be disclosed to:

(A) Attorneys actively working on this case;

(B) Persons regularly employed or associated with the attorneys actively working on the case whose assistance is required by said attorneys in the preparation of trial, at trial, or at other proceedings in this case;

(C) The parties and representatives of the corporate parties;

(D) Expert witnesses and consultants retained in connection with this proceeding, to the extent such disclosure is necessary for preparation, trial, or other proceedings in this case;

(E) The Court and its employees ("Court Personnel");

(F) Stenographic reporters who are engaged in proceedings necessarily incident to the conduct of this action;

(G) auditors, accountants, and insurers of any of the parties who have been advised of their obligation with respect to the Confidential Information provided to them hereunder, provided that the respective party directs each of its auditors, accountants, and insurers to whom Confidential Information is provided to maintain such Confidential Information as confidential subject to all terms of this Protective Order;

(H) Deponents, witnesses, or potential witnesses; and

(I) Other persons by written agreement of the parties.

6. Prior to disclosing any Confidential Information to any person listed above (other than those identified below), counsel shall provide such person with a copy of this Protective Order and obtain from such person a written acknowledgment in the form appended hereto as Exhibit A stating that he or she has read this Protective Order and agrees to be bound by its provisions. All such acknowledgements shall be retained by counsel and shall be subject to *in camera* review by the Court if good cause for review is demonstrated by opposing counsel.

Counsel need not obtain a written acknowledgement prior to showing Confidential Information to persons falling in the following categories:

a. Counsel;

b. Persons employed by, contracted with, or assisting counsel, including consulting experts, copy services, vendors assisting with transmission or electronic storage of documents, or others;

c. auditors, accountants, and insurers of any of the parties who have been advised of their obligation with respect to the Confidential Information;

d. Court Personnel and stenographic reporters;

e. Jurors;

f. Parties in the case, including those who have defaulted, and contractors, employees, or agents of any of them; and

g. Persons who had or have access to the Confidential Information in question through means independent of their production in this lawsuit.

If counsel wishes to show Confidential Information to a person other than those identified above, and that person refuses to timely sign the written acknowledgement, then all parties agree that the deposition of that party may be taken without counting against the total depositions allowed under the Civil Rules. At this deposition, the Confidential Information may be used under the procedures set forth in this protective order.

7. Whenever a deposition involves the disclosure of Confidential Information, the deposition or portions thereof shall be designated as Confidential Information and shall be subject to the provisions of this Protective Order. Such designations shall be made on the record during the deposition whenever possible, but a party may designate portions of depositions as Confidential after transcription, provided written notice of the designation is promptly given to all counsel of record within (30) days after notice by the court reporter of the completion of the transcript.

8. Any Confidential Information (or extract or summary prepared from such information) to be filed with the Court as part of a motion, brief, memoranda, exhibit, or any other writing shall be filed under seal.

9. In the event that any Confidential Information is to be used at any hearing or trial relating to this case, the party proposing to use it must notify the party who produced it at least twenty (20) business days before the date of the hearing or trial, and the parties are directed to work together to determine measures reasonably calculated to protect its confidentiality during such use and to propose those measures to the Court for approval no later than ten (10) business days before the hearing or trial. In the event that the parties are unable to reach agreement on such measures, each party shall submit a proposal to the Court no later than ten (10) business days before the hearing or trial. In any event, the Confidential Information shall not lose its status as Confidential through such use.

10. A party may object to the designation of particular Confidential information by giving written notice to the party designating the disputed information. The written notice shall identify the information to which the objection is made. If the parties cannot resolve the objection within ten (10) business days after the time the notice is received, it shall be the obligation of the party designating the information as Confidential to file an appropriate motion requesting that the Court determine whether the disputed information should be subject to the terms of this Protective Order. If such a motion is timely filed, the disputed information shall be treated as Confidential under the terms of this Protective Order until the Court rules on the motion. If the designating party fails to file such a motion within the prescribed time, the disputed information shall lose its designation as Confidential and shall not thereafter be treated as Confidential in accordance with this Protective Order. In connection with a motion filed under this provision, the party designating the information as "Confidential" shall bear the burden of establishing that good cause exists for the disputed information to be treated as "Confidential."

11. At the conclusion of this case, unless other arrangements are agreed upon, each document and all copies thereof which have been designated as Confidential shall be returned to the party that designated it Confidential, or the parties may elect to destroy Confidential documents. Where the parties agree to destroy Confidential documents, the destroying party shall provide all parties with an affidavit confirming the destruction.

12. By agreeing to the entry of this Protective Order, the parties adopt no position as to the authenticity or admissibility of documents produced subject to it.

13. This Protective Order may be modified by the Court at any time for good cause shown following notice to all parties and an opportunity for them to be heard.

Dated _____.

Entered:

_____
United States District Court Judge

STIPULATED TO AND APPROVED BY:

_____

Counsel for Plaintiff

_____

Counsel for Defendant

EXHIBIT A

<u>AFFIDAVIT</u>

STATE OF NEW YORK   )

)   ss:

COUNTY OF _____   )

_____, being first duly sworn, states that:

1. I have read the Protective Order in *ABC Group, LLC v. XYZ Holdings, Inc.* (Case No. 00-cv-00000), a copy of which is attached to this Affidavit, and I agree to be bound by its terms.

2. I have been informed by _____, Esq., counsel for _____, that the materials described in the list attached to this Affidavit are "Confidential" information as defined in the Protective Order.

3. I have not and will not disclose any information designated or marked as "Confidential" to any other person, firm, or concern, and will not use any such information for any purpose other than the above-captioned action.

4. I hereby submit to the jurisdiction of the United States District Court, Southern District of New York, for the resolution of any dispute regarding the Protective Order or any violations of its provisions.

_____

SIGNATURE

_____

NAME (Print)

_____

_____

_____

ADDRESS AND PHONE NUMBER

SUBSCRIBED AND SWORN to before me this _____ day of _____, 201__, by _____.

WITNESS my hand and official seal.

_____

Notary Public

My Commission Expires:_____

Appendix E:
Sample Rule 502(d) Order

**IN THE UNITED STATES DISTRICT COURT
FOR THE NORTHERN DISTRICT OF ILLINOIS
EASTERN DIVISION**

ABC GROUP LLC,	)))))))))))))	
Plaintiffs,		
v.		Case No. 00-cv-00000
XYZ HOLDINGS, INC.,		
Defendant.		

**STIPULATION AND ORDER
CONCERNING NONWAIVER OF ATTORNEY-CLIENT
PRIVILEGE AND WORK PRODUCT PROTECTION**

WHEREAS, in accordance with Federal Rule of Civil Procedure 26(f)(3)(D) and Federal Rule of Evidence 502, counsel for plaintiff ABC Group, LLC ("Plaintiff") and counsel for defendant, XYZ Holdings, Inc. ("Defendant," together with Plaintiff, the "Parties") have met and conferred regarding application of the discovery process set forth in the Federal Rules of Civil Procedure and the Local Rules of the Northern District of Illinois to this case;

WHEREAS, the Parties have reached agreement on certain issues concerning nonwaiver of attorney-client privilege and work-product protection; and

WHEREAS, the Parties have entered into this Stipulation and Order Concerning Nonwaiver of Attorney-Client Privilege and Work-Product Protection to facilitate the just, speedy, and inexpensive conduct of discovery;

IT IS HEREBY ORDERED that:

Privilege Logging Protocol

1.1 <u>Post-Complaint Documents</u>. Documents generated after the filing of the original complaint in this litigation need not be logged.

1.2 <u>Presumptively Privileged Documents</u>. Documents that are presumptively privileged need not be logged. These are:

   a.   Internal communications within a law firm; and

   b.   Communications solely between outside counsel (including their staff) and in-house counsel (including their staff) related to this litigation or to the related action *ABC Group, LLC v. XYZ Holdings, Inc.,* Case No. 00-cv-00000, in the Northern District of Illinois.

1.3 <u>Asserting Privilege or Protection</u>. The Parties will exchange information regarding claims of attorney-client privilege and/or work-product protection in an efficient manner.

   a.   When asserting privilege on the same basis with respect to multiple documents, it is presumptively proper to provide the information required by FED. R. CIV. P. 26(b)(5)(A)(ii) by group or category. A Party receiving a privilege log that groups documents or otherwise departs from a document-by-document or communication-by-communication listing may not object solely on that basis, but may object if the substantive information required by FED. R. CIV. P. 26(b)(5)(A)(ii) has not been provided in a comprehensible form.

   b.   For documents and ESI that cannot be grouped or categorized and for which individual log entries are necessary, the withholding Party shall provide a listing of such documents and ESI in electronic spreadsheet format, providing as much objective metadata as is reasonably available (e.g., document control number, date, author(s), recipient(s), file type, etc.) and an indication of the privilege and/or protection being asserted. "Objective metadata" does not include substantive content from, or a subjective description of, the document or ESI being withheld.

   c.   Where an individual log entry is necessary for an e-mail thread, the Party's privilege log should reflect only the most inclusive message and need not include earlier, less inclusive messages that are fully contained, including attachments, within the most inclusive message.

1.4 <u>Redactions</u>. Redacted documents need not be logged so long as (i) for emails, the bibliographic information (i.e., to, from, cc: and bcc: recipients, date, and time) is not redacted, and the reason for the redaction is noted on the face of the document; and (ii) for non-e-mail documents, the reason for the redaction is noted on the face of the document. Upon request, made on an individualized basis as to particular redacted documents, and within reason, the producing Party will provide log entries for such particular redacted documents in the manner set forth in paragraph 1.3, above.

1.5 <u>Challenging Asserted Privilege and Protection</u>. If a Party challenges an assertion of privilege or protection from discovery, then the Parties shall meet and confer and make a good-faith effort to resolve such challenges without Court intervention. In the event that the Parties are not able to resolve such challenges, they shall make a good-faith effort cooperatively to classify the challenged documents and ESI into categories that are subject to common factual and legal issues insofar as practicable. Thereafter, the Parties shall jointly present their dispute to the assigned Magistrate Judge in accordance with Local Civil Rule 37.2.

Nonwaiver and Clawback Protocol (Fed. R. Evid. 502(d))

2.1 <u>Nonwaiver By Production</u>. Disclosure of communications and information in this case, in any form and regardless of whether made by agreement or otherwise, shall be without prejudice to and shall not waive for purposes of this proceeding or any other Federal or State proceeding, any attorney-client privilege, work-product protection, or any other applicable privilege, immunity, or protection afforded by law. For the avoidance of doubt, the provisions of this paragraph 2.1 shall apply to all disclosures, privileges, and protections within the scope of Fed. R. Civ. P. 502(d), and further shall apply to all disclosures, privileges, and protections within this Court's authority, to the fullest extent permitted under law.

2.2 <u>Time For Asserting Privilege And Protection</u>. A producing Party may assert privilege or protection over produced documents and ESI at any time by notifying the receiving Party or Parties in writing of the assertion of privilege or protection, except that:

a.   Affirmative use of ESI or a document by the producing Party in the case waives privilege and protection with respect to that ESI or document; and

b.   Upon use in the case by another of ESI or a document that was produced by a Party, where such use is known to the Party, that producing Party must promptly (within 10 business days) assert any claimed privilege and/or protection over it and request return or destruction thereof.

2.3 <u>Disputing Claims of Privilege/Protection Over Produced Documents</u>. Upon receipt of notice of the assertion of privilege or protection over produced documents or ESI, the receiving Party shall either:

a.   Promptly certify in writing to the producing Party that it has returned or destroyed the applicable document(s) and/or ESI, and has made reasonably diligent efforts to identify and destroy each copy thereof and all information derived therefrom; or

b.   Promptly meet and confer and, to the extent the assertion of privilege or protection cannot be resolved amicably after meeting and conferring in good faith, promptly move the Court for an order that the documents and/or ESI be produced. The documents and/or ESI in question may be submitted to the Court. If the receiving party promptly files such a motion, it may maintain the contested documents and ESI pending resolution of the contest by the Court. The party asserting privilege shall have the burden of proving that the privilege or protection exists if any such motion is filed.

Attorneys for Plaintiff   Attorneys for Defendant

_____   _____

SO ORDERED:

_____

United States District Judge

Chapter 11

In-House Counsel's Guide to Insurance Coverage

By Joseph M. Saka and Courtney E. Alvarez

Legal departments at companies often unfairly are considered "cost centers." In truth, the advice and counsel that in-house attorneys provide save their companies substantial sums. With insurance, however, the benefit is measurable. Insurance coverage provides a unique way for legal departments to recover money for their organizations. Most businesses have broad portfolios of insurance policies that may pay for, among other things, costs for investigating a claim or defending a lawsuit, costs for settlements or judgments, loss resulting from property damage, including costs for interruption of a company's business operations, and loss resulting from a theft or data breach. Whenever assessing a claim or loss, in-house counsel should consider whether there is insurance in play. This chapter will provide the tools to conduct an informed analysis.

I. FUNDAMENTALS OF INSURANCE COVERAGE

A. Different Types of Insurance Policies for Different Risks and Liabilities

Just as individuals purchase different types of insurance to protect against different risks and accidents, companies have many types of insurance policies. Common commercial insurance includes commercial general liability, directors and officers (D&O) liability, employment practice liability, first-party property, and fidelity policies. In addition to these common policies, there are a number of policies that are becoming more widespread to address emerging risks, including representations and warranties insurance, political risk insurance, and cyber insurance.

Unlike many personal insurance policies, however, there are significant differences among the policy forms available to businesses. There are wide variations from policy form to policy form, and even seemingly minor differences in language can have drastic ramifications on the scope of coverage. As a result, a careful review of language is necessary in assessing whether coverage is available, and it is best never to assume that a claim or loss is not covered. An examination of language should be done after a claim or loss, of course, but *prudent in-house counsel should review language before a claim is even made.* Corporate policyholders often can request, and insurance companies will accept, revisions to policy language, but companies do not get what they do not ask for.

B. More Than One Policy May Provide Coverage for the Same Liability

Not only are there many types of insurance policies, but more than one policy also may respond to the same risk. A common example comes up in the context of personal insurance. If an employee is backing out of his or her home driveway while talking on a work telephone call and has a collision, the employee's personal automobile insurer, homeowners insurer, or employer's commercial general liability insurer may respond, depending on the facts and circumstances. Former President Bill Clinton famously found coverage for Paula Jones's suit alleging sexual harassment under his umbrella homeowner's policy. More recently, the United States Court of Appeals for the First Circuit found that Bill Cosby had coverage for suits by sexual assault victims alleging defamation under his homeowners and umbrella insurance policy.[1]

Practice Pointer

Coverage can be found in unexpected places. The first step in maximizing insurance is to understand the organization's insurance portfolio and know which policies may respond to a loss or claim.

C. Insurance Law Is State Law Determinative

Practice Pointer

One important point to understand in assessing the availability of coverage is that insurance law is state-law specific. Remarkably, this could mean that a court construing the same exact language and the same exact set of facts could reach an

---

1. AIG Prop. Cas. Co. v. Cosby, 892 F.3d 25, 29 (1st Cir. 2018).

entirely different outcome depending on which state's law applies. Given that there may be significant differences in the law from one state to another, this means that it is important to identify which state's law applies in evaluating whether there may be coverage available for any particular claim or loss.

D. Reading an Insurance Policy Need Not Be Overwhelming

Insurance policies are intimidating. They often are thick documents comprising scores of pages with small, single-spaced font, but once you understand the basic structure, you need not be overwhelmed. Most policies contain five basic sections: (1) a declarations page that sets forth the names of the insured and the insurance company, limits of the insurer's liability, and policy period; (2) the insuring agreements; (3) the exclusions sections; (4) the policy conditions; and (5) the policy endorsements. With an understanding of these five sections, reading an insurance policy will be much more manageable. Even with this knowledge, however, one should not be surprised to find that the language of an insurance policy is unclear—insurance underwriters can be sloppy if not purposefully confusing.

E. Rules of Construction: Tie Goes to the Policyholder

Practice Pointer

Under the law of most states, there are several common rules regarding the interpretation of insurance policies that favor the policyholder. If the language of the policy is clear on its face and there are no ambiguities (including latent ambiguities), the policy will be construed as written.[2] Depending on the state, the court may look to extrinsic evidence submitted by the policyholder to determine whether the language is ambiguous and whether an ambiguity exists.[3] The language should be interpreted to protect the reasonable expectations of the policyholder.[4] Thus, if the language is ambiguous and subject to two reasonable

---

2. Hallowell v. State Farm Mut. Auto. Ins. Co., 443 A.2d 925, 926 (Del. 1982) ("when the language of an insurance contract is clear and unequivocal, a party will be bound by its plain meaning because creating an ambiguity where none exists could, in effect, create a new contract with rights, liabilities and duties to which the parties had not assented").

3. Ahsan v. Eagle, Inc., 287 Ill. App. 3d 788, 790, 678 N.E.2d 1238, 1241 (3d Dist. 1997) (Illinois courts can consider "parole evidence provisionally to determine if an agreement that appears to be clear on its face is actually ambiguous").

4. Terra Indus. v. Nat'l Union Fire Ins. Co. of Pittsburgh, PA, No. C02-4003-MWB, 2003 WL 22023105, at *6 (N.D. Iowa 2003) (policy terms should be ascribed the meaning that a reasonable insured would ascribe to them); Dishman v. Am. Gen. Assur. Co., 187 F. Supp. 2d 1073, 1093 (N.D. Iowa 2002) ("the objectively reasonable expectations of applicants and intended beneficiaries regarding insurance policies will be honored even though painstaking study of the policy provisions would have negated those expectations"); Boelman v. Grinnel Mut. Reins. Co., 826 N.W.2d 494, 506 (Iowa 2013) (Iowa courts invoke the reasonable expectations doctrine when a policy exclusion "(1) is bizarre or oppressive, (2) eviscerates terms explicitly agreed

interpretations, it will be construed against the insurance company as drafter and in favor of coverage.[5] This is true even if the insurance company's proposed interpretation is a better interpretation, so long as the policyholder's interpretation is a reasonable one.[6] At the same time, whereas coverage grants in insurance policies will be construed broadly, exclusions in insurance policies typically are construed narrowly.[7] The insurance company bears the burden of proving that exclusions and limitations in its policy form bar coverage.[8] To meet this burden, the insurer generally must show that the exclusionary language is unambiguous and clearly bars coverage.[9] Policyholders with a good understanding of these fundamental rules may have an early advantage.

F.   Avoid Land Mines in Completing the Application

Even where a claim is clearly covered, insurance companies may seek to avoid their coverage obligation by claiming that there was a misrepresentation in the application for the policy. Policyholders, of course, are well served to be truthful in their applications, but there is language that businesses can include in their insurance policies to reduce the likelihood of an insurer denying coverage based on a misrepresentation. First, the definition of "application" in the policy may include not only the formal application that the business is required to fill out to obtain the policy, but also other materials such as filings with the SEC or other regulators; the narrower this definition, the better for the policyholder. Second, policyholders can request nonimputation or severability clauses.

to, or (3) eliminates the dominant purpose of the transaction"); Hallowell v. State Farm Mut. Auto. Ins. Co., 443 A.2d 925, 927 (Del. 1982) ("the Court will look to the reasonable expectations of the insured at the time when he entered into the contract if the terms thereof are ambiguous or conflicting, or if the policy contains a hidden trap or pitfall, or if the fine print takes away that which has been given by the large print"); Jordan v. Allstate Ins. Co., 116 Cal. App. 4th 1206, 1214 (2004) (ambiguous policy terms should be construed to protect the objectively reasonable expectations of the insured).

    5.   Hercules, Inc. v. AIU Ins. Co., 784 A.2d 481, 492 (Del. 2001) (Delaware courts apply the doctrine of *contra proferentem* and resolve ambiguities against insurers and in favor of coverage).

    6.   PMI Mortg. Ins. Co. v. Am. Int'l Specialty Lines Ins. Co., 394 F.3d 761, 765 n.5 (9th Cir. 2005); Bodell v. Walbrook Ins. Co., 119 F.3d 1411, 1413 (9th Cir. 1997).

    7.   Manzarek v. St. Paul Fire & Marine Ins. Co., 519 F.3d 1025, 1032 (9th Cir. 2008) (insurance coverage is interpreted broadly and policy exclusions are construed narrowly); MacKinnon v. Truck Ins. Exchange, 31 Cal. 4th 635, 648 (2003) (insurance policies are interpreted broadly "to afford the greatest possible protection," whereas exclusions and other coverage-limiting provisions are "interpreted narrowly against the insurer"); Bituminous Cas. Corp. v. Sand Livestock Sys., Inc., 728 N.W.2d 216, 220 (Iowa 2007) (insurance policies are interpreted broadly "to afford the greatest possible protection," but exclusions and other coverage-limiting provisions are "construed strictly against the insurer").

    8.   MacKinnon v. Truck Ins. Exch., 31 Cal. 4th 635, 648, 73 P.3d 1205, 1213 (2003), *as modified on denial of reh'g* (Sept. 17, 2003) (the burden is on "the insurer to establish that the claim is specifically excluded"); Safeco Ins. Co. v. Robert S., 26 Cal. 4th 758, 766 (2001); Hometown Plumbing & Heating Co. v. Secura Ins. Co., 815 N.W.2d 779, 2012 WL 1245755, at *4 (Iowa Ct. App. 2012) ("The burden of proving that coverage is excluded by an exclusion or exception in the policy rests upon the insurer").

    9.   Safeco Ins. Co. of Am. v. Robert S., 26 Cal. 4th 758, 766, 28 P.3d 889 (2001) ("The 'burden rests upon the insurer to phrase exceptions and exclusions in clear and unmistakable language'").

These provisions limit the impact of any misrepresentation to the person with knowledge and preserve coverage for those that did not know of the misrepresentation. In addition, keep in mind that even where there is a misrepresentation, the insurer usually has the obligation to prove that the misrepresentation was material and that the insurer relied on the misrepresentation in selling the policy.[10]

G. Importance of Notice

Too often corporate policyholders forfeit their right to coverage simply because they fail to take one simple step: provide notice to their insurance company of the claim or loss. It is imperative for legal departments to understand what they are required to do in the event of a claim, accident, or loss. Some policies require notice within a certain number of days, some "as soon as practicable," and some within a reasonable time period. Policies also commonly provide specific information on how notice must be provided, including in some instances in a specified form and to a specific location.

Practice Pointer

Even before a claim comes in, companies should have a thorough understanding of what notice is required and a plan in place to meet those requirements. Providing notice is not difficult, and no one wants to be responsible for costing their company millions of dollars simply by failing to check the proverbial box. Importantly, although strict compliance with notice provisions is the best practice, the failure to do so does not always result in forfeiture of coverage. In some states, the insurer has the burden to prove that it was prejudiced by late notice before its obligation will be excused.[11]

H. Settling Lawsuits with Insurance in Mind

Often in high-stakes, complex litigation there are opportunities to enter into an early settlement to resolve a complex claim and avoid the associated expenses and publicity. In the context of liability insurance, before entering into a settlement, businesses must consider carefully the implications on insurance. For example, most policies require the policyholder to obtain the insurer's consent prior to settlement. Although some states will not enforce this requirement where an insurer has denied coverage or unreasonably refuses consent,[12] companies should review the applicable law on the "consent to settle"

---

10.   *See, e.g.*, DEL. CODE ANN. tit. 18, § 2711.

11.   Nationwide Mut. Ins. Co. v. Starr, 575 A.2d 1083 (Del. 1990) (under Delaware law, even if notice is untimely, late notice will not result in a forfeiture of coverage unless the insurer establishes that it was materially prejudiced by the late notice).

12.   Rhodes v. Chicago Ins. Co., a Div. of Interstate Nat. Corp., 719 F.2d 116, 120 (5th Cir. 1983) ("[a] consequence of a breach of the duty to defend is the inability to enforce against the insured any conditions

provision before settling. Additionally, the underlying lawsuit may allege both covered and uncovered claims. In those instances, the policy and the applicable law should be evaluated as to whether the settlement will be allocated between the insurer and the policyholder.

I. Protection in Commercial Agreements: Additional Insured Coverage and Indemnification

In addition to the company's own insurance policies, in-house counsel should not lose sight of protection established by commercial agreements. In a company's business agreements, the other contracting party often agrees to indemnify the company and/or name the company an additional insured under its insurance policies. This is another source of protection that is often forgotten until it is too late.

II. MAJOR COMMERCIAL INSURANCE POLICIES

A. Commercial General Liability (CGL) Insurance

CGL insurance policies are an important protection for corporate policyholders against third-party liability claims, broadly providing defense and indemnity coverage against claims for bodily injury, property damage, personal injury (e.g., false arrest, libel and slander, invasion of privacy), and advertising injury. CGL policies typically are written on standard policy forms developed by nationwide insurance-industry organizations.

1. Explanation of Coverage

Although there may be some variance in language, standard primary CGL policies typically provide the following promises:

> The Company will pay on behalf of the insured all sums which the insured shall become legally obligated to pay as damages because of bodily injury or property damage to which this insurance applies caused by an occurrence and the Company shall have the right and duty to defend any suit against the insured seeking damages on account of such bodily injury or property damage . . . .

As the language suggests, the coverage is triggered when bodily injury or property damage takes place during the policy period. By contrast, "claims made" policies generally are

---

in the policy; the insured is no longer constrained by "no action" or "no voluntary assumption of liability" clauses"); J.P. Morgan Sec. Inc. v. Vigilant Ins. Co., 53 Misc. 3d 694, 701, 39 N.Y.S.3d 864, 869 (N.Y. Sup. 2016), *aff'd*, 151 A.D.3d 632, 58 N.Y.S.3d 38 (N.Y. App. Div. 2017) ("The Court concludes that there is no triable issue that the Insurers effectively disclaimed coverage prior to Bear Stearns settlement with the SEC, which excused Bear Stearns from complying with that term of the policies obligating it to obtain the Insurers' consent before settlement of any matter").

triggered by a claim asserted against the policyholder during the policy period. When a policy is triggered, an insurer owes its policyholder two principal obligations: a duty to defend and a duty to indemnify.

The duty to defend. The insuring agreement gives the insurer the right and imposes upon the insurer the duty to defend any suit seeking covered damages from the policyholder. The obligation to defend is determined by comparing the allegations of the underlying complaint with the language of the policy.[13] If even a single claim potentially falls within coverage, under the law of many states, the insurer must defend the entire action.[14] The insurer's duty arises even when the underlying lawsuit or claim is groundless, false, or fraudulent.[15] Notably, if an insurance company reserves its rights to disclaim an indemnity obligation, a conflict of interest is created, which courts in most jurisdictions resolve by permitting a policyholder to retain independent defense counsel at the insurer's expense.[16]

Unsurprisingly, the insurer's defense obligation generally is extremely valuable to the policyholder. As a practical matter, a policyholder may incur tens of millions of dollars in legal fees for large-scale environmental or product liability claims, even where the policyholder faces a frivolous claim or ultimately avoids liability. Depending on the language of the policy, defense costs may or may not erode the limits of CGL coverage.

The duty to indemnify. In contrast to the duty to defend, the insurer's duty to indemnify more narrowly turns on the actual facts of the third-party claim as developed in the underlying case. The duty to indemnify arises upon the policyholder's legal obligation to pay a judgment or settlement.[17]

2.   Key Exclusions

CGL policies have a number of significant exclusions based on insurance-industry claims experience. The following exclusions are some of the most important to consider:

Pollution exclusions. Beginning in the 1960s and 1970s, the insurance industry began to recognize the potential for exposure for significant environmental liability

---

13.   Brohawn v. Transamerica Ins. Co., 276 Md. 396, 408, 347 A.2d 842, 850 (1975) (under Maryland law, the obligation of an insurer to defend is broad and is judged by whether there is a potential that the allegations of the claim fall within coverage); Aetna Cas. & Sur. Co. v. Cochran, 337 Md. 98, 102, 651 A.2d 859, 861 (1995) ("[A]n insurance company has a duty to defend its insured for all claims which are potentially covered under an insurance policy").

14.   United Servs. Auto. Ass'n v. Morris, 154 Ariz. 113, 117, 741 P.2d 246, 250 (1987) ("the insurer must defend claims potentially not covered and those that are groundless, false, or fraudulent").

15.   Aetna Ins. Co. v. Aaron, 112 Md. App. 472, 481–82, 685 A.2d 858, 862–63 (Ct. Spec. App. 1996) ("[T]he duty to defend arises as long as the complaint against the insured alleges 'action that is potentially covered by the policy, no matter how attenuated, frivolous, or illogical that allegation may be'").

16.   Rhodes v. Chicago Ins. Co., 719 F.2d 116, 120–121 (5th Cir. 1983) ("When a reservation of rights is made, however, the insured may properly refuse the tender of defense and pursue his own defense. The insurer remains liable for attorneys' fees incurred by the insured and may not insist on conducting the defense."); Moeller v. Am. Guarantee & Liab. Ins. Co., 707 So. 2d 1062, 1071 (Miss. 1996) (insurer that provided a defense under a reservation of rights to disclaim coverage was obligated to let its policyholder select its own defense counsel at the expense of the insurer).

17.   Perdue Farms, Inc. v. Travelers Cas., 448 F. 3d 252 (4th Cir. 2006).

claims. The insurance industry responded by adding an exclusion that barred coverage for environmental contamination unless the discharge of pollutants was "sudden and accidental." The language of this exclusion resulted in many lawsuits regarding whether this form of the pollution exclusion barred coverage for gradual, unexpected contamination, with many cases finding in favor of policyholders.[18] Subsequently, the insurance industry modified the exclusion in the 1980s and introduced what is known as the "absolute pollution exclusion." As the name suggests, the exclusion is broad but not without limits. Litigation continues today as to whether this exclusion bars coverage for only traditional pollution or whether it should have broader application. Many courts have reached policyholder-friendly results based on the scope of the exclusion.[19]

Assault and battery exclusions. A typical assault and battery exclusion provides that coverage does not apply to injury directly or indirectly arising from any actual or alleged assault and/or battery. A common dispute relates to whether an underlying suit alleges negligence claims that fall outside the scope of the exclusion, and whether the claims fall within any exception to the exclusion.

Expected or intended limitations. Nearly all CGL policies limit coverage for injury expected or intended from the standpoint of the insured.

Practice Pointer

Insurance companies commonly try to extend the reach of this language so that it applies to all intentional acts, but most courts hold that the language bars coverage only when the damage itself was expected or intended.[20]

Contractual liability exclusions. Many CGL policies contain an exclusion barring coverage for damages that the policyholder is obligated to pay by reason of assumption of liability in a contract. However, there typically are two significant exceptions. First, the exclusion often excepts liability that "the insured would have in the absence of the contract or agreement." Second, to preserve coverage in instances where the policyholder is required to indemnify another business, the exclusion often excepts liability "[a]ssumed in a contract or agreement that is an 'insured contract.'"

---

18.   Hecla Mining Co. v. New Hampshire Ins. Co., 811 P.2d 1083, 1091–92 (Colo.1991); Claussen v. Aetna Casualty & Surety Co., 259 Ga. 333, 335, 380 S.E.2d 686, 688 (Ga. 1989)); Outboard Marine Corp. v. Liberty Mut. Ins. Co., 154 Ill. 2d 90, 120–21, 607 N.E.2d 1204, 1218 (1992).

19.   Century Sur. Co. v. Casino W., Inc., 329 P.3d 614, 618 (Nev. 2014) ("the absolute pollution exclusion does not bar coverage for the injuries caused by carbon monoxide"); Andersen v. Highland House Co., 757 N.E.2d 329 (Ohio Sup. Ct. 2001); Am. States Ins. Co. v. Koloms, 177 Ill. 2d 473, 687 N.E.2d 72 (Ill. Sup. Ct. 1997).

20.   Lassen Canyon Nursery, Inc. v. Royal Ins. Co. of Am., 720 F.2d 1016, 1017 (9th Cir. 1983); Shell Oil Co. v. Winterthur Swiss Ins. Co., 12 Cal. App. 4th 715, 748, 15 Cal. Rptr. 2d 815, 836 (1993).

Cyber and data exclusions. After courts found coverage under CGL policies for liability resulting from several data breaches,[21] the insurance industry in 2014 introduced a broad exclusion "for injury or damage arising out of any access to or disclosure of any person's or organization's confidential or personal information, including patents, trade secrets, processing methods, customer lists, financial information, credit-card information, health information, or any other type of nonpublic information." Policyholders that have policies with this exclusion may have an uphill battle seeking coverage for liability from a data breach, but in-house counsel should not assume that this exclusion necessarily is part of the policy, and several courts have found coverage for cyber liability where policies omit this language.

3. Other Important Conditions and Considerations

Other policy terms may impact the coverage initially promised in the insuring agreement. CGL policies impose various duties and conditions on policyholders, including requirements concerning when and how policyholders must give notice to their insurers of occurrences or claims.

Trigger of coverage. One issue that comes up frequently in disputes regarding CGL policies is determining when the event that gives rise to coverage takes place. In contrast to a "claims made" policy, which is triggered by claims made during the policy, CGL policies typically are "occurrence" policies, which require the injury to occur during the policy period. Where injury is latent and occurs over the course of many policy periods, the "trigger" issue is identifying which policy or policies will respond to a claim. It is important to assess carefully which state or states' law applies in conducting this analysis. Where the date of the injury is uncertain or ongoing, coverage may be available under multiple policy years.

Number of occurrences. Determining the number of occurrences can be a key consideration in assessing coverage under CGL policies. This issue has broad ramifications, including how many deductibles the policyholder must pay and whether a claim is subject to a single limit or multiple limits. Interestingly, sometimes insurance companies will favor a finding of multiple occurrences (so that the policyholder must separately pay many deductibles), whereas other times insurance companies will favor a finding of a single occurrence (so that the insurer's liability is limited to a single limit). As a result, helpful admissions often can be found in past court filings by the insurance industry.

Allocation. Where multiple policies respond to the same claim, questions often arise regarding how liability should be allocated among insurers. Courts have reached varying conclusions regarding this issue. Some have determined that the policyholder can select any triggered policy, and the insurer is required to pay "all sums" for which the policyholder is legally obligated to pay.[22] Other courts, to the detriment of policyholders,

---

21. Travelers Indem. Co. of Am. v. Portal Healthcare Sols., L.L.C., 644 F. App'x 245, 248 (4th Cir. 2016) (applying Virginia law).

22. Keene Corp. v. Ins. Co. of N. Am., 667 F.2 1034 (D.C. Cir. 1981); Nooter Corp. v. Allianz Underwriters Ins. Co., 536 S.W.3d 251, 266 (Mo. Ct. App. 2017).

have found that a "pro rata" allocation applies meaning that the loss is allocated among all applicable policy periods, with each insurer paying a pro rata share of the policyholder's total liability.[23]

B. D&O Liability Insurance

One of the important protections available to directors and officers and companies is D&O insurance. The extent of insurance coverage provided varies considerably among D&O policies. However, these policies often provide valuable protection for cases ranging from mismanagement claims to antitrust cases.

1. Explanation of Coverage

Whereas many CGL policies are written on a form used throughout the insurance industry, D&O insurance is not sold on any one standard form. Rather, each insurance company uses different language for its D&O policy forms. As circumstances have evolved in recent years, each insurance company has continued to modify its policy language. However, there are typically some commonalities among D&O insurance policies.

Practice Pointer

There generally are three main coverage grants: Side A coverage, Side B coverage, and Side C coverage.

Side A coverage provides insurance to protect directors and officers from claims made against them. It does not provide insurance for claims against the entity itself. Under a typical D&O insurance policy, the insurance company agrees to indemnify, or to pay on the behalf of, the individual directors or officers for all "loss" that those individuals become legally obligated to pay arising from a "wrongful act" committed in their capacity as a director or officer. One typical provision provides:

> This policy shall pay the Loss of any Insured Person arising from a Claim made against such Insured Person for any Wrongful Act of such Insured Person, except when and to the extent that an Organization has indemnified such Insured Person.

The individuals covered under a D&O policy often include past, present, and future directors and officers, but the individuals are covered only for claims that allege wrongdoing performed by the director or officer while acting in his or her capacity as a director or officer. This coverage also generally insures individuals who serve as outside

---

23. Boston Gas Co. v. Century Indem. Co., 910 N.E.2d 290, 301, 454 Mass. 337, 351 (2009); *In re Viking Pump, Inc.*, 52 N.E.3d 1144, 1150, 33 N.Y.S.3d 118, 27 N.Y.3d 244, 256–57 (2016).

directors of other corporations at the request of their corporate employer. Coverage also may extend to the spouses of current or former directors and officers.

Side B coverage, sometimes referred to as "reimbursement" coverage, obligates the insurance company to reimburse the corporate entity for all "loss" for which the company is required to indemnify, or has legally indemnified, the directors or officers for a claim alleging a wrongful act. A common Side B insuring agreement provides:

> [T]he Insurer shall pay on behalf of the Company or any Subsidiary, Loss for which the Company or any Subsidiary is required, or has determined as permitted by law, to indemnify the Insured Persons and which results from any Claim first reported by the Company to the Insurer during the Policy Period or Extended Reporting Period, if applicable, and made against the Insured Persons for a Wrongful Act.

Again, Coverage B does not provide insurance for the corporate entity's own liability for claims. Rather, it requires the insurer to reimburse the corporate entity for amounts it has spent to protect individual insureds.

Finally, Side C coverage requires the insurer to pay the corporate entity for the entity's own liability in defending or resolving claims against it alleging wrongful acts. For example, one typical provision provides:

> The Insurer will pay on behalf of the Company, Loss resulting from Claims first made during the Policy Period or the Discovery Period against the Company for which the Company is legally obligated to pay for Wrongful Acts.

The term "Wrongful Acts" often is broadly defined to include "any act, error, misstatement or omissions, neglect, or breach of duty." However, the manner in which terms are defined in D&O policies can be important and warrant special attention.

2. Key Exclusions

Unsurprisingly, D&O insurance policies, like all policies, contain a section that sets forth exclusions that limit coverage for certain types of claims or losses. However, not all policies are the same, and some policies are far less restrictive. Depending on market conditions, insurers often agree to changes requested by their policyholders to eliminate, or narrow the scope of, certain exclusions.

Practice Pointer

Consider working with your broker or experienced coverage counsel to obtain the most favorable language. Some of the most significant exclusions typically found in D&O policies include the following:

Conduct exclusions. These include exclusions that restrict coverage due to a policyholder's misconduct, such as exclusions for illegal personal gain, dishonest acts, or fraudulent or illegal conduct. For more favorable language, policyholders should request that any conduct-based exclusion be removed or, at a minimum, limited to instances in which intentional misconduct is established by final adjudication in the underlying case. Assuming that change is made, the conduct-based exclusions generally will not relieve the insurer from providing defense coverage, regardless of how egregious the allegations of misconduct, nor will they preclude coverage in the case of settlements. Policyholders also should closely examine the allegations of any underlying complaints. If any of the claims in the underlying case are based on nonintentional conduct, a conduct-based exclusion likely will not absolve an insurer of its duty to defend.

"Prior acts" or "prior litigation" exclusions. These include exclusions for claims relating to wrongful acts that occurred prior to a specific date set forth in the policy, or for claims relating to a specified claim or circumstance. Policyholders should be cognizant of any prior acts exclusions and their impact on any existing but unknown claim, and attempt to limit the application of such exclusions.

Insured versus insured exclusions. The "insured vs. insured" exclusion typically bars coverage for claims "by, on behalf of, or at the behest of" the insured company or any insured person against another insured. This exclusion was designed by insurance companies in response to collusive "disputes" between or among companies and directors and officers. However, some insurers have relied on this exclusion beyond its intended purpose to bar coverage for claims by bankruptcy trustees and others following a corporate insolvency. Many courts have rejected this position,[24] but during the underwriting and purchase of D&O insurance, corporate policyholders should consider seeking endorsements from the insurer clarifying that the insurer will not invoke the insured vs. insured exclusion for claims by trustees or receivers in the event of bankruptcy or insolvency.

Hidden limitations on coverage. Intuitively, policyholders may assume that the major limitations on coverage are spelled out in the exclusions section, but with increasing frequency, insurance companies are hiding limitations on coverage in definitions and elsewhere in the policy. For example, the definition of "loss" generally includes settlements, verdicts, and judgments. However, the definition of "loss" may "carve out" not only punitive damages, but also disgorgement and the depreciation of investments. In most states, exclusions must be clear and unambiguous; therefore, these limitations may not pass the test.[25] To avoid these issues, policyholders should carefully review the definitions section to assure that there are no hidden limitations on coverage.

---

24.   Certain Underwriters at Lloyd's of London v. Fed. Deposit Ins. Corp., 16-16702, 2018 WL 509095, at *2 (11th Cir. Jan. 23, 2018); St. Paul Mercury Ins. Co. v. Miller, 774 F.3d 702 (11th Cir. 2014); St. Paul Mercury Ins. Co. v. FDIC as Receiver for Pacific Coast Nat'l Bank, 2016 U.S. App. LEXIS 18811, 2016 WL 6092400 (9th Cir. Cal. Oct. 19, 2016).

25.   Progressive Cas. Ins. Co. v. F.D.I.C., No. C 12-4041-MWB, 2015 WL 310225, at *22 (N.D. Iowa Jan. 23, 2015); *St. Paul Mercury*, 2016 U.S. App. LEXIS 18811, 2016 WL 6092400.

3. Other Important Conditions and Considerations

"Claims-made" coverage. D&O coverage is written on a claims-made basis, which requires that a claim be made against the policyholders during the policy period. Some policies also may require that the claim be reported to the insurer during the policy period. One question that often arises regarding the trigger of the claims-made policy is what constitutes a claim. The definition of "claim" varies from policy form to policy form. The definition will undoubtedly include civil lawsuits; however, it also may include civil investigation demands and subpoenas.

Practice Pointer

The expanded definition of "claim" can be beneficial to policyholders, but in-house counsel should recognize that with an expanded definition of "claim," there correspondingly is an expanded obligation to provide notice to the insurer(s). Note that even if a claim is not made during the policy period, there may be coverage under some D&O policies so long as notice of potential circumstances that could give rise to a claim is provided to the insurer during the policy period.

Be careful during renewal and in replacing insurers. One of the times policyholders must be most careful is when they renew their policies or decide to replace their insurance company. The issue is that existing policies may not cover claims reported after the policy period, and the replacement policies may contain prior acts or prior litigation exclusions. Additionally, some replacement policies may contain a retroactive date limitation barring coverage for claims arising from acts taking place after a specified date. Companies must be aware of the implications of these provisions in view of existing claims and potential claims.

C. First-Party Property Insurance

1. Explanation of Coverage

First-party property policies typically provide two types of coverage: coverage for property damage and coverage for business interruption. The first protects against the risk of physical damage to a company's property. The second is designed to compensate for the financial loss stemming from the disruption of an entity's business and can be either direct (i.e., damage sustained by the policyholder itself) or contingent (i.e., damage sustained by the policyholder's integral third parties, such as suppliers, customers, etc.).

Some property policies cover "all risks" except those that are expressly excluded. Other policies are written on a "covered peril" basis, which means they respond only to losses caused by specifically enumerated events. A typical all-risk policy will provide coverage for loss mitigation, business income losses (including losses caused by damage to any suppliers), extra expenses, debris removal, and blocked access to company facilities. For coverage to be triggered, physical damage is an essential prerequisite in most first-party property policies.

2. Key Exclusions

Corporate policyholders must be acutely aware of potentially applicable exclusions in their property insurance policies. The most significant exclusions include:

Intentional act exclusions. These exclusions bar coverage for loss intentionally caused by the policyholder. This obviously bars coverage when the policyholder intentionally damages property, but depending on the scope of the exclusion it also could extend to damage that was expected based on the insured's conduct.

Water and flood exclusions. At a high level, water and flood exclusions bar coverage for loss caused by flooding, but there are a number of potential exceptions and issues regarding its application. For example, depending on which law applies and the language of the policy, the exclusion may or may not apply to man-made flooding. Given the increasing severity of damaging weather events, corporate policyholders should consider seeking coverage for flood losses.

Enforcement of ordinances exclusions. These exclusions bar coverage for losses resulting from compliance with government-issued ordinances; however, if the ordinance results from an otherwise covered loss, the exclusion may not apply.

Wear-and-tear exclusions. These exclusions bar coverage for loss caused by ordinary wear and tear expected from the use of the property.

3. Important Conditions and Other Considerations

There are a number of important steps that prudent in-house counsel should take in securing coverage for a property loss:

Protect property if possible. Protect material assets by boarding up windows and doors, moving raw materials and finished products to higher ground, and relocating portable property. These steps are not only necessary to minimize a loss, they may be important for maximizing coverage. There are two basic reasons for this. First, loss mitigation may be a prerequisite to coverage. Second, many policies will actually reimburse storm preparation costs.

Promptly notify your carrier. All policies require notice to the insurer following a loss and most provide specific details regarding the timing and manner of that notice. Although policyholders should follow the mandate of each particular policy, it is imperative to provide the required notice as promptly as possible. Depending on the language of the policy and which state's law applies, failing to do so may result in forfeiture of coverage.

Document your losses. It is essential to carefully document all property damaged as well as any resulting expenses. In addition, in the event of an interruption to the operations of a business, organizations should have a protocol in place, such as a daily diary, for recording all actions taken from the time of the loss, including mitigation efforts and extra expenses. Such protocols will ensure accurate and concise records to present to the insurer.

Rely upon insurance professionals. Understanding the applicable policy provisions, comprehensively documenting losses, tendering a formal proof of loss, and interacting with the carrier's representatives can be a complicated and confusing process. Mistakes in the early stages can have a drastic effect on the ultimate recovery.

Practice Pointer

Given the potential complexity of tendering a loss, coverage counsel, insurance brokers, and forensic accountants should be consulted from the outset. For example, in measuring a business interruption loss, there may be several complex ways in which the loss can be calculated. It behooves policyholders to retain an expert who can articulate defensible calculations for measuring the loss to the business.

D. Cyber Insurance

1. Explanation of Coverage

The cyber-insurance market has been described as the "wild west." As one of the fastest growing forms of coverage, there are more than 60 insurers selling dozens of different insurance policy forms with no standardization. Cyber-insurance policy forms are complex legal instruments with extremely technical language.

Given the various policies on the market, policyholders should look for a product that is tailored to their risk, beginning with an understanding of the organization's exposures. Each company will have a different risk profile, depending on several factors such as industry, type of records maintained, and payment collection methods.

Although the specifics of coverage will change, cyber-insurance policies generally provide two forms of protection: (1) third-party liability coverage, i.e., amounts paid in defending or resolving claims by third parties; and (2) first-party coverage, i.e., the business's own losses. Legal departments should assess the risk of third-party claims broadly and look for cyber policies to provide coverage for: (1) lawsuits and written demands from customers or suppliers resulting from a cyber breach; (2) liability for regulatory claims—an increasing risk with the European Union's implementation of the General Data Protection Regulation and the SEC instituting investigations and seeking fines from companies for failing to disclose cyber events; and (3) online media liability for claims alleging that the organization's website contains defamatory or infringing statements. For first-party coverage, policyholders will want to focus on breach response costs, business interruption costs, and costs for data loss and restoration. In addition, businesses that collect payment cards should ensure that coverage extends to payment-card industry fines or fees imposed by bank or credit-card companies for failing to comply with security requirements. Given that cyber risks evolve rapidly, coverage provided by these policies necessitate regular updating. For example, in 2017 and 2018, ransomware attacks and social engineering attacks were the most common cyber attacks, but other risks are anticipated in the years ahead. Companies must remain vigilant for what comes next.

2. Key Exclusions

Just as the scope of coverage varies from cyber policy to cyber policy, exclusions likewise vary by policy form. Although the language of exclusions in different policy forms is not identical, the following are common exclusions included in cyber-insurance policies.

Intentional, dishonest, or fraudulent acts exclusions. Cyber policies frequently include exclusions for intentional, dishonest, or fraudulent acts.

Practice Pointer

To ensure that this exclusion is narrowly tailored, policyholders should seek an exclusion that is applicable only upon a final, nonappealable determination of a court.

Civil fines and penalties limitations. If these losses are excluded, it may be done as a stand-alone exclusion or a carve-out from the "loss" definition. Policyholders should avoid these limitations if possible because these are one of the costs that a policyholder is most susceptible to incur following a data breach.

Acts of war or terrorism exclusions. Some cyber-insurance policies bar coverage for loss resulting from acts of war or terrorism. Given that state actors often have been the culprits behind cyber attacks and data breaches, policyholders should seek policies that do not have such an exclusion or limit the exclusion to narrow factual scenarios.

Laptop exclusions. Cyber policies frequently limit coverage for portable devices. Policyholders can often negotiate to have this coverage added back into the policy by agreeing to provide satisfactory encryption for data on portable devices.

Prior knowledge and/or retroactive coverage limitations. Most cyber policies exclude loss arising from events occurring before a specified "retroactive date," regardless of when a claim is made or a loss is discovered. Policyholders should negotiate the earliest retroactive date possible. The problem is that events thought to be blips often turn into catastrophic events. Sometimes hackers may be inside a company's system for months before the company becomes aware of it. Other times, companies will learn about a cyber event but not appreciate the ramifications. Legal departments should protect their organizations from these contingencies.

3. Important Conditions and Other Considerations

Understand the Underwriting Process. The underwriting process for cyber liability insurance is detailed and comprehensive. Cyber-policy applications typically require the applicants to, among other things, attach their most recent financial statements; answer questions about their practices in connection with vendor contracts; provide information about whether they are compliant with payment-card industry data-security standards; and provide information about the type of data they collect. Cyber-policy applications also seek information about any prior data breach the company has experienced.

Practice Pointer

It is important that policyholders provide thoughtful and accurate information during this process because some cyber insurance companies have focused on policy applications to dispute coverage following a data breach. Additionally, prudent policyholders will take steps at the front end of the underwriting process that can reduce premiums, such as providing additional information where application questions are vague, working with brokers and consultants who understand cyber coverage and technology-related issues, and involving individuals from the information-security department to ensure responses about security practices are accurate.

Beware of sublimits. In some instances, sublimits in endorsements may add coverage that does not exist, but in many instances insurers add sublimits that actually reduce coverage already provided. In-house counsel should carefully review sublimited coverage to ensure that: (1) it is not reducing coverage that the policy otherwise would have provided, and (2) it is sufficient to address the organization's risk and potential exposure.

Understand what to do in the event of a loss or breach. Focused legal departments will have a plan before a loss occurs. Many companies retain a SWAT team—consisting of a cyber coach, attorneys, forensic accountants, and engineers—to take action in the event of a breach. During underwriting, policyholders should ensure that this preferred SWAT team is approved for use by the insurer. Insurance must be part of the plan. In the aftermath of a breach or a loss, policyholders also should have coverage counsel in place that will assess which insurance policies may respond, provide notice to applicable insurers as required under the policies, and document corporate losses in a manner that is likely to be paid. The worst-case scenario is both to have a cyber loss and fail to properly access and maximize insurance.

E. Other Significant Commercial Insurance Policies

Although the foregoing sections discussed four types of insurance policies at length, in-house counsel should not lose sight of other common insurance policies that their organizations may have. To name a few, these include employment practices liability insurance (covering claims by employees alleging wrongful termination, harassment, discrimination, and similar conduct); fidelity insurance (covering loss resulting from dishonest or fraudulent acts by employees or others); pollution liability insurance (covering liability resulting from pollution); fiduciary liability insurance (covering claims alleging mismanagement of an organization's benefit plans); representations and warranty insurance (covering loss resulting from a breach of a representation or warranty in a purchase and sale agreement); and inland marine insurance (covering loss to property in transit). Again, depending on the facts of the specific loss or claim, coverage may be found in more than one policy and sometimes in unexpected places.

III. SEEKING COVERAGE FOR A CLAIM OR LOSS

A. Dealing with a Claim

There are a number of steps that all in-house counsel should ensure are taken in the event the company plans to seek coverage for a claim:

1. **Review notice provisions to ensure notice is provided in a timely manner and any specific requirements are met.** Notice should be provided not just to primary insurers, but also to excess insurers whose policies potentially will be implicated by the loss. Unless called for by the policy, policyholders generally should avoid summarizing or characterizing the claim made against them.

2. **Be careful in communications with the insurance company regarding the claim.** Keep detailed notes of any oral communications and maintain copies of communications with the insurer. Note that depending on the coverage position taken by the insurer and the applicable law, the underlying claimants may be able to discover information shared with the insurance company.

3. **Promptly communicate any offers to settle, especially any offer to settle within limits.** As noted above, many policies contain consent-to-settle provisions requiring an insurer's consent before the policyholder enters into a settlement. The failure to comply with such provisions may result in the forfeiture of coverage. At the same time, a settlement offer within limits may put pressure on an insurer to agree to coverage to avoid exposure for bad faith claims and consequent damages in excess of policy limits.

B. Dealing with a Denial

It will come as no surprise that in some instances, insurance companies might deny coverage for a claim or loss. There are a number of steps that legal departments should consider, short of litigation, to persuade an insurer to revisit its denial:

1. **Build the case for coverage.** In doing so, consider all facts showing that the claim or loss was intended to be covered and is not barred by any exclusion asserted by the insurer. Policyholders should review other language available in the marketplace that insurance companies could have used, but did not use, to clearly bar coverage. In addition, marketing materials and underwriting information should be revisited. Unsurprisingly, the insurer's representations when marketing and selling a policy are frequently inconsistent with positions taken following a claim or loss. Once this information has been collected,

policyholders should educate the claims handler about the case for coverage and speak to a supervisor if necessary.

2. **Bring business relationships to the table.** The insurance industry is a business built on relationships. Policyholders seeking coverage should lean on business relationships with brokers, insurance companies, and coverage counsel to try to reach a positive result.

3. **Demand to settle within limits.** In the context of a third-party liability claim, if the insurer receives a demand to settle within limits and refuses, and a verdict later comes back in excess of the limits, the insurer may be liable to pay the full amount of the judgment, including the amount in excess of the insurer's policy limits.

4. **Submit an insurance department inquiry.** Many states have a process whereby complaints can be filed against insurers based on improper claims handling. Although the approach of regulators varies by state, the inquiry alone may put pressure on the insurance company and force it to focus on the claim.

5. **Request mediation.** Many policies now have provisions requiring mediation before a lawsuit can be filed. Even where such language is not included, there may be a benefit to requesting an early mediation. Although the mediator's views are not binding on either side, mediation often forces parties to focus on the strengths and weaknesses of their cases. There are a few important points to consider in moving forward with mediation. First, the selection of the mediator can be crucial. Given that the insurance industry has hundreds of mediators on its roster, it is important to find someone who does not treat the insurance industry as a client. Second, the identity of the insurer's representatives at the mediation can be important. Those attending for the insurer should have authority to settle at the full amount of the demand. Finally, corporate policyholders should articulate the amount of their full claim without leaving anything on the table, including attorney's fees, prejudgment interest, and any bad-faith damages.

6. **Litigating insurance disputes.** In some instances, litigation will be necessary to obtain coverage. Before proceeding with litigation, in-house counsel should evaluate and understand whether litigation is likely to move the case toward resolution or lead to years of disputes. As a plaintiff seeking coverage, corporate policyholders should seek an early trial date and attempt to keep the schedule. However, businesses should not lose sight of the potential benefit of discovery from insurance companies. Sources of discovery from an insurer's files, such as drafting history, claims documents, reinsurance communications, and loss reserve information, often contain a treasure trove of helpful admissions.

When an organization experiences a significant claim or loss, in-house counsel undoubtedly has multiple priorities. The organization's insurance coverage should not get lost in the flurry. Corporate counsel's focus on available insurance may provide the best opportunity to recoup losses and to minimize the organization's exposures.

Chapter 12

What Is a Trademark or Service Mark?

By Terese L. Arenth

This chapter is intended to provide an overview of basic trademark rights and registrations in the United States. It covers the legal framework for trademark protection, what a trademark protects, and the requirements for obtaining federal trademark protection. It also discusses the process for applying for, securing, and maintaining federal trademark registrations with the U.S. Patent and Trademark Office. It further addresses trademark protection in the digital age, cybersquatting, and one of the most utilized administrative proceedings for the resolution of domain name disputes.

A trademark is a word, phrase, symbol, or design, or a combination thereof, used in commerce to identify and distinguish the goods of one manufacturer or seller from those of another, and to indicate the source of the goods.[1] Put more simply, a trademark is nearly anything that can serve to identify the source of goods. Although traditional types of trademark are words, names, phrases, symbols, images, designs, logos, or slogans, or any combination thereof, there are also nontraditional types of trademark, such as sound, scent, product packaging, shape, or color.

A service mark is the same as a trademark, except that it identifies and distinguishes the source of services rather than goods. For purposes of this chapter, use of the terms "mark" and "trademark" refers to both trademarks and service marks.

---

1. *See* 15 U.S.C. § 1127.

A website domain name can function as a trademark if it is used to identify goods or services and not simply as a website address.

A trade name is the name of a company or business. A trade name does not typically function as a trademark when it is used only to identify the company or business and not any particular product or service. However, a trade name can receive trademark protection if it is used to identify the source or origin of a product or service.

Trade dress refers to the look and feel of a product, service, or product packaging or labeling. It is the overall appearance or impression created by the design and appearance elements. To be protected as a trademark or service mark, trade dress must be both distinctive and nonfunctional. Trade dress includes such features as color schemes, textures, sizes, designs, shapes, graphic decorations, and placement of words. Trade dress protection has been legally found for things such as a restaurant's décor, menu, and style; the appearance of a piece of furniture; and the shape of a beverage bottle. To demonstrate the distinctiveness of trade dress, the required proof differs based upon whether protection is sought for packaging/labeling or product design. Packaging and labeling may either be inherently distinctive or acquire distinctiveness through use. Product design, however, can never be inherently distinctive and is protectable only on a showing of secondary meaning.

I.   THE SCOPE OF TRADEMARK PROTECTION

Generally speaking, trademark protection extends to the scope of use, which is defined both geographically and by the goods or services for which the mark is used.

A. Geographic Scope

A trademark registered on the federal register provides nationwide protection of the mark. This is in contrast to common-law rights, which are limited to the geographic region in which the mark is used. For use of the mark outside the United States, a trademark owner should consider conducting trademark clearance and registering the mark in the relevant foreign jurisdictions.

B. Goods and Services

In general, a trademark protects, and may be registered for, the specific goods and services for which the mark is used. The likelihood-of-confusion standard for trademark infringement allows trademark owners to prevent others from using the mark on goods or services that are similar or related, but not identical, to those of the trademark owner.

C. Famous Marks

Famous marks have a broader scope of protection, including under the federal Trademark Dilution Revision Act of 2006 (TDRA)[2] and state trademark dilution statutes. Dilution of a trademark occurs when the unauthorized use of a mark impairs its distinctive quality by (1) blurring, where the mark is weakened by its identification with dissimilar goods, or (2) tarnishment, where the mark is damaged by reason of its association with inferior or unseemly goods or services. Unlike trademark infringement, trademark dilution does not require a showing of likelihood of confusion.

II. REQUIREMENTS FOR FEDERAL TRADEMARK PROTECTION

To obtain federal trademark protection for a mark, the following requirements must be met: (1) use in commerce; (2) distinctiveness; (3) no likelihood of confusion; and (4) eligibility for trademark registration under the Lanham Act, which is the primary federal trademark statute under U.S. law.[3]

A. Use in Commerce

For federal trademark protection, trademark rights are obtained by being the first to use the mark in commerce for the relevant goods or services. Under the Lanham Act, "use in commerce" means the bona fide use of a mark in the ordinary course of trade. It does not include use merely to reserve a right in the mark.

A mark is deemed to be used in commerce when:

1. goods are sold or transported in commerce and the mark is displayed: (a) on the goods or their containers; (b) in association with the goods or on tags or labels affixed to the goods; or (c) on documents associated with the goods, if the nature of the goods makes placement of the mark on the goods impracticable; and

2. services are rendered in commerce, and the mark is used or displayed on materials to advertise or sell the services.

In order to obtain federal trademark protection, the goods or services must be provided, advertised, or sold either in interstate commerce or in commerce between the United States and a foreign country.

B. Distinctiveness

To be protectable as a trademark, a mark must be distinctive, meaning that it identifies a good or service as originating from a single source. There are five general categories

---

2. Pub. L. No. 109-312, § 2, 120 Stat. 1730 (2006) (codified at 15 U.S.C. §1125(c)(2)(A)).
3. 15 U.S.C. § 1051 *et seq.*

for evaluating whether a mark is distinctive and may be protectable as a trademark: (1) fanciful; (2) arbitrary; (3) suggestive; (4) descriptive; and (5) generic.

Fanciful, arbitrary, and suggestive marks are deemed to be inherently distinctive and can immediately identify the source of a specific product or service. These types of marks can be registered on the Principal Register of the United States Patent and Trademark Office (USPTO) (see Part IV-A, *infra*) without showing that they are recognized as identifying the source of a good or service. Descriptive marks are not inherently distinctive and can be protected as trademarks only if they can be shown to have attained distinctiveness (referred to as "secondary meaning,") through use in commerce. Generic terms are unprotectable and can never function as a trademark.

1. Fanciful Marks

Fanciful marks are terms that are coined for use as a trademark and have no previous common meaning in the dictionary. Examples of fanciful marks include: POLAROID for instant photo cameras; KODAK for film and cameras; and EXXON for oil and gas. Fanciful marks receive the broadest trademark protection and are generally considered the strongest marks. The reasons for this include that a coined term is capable of creating a strong association with the product because it has no other meaning, and it is more likely and generally easier to prove that a second user of a coined term is trading on the goodwill of the owner's mark.

2. Arbitrary Marks

Arbitrary marks use words that are in common use but bear no relationship to the associated goods or services. They may have common meaning, but they do not suggest or otherwise describe the goods or services for which they are used. Examples of arbitrary marks include: APPLE for computers and IVORY for soap.

3. Suggestive Marks

Suggestive marks suggest some quality or character of the associated goods or services, but do not directly describe the goods or services. Rather, thought and imagination are needed to connect the goods or services to the trademark. Examples of suggestive marks include: COPPERTONE for suntan lotion or EVEREADY for batteries.

4. Descriptive Marks

Descriptive marks are marks that describe a good or service or one or more of its features, such as its qualities, ingredients, function, purpose, or use. Descriptive marks are not inherently distinctive and are not automatically entitled to trademark protection because they do not immediately identify the source of the good or service, but immediately convey information about the nature of the goods or services. However, through use over time, a descriptive mark may come to be associated in consumers' minds with a single source of a good or service, in which case the mark acquires "secondary meaning" and can be protected as a trademark. Examples of descriptive terms that have acquired secondary meaning include: INTERNATIONAL BUSINESS MACHINES for computers; SHARP for televisions and monitors; and BEST BUY for a store that sells electronics. Descriptive marks cannot be registered on the Principal Register unless they have acquired secondary meaning. However, if a descriptive term is capable of distinguishing the goods and services, they may be registered on the USPTO's Supplemental Register (see Part IV-B, *infra*).

5.   Generic Terms

A generic term is a common group or class name to which a particular product belongs. It defines or is the dictionary term for a product or service. A generic term can never function as a trademark because it cannot designate a particular source for the identified goods or services. Certain terms are generic by their nature. Examples of generic terms are "shoes," "beer," or "automobile." Some trademarks become generic and lose their trademark protection because consumers use the mark to describe an entire class of products or services. Examples of trademarks that were once famous and have now become generic terms include: ASPIRIN (which was once a trademark of Bayer but is now used generically to describe the pain relieving drug acetylsalicylic acid) and ESCALATOR (which was once a trademark of Otis Elevator but is now used generically to describe a moving stairway).

A term's distinctiveness must be evaluated in the context of the goods and services for which it is used. By way of example, although the term APPLE is generic for the fruit, it is arbitrary for computers.

C.   No Likelihood of Confusion

Trademark protection can only be granted to a mark in which there is no likelihood of confusion with another mark.[4] Likelihood of confusion is the standard for trademark infringement and exists if marks used by two unrelated parties are so similar that consumers are likely to believe that the products or services have a single source. In determining likelihood of confusion, marks may be examined to see if they (1) look the same, (2) sound the same, or (3) have the same meaning.

Although any one of these elements may be sufficient to establish a likelihood of confusion, other factors may also be taken into consideration. A finding of likelihood of confusion does not require that the conflicting marks, or the goods and services on which they are used, be identical.

In the case of *In Re E. I. du Pont de Nemours & Co.*,[5] the court set forth 13 factors (the *DuPont* factors) to be weighed in determining whether one mark is likely to be confused with another: (1) the similarity or dissimilarity of the marks in their entireties as to appearance, sound, connotation, and commercial impression; (2) the similarity or dissimilarity of the goods for which the marks are used; (3) the similarity of the

---

4.   *See id.* § 29(d).
5.   476 F.2d 1357, 177 U.S.P.Q. 563 (C.C.P.A. 1973).

channels of trade of the goods for which the marks are used; (4) the sophistication of purchasers—impulse buying versus careful, sophisticated purchasing; (5) the fame of the senior mark; (6) the number and nature of similar marks in use on similar goods; (7) the nature and extent of any actual confusion; (8) the length of time under which there has been concurrent use without evidence of actual confusion; (9) the variety of goods on which a mark is used; (10) the market interface between the junior and senior users (consents to use, agreements designed to preclude confusion); (11) the extent to which the applicant has the right to exclude others from use of its mark on its goods— the strength of the mark; (12) the extent of potential confusion; and (13) any other established fact probative of the effect of use.

D. Eligibility for Trademark Registration under the Lanham Act

The Lanham Act and USPTO regulations specify the eligibility of marks for federal registration. Not all words, symbols, logos, and devices can be registered as trademarks, and certain types of subject matter cannot be registered at all.

Aside from confusingly similar marks and generic terms, other types of marks that cannot serve as trademarks are deceptive marks, which falsely describe the material content of a product or marks that are geographically deceptive, as well as marks that "disparage, falsely suggest a connection, or bring into contempt or disrepute" any person, institution, belief, or national symbol.[6] Other types of marks that cannot serve as trademarks are: (1) marks that contain the flag or coat of arms or other insignia of the United States, or of any state or municipality, or of any foreign nation, or any simulation thereof; and (2) marks that contain a name, portrait, or signature identifying a particular living individual except by his or her written consent, or that of a deceased president during the life of his or her widow/widower, except by the widow's/widower's written consent.

Product or package design elements that are functional and not purely decorative are also unregistrable. A feature of a product or its package is functional if it is either essential to the use or purpose of the product, or affects the cost or quality of the product.

III. ACQUIRING RIGHTS IN MARKS

Trademark protection can arise at both the state and federal level. At the state level, trademarks may be protected in some states by statute, including state trademark and unfair competition statutes. They may also be protected by common-law rights that arise from actual use of a mark in commerce, whether it is the subject of a federal registration or not. In the United States, common-law trademark rights generally belong to the first party to use the mark. Although a federal application may be filed with the USPTO based on intent to use, this does not grant registration, and no rights attach to the mark until the applicant begins using it on the products or services specified in the application.

---

6. Matal v. Tam, 137 S. Ct. 1744 (2017).

Rights in unregistered marks, however, are limited in scope and generally extend only to the territory in which the mark is used.

At the federal level, trademarks are protected primarily under the Lanham Act. The USPTO is the federal agency that administers the Lanham Act and regulates registration of trademarks on the federal trademark register.

The Lanham Act allows trademark owners to enforce their trademark rights through statutory causes of action for trademark infringement and similar unfair competition claims, including infringement of a registered trademark, counterfeiting of a registered trademark, trademark dilution, false advertising, and passing off.

The Lanham Act also sets forth the procedures and requirements for registering trademarks on the federal trademark register.

Practice Pointer

Although federal registration is not required for protection under the Lanham Act, it does provide a trademark owner with significant benefits and more expansive rights than those available to the owner of an unregistered mark under either the Lanham Act or state law.

IV. FEDERAL TRADEMARK REGISTRATION BENEFITS AND PROCESS

Although it is not necessary to register a trademark on the federal trademark register, federal registration does provide a trademark owner with substantial benefits and more expansive rights than those available to unregistered marks under the Lanham Act or state law.

A. The Principal Register

Federal registration on the Principal Register has many advantages, which include prima facie evidence of validity and the registrant's ownership of the mark; presumed nationwide use of the mark; federal court subject-matter jurisdiction over infringement and other trademark claims, without a showing of diversity or minimum amount in controversy; statutory remedies for federal infringement claims, including, under certain circumstances, treble damages and recovery of attorney's fees and costs; constructive notice of ownership, which eliminates the defenses of good-faith use and innocent adoption by an infringer; the right to use the designation ® and other notices of federal registration; a basis for registering the mark in foreign jurisdictions; a recording with U.S. Customs to stop the importation of infringing, counterfeit, and gray-market goods; and after five years, subject to limited exceptions, incontestable, conclusive evidence of the trademark owner's exclusive rights to use the mark.

B. The Supplemental Register

If a term does not qualify for registration on the Principal Register, it may be eligible for registration on the Supplemental Register. For inclusion on the Supplemental Register, a mark must be capable of distinguishing the applicant's goods or services; unregistrable on the Principal Register; not otherwise registrable; and either lawfully used in commerce or registered in a foreign country where the trademark owner has an office.

Registration on the Supplemental Register is most common for marks that are merely descriptive and the applicant cannot yet demonstrate secondary meaning. Benefits of registration on the Supplemental Register include federal court subject-matter jurisdiction over infringement and related unfair-competition claims; the ability to be cited by trademark examiners against later applications to register similar marks; inclusion in trademark search results, which may deter third parties from adopting similar marks; and the right to use the designation ® and other notices of federal registration.

Practice Pointer

Registration on the Supplemental Register does not, however, provide trademark rights beyond common-law rights and the advantages provided by registration on the Principal Register (see discussion *supra*).

It is possible to file an application requesting registration on the Supplemental Register. In most cases, however, applicants apply for registration on the Principal Register and can then amend the application to the Supplemental Register if the USPTO refuses registration because of descriptiveness. A trademark must be used in commerce or based on a foreign registration to qualify for registration on the Supplemental Register.

Practice Pointer

Applications based on intent to use cannot be filed for or converted to the Supplemental Register until a Statement of Use or Amendment to Allege Use is filed.

The Lanham Act permits the filing of an intent-to-use trademark application for a mark that is not yet in use if the applicant has a bona fide intent to use it for the goods or services listed in the application. Benefits of filing intent-to-use applications include the fact that if the mark becomes registered, the filing date of the application is deemed to be the date of first use, the provision of a priority date that is earlier than actual use, and the fact that the owner can determine whether the mark is registrable and address any obstacles to registration before making substantial investments in the mark.

C. The Registration Process

The trademark registration process generally consists of three phases: (1) clearing the trademark for use and registration; (2) preparing and filing the trademark registration application; and (3) responding to and addressing issues raised, if any, during the application review process. Issues may be raised by the trademark examiner in an Office Action and by third parties in opposition proceedings.

Assuming the application proceeds to registration, the entire process of obtaining a federal trademark registration usually takes one to two years from the filing of the application. That timing is dependent upon several factors, however, including the extent, if any, to which the USPTO or third parties object to registration of the mark, and any backlog of pending applications.

1.   Trademark Clearance

Before applying for federal trademark registration or using the mark, the brand owner should conduct trademark clearance. The clearance process involves conducting one or more trademark searches, analyzing the search results, and issuing an opinion. Trademark clearance helps brand owners evaluate whether the proposed mark qualifies for trademark protection and federal registration. It also helps identify and address risks presented by existing or proposed uses of the mark.

Advantages of trademark clearance in the initial phases of adopting a new mark include avoiding or reducing investment in a trademark that is unavailable for use or registration, reducing the risk of third-party objections to use and registration of the proposed mark, assisting in drafting the application to address issues uncovered in the search, and helping to evaluate the strength of a proposed trademark.

A well-structured trademark search should identify the most significant risks of using a mark.

Practice Pointer

Trademark owners should be cognizant that searches and clearance cannot identify all issues. An analysis of eligibility and availability for use and registration requires knowledge of trademark law and is typically performed by an experienced trademark attorney.

2.   Trademark Search

Although the scope can vary, trademark searches generally include a search of the federal trademark register administered by the USPTO, state trademark registers, various other publicly available publications and databases relating to relevant products and services, and the internet. A trademark search is usually performed in two stages: a preliminary (knock-out) search, followed by a comprehensive (full) search.

A knock-out search aims to identify marks that are visually, conceptually, and phonetically similar to the proposed mark and that cover the same or similar goods or services. Although the scope of knock-out searches is limited, they can help the brand owner avoid the expense of a full search, for example if a clearly blocking trademark is uncovered, and choose from a selection of alternative trademarks, especially if there are budgetary issues.

The scope of a knock-out search is typically limited to information that is free and easy to access online, including online searches of the USPTO database of federal trademark registrations and applications using the USPTO's Trademark Electronic Search System (TESS), basic internet searches for direct hits, and WHOIS domain-name registry searches for specific domain names.

Full searches are necessary to conduct a more thorough risk assessment of existing registrations, applications for registration, and common-law uses of similar marks. They involve a more thorough search of federal applications and registrations, and cover a wide range of additional publicly available information, including databases of state trademark registrations maintained by state trademark offices, and common-law uses, including searches of the internet, business/trade name directories, databases of periodicals, domain name registries, and dictionaries. If the business expects to use the mark internationally, a full search may also include registries and common-law uses in selected foreign jurisdictions.

Some law firms that specialize in trademark law have in-house search capabilities, and several third-party vendors also offer trademark searching services.

Practice Pointer

Most third-party vendors do not provide an analysis of the search results or an opinion on the risks associated with using and registering a proposed mark, however.

---

3.   Analyzing Search Results and Opinion

Analyzing search results focuses on whether the proposed mark meets the criteria for federal registration and is likely to cause confusion about source, sponsorship, or affiliation with a previously used or registered trademark. The most obvious issues identified by trademark searches involve identical marks for similar goods or services (referred to as direct hits). However, evaluating likelihood of confusion requires consideration of many other issues, including that:

- marks that share a prefix or suffix with the proposed mark may present a likelihood of confusion, especially if the goods or services are similar or related, or the senior owner has several marks with that prefix or suffix;
- abandoned, canceled, or expired applications or registrations may continue to indicate obstacles because the mark may still be in actual use despite the lack of a valid federal trademark registration, or if the abandonment, cancellation,

or expiration resulted from a USPTO rejection or adversarial action by another party, then the proposed mark may face a similar objection; and

- well-known registered marks could be an obstacle to use and registration of the proposed mark.

Properly evaluating search results often requires further investigation to determine, among other things, whether a mark is in use or whether the owner of a mark has defended its rights against marks similar to the proposed mark. Both likelihood of confusion and distinctiveness are fact-based determinations that involve subjective judgment and require knowledge of trademark law.

Practice Pointer

It is therefore advisable to have trademark search results analyzed by an experienced trademark attorney.

---

4.   Application Process and Considerations

After trademark clearance is complete, if the business decides to proceed with registering a mark, it should prepare and file the application with the USPTO. Most applications are now filed online using the USPTO's Trademark Electronic Application System (TEAS), although applicants can still file paper applications. All information submitted to the USPTO at any point in the application and/or registration process will become public record.

5.   Filing Basis

To file a trademark application, you must claim any of the following as a filing basis: (1) use in commerce; (2) intent to use; (3) qualified foreign applicant; and (4) extension of protection to the United States under the Protocol Relating to the Madrid Agreement Concerning International Registration of Marks. Use in commerce and intent to use are the two most common bases.

1. **Use in Commerce.** A use-based (section 1(a)) application is based on existing use of the mark in interstate commerce.[7] The claimed use must be a bona fide use in the ordinary course of trade and not use solely made to reserve trademark rights.

2. **Intent to Use.** An intent-to-use (ITU or section 1(b)) application is based on a bona fide intent to use the mark in connection with the goods or services, or both, listed in the application even though actual use has not yet taken place.[8] The USPTO examines and publishes ITU applications in the same manner

---

7. 15 U.S.C. § 1(a).
8. *Id.* § 1(b).

as use-based applications. However, the USPTO will not issue a registration until the applicant files an Amendment to Allege Use or Statement of Use and appropriate evidence showing that the mark has been used in commerce.

3. **Qualified Foreign Applicant.** A foreign entity that owns an application or registration for the mark in another country can use this basis (section 44 applications).[9] Unlike applications based on use and intent to use, section 44 applications do not require the filing of evidence of use before registration issues. Use is not required to obtain the registration, but the owner must eventually use the mark to maintain the registration. Section 44(d) of the Lanham Act[10] provides for a priority filing date to eligible applicants who have filed an application in a treaty country as defined by section 44(b). If an eligible applicant files the U.S. application claiming section 44(d) priority within six months of filing the first application to register the mark in a treaty country, the filing date of the first-filed foreign application is the effective filing date of the U.S. application. To be eligible for a priority filing date under section 44(d), an applicant must meet the following requirements: (1) the applicant's country of origin must be a party to an international treaty or agreement with the United States that provides a right of priority, or must extend reciprocal rights to priority to U.S. nationals; and (2) the foreign application that is the basis for the priority claim must be filed in a country that either is a party to a treaty or agreement with the United States that provides a right of priority, or extends reciprocal rights to priority to U.S. nationals.[11]

4. **Extension of Protection to the United States under the Madrid Protocol.** The Madrid Protocol[12] is a trademark filing treaty that facilitates registering trademarks in several countries. Under the treaty, an owner of a trademark application or registration in its home country can file a single application to seek registration in other countries that are parties to the treaty, including the United States. WIPO administers the international registration process. The owner of an international registration may seek to extend the protection of the home registration to other countries, including the United States.

6. The Trademark Application and its Elements

To receive a filing date for the application (generally the effective filing date for determining priority for publication or issue, or for constructive use), the application must include at least: (1) the applicant's name and address; (2) the applicant's citizenship and type of entity; (3) a name and address for correspondence; (4) a clear drawing of the mark; (5) a listing of the goods or services; (6) the goods' or services' classification;

---

9. *Id.* § 1126.
10. *Id.* § 1126(d).
11. *Id.* § 1126(b), (d).
12. *See* https://www.uspto.gov/trademark/laws-regulations/madrid-protocol.

(7) the applicant's verified statement; (8) the filing fee for at least one class of goods or services; and (9) additional use-in-commerce application requirements.[13]

Practice Pointer

This is not an exhaustive list, and certain additional requirements may apply depending on the mark being registered, including whether the application is for a certification mark or collective mark.

---

1. **Applicant's Name and Address.** The owner of the trademark is the individual or entity that controls the nature or quality of the goods or services identified by the trademark. The trademark owner must be the applicant for registration.

2. **Type of Legal Entity and Citizenship.** The applicant can be any type of legal entity, including an individual, partnership, or corporation. The application must state both the type of entity filing and the applicant's citizenship, or the state or nation under which laws the applicant is organized (for example, a U.S. corporation must specify the state in which it is incorporated). Partnerships must include the names and citizenships of the general partners.

3. **Name and Address for Correspondence.** The application must include the applicant's (or its legal representative's) name and address for correspondence from the USPTO regarding the application. Foreign applicants should appoint a domestic representative to receive notices and service of process.

4. **Drawing of the Mark.** The application must include a clear drawing or depiction of the mark. If the trademark is not used or intended to be used in a particular format, the applicant can use a standard character (block letter) format. The applicant should use a special form drawing if the trademark includes a particular style, lettering, color and/or design.

5. **Specification of the Goods or Services.** The trademark application must include a description of the goods or services for which the mark is used or, for an ITU application, will be used. The description must be in specific detail and use common, clear, and concise terms. For example, "clothing" is unacceptably broad. Instead, the application should list specific items of clothing, for example, t-shirts, pants, skirts, and so on. The USPTO's Acceptable Identification of Goods and Services Manual, a searchable database, provides examples of language that has been accepted for particular types of goods and services.

---

13.   37 C.F.R. § 2.21.

Practice Pointer

It is important to carefully consider the description of the goods and services. USPTO rules permit an applicant to clarify and limit, but not expand or broaden, the goods or services. For example, shirts may be limited to "t-shirts and blouses," but cannot be broadened to include "pants."

6. **Classification.** Goods and services are classified in accordance with the 45 categories set out in the *Nice Classification*. An application may include goods or services in more than one class, and the applicant should identify one or more classifications if known.

7. **Verified Statement.** The applicant or its authorized representative must sign a verified statement, which may be done by declaration.[14] The verification must state that: (1) to the best of the applicant's knowledge, the facts in the application are true; (2) the applicant believes it is the owner of the mark and to the best of its knowledge, no other entity has the right to use the applied-for mark or any similar trademark in commerce; (3) for use-based applications, the mark is in use in commerce on or in connection with the claimed goods or services; and (4) for ITU applications, the applicant has a bona fide intent to use the mark in commerce in connection with the claimed goods or services.

8. **Filing Fee.** Filing fees are based on the number of classes covered in the application and must be paid when the application is filed. It is important to note that the filing fee is a fee for processing the application. This fee will not be refunded, even if no registration ultimately issues.

9. **Additional Use-in-Commerce Application Requirements.** A use-based application must also include the following information:

   a. **Date of first use anywhere.** This is the date of the applicant's first use of the mark anywhere on or in connection with the specified goods or services.

   b. **Date of first use in commerce.** This is the applicant's first use of the mark in commerce that Congress may lawfully regulate (for example, interstate commerce or commerce between the United States and another country) as a trademark or service mark on or in connection with the specified goods or services.

   c. **Specimen of use.** For each class of claimed goods or services, the applicant must submit a specimen showing the mark as actually used in connection with that class of goods or services. For goods, acceptable specimens of use include tags, labels, or images of the goods displaying the mark. For services, acceptable specimens include advertisements, correspondence

---

14. *Id.* § 2.193(e)(1).

displaying the mark and referring to the services, or web pages showing the mark and referring to the services.

D. Post-Application Considerations and Procedures

Once the application is filed and the USPTO determines that you have met the minimum filing requirements, the application is assigned a serial number, and the USPTO will issue a filing receipt by e-mail for electronic applications, and by mail for hard-copy applications. The filing receipt includes a summary of the filed information and the assigned serial number. After the application is filed and a serial number is assigned, the application is assigned to a USPTO trademark examining attorney. The examining attorney reviews the application to determine whether: (1) the application meets formal examination requirements (for example, that it includes the elements listed in "Application Elements"; (2) the trademark is eligible for registration in accordance with the federal Lanham Act and USPTO's regulations; and (3) the trademark is likely to cause confusion with any other previously applied-for or registered trademark.

The USPTO advises that applicants check the status of pending applications every three to four months after the initial filing of the application to avoid missing any filing deadlines. An applicant can check an application's status online through the USPTO's Trademark Status and Document Retrieval (TSDR) system.

An initial response from the USPTO generally takes anywhere from three to six months (sometimes longer). If the application meets all formal requirements and the examining attorney has no further objections, the examining attorney issues a Notice of Publication, which is followed by publication of the mark in the *Official Gazette*.

1. Office Actions

Sometimes, however, the first response is a letter, or Office Action, from the examining attorney explaining any substantive objections to the application or any technical or procedural deficiencies in the application. The first Office Action usually issues about six months after the application is filed. Office Actions can include objections arising from: (1) a defect in the formal application requirements, e.g., if the required identification of goods or services is unacceptable; (2) ineligibility for registration; (3) descriptiveness; and/or (4) a likelihood of confusion with a previously registered or applied-for mark.

The first Office Action raising an issue is a nonfinal Office Action. The applicant must file a response within six months after the date of the Office Action, addressing each issue raised by: (1) correcting any technical defects; (2) modifying the application to address substantive refusals; or (3) providing arguments to refute any substantive refusals. If a timely response is not submitted, the USPTO will declare the application abandoned.

After the applicant files a timely response to a nonfinal Office Action, the trademark examiner will issue either a Notice of Publication or, if the examining attorney does not believe all of the issues have been addressed, another (typically final) Office Action.

The examiner also may issue another nonfinal Office Action if the examiner identifies any new issues raised by the applicant's response. As with nonfinal Office Actions, the applicant has six months from the date of the final Office Action to respond.

2.   Appeals

A trademark registration applicant may appeal a final refusal of its application by filing a request for reconsideration by the examining attorney or by filing an appeal with the Trademark Trial and Appeal Board (TTAB). Adverse decisions by the TTAB can be appealed to the U.S. Court of Appeals for the Federal Circuit, or the applicant can instead file a civil action in a federal district court.

3.   Amendment to Allege Use for ITU Applications

If the applicant begins using the mark in commerce before it is approved for publication, the applicant can amend the ITU application to a use-based application by filing an Amendment to Allege Use. The amendment must include: (1) a verified statement, which may be done by declaration, that the applicant believes it is the owner of the mark and the mark is in use in commerce, specifying the date of the first use and first use in commerce; (2) identification of the goods and services specified in the application on which the mark is used; (3) a specimen of the mark as used for each class of goods and services covered by the amendment; and (4) a fee based on the number of classes encompassed by the amendment.

4.   Publication

If an application passes through the examining attorney's review without being rejected or abandoned, the examining attorney will approve the mark for publication in the *Official Gazette*, a weekly publication of the USPTO.

After the mark is published in the *Official Gazette*, any party who believes it may be damaged by registration of the mark can file an opposition to the mark's registration on the Principal Register within 30 days after the date of publication. The USPTO will extend the time period to oppose a mark's registration on the Principal Register once for an additional 30 days if the party files an extension request with the TTAB within the initial 30-day period. Interested parties can file additional extension requests for good cause, but the total period of all extensions cannot exceed 180 days from the date of publication.

If no opposition is filed or if the opposition is unsuccessful, the application enters the next stage of the registration process. It can take three to four months from the time the notice of publication is sent before the applicant will receive official notice of the next status of the application.

5.   Opposition

An opposition is a proceeding in which an interested party seeks to prevent registration of another party's mark. Most oppositions are filed by an owner of a prior mark claiming the applied-for mark is likely to cause confusion with the prior mark. Other claims, however, can be raised in an opposition, such as, by way of example, that the proposed mark is scandalous or immoral.

If an opposition is filed, the trademark registration applicant will be provided with a copy of the "notice of opposition" and will have 30 days to file an answer. If an answer is not filed, the application is deemed abandoned. The opposition procedure is similar to litigation in civil court, but the TTAB has specific rules governing the conduct of an opposition. Most matters are resolved by written records; the TTAB usually does not conduct oral hearings. Adverse TTAB decisions may be appealed to the U.S. Court of Appeals for the Federal Circuit or to a federal district court.

E. Registration

If no opposition is filed against a use-based application for a mark on the Principal Register, the USPTO registers the mark. The USPTO will not register a mark applied for on an ITU basis until the applicant files a Statement of Use and an acceptable specimen showing use of the mark in the claimed class of goods or services with the USPTO. Therefore, if no opposition is filed against an ITU application, the USPTO issues a Notice of Allowance. The applicant then has six months to file a Statement of Use and an acceptable specimen and pay the required fee.

An applicant can receive up to five, six-month extensions to file a Statement of Use (including an acceptable specimen of use for the claimed class of goods or services). For each extension, the applicant must properly file a request within the immediately preceding six-month period and pay the required fee.

An extension request is often filed along with the Statement of Use and the specimen evidencing use. This ensures that if the Statement of Use or specimen is defective, the application is not deemed abandoned. The USPTO deems an ITU application abandoned if the applicant fails to timely file either the Statement of Use (including an acceptable specimen of use) or any individual extension request.

1. Certificate of Registration

If a mark proceeds to registration, the USPTO mails the owner a Certificate of Registration (the official document issued by the USPTO evidencing the mark's registration). The mark owner should make copies of the certificate and store the original in a safe place.

2. Maintaining Trademark Registrations

Once a trademark is registered with the USPTO, the trademark owner must take affirmative action to maintain the registration by filing specific maintenance documents. The USPTO may cancel a registration if the owner fails to make the required filings. In addition, any interested party can petition to have a trademark canceled based on one of several grounds, including genericism and abandonment.

Practice Pointer

To keep a federal trademark registration in effect, the trademark owner must periodically file the following documents and pay filing fees: (1) Declarations of Continued Use or Excusable Nonuse; and (2) Renewal Applications.

A trademark can be deemed abandoned if the owner discontinues use with the intent not to resume use, or if the owner, by its conduct, causes the mark to lose meaning as a trademark, e.g., the mark becomes generic or the owner fails to control use by a licensee or assert rights against infringers.

Practice Pointer

The trademark owner should also consider filing a Declaration of Incontestability once the mark has been in continuous use in commerce for at least five consecutive years after the registration date.

---

3. Declaration of Continued Use or Excusable Nonuse

To maintain the federal registration, the current trademark owner must file with the USPTO a Declaration of Continued Use or Excusable Nonuse (Section 8 Affidavit or Declaration) within one year before the end of each of the: (1) sixth year of registration; and (2) tenth year of registration and each successive 10-year period after that.

A six-month grace period following each deadline is provided to the trademark owner, subject to payment of an extra fee. Failure to file a Section 8 Declaration results in the cancellation of the registration. Each Section 8 Declaration must include an acceptable specimen showing use.

4. Declaration of Incontestability

A trademark owner also can file a Declaration of Incontestability (Section 15 Affidavit or Declaration) once a mark registered on the Principal Register has been in continuous use in commerce for at least five consecutive years after the registration date. Incontestability status offers many advantages, including that third parties can no longer challenge ownership of the trademark, and the mark can no longer be challenged on the basis that it is merely descriptive of the goods or services or was improperly registered. A trademark owner can file a Declaration of Incontestability separately or combined with a six-year Declaration of Continued Use.

5. Renewal Application or Combined Declaration of Use and Renewal Application

Trademark registrations must be renewed every 10 years. A written renewal application (Section 9 Renewal Application) must be made during the last year of each successive 10-year period for which the registration is issued or renewed, and must be accompanied by payment of the required fee.

The registration will expire if a timely renewal application is not filed. The registrant also must file a Declaration of Continued Use or Excusable Nonuse to maintain the registration and has the option to file a combined Declaration of Use or Excusable Nonuse and Renewal Application form with the USPTO.

6. Cancellation

A cancellation is a proceeding before the TTAB in which a party seeks to cancel an existing registration. A cancellation proceeding is similar to an opposition except it is brought against a registered mark, not an application for registration.

As with oppositions, any entity that believes it is or will be damaged by the registration can file a petition to cancel. The most common arguments for cancellation are that: (1) the trademark owner abandoned the registered mark through nonuse or failure to exercise quality control; (2) the registered mark has become generic; or (3) the trademark owner committed fraud on the USPTO.

7. Notice of Trademark Rights

The ™ symbol is used by trademark owners before they obtain a federal registration for their trademark.

Practice Pointer

Although not required by trademark law, the use of the ™ symbol can serve many useful purposes for a trademark owner, including: (1) putting a third party on notice that the owner is claiming trademark rights; (2) helping defeat an infringer's claim that it was unaware that the owner claimed rights in the mark; and (3) helping prevent the mark from becoming generic.

The ® symbol is used by trademark owners to give notice that a particular mark is registered with the USPTO for particular goods or services. It may only be used after a federal registration has been granted. Even if a trademark application is pending with the USPTO, the ® symbol may not be used until the mark becomes federally registered. The improper use of a federal registration symbol is grounds for denying registration of an otherwise registrable mark if it is done with the intent to deceive the public or others in the trade into believing that the mark is registered.

V. TRADEMARK PROTECTION IN THE DIGITAL AGE: PROTECTING TRADEMARKS FROM CYBERSQUATTING

With the growing use and popularity of the internet, more and more people and businesses have made the leap into cyberspace to sell, advertise, or promote their company, name, products, or services. With this growing evolution, the inevitable clash over domain names has also grown.

What exactly is a domain name? Simply put, a domain name is essentially the user-friendly form of the internet equivalent to a telephone number or street address. It is the address of a person or organization on the internet where other people can find them online, and it can also become the online identity of that person or organization. For example, many businesses will register their company name as their domain name. A domain name can function as a trademark if it is used to identify goods or services and is not used simply as a website address. Although providing a staggering global market forum, the internet also provides fertile ground for trademark infringers. One of the most common avenues for infringement on the web is that traveled by "cybersquatters."

A cybersquatter, sometimes referred to as a cyberpirate, is a person or entity that engages in the abusive registration and use of trademarks as domain names, commonly for the purpose of selling the domain name back to the trademark owner or to attract web traffic to unrelated commercial offers. To provide trademark owners with a remedy and a means by which to evict cybersquatters, two alternatives developed: the Anti-Cybersquatting Consumer Protection Act, a federal statute providing the basis for a court action against cybersquatters, and the Uniform Domain Name Dispute Resolution Policy, which provides for an administrative proceeding for the resolution of domain name disputes, much like an arbitration.

A. The Anti-Cybersquatting Consumer Protection Act (ACPA)

As relevant to this discussion, the ACPA[15] was enacted in 1999 to redress cybersquatting by allowing trademark owners to bring a civil action against a cybersquatter if that person: (1) has a bad-faith intent to profit from the mark; and (2) registers, traffics in, or uses a domain name that in the case of a distinctive mark, is identical or confusingly similar to that mark, or in the case of a famous mark, is identical or confusingly similar to, or dilutive of, that mark.

Remedies for violation of the ACPA include statutory damages between $1,000.00 and $100,000.00 per domain name for which the cybersquatter is found liable, actual damages, the transfer or cancellation of the domain name, and/or attorney's fees.[16]

---

15. 15 U.S.C. § 1125(d).
16. *See id.* §§ 1114, 1117.

B. Uniform Domain Name Dispute Resolution Policy

A less costly and more efficient alternative to the court system is the Uniform Domain Name Dispute Resolution Policy (UDRP or Policy), a mandatory administrative procedure for resolving complaints regarding abusive domain name registration and usage.

Effective December 1, 1999, the UDRP was implemented by the Internet Corporation for Assigned Names and Numbers (ICANN), an internationally organized, nonprofit corporation created in 1998. ICANN is responsible for managing and coordinating the Internet Domain Name System by, among other things, overseeing the distribution of unique internet protocol (IP) addresses and domain names, and ensuring that each domain name maps to the correct IP address. ICANN is also charged with accrediting the domain name registrars, each of which is required by ICANN to incorporate the UDRP into its domain name registration contract with its customers, the domain name owners. Accordingly, the UDRP has been adopted by all accredited domain name registrars for generic, top-level domain names (gTLDs), such as domain names ending in .com, .net, and .org.

1. The Required Elements of Proof

Under the UDRP, ICANN has the power to order the cancellation or transfer of a domain name in resolution of a dispute between the domain name registrant and a trademark owner. Consistent with the ACPA, under the UDRP, the trademark owner (complainant) must prove that: (1) the allegedly infringing domain name is identical or confusingly similar to a trademark or service mark in which the complainant has rights; (2) the alleged infringer has no rights or legitimate interests in respect of the domain name; and (3) the allegedly infringing domain name has been registered and is being used in bad faith.

2. Identical or Confusing Similarity

Initially, the allegedly infringing domain name must be identical or confusingly similar to a trademark or service mark in which the complainant has rights. Marks in which a complainant has rights include both marks that are federally registered with the USPTO, as well as unregistered marks that have acquired common-law rights. Common-law rights are acquired when the mark becomes a source indicator in commerce through its usage, promotion, marketing, and advertising. For example, "it has been accepted in a succession of UDRP decisions that authors and performers may have trademark rights in the names by which they have become well-known . . . . [P]erformers can establish trademark rights either by showing that they have registered their names as marks for certain goods or services, or because, through deployment of the names as source indicators in commerce, they have unregistered or 'common law' rights to protection against misleading use".[17]

---

17. *See, e.g.,* Celine Dion & Sony Music Entm't (Canada) Inc. v. Jeff Burgar operating or carrying on business as Celine Dion Club, WIPO Case No. D2000-1838 (and decisions cited therein).

For example, the recording artist professionally known as Sade was successful in obtaining the transfer of the domain "sade.com," despite the fact that she had not registered her mark SADE. However, she sufficiently demonstrated her usage of the stage name "Sade" as a mark to distinguish her goods and services as a singer, songwriter, performer, and recording artist, and the establishment of substantial goodwill in that mark in connection therewith, based upon evidence of her sales of records, CDs, clothing, and other merchandise using the mark SADE, as well as live tours, performances, advertising, and promotion.[18]

Once the complainant has established its rights in the mark, it must establish that the disputed domain name is "identical or confusingly similar" to its mark. Not too surprisingly, where the domain name is identical to the complainant's mark, the requirement of identity or confusing similarity as required by paragraph 4(a)(i) of the UDRP has been found satisfied.[19] The addition of ".com" or some other gTLD suffix is not a distinguishing difference where the domain name is otherwise identical to the complainant's mark.[20]

In determining "confusing similarity," jurisprudence under the UDRP is decided on a case-by-case basis. One particular scenario that continues to confound the UDRP Panels is the appendage of the term "-sucks" to another's trademark. In a decision that discusses at length the various approaches taken to analyze this issue,[21] the UDRP Panel transferred to the complainant, a company best-known for its sale of alcoholic beverages under the trademark "Guinness," the disputed domain names: "guinness-really-sucks.com," "guinness-really-really-sucks.com," "guinness-beer-really-sucks.com," and "guinness-beer-really-really-sucks.com" in addition to a host of other similar variations.[22]

Another common scenario involving confusing similarity is that involving a form of cybersquatting known as "typosquatting," where the registered domain name is a misspelling of a trademark. In a WIPO case involving a typosquatter notorious for registration of infringing domain names that contain slight misspellings of famous trademarks, Disney Enterprises successfully obtained transfer of a myriad of domain names that infringed on its famous DISNEY mark by fully incorporating the DISNEY mark, coupled with slight misspellings of other DISNEY-formative marks, like "Walt Disney World" (for example, the disputed domain names included "disneywold.com,"

---

18. Helen Folsade Adu known as Sade v. Quantum Computer Services Inc., WIPO Case No. D2000-0794.

19. *See, e.g.,* Julia Fiona Roberts v. Russell Boyd, WIPO Case No. D2000-0210 (transferring "juliaroberts.com"); *see also* Bell-Phillip Television Prod. v. Make A. Aford, WIPO Case No. D2000-0180 (although Complainant did not offer evidence that members of the public were actually confused by the Respondent's domain name registration, "given that Respondent's domain name, www.theboldandthebeautiful.com, is identical with Complainant's service mark, this Panel finds that confusion is ineluctable").

20. Michael J. Feinstein v. PAWS Video Prod., WIPO Case No. D2000-0880 (and decisions cited therein).

21. For example, whether the domain fully incorporates the trademark in its entirety, or an analysis of eight factors to determine "likelihood of confusion," including strength of the mark, proximity of the goods, similarity of the goods, evidence of actual confusion, the marketing channels used, the type of goods and degree of care likely to be used by a purchaser, defendant's intent in selecting the mark, and the likelihood of expansion of product lines.

22. Diageo plc v. John Zuccarini, Individually and t/a Cupcake Patrol, WIPO Case No. D2000-0996.

"disneywolrd.com," and "disneyworl.com"). When internet users mistakenly entered the disputed domain names into their web browsers, a number of pop-up windows appeared containing third-party websites and advertisements for goods and services like music, games, credit approval, and casinos. When the internet user would close these windows, additional pop-up windows would appear, containing still more third-party advertisements or websites in a continuous cycle, despite the fact that Disney was not affiliated with, nor had given permission to use its trademarks to, any of the websites appearing in the perpetual stream of pop-up windows (a tactic which, as an aside, is curiously known as mousetrapping, but having no affiliation with or relation to Disney's icon Mickey Mouse).[23]

3.   Lack of Rights or Legitimate Interests

Any number of factors has been held to establish a domain name registrant's lack of rights or a legitimate interest in the disputed domain name. For example, one common factor is where it may be inferred or established that the registrant's motive for registering the domain name was to sell it at auction on the internet, without any other apparent right or interest in the domain.[24]

Pursuant to the UDRP, a domain name registrant can establish its rights or legitimate interest in the disputed domain name by demonstrating any of the following circumstances, in particular but without limitation that:

(i)   The registrant used, or made demonstrable preparations to use, the domain name or a name corresponding therewith in connection with a bona fide offering of goods or services prior to the registrant's receipt of notice of the dispute. For example, the owner of the domain and mark "sexplanet.com" lost its dispute over the domain name "sexplanets.com," despite its claim that it was the first and most popular adult website for the download of live, streaming video, where the registrant of "sexplanets.com" demonstrated that the domain was registered without prior knowledge of the complainant's domain name "sexplanet.com" and was immediately used to further its business plan of providing bona-fide free hosting services to webmasters of adult websites in exchange for advertising revenue generated from banners displayed on the adult sites hosted.[25] In contrast, the recording artist and performer Peter Frampton successfully obtained transfer of the domain name "peterframpton.com" where the evidence clearly demonstrated that the registrant had deliberately chosen to include Peter Frampton's well-known trademarked name with the goal of

---

23.   *See* Disney Enter., Inc. v. John Zuccarini, Cupcake City and Cupcake Patrol, WIPO Case No. D2001-0489.

24.   *See* Bell-Phillip Television Prod. v. Make A. Aford, WIPO Case No. D2000-0180 (evidence demonstrating Respondent's attempt to auction the disputed domain name was sufficient to infer that Respondent's motive for registering the domain was to sell it at auction, which is not a legitimate right or business interest under the policy).

25.   Global Media Res. SA v. Sexplanets aka SexPlanets Free Hosting, WIPO Case No. D2001-1391.

creating opportunities and commercially benefitting itself from the inevitable user confusion that would result from their concurrent usage of the domain name and Peter Frampton's mark. In particular, the registrant, who coincidentally shared the name "Frampton," clearly sought to capitalize on Peter Frampton's fame and celebrity reputation where he used the domain to post a website that offered goods directly competitive with Peter Frampton in the music industry. Such use, which was deemed "to exploit user confusion," "cannot and does not constitute bona fide commercial use. . . ."[26]

(ii) The registrant (either as an individual, business, or other organization) has been commonly known by the domain name, even if it has acquired no trademark rights. For example, the musician Sting almost got stung by the registrant of the domain "sting.com" where the registrant argued that he had been using the nickname "Sting" for eight years, most recently on the internet in connection with global online gaming services. However, the UDRP Panel was not persuaded that the registrant had established that he has been "commonly known" by the domain as contemplated by the UDRP; rather, it determined that the word "sting" is not distinctive, most likely used by numerous other people in cyberspace and, in practice, merely provided the registrant with anonymity rather than with a name by which he was commonly known. Unfortunately for the musician Sting, these findings were not sufficient to prevent the denial of his complaint where the UDRP Panel accepted that he was world famous under the name "Sting," but had not demonstrated his rights in the name "Sting" as an unregistered trademark or service mark, given the fact that the personal name in this case (unlike "Pat Benatar," *infra*, or "Sade," *supra*) is also a common word in the English language with a number of different meanings.[27]

(iii) The registrant is making a legitimate noncommercial or fair use of the domain name without intent for commercial gain to misleadingly divert consumers or to tarnish the trademark at issue. Examples of a "legitimate noncommercial or fair use" include parody sites, fan sites, and sites dedicated to criticism or commentary. The recording artist Pat Benatar, for example, was denied transfer of the domain name "patbenatar.com" where the registrant had created a fan website that provided a wide range of information concerning Pat Benatar, including a detailed history of her band, a chronology of her albums, and past and future appearances. The website contained clear disclaimers that it was strictly operated as a fan site and was unauthorized by, had no affiliation with, and was not endorsed by, Pat Benatar, her band, or agents. Equally important, there was no evidence that the registrant obtained any commercial benefit from the website, which may well have led to a different result. In a more extreme case, Eddie Van Halen of legendary rock fame was denied transfer of the domain "edwardvanhalen.com" from a fan who registered the domain with the alleged intent of putting up a fan site, even though the fan site never

---

26. Peter Frampton v. Frampton Enter., Inc., WIPO Case No. D2002-0141.
27. Gordon Sumner p/k/a Sting v. Michael Urvan, WIPO Case No. D2000-0596.

had any content added to it.[28] In contrast, the law firm Hunton & Williams successfully obtained transfer of the domains "huntonandwilliams.com" and "huntonwilliams.com" where the registrant made a failed attempt at a parody website by posting content that was found to merely disparage the law firm as greedy, parasitical, and unethical, including the text "PARASITES—no soul . . . no conscience . . . no spine . . . NO PROBLEM!!!" against a background of human skulls, together with a myriad of definitions of the term "parasite" and of advertised products, as opposed to imitating any distinctive style of the firm for comic effect or in ridicule.[29]

4.   Registration and Use in Bad Faith

The UDRP requires that both the registration *and* use of the disputed domain must be in bad faith. Pursuant to the express terms of the UDRP, evidence of the registration and use of a domain name in bad faith shall include, in particular but without limitation:

(i)   circumstances indicating that the domain name was registered or acquired primarily for the purpose of selling, renting, or otherwise transferring the domain name registration to the trademark owner or its competitor, for valuable consideration in excess of the registrant's documented out-of-pocket costs directly related to the domain name (e.g., in the UDRP proceeding initiated by the famous actress Julia Roberts, wherein she successfully obtained transfer of the domain "juliaroberts.com," it was found that the registrant had registered and used the domain in bad faith where, among other things, he had placed the domain up for auction on the commercial website eBay).[30]

(ii)   registration of the domain name in order to prevent the trademark owner from reflecting the mark in a corresponding domain name, provided that the registrant has engaged in a pattern of such conduct (e.g., also in the "juliaroberts.com" case, the registrant had admittedly registered other domain names, including several famous movie and sports stars which actions, according the Panel deciding that case, necessarily prevented the complainant from using the disputed domain name and demonstrated a pattern of such conduct).[31]

(iii)   registration of the domain name primarily for the purpose of disrupting the business of a competitor (e.g., Ticketmaster, dubbed the "global leader in live event ticket sales," successfully obtained transfer of the domains "ticketmasters.com," "wwwticketsmaster.com," and "ticketsmasters.com" where the registrant had deliberately used various misspelling of the well-known Ticketmaster mark (typosquatting) to attract internet users who mistype or misspell Ticketmaster's name when seeking to find Ticketmaster's website

---

28.   Edward Van Halen v. Deborah Morgan, WIPO Case No. D2000-1313.
29.   Hunton & Williams v. Am. Distrib. Sys., Inc. et al., WIPO Case No. D2000-0501.
30.   Julia Fiona Roberts v. Russell Boyd, WIPO Case No. D2000-0210.
31.   *Id.*

and, instead, were redirected to the registrant's competing website offering the same products and services as Ticketmaster).[32]

(iv) by using the domain name, the domain name registrant has intentionally attempted to attract, for commercial gain, internet users to its website or other on-line location, by creating a likelihood of confusion with the complainant's mark as to the source, sponsorship, affiliation, or endorsement of its website or location or of a product or service on its website or location (e.g., the registrant's automatic hyperlink of the domain to a competing website or a pornographic site, such as in a case disputing the domain name "bodacious-tatas.com," an Indian corporation known as Tata Sons Limited successfully obtained cancellation of the domain, which directed to a pornographic website, and in so doing, the registrant was held to have registered and used the domain in bad faith where, among other things, it had unlawfully placed the complainant's trademarked "TATA" in the meta-tags of its domain address so that when internet users performed an internet search using the "TATA" trademark in any internet search engine (e.g., Google), the search results would include the registrant's unauthorized pornographic website which, the UDRP Panel held, could induce a potential customer or client of Tata Sons into believing that the porn site was licensed, authorized, or owned by Tata Sons.[33]

Practice Pointer

The above factors cited by the UDRP were not intended to be exclusive to a finding of bad faith, and numerous other factors have been considered indicative of bad faith, including actual or constructive knowledge of a commonly known mark,[34] attempts to sell the domain at auction on the internet,[35] failure to take affirmative action to post content,[36] and provision of false contact information associated with the domain name registration.[37]

---

5. Proceedings under the UDRP

Proceedings under the UDRP are conducted in accordance with the Rules for Uniform Domain Name Dispute Resolution Policy (the Rules of Procedure). Pursuant to the Rules of Procedure, a dispute under the UDRP may be filed with any one of the

---

32. Ticketmaster Corp. v. Woofer Smith, WIPO Case No. D2003-0346.

33. Tata Sons Ltd. v. D & V Enterprises, WIPO Case No. D2000-0479.

34. Barney's Inc. v. BNY Bulletin Board, WIPO Case No. D2000-0059 (charging knowledge of complainant's rights in its registered mark BARNEY'S NEW YORK).

35. Julia Fiona Roberts v. Russell Boyd, WIPO Case No. D2000-0210); Bell-Phillip Television Prod. v. Make A. Aford, WIPO Case No. D2000-0180.

36. Michael J. Feinstein v. PAWS Video Prod., WIPO Case No. D2000-0880 (and decisions cited therein).

37. Ticketmaster Corp. v. Dmitri Prem, WIPO Case No. D2000-1550.

ICANN-approved dispute resolution service providers for the UDRP, which providers currently include the World Intellectual Property Organization (WIPO) and the National Arbitration Forum (NAF), among others. Each provider has its own rules supplemental to the Rules of Procedure. For purposes of this chapter, we will discuss only proceedings filed with WIPO, which agency (as discussed below) is credited for the UDRP. Based in Geneva, Switzerland, WIPO is a self-funding agency of the United Nations, which is currently comprised of 191 member states, including the United States.

As an alternative to court litigation, WIPO's Arbitration and Mediation Center was established in 1994 to offer alternative dispute resolution for commercial disputes between private parties involving intellectual property. Commencing in 1998, in response to a request first initiated by the U.S. government, WIPO undertook an international process to develop recommendations concerning intellectual property issues associated with internet domain names, including domain name dispute resolution. That process was finalized on April 30, 1999, with WIPO's issuance of its Final Report and its recommendations for dealing with domain name and trademark issues, which included the institution of a policy to be followed uniformly by all registrars that would provide an administrative remedy for domain-name disputes in all gTLDs, and that the scope of such administrative procedure be limited to cases of bad-faith, abusive registration of domain names that violate trademark rights. Following WIPO's recommendations, ICANN adopted the UDRP on August 26, 1999.

Effective December 1, 1999, WIPO became the first domain-name dispute resolution service provider to be accredited by ICANN and the first to receive a case under the UDRP. Since WIPO administered its first UDRP case in 1999, total WIPO case filings passed the 39,000 mark in 2017, encompassing over 73,000 domain names.[38]

6. Who's Who?

The "complainant" is essentially the UDRP version of a plaintiff in a court proceeding. It is the person or entity claiming trademark rights and initiating a complaint concerning a disputed domain-name registration in accordance with the UDRP.

The "respondent" is essentially the UDRP version of a defendant in a court proceeding. It is the holder of the disputed domain-name registration that is subject of the complaint initiated by the complainant. Pursuant to the terms of the domain-name registration agreement that the respondent enters into with its registrar, the respondent is required to participate in the UDRP proceeding.

The "panel" consists of one or three independent and impartial arbitrators appointed by WIPO to decide a UDRP proceeding. In its complaint, the complainant has the opportunity to designate whether it prefers a single-member or three-member panel, in addition to nominating its preferred panelists chosen from a list of WIPO-approved participating panelists. Information regarding the panel process, available panelists, and their qualifications is found on the WIPO website at http://arbiter.wipo.int/domains/

---

38. *See* http://www.wipo.int/pressroom/en/articles/2018/article_0001.html.

panel/index.html. In its response, the respondent has a corresponding opportunity with respect to the panel designation.

The "registrar" is the entity with which the respondent registered the domain name subject of the complaint. As previously discussed, the registrar must be accredited by ICANN, and a condition of accreditation is the incorporation of the UDRP into the registrar's domain-name registration agreement with its registrants. The registrar does not participate in the UDRP proceeding and cannot be held liable under any decision rendered by a panel. However, the registrar is put on notice of the commencement of a UDRP proceeding and is instrumental in that it must lock the domain-name registration pending the proceeding (i.e., prevent the transfer or cancellation of the disputed domain during the proceeding pendency) and thereafter implement any decision rendered by the panel (i.e., by either cancelling the domain name registration or transferring it to a prevailing complainant).

7. Overview of the General Stages of a UDRP Proceeding

Similar to a court action, a UDRP proceeding is initiated by the filing of a complaint. However, the complainant files the complaint with WIPO and not a court. Given that UDRP rules and criteria are fairly narrow and specific, WIPO makes available an online Model Complaint to serve as a framework. A copy of the Model Complaint may be found on the WIPO website.[39]

WIPO's website makes optional either downloading the Model Complaint as a Word document for subsequent submission upon its completion, or completing the Model Complaint online. In either case, the complainant must submit the completed complaint to WIPO electronically, together with WIPO's form Complaint Transmittal Coversheet.[40] A filing fee must be paid by the complainant at the time of its initiation of the proceeding, the amount of which is dependent upon the number of domain names subject of the dispute and the number of panelists elected. For cases involving one to five domain names, there generally is a $1,500.00 fee for a single-member panel, and a $4,000.00 fee for a three-member panel.[41]

Subsequent to the complainant's submission of the complaint, WIPO shall submit a verification request to the concerned registrar. The verification request will include a request to lock the domain name, which prevents any modification to the registrant and registrar information, as well as prevents the transfer of the domain during the pendency of the UDRP proceeding. The lock remains in place through the remaining pendency of the UDRP proceeding. Any updates to the respondent's data, such as through the result of a request by a privacy or proxy provider to reveal the underlying customer data, must be made before the conclusion of a two-business-day period or before the registrar verifies the information requested and confirms the lock to WIPO, whichever occurs first.

---

39. *See* http://www.wipo.int/amc/en/domains/complainant/.
40. http://www.wipo.int/amc/en/domains/complainant/coversheet.html.
41. *See* http://www.wipo.int/amc/en/domains/fees/ for WIPO's fee schedule.

Any modification(s) of the respondent's data following the two-business-day period may be addressed by the panel in its decision.

WIPO then reviews the complaint for administrative compliance with the Policy and the Rules of Procedure and, if in compliance, shall forward the complaint, including any annexes, electronically to the respondent and registrar and shall send written notice of the complaint to the respondent, within three calendar days following receipt of the fees to be paid by the complainant. Within 20 days of the date of commencement of the administrative proceeding, the respondent shall submit a response to the complaint. Like the complaint, WIPO makes available an online Model Response.[42]

Upon WIPO's acknowledgment of receipt of the filed response (or, as the case may frequently be, issuance of notification of respondent's default), WIPO will appoint the panel to review the complaint and response. Within 14 days from the panel's appointment, a decision on the case is submitted to WIPO by the panel, upon which WIPO will notify the parties, the registrar, and ICANN of the decision. A decision by the panel can go one of three ways: (1) denial of the complaint; (2) cancellation of the disputed domain name; or (3) transfer of the disputed domain name to the complainant. If the panel decides that the domain name should either be cancelled or transferred, pursuant to paragraph 4(k) of the UDRP, there is a 10-business-day grace period prior to which ICANN will implement the decision with the registrar. During that grace period, a respondent may provide ICANN with "official documentation" (such as a filed-stamped copy of a complaint) of its commencement of a lawsuit against the complainant. In the event thereof, ICANN will take no action with regard to the panel's decision until it receives: (1) satisfactory evidence of a resolution between the parties; (2) satisfactory evidence of the dismissal or withdrawal of the lawsuit; or (3) a court order dismissing the lawsuit or ordering that the respondent does not have the right to continue to use the disputed domain name.

Assuming the passing of the 10-day grace period without event, the entire process of the UDRP proceeding from its commencement through implementation of decision should take approximately 60 days.

8.   WIPO—A Source and a Resource

All panel decisions are fully indexed and posted on WIPO's website, which also provides an overview of WIPO panel views on selected UDRP questions.[43]

---

42.   *See* http://www.wipo.int/amc/en/domains/respondent/.

43.   *See* http://www.wipo.int/amc/en/domains/search/. *See also* http://www.wipo.int/amc/en/domains/search/overview3.0/.

Chapter 13

Patents

By Steven S. Rubin and Stephen E. Breidenbach

Innovative people come up with new inventions every day. This chapter's goal is to educate in-house counsel on the intellectual property rights afforded inventors in relation to their inventions, which are protected through the patent process, by providing the necessary knowledge to understand how inventions are protected, the process necessary to obtain those protections, and the means by which to enforce their rights.

With the percentage of a company's value attributable to intangible assets continually increasing, there is an increased interest in protecting that intellectual property. Our Founding Fathers had the foresight to predict this interest as patent law in our Constitution. Article I, Section 8 of the U.S. Constitution provides Congress with the power "To promote the progress of science and useful arts, by securing for limited times to authors and inventors the exclusive right to their respective writings and discoveries." Patent law is a subset of intellectual property law, which encompasses copyrights, trademarks, and trade secrets. Under patent law, an inventor is afforded a limited monopoly for his or her invention in exchange for sharing the details of his or her invention to the world. The idea is that others can read a patent, learn from it, and science will continue to evolve.

I.   WHAT IS A PATENT?

A patent grants a property right to the inventor or inventors. The right conferred by the patent is the right to *exclude* others from making, using, selling, offering for sale, or importing the claimed invention into the United States.[1]

Practice Pointer

Thus, a patent is an *exclusionary* right, and not a right to practice the invention. A U.S. patent is effective only in the United States. If an invention were to be practiced outside of the United States, the patent owner may not have any legal recourse, unless the patent owner has secured patent rights in the applicable country. If all maintenance fees are paid on the patent, the right usually lasts for a period of 20 years.[2]

II.   WHAT DOES A PATENT ALLOW?

Practice Pointer

It is important to understand that a patent does not grant the inventor the right to make, use, offer for sale, sell, or import the invention; rather, the inventor is provided only the right to *exclude others* from such acts. This is an important distinction because obtaining a patent does not provide the inventor the right to make the patented work; it only allows the inventor the power to prevent others from making the patented work, and it does not supersede the rights of other individuals. For example, the owner of a patent would still be subject to state laws that could restrict the creation or distribution of that invention within its jurisdiction. In addition, the owner of a patent must respect the rights of other patent holders. For example, if an invention is an improvement on another patented invention, the patent owner could be excluded from making his or her patented invention subject to the other patented invention.

III.   DISCUSSION OF THE LAW

Under Article I, section 8 of the U.S. Constitution, Congress has the "power . . . to promote the progress of science and useful arts, by securing for limited times to authors and inventors the exclusive right to their respective writings and discoveries." Under this

---

1.   35 U.S.C. § 154.
2.   *Id.*

power, Congress enacted various laws to protect intellectual property. The first patent law was the Patent Act of 1790.[3] Thereafter, patent law was revised with the enactment of the U.S. Patent Act of 1952 that became effective January 1, 1953,[4] followed by the American Inventors Protection Act of 1999.[5]

Patent law specifies the subject matter and the conditions necessary for obtaining a patent and authorized the creation of the United States Patent and Trademark Office (USPTO) to oversee the granting of patents, which is governed by title 37 of the Code of Federal Regulations. Under that authority, the USPTO issues rules of practice in its *Manual of Patent Examination and Procedure* (MPEP).[6]

IV.   SCOPE OF RIGHTS CONFERRED

The term of the patent is generally 20 years from the date on which the application for the patent was filed in the United States, subject to the payment of maintenance fees as provided by law. A maintenance fee is due 3.5, 7.5, and 11.5 years after the original grant for all utility patents issuing from applications filed on and after December 12, 1980. If a patent's maintenance fee is not paid at the required times, then the patent will be deemed to have expired.

Practice Pointer

After the patent has expired, anyone may make, use, offer for sale, sell, or import the invention without permission of the patentee, provided that matter covered by other unexpired patents is not used.

Practice Pointer

On March 16, 2013, the American Invents Act (AIA) changed U.S. law from a "first to invent" jurisdiction to a "first to file" jurisdiction. This is a significant change. Prior to the AIA, an inventor could still acquire patent protection even if he or she did not file in the USPTO first, provided the inventor could show that he or she was the first to invent it. At the time, a complex procedure called an interference would probe into this inventorship issue. The AIA removed that procedure, and inventorship rights are now based on the filing date with the USPTO.

---

3.   Patent Act of 1790, 1 Stat. 109 (1790).
4.   *See* Pub. L. No. 593, 66 Stat. 792 (1952).
5.   *See* Pub. L. No. 106-113, 113 Stat. 1501 (1999).
6.   Manual of Patent Examining Procedure, Ninth Edition, Revision 08.2017, Last Revised Jan. 2018, https://www.uspto.gov/web/offices/pac/mpep/index.html (hereinafter MPEP).

V.   U.S. PATENTS

A. Types of Inventions

There are three types of patents: (1) utility patents, (2) design patents, and (3) plant patents.

1.   Utility Patents

A utility patent protects the functional aspects of an invention. A utility patent may be granted to anyone who invents or discovers any new and useful process, machine, article of manufacture, or composition of matter, or any new and useful improvement thereof.[7] The term of a utility patent is generally 20 years from the filing date. Most discussion of patent law relates to utility patents because they are the most common.

2.   Design Patents

A design patent protects new, original, and ornamental designs for an article of manufacture.[8] This is an important difference from a utility patent because design patents protect only the appearance of the article and do not protect any structural or functional features. Any design patent filed prior to May 13, 2015, has a term of 14 years from grant, and no fees are necessary to keep a design patent in force.[9] However, on May 13, 2015, the patent term for a design was revised to 15 years from the date of patent grant.[10] Maintenance fees are generally not required to maintain a design patent in force.

3.   Plant Patents[11]

A plant patent can be granted to anyone who invents or discovers and asexually reproduces any distinct and new variety of plant. The plant patent applies to the entire plant; therefore, only one claim is required, as discussed below. The term of a plant patent is usually 20 years.[12]

B. What Qualifies as an Invention?

There are essentially four doors through which an individual must pass to prove his or her contribution is patentable. A contribution that passes through these four doors is then

---

7.   35 U.S.C. § 101 ("Whoever invents or discovers any new and useful process, machine, manufacture, or composition of matter, or any new and useful improvement thereof, may obtain a patent therefor, subject to the conditions and requirements of this title.").

8.   35 U.S.C. § 171, Vas-Cath, Inc. v. Mahurkar.

9.   Patent Act of 1790, 1 Stat. 109 (1790).

10.   35 U.S.C. § 173; Patent Law Treaties Implementation Act, 126 Stat. 1531-32 (2012).

11.   35 U.S.C. § 161.

12.   35 U.S.C. § 161; 35 U.S.C. § 154.

deemed an invention. The concepts of inventor, invention, and patentability are thus intertwined. The doors are:

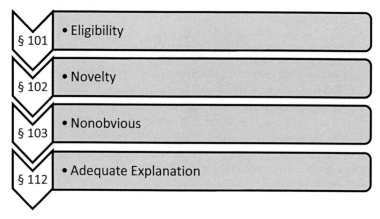

1. Eligibility

The first of these doors is eligibility. Eligible subject matter is defined under title 35, section 101 of the U.S. Code as "any new and useful process, machine, manufacture, or composition of matter, or any new and useful improvement thereof."[13]

The Supreme Court addressed, and completely obfuscated, the question for eligibility in the 2014 case of *Alice Corp v. CLS Bank*.[14] *Alice* set forth a two-part test to determine the types of subject matter eligible for patent protection: (1) determine whether the claim is directed to an abstract idea; and (2) if so, determine whether the claim's elements, considered both individually and as an ordered combination, transform the nature of the claim into a patent-eligible application.

The courts, the USPTO, and the patent bar have all struggled in understanding how this test works and how it should be applied. The determination of what "abstract" means could not be more abstract. In a gross oversimplification, inventions that have technical problems and technical solutions, or inventions that are solely mechanical, may be eligible, but consultation with counsel is advisable.

2. Novelty

The second door is novelty. Novelty is defined under title 35, section 102 of the U.S. Code, which provides that a person may receive a patent, provided that the claimed invention was not "described in a printed publication, or in a public use, on sale, or otherwise available to the public before the effective filing date of the claimed inventions. . . ."[15] However, there is a one-year grace period in the United States during which disclosures by the inventor do not prevent patentability.[16] Stated differently, the disclosure begins a

---

13. 35 U.S.C. § 101.
14. Alice Corp. v. CLS Bank Int'l, 573 U.S. __, 134 S. Ct. 2347 (2014).
15. 35 U.S.C. § 102(a)(1).
16. 35 U.S.C. § 102(b)(1)(A); 35 U.S.C. § 102(a)(1).

one-year clock during which the inventor must file an application before the end of the year to avoid having that disclosure bar patent protection.

Practice Pointer

An invention is considered published when the invention is described in a printed publication or is described in an issued patent or application. In general, the courts look to whether the invention was made available to the interested public. In *Suffolk Tech v. AOL*, users posted answers to a question on a Usenet group.[17] One of the answers was deemed to have anticipated a claimed invention. The Federal Circuit held that public accessibility is the cornerstone for determining whether a reference in a printed publication has been made available to the public. Given that the post was sufficiently disseminated to those of ordinary skill in the art, the post was considered to be publicly accessible. Public accessibility means that the document was disseminated, or other otherwise made available, to the extent that persons interested and ordinarily skilled in the subject matter, exercising reasonable diligence, could locate it.[18]

Practice Pointer

An inventor cannot obtain a patent if the invention has been *on sale* before the effective filing date of a patent application with the USPTO. In order to place an invention "on sale," there must first be an invention, and the sale must be commercial. Although usually an invention is considered complete when it is reduced to practice, it may also be complete when the invention is ready for patenting. The Supreme Court has ruled that an invention will be considered completed when there is "proof of reduction to practice before the critical date" or "the inventor had prepared drawings or other descriptions of the invention that were sufficiently specific to enable a person skilled in the art to practice the invention."[19] When considering whether an invention is on sale, a court will consider "all of the circumstances surrounding the sale or offer to sell, including the stage of development of the invention and the nature of the invention" against the policies underlying section 102(b).[20]

---

17. 752 F.3d 1358 (Fed. Cir. 2014).

18. *In re* Wyer, 655 F.2d 221, 210 U.S.P.Q. 790 (C.C.P.A. 1981) (quoting I.C.E. Corp. v. Armco Steel Corp., 250 F. Supp. 738, 743, 148 U.S.P.Q. 537, 540 (SDNY 1966)).

19. Pfaff v. Wells Elecs, 525 U.S. 55, 67-68, 119 S. Ct. 304, 312 (1998).

20. *Id.* at 66 n.11 (quoting Micro Chem., Inc. v. Great Plains Chem. Co., 103 F.3d 1538, 1544 (1997).

3.   Nonobviousness

The third door requires that the invention not be obvious to someone of ordinary skill in the art. The statute provides that a patent may not be granted "if the differences between the claimed invention and the prior art are such that the claimed invention as a whole would have been obvious before the effective filing date of the claimed invention to a person having ordinary skill in the art to which the claimed invention pertains."[21]

To put this into context, an invention is not patentable when it is embodied in previous teachings or publications. For example, if you invented a table that included a top and four legs, then the table would be deemed anticipated by someone else's creation if the creation embodied all of the parts of your table and was available to the public before your table. In the example below, Invention B cannot be patented (based on novelty) because of the publication of Invention A:

Invention A	Invention B
A chair comprising: ▪ a back, ▪ a seat, and ▪ four legs.	A chair comprising: ▪ a back, ▪ a seat, and ▪ four legs with wheels attached the bottoms of each leg.
Published March 1, 2013	Filed March 10, 2016

Obviousness becomes an issue when an invention embodies the parts of a combination of multiple prior publications. The question then presented is whether the new purported invention is an obvious modification of the prior teachings at the time the new invention was created. Consider the following scenario:

Publication A	Publication B	Invention C
A table comprising: ▪ a top, and ▪ three legs.	A chair comprising: ▪ a back, ▪ a seat, and ▪ four legs.	A school desk/chair combination comprising: ▪ a top, ▪ a back, ▪ a seat, and ▪ four legs.
Published March 10, 2013	Published March 9, 2016	Filed March 10, 2016

In hindsight, one could say a person of ordinary skill in the art would easily come to the conclusion, but to truly understand the situation, the court must stand in the shoes of the inventor at the time the invention was created. To help avoid the notion of 20/20

---

21.   35 U.S.C. § 103.

hindsight, the Supreme Court in *KSR Int'l Co. v. Teleflex, Inc.* laid out the following list of factors to be considered in determining obviousness:[22]

- the scope and content of the prior art
- the difference between the prior art and the claims at issue
- the level of ordinary skill in the pertinent art
- secondary considerations (i.e., long-felt need in the industry, recognition in the industry, the cause of the commercial success, etc.)

4. Explanation

The final door through which an inventor must pass to obtain and maintain a patent relates to an adequate explanation. Title 35, section 112 of the U.S. Code requires that "[t]he specification shall contain a written description of the invention, and of the manner and process of making and using it, in such full, clear, concise, and exact terms as to enable any person skilled in the art to which it pertains, or with which it is most nearly connected, to make and use the same."[23] Section 112 further requires that the specification end with a set of claims.

In brief, this means the patent application must explain the invention in sufficient detail so that a person of ordinary skill in the art can practice the invention without undue experimentation. This description helps promote progress and distinguishes patents from trade secrets. This is called "enablement."[24]

The patent application ends with a claims section. The claims define the metes and bounds of the invention; this section must distinguish the invention over the prior art in order for the invention to pass through the USPTO and to maintain validity. The claims are also used to determine infringement. Infringement by an accused device means the accused device has something corresponding to every element in the claim. Infringement is covered in more detail below.

VI. TREATIES AND FOREIGN PATENTS

Practice Pointer

It is important to understand that a U.S. patent will protect the patented invention only in the United States and has no effect in a foreign country. An inventor who wishes to protect his or her invention abroad must also apply for patents in each

---

22. KSR Int'l Co. v. Teleflex, Inc., 127 S. Ct. 1727 (2007).
23. 35 U.S.C. § 112.
24. CFMT, Inc. v. Yieldup Int'l Corp., 349 F.3d 1333, 1338, 68 U.S.P.Q.2d 1940, 1944 (Fed. Cir. 2003) (to "enable one of ordinary skill in the art to make and use a perfected, commercially viable embodiment absent a claim limitation to that effect.").

of those foreign countries. One option such a party should consider is the Paris Convention for the Protection of Industrial Property.[25] The treaty is adopted by at least 176 countries (at the time of this printing), including the United States, and provides that each country shall respect the other countries' patent rights. In brief, an inventor may file an application in the United States and then file that same application in a second country who is a member of the Paris Convention. If the second filing is within 12 months of the first filing, the foreign country will afford the priority date of the first filing.

Another treaty, known as the Patent Cooperation Treaty, was negotiated at a diplomatic conference in Washington, D.C. in June 1970.[26] The treaty came into force on January 24, 1978, and as of 2014 is adhered to by over 148 countries, including the United States. The treaty facilitates the filing of applications for patent on the same invention in member countries by providing, among other things, for centralized filing procedures and a standardized application format. Filing pursuant to the Patent Cooperation Treaty effectively extends the 12-month Paris Convention timing requirements to 30 months.

VII. HOW TO GET A PATENT

A. Who Has the Rights to a Patent? (Inventor Versus Company)

The natural person, and not a company, who invents the patentable subject matter is entitled to the invention.[27] When two or more people come up with an invention, they must apply jointly for the patent. In contrast, people who make only a financial contribution to an invention may not be joined in the application as an inventor. For applications filed on or after September 16, 2012, the original applicant is presumed to be the initial owner of an application for an original patent.[28] For applications filed before September 16, 2012, the ownership of the patent initially vested in the named inventors of the invention.[29]

In the absence of an agreement to the contrary, each of the owners of a patent may make, use, offer to sell, or sell the patented invention without the consent of, and without accounting to, the other owners.[30] If an employee were to resign during the development process, the employee may still have rights as an inventor. A stray inventor could thus grant a third party the right to use the patent and make the patent harder to enforce if he

---

25. Paris Convention for the Protection of Industrial Property, Mar. 20, 1883, as revised at Stockholm, July 14, 1967, 21 U.S.T. 1583, 828 U.N.T.S. 305.

26. Patent Cooperation Treaty, 28 U.S.T. 7645.

27. 35 U.S.C. § 101.

28. *See* 37 C.F.R. § 3.73(a).

29. *See* Beech Aircraft Corp. v. EDO Corp., 990 F.2d 1237, 1248, 26 U.S.P.Q.2d 1572, 1582 (Fed. Cir. 1993).

30. 35 U.S.C. § 262.

or she refuses to join a suit. In general, patent suits will not move forward, and could be dismissed, unless all interested parties are named in the suit.

B. Types of Filings

When applying for a patent, there are a couple of options: an applicant can choose to file a provisional application or a nonprovisional application. The former is usually faster and cheaper but affords the applicant only a 12-month period of potential protection, after which he or she must file a nonprovisional application. A description of each type of application is provided below.

1. Provisional Application for a Patent

A provisional application provides a low-cost alternative to inventors. In theory, unlike a traditional nonprovisional application, the applicant does not have to provide claims, an oath, or a declaration. The inventor must provide only a cover sheet, a written description of the invention, and any necessary drawings.

Practice Pointer

However, there are downsides to a provisional application. Provisional applications may not be filed for designs, and they afford the applicant protection for only 12 months. Further, the applicant is not actually given patent protection; rather, the applicant is given a possibility of patent protection. In order for the applicant to enforce his or her rights, the applicant must still file a traditional nonprovisional application during the 12-month period of the provisional application. If the applicant fails to then file, the provisional application will expire, and the applicant will no longer have the possibility of patent protection. If the applicant decides to move forward with a nonprovisional application, the nonprovisional application must refer to the provisional application.[31] The nonprovisional application may be afforded the filing date of the provisional application if the provisional application has appropriate support for the invention, i.e., the provisional application explains the invention with sufficient clarity so as to teach the invention to a person of ordinary skill in the art. Thus, although on paper a provisional application is less expensive, the provisional application must satisfy certain written requirements, and it becomes part of the patent's record. This means any problems with a provisional application will infect an eventually issued patent.

---

2. Nonprovisional Application

Unlike the provisional application, applying for a nonprovisional application is a much more complex process, and is ultimately necessary to afford an applicant patent

---

31.   35 U.S.C. § 119(e).

protection. Also unlike a provisional application, a nonprovisional application includes several required sections and is subjected to an examination by the USPTO.

Practice Pointer

The nonprovisional application must include all required parts or it will not be forwarded for examination.

VIII. PARTS OF AN ISSUED PATENT

An issued patent is comprised of multiple parts, including a summary page, drawing set, background of the invention, brief summary of the invention, brief description of the drawings, detailed description of the invention, and claims, all of which are discussed below.

A. Summary Page

The summary page is the first page of the patent. It includes such useful information as the patent number, name(s) of inventor(s), serial number, abstract, prior-art references, and representative drawings. The patent number is the number granted to the patent upon issuance. The serial number is the number given to the patent while it was an application in the USPTO. The references cited show the art the USPTO considered while it was deciding whether to grant the patent. The representative drawing shows the picture the examiner felt best represented the invention. Finally, the abstract is quick summary of the patented subject matter.[32]

---

32. 37 C.F.R. § 1.72; MPEP, *supra* note 6, at 608.01(b).

US009816280B1

(12) **United States Patent**
Reitnauer

(10) **Patent No.:** **US 9,816,280 B1**
(45) **Date of Patent:** **Nov. 14, 2017**

(54) **PORTABLE FLOOR**

(71) Applicant: **Matthew Reitnauer**, Emmaus, PA (US)

(72) Inventor: **Matthew Reitnauer**, Emmaus, PA (US)

(*) Notice: Subject to any disclaimer, the term of this patent is extended or adjusted under 35 U.S.C. 154(b) by 0 days.

(21) Appl. No.: **15/341,728**

(22) Filed: **Nov. 2, 2016**

(51) **Int. Cl.**
E04G 9/08 (2006.01)
E04G 11/36 (2006.01)

(52) **U.S. Cl.**
CPC *E04G 11/36* (2013.01); *E04G 9/083* (2013.01)

(58) **Field of Classification Search**
CPC . E04G 9/08; E04G 9/083; E04G 11/36; E04F 15/00; E04F 15/02; E04F 15/02183; E04F 15/02033; E04F 15/02038; E04F 15/163; E04F 15/166; E04F 15/16; E04F 2201/0594; B62D 55/00; B62D 55/02; B62D 55/04; B62D 55/06; B62D 55/062; B62D 55/0655; B62D 55/08; B62D 55/18; B62D 55/20; B62D 55/202; B62D 55/205; B62D 55/21; B62D 55/213
USPC 404/35, 39, 41
See application file for complete search history.

(56) **References Cited**

U.S. PATENT DOCUMENTS

3,295,269 A * 1/1967 Schuster A45B 9/00
182/41
3,611,655 A 10/1971 Loebner

4,315,345 A	2/1982	Schifj
5,168,678 A *	12/1992	Scott, Jr. A01G 1/08 47/33
5,833,386 A	11/1998	Rosen et al.
7,090,430 B1	8/2006	Fletcher et al.
7,364,383 B2	4/2008	Fletcher et al.
8,534,003 B2	9/2013	Curry, III
2004/0010983 A1*	1/2004	Eshpar E06B 9/15 52/71
2007/0062147 A1	3/2007	Wright
2014/0161525 A1*	6/2014	Smith E01C 5/18 404/41
2015/0056013 A1*	2/2015	Brown E01C 5/005 404/35
2016/0115653 A1*	4/2016	Forbes E01C 5/14 404/35

* cited by examiner

Primary Examiner — Jessica Laux
(74) *Attorney, Agent, or Firm* — Altman & Martin; Steven K Martin

(57) **ABSTRACT**

A portable floor composed of a plurality of rectangular sections attached by hinges so that adjacent sections pivot between a rolled configuration for transportation and storage and a flat configuration to bear weight. A finger edge of the section has a plurality of spaced fingers with a beveled surface that extends from the bottom of the finger upwardly to the tip of the finger. The opposed notch edge of the section has a plurality of spaced notches with a beveled surface from the top of the section downwardly into the notch. The beveled surfaces are at an angle of 15° to 75°. The finger edge meshes with the notch edge of the adjacent section. Adjacent top surfaces are planar when the notch and finger beveled surfaces abut each other. The hinge is a pin extending through aligned holes in the fingers and cogs between notches.

15 Claims, 8 Drawing Sheets

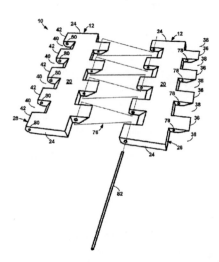

B. Drawing Set

The drawings include the figures provided by the applicant and are used to describe the invention. Each element in the drawings should be labeled with a corresponding number. The numbers are addressed in the detailed description.

U.S. Patent   Nov. 14, 2017   Sheet 1 of 8   US 9,816,280 B1

U.S. Patent   Nov. 14, 2017   Sheet 2 of 8   US 9,816,280 B1

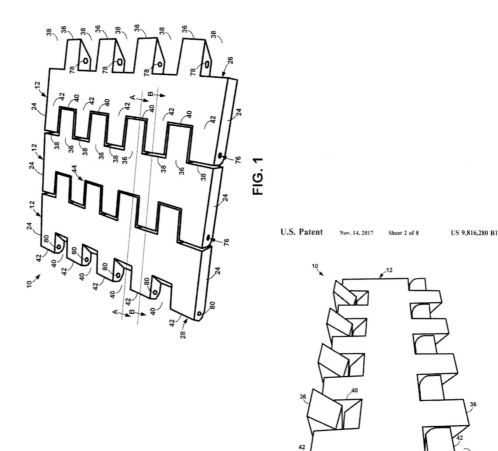

FIG. 1

FIG. 2

US 9,816,280 B1

1

PORTABLE FLOOR

STATEMENT REGARDING FEDERALLY
SPONSORED RESEARCH OR DEVELOPMENT

Not Applicable

REFERENCE TO A SEQUENCE LISTING, A
TABLE, OR A COMPUTER PROGRAM LISTING
COMPACT DISK APPENDIX

Not Applicable

BACKGROUND OF THE INVENTION

1. Field of the Invention

The present invention relates to building construction, more particularly, to portable, temporary flooring for working in areas where only joists are installed.

2. Description of the Related Art

Many homes and building have attics and other spaces that without permanent flooring. The floor area is composed of parallel joists with exposed drywall or blueboard. There may be insulation in between. This arrangement makes it very difficult for walking around in the attic area when using it for storage or for other work on the building.

Often the building owner will lay sheets of plywood or other flat material over the top of the joists to create a passable floor surface. However, this in usually inconvenient because access to an attic is often through relatively small openings, thereby making it difficult to move plywood to the attic. Also, these sheets of plywood are not very sturdy and will not support a large amount of weight or movement.

What is desired is a portable, folding flooring unit that is capable of being easily carried into small areas, such as attics, and is sturdy enough to support a significant amount of weight regardless of its orientation relative to the joists.

BRIEF SUMMARY OF THE INVENTION

The portable floor of the present invention rolls up for transportation and storage and to flatten out to bear weight. It is composed of a plurality of rectangular sections that are attached to each other by hinges. The hinge permits adjacent sections to pivot between a flat operational configuration and a rolled storage configuration.

The finger edge of the section has a plurality of spaced fingers alternating with gaps. The notch edge of the section has a plurality of spaced notches alternating with cogs. The finger edge of one section meshes with the notch edge of the adjacent section.

Each finger has a beveled surface that extends inwardly from the tip of the finger to the bottom surface at an angle in the range of from 15° to 75° and preferably approximately 45°. Each notch has a corresponding beveled surface from the top surface of the section outwardly into the notch to the bottom surface. The top surfaces of adjacent sections are substantially planar when the notch beveled surface abuts the finger beveled surface in the operational configuration.

Adjacent sections are attached by a hinge. Each finger and each cog has a transverse hole that are aligned. A hinge pin extends through the aligned holes to form the hinge. Any method known to retain the hinge pin can be used.

The various parameters of the section are determined based on the design load and resulting moment created at the hinge, the materials used for construction and the method of manufacturing used.

2

The rolled portable floor of the present invention is transported to where it is needed and then rolled out flat and then flipped over.

Objects of the present invention will become apparent in light of the following drawings and detailed description of the invention.

BRIEF DESCRIPTION OF THE DRAWINGS

For a fuller understanding of the nature and object of the present invention, reference is made to the accompanying drawings, wherein:

FIG. 1 is a perspective view of the portable floor of the present invention with three sections installed;

FIG. 2 is a perspective view of the portable floor of the present invention with three sections rolled;

FIG. 3 is an exploded, perspective view of two sections;

FIG. 4 is a cross-sectional view of two sections taken at A-A;

FIG. 5 is a cross-sectional view of two sections taken at B-B;

FIG. 6 is a top view of part of a section showing various parameters related to the fingers and notches;

FIG. 7 is a top view of two sections showing different parameters related to the fingers and notches;

FIG. 8 is a top view of two sections showing different parameters related to the fingers and notches;

FIG. 9 is an end view of a rolled portable floor with sections having decreasing lengths;

FIG. 10 is a perspective view of a configuration of the underside of a section;

FIG. 11 is a perspective view of a finger terminal section; and

FIG. 12 is a perspective view of a notch terminal section.

DETAILED DESCRIPTION OF THE
INVENTION

The portable floor **10** of the present invention is designed to roll up for transportation and to flatten out to bear weight. The portable floor **10**, shown in the figures, is composed of a plurality of rectangular sections **12** that are attached to each other by hinges **76**. Each section **12** has a top surface **20**, a bottom surface **22**, opposed, parallel side edges **24**, a finger edge **26**, and a notch edge **28** opposed to the finger edge **26**. The hinge **76** permits adjacent sections **12** to pivot between an operational configuration, shown in FIG. **1**, where the top surfaces **20** are substantial co-planar, and a storage configuration, shown in FIG. **2**, where the top surfaces **20** are not generally co-planar to each other.

As shown in FIG. **3**, the finger edge **26** has a plurality of spaced fingers **36** alternating with gaps **38**. The notch edge **28** has a plurality of spaced notches **40** alternating with cogs **42**. Preferably, the fingers **36** and notches **40** are evenly spaced. The finger edge **26** of one section **12** meshes with the notch edge **28** of the adjacent section **12**, as at **44**, such that the fingers **36** fit into the notches **40** and the cogs **42** fit into the gaps **38**.

As shown in FIG. **4**, each finger **36** has a beveled surface **50** that extends inwardly from the tip **54** of the finger **36** to the bottom surface **52** at an angle **56** in the range of from 15° to 75°, preferably in the range of from 30° to 60°, and most preferably approximately 45°. The angle **56** can vary depending on the size and strength of the finger **36** in combination with the maximum load that the portable floor **10** is designed to carry.

C.   Background of the Invention

This section usually describes the general nature of the problem that the invention was made to solve and discusses the state of the existing technology.

D.   Brief Description of the Drawings/Brief Summary

This section provides a summary of what is covered in the detailed description and provides a brief description of the figures.

E.   Detailed Description of the Invention

This section describes the invention in detail and is designed, along with the drawings, to enable one of ordinary skill in the art to practice the invention without undue experimentation.[33]

F.   Claims

The patent concludes with the claims section. This section usually begins with the words, "I claim," "We claim," or "What is claimed is." The claim section sets forth one or more claims, which define the scope of the subject matter that the patent protects. For a basic filing fee, the applicant may include up to 20 claims. Three of those 20 claims may be independent claims, and 17 of those claims should be dependent claims. A claim is dependent if it incorporates by reference a preceding claim.[34]

---

33.   MPEP 608.01(g).
34.   37 C.F.R. § 1.75; MPEP, *supra* note 6, at 608.01(i).

US 9,816,280 B1

3

As shown in FIG. 4, each notch 40 has a beveled surface 60 that extends outwardly from the top surface 20 of the section 12 into the notch 40 to the bottom surface 52 at an angle 62 in the range of from 15° to 75°, preferably in the range of from 30° to 60°, and most preferably approximately 45°. The angle 62 can vary for the reasons described above for the finger bevel angle 56.

The notch bevel angle 62 is the same as the finger bevel angle 56 so that the top surfaces 20 of adjacent sections 12 are substantially planar when the notch beveled surface 60 abuts the finger beveled surface 50 in the operational configuration, as in FIG. 4.

In the illustrated configuration, the width 68 of the finger 36 and notch 40 is the same as the width 70 of the gap 38 and cog 42, as in FIG. 6. However, the present invention contemplates that the finger/notch width 68 can be smaller that the gap/cog width 70, as in FIG. 7, or the finger/notch width 68 can be larger than the gap/cog width 70, as in FIG. 8.

As indicated above, adjacent sections 12 are attached by a hinge 76 so that each section 12 can pivot relative to the adjacent section 12. Each finger 36 has a transverse hole 78 and each cog 42 has a transverse hole 80. When the finger edge 26 and notch edge 28 of adjacent sections 12 are meshed, the finger holes 78 and the cog holes 80 align. A hinge pin 82 extends through the aligned holes 78, 80 to form the hinge 76. The hinge pin 82 must be robust enough to handle the weight for which the portable floor 10 is designed. Typically, the hinge pin 82 is a metal rod, either solid or hollow.

There are a number of ways known in the art to retain the hinge pin 82. In one, the finger holes 78 are slightly larger than the diameter of the hinge pin 82 and the cog holes 80 are the same size or slightly smaller than the hinge pin diameter. The hinge pin 82 is forced through the cog holes 80 and are retained by friction. Because the finger holes 78 are larger than the hinge pin diameter, the fingers 36 pivot on the hinge pin 82.

In another method of retaining the hinge pin 82, both the finger holes 78 and cog holes 80 are slightly larger than the hinge pin diameter. The hinge pin 82 is fit through the holes 78, 80 and the ends of the hinge pin 82 are expanded to larger than the cog holes 80 in order to retain the hinge pin 82. Expansion of the hinge pin ends can take the form of, for example, stretching the diameter of the hinge pin or attaching a larger diameter component to the end of the hinge pin 82. A larger diameter component can be, for example, a nut threaded onto the hinge pin end or a disk-shaped component welded or otherwise adhered to the hinge pin end.

The present invention contemplates that any method known to retain the hinge pin 82 that permits adjacent sections 12 to pivot relative to each other can be used.

In order to facilitate pivoting about the hinge 76, the lower corner 86 of the end 84 of the cog 42 is rounded, as in FIG. 5. Alternatively, the cog 42 can be shorter than the finger 36 so that the end 84 does not interfere with the hinge 76.

The length 88 of the section 12 depends on the particular design, the materials from which it is composed, and ease of manipulation. The present invention contemplates that the sections 12 can all have the same length 88, as in FIG. 1, or that they can have different lengths 88. In an example of different lengths 88, the lengths increase in steps from one end of the portable floor 10 to the other end. This facilitates rolling the portable floor 10 into a more compact storage configuration, as shown in FIG. 9.

4

The width 90 of the section 12 depends on the particular design. The present invention does not contemplate any minimum or maximum width 90.

The thickness 92 of the section 12 is appropriate for a combination of the material that it is composed of and the maximum weight that the portable floor 10 is designed to accommodate. In order the reduce the weight of the portable floor 10, the section 12 can be hollow and include ribs 94 for reinforcement, as in FIG. 10.

The present invention contemplates that there can be terminal sections. A finger terminal section 14, shown in FIG. 11, has only a finger edge 26. The opposed edge 30 is flat with no features. A notch terminal section 12, shown in FIG. 12, has only a notch edge 28. The opposed edge 32 is flat with no features. The terminal sections 14, 16 make the portable floor 10 easier to manipulate because there are no fingers and cogs at the ends to get caught on other things.

The sections 12, 14, 16 can be composed of any rigid material that can accommodate the weight the portable floor 10 is designed for. Contemplated materials include plastics, metals, wood, and composites.

The number and parameters of the fingers 36 and notches 40 is determined by coming up with a bearing area at the given bevel angle 56, 62 that can carry the moment created by the chosen design load without exceeding the yield stress of the potential materials. Once the total area is determined, the actual material and method of manufacture are incorporated. In the present design, the section 12 is designed for injection-molded with a fairly uniform thicknesses that is removable from an injection-molding die. The result is multiple fingers 36 on multiple sections 12 that press against each other and transfer the load through the rest of the structure with a simple load path. The gaps 38 and cogs 42 are sized to have similar stress levels created by the bearing load of the hinge pin 82.

In summary, the parameters of the section 12 are determined based on the length 88, width 90, and thickness 92 of the section 12, the design load, and resulting moment created at the hinge 76, the materials used for construction and the method of manufacturing used. The goal is to minimize high stress areas while keeping the structure as light as possible for portability and cost reduction.

The portable floor 10 of the present invention is designed to be able to be taken into an unfinished area where no floor is provided, such as an attic. The rolled floor 10 is transported to where it is needed. Once the floor 10 is where needed, it can be rolled out flat and then flipped over. Because of its design, the floor of the present invention can bear weight regardless of its orientation relative to the joists.

Thus it has been shown and described a portable floor. Since certain changes may be made in the present disclosure without departing from the scope of the present invention, it is intended that all matter described in the foregoing specification and shown in the accompanying drawings be interpreted as illustrative and not in a limiting sense.

What is claimed is:

1. A portable floor comprising:
(a) a plurality of rectangular sections each having a length, a width, a top surface, a bottom surface, a finger edge, and a notch edge opposed to the finger edge;
(b) the finger edge having a plurality of spaced fingers separated by gaps, each finger having a tip and a beveled surface extending inwardly at a bevel angle from the top surface at the tip to the bottom surface;
(c) the notch edge having a plurality of spaced notches separated by cogs, each notch having a beveled surface

IX. AFTER THE APPLICATION

A. Maintenance Fees

To keep a patent in good standing, a patent holder must pay maintenance fees. All utility patents require the payment of maintenance fees every 3.5, 7.5, and 11.5 years from the date the patent is granted. Maintenance fees cannot be paid in advance. Instead, they must be paid within the "window period." The window period includes the six-month period before each due date. These window periods consist of the following:

- First maintenance fee payment: 3 to 3 1/2 years after the date of issue;
- Second maintenance fee payment: 7 to 7 1/2 years after the date of issue; and
- Final maintenance fee payment: 11 to 11 1/2 years after the date of issue.[35]

If the patent holder fails to make the required maintenance fee payment within the window period, the patent holder can still make the payment within a "grace period," but must pay a surcharge. The grace period consists of the six months immediately following each due date:

- First grace period: 3 1/2 years and through the day of the fourth anniversary of the grant of the patent;
- Second grace period: 7 1/2 years and through the day of the eighth anniversary of the grant of the patent; and
- Final grace period: 11 1/2 years and through the day of the 12th anniversary of the grant of the patent.[36]

If the patent holder fails to make the payment by the end of the applicable grace period, then the patent will expire and the patent holder will no long have protection under the patent. A list of fees can be found on the USPTO's website at https://www.uspto.gov/learning-and-resources/fees-and-payment/uspto-fee-schedule.

X. ASSIGNMENTS AND LICENSES

A patent is personal property. A patent's ownership may be transferred like other forms of personal property, such as by inheritance or even as collateral. Patent law provides that when assigning rights in patent applications, patents, or any interest therein to another party, the assignment must be in writing. The assignor may transfer all or a part of the rights, title, or interest in the patent.[37] When a patent is assigned, the assignee becomes the owner of the patent. As an owner, the assignee may make, use, offer to sell, or sell the patented invention without the consent of, and without accounting to, the other owners.[38] An assignment, grant, or conveyance of any patent or application for patent should be

---

35. 37 C.F.R. § 1.362(d).
36. 37 C.F.R. § 1.362(e).
37. 37 C.F.R. § 3.1.
38. 35 U.S.C. § 262.

acknowledged before a notary public. The certificate of acknowledgment constitutes prima facie evidence of the execution of the assignment, grant, or conveyance.[39] A conveyance of less than all of the rights in a patent is called a license, which can be complex. Assignment of all patent rights can be addressed in a short, two- to three-paragraph document. In contrast, a license may address a myriad of issues, such as duration of the license, geographic scope, products, fees, accounting, enforceability, etc.

A. Recording of Assignments

Practice Pointer

Any assignment or license should also be recorded with the USPTO. If an assignment or license is not recorded in the USPTO within three months from its date, it is void against a subsequent purchaser for a valuable consideration without notice, unless it is recorded prior to the subsequent purchase.[40]

An instrument relating to an ownership interest in a patent should identify the patent by number and date, and the name of the inventor as well as the title of the invention as stated in the patent should also be given. An instrument relating to an application should identify the application by its application number and date of filing, and the name of the inventor as well as the title of the invention as stated in the application should also be given. Sometimes an assignment of an application is executed at the same time that the application is prepared and before it has been filed with the USPTO. Such assignment should adequately identify the application by its date of execution, inventor name, and invention title so that there can be no mistake as to the application intended. If an application has been assigned and the assignment has been recorded or filed for recordation, the patent will be issued to the assignee as owner if the name of the assignee is provided when the issue fee is paid and the patent is requested to be issued to the assignee.

XI. INFRINGEMENT

A patent can be infringed when someone without authorization makes, uses, offers for sale, or sells any patented invention within the United States or U.S. territories. A patent may also be infringed when someone imports into the United States a patented invention. There are a few remedies to patent infringement that a patent holder can seek, such as an injunction stopping the infringing party from practicing the patent holder's invention

---

39. 35 U.S.C. § 261.
40. 35 U.S.C. § 261.

or monetary damages. If the infringing party is the U.S. government, the remedies for the patent holder are a little different. The government is permitted to use any patented invention without the permission of the patent holder, but the government must compensate the patent holder for the use. The USPTO does not hear matters related to patent infringement; instead, actions for infringement must be brought before the courts.

A. Marking Requirement

Under 35 U.S.C. § 287, a patent owner can receive damages against an infringing party only if the infringing party was adequately notified of the patent owner's patents.[41] A patent owner can notify an infringing party by providing actual notice or constructive notice. Actual notice occurs when the infringing party is directly informed of his or her infringing activity, and constructive notice usually occurs when a patent owner has marked his or her product with a patent number. Marking traditionally was done by placing "Made under U.S. Pat." or "For Use under U.S. Pat.," followed by the actual patent number on the invention. However, under rules set out in the AIA, patent holders can use virtual marking. In virtual marking, the patent holder marks the invention with the indicator "Patent" or "Pat." together with a URL address. The URL address should resolve to a page containing the associated patent numbers. This serves a benefit in that it allows companies to place a single notice on all its patents.

Practice Pointer

However, companies should be cautious because marking an item patented when it is not patented is illegal. Companies should remember that a patent's protection does not begin until the patent is granted.

B. All-Elements Test

There are two types of infringement: direct and indirect. Direct infringement occurs when someone without authority makes, uses, offers to sell, or sells any patented invention within the United States or imports the invention into the United States.[42] Indirect infringement occurs when someone induces another to commit patent infringement or when a person contributes to a patent infringement committed by another person.[43]

In order to satisfy a cause of action for direct infringement, the accusing party must prove that the infringing device embodies each and every element of the patent holder's claim. This is called the all-elements test. Take, for example, the following hypothetical inventions:

---

41. 35 U.S.C. § 287.
42. 35 U.S.C. § 271(a).
43. 35 U.S.C. § 271(b)-(c).

Patent 1	Product 2	Product 3
A device comprising: • a top, and • four legs.	A device comprising: • a top, • four legs, and • wheels.	A device comprising: • a top, • three legs, and • an extendable support.

Under the all-elements test, Product 2 would infringe Patent 1; however, Product 3 may not infringe either Patent 1 or Patent 2 under the all-elements test. This is because Product 2 contains all the parts present in Patent 1: (1) a top and (2) four legs. Therefore, all the elements of Patent 1 are present in Product 2. Importantly, the device must embody all elements of the patented invention to infringe a patent. For the device to embody the elements of a patent, it must be assembled and capable of being used. Therefore, although the manufacturer may not be directly liable for infringement, the individual who actually assembles the invention, after receiving the parts, would be making the patented invention and committing patent infringement. This does not mean, however, that a party can simply avoid patent infringement by having someone else perform the tasks that infringe. A first party would still be liable for infringement when he or she contracts with a second party to take actions that lead to patent infringement.[44]

C. Doctrine of Equivalents

To find infringement under the all-elements rule, an accused device must contain each limitation of a claim, *either literally or by an equivalent.*[45] To determine whether an element of a claim is equivalent to an aspect of a device, courts use the doctrine of equivalents. The Supreme Court defines equivalency as follows:

> What constitutes equivalency must be determined against the context of the patent, the prior art, and the particular circumstances of the case. Equivalence, in the patent law, is not the prisoner of a formula and is not an absolute to be considered in a vacuum. It does not require complete identity for every purpose and in every respect. In determining equivalents, things equal to the same thing may not be equal to each other and, by the same token, things for most purposes different may sometimes be equivalents. Consideration must be given to the purpose for which an ingredient is used in a patent, the qualities it has when combined with the other ingredients, and the function which it is intended to perform. An important factor is whether persons reasonably skilled in the art would have known of the interchangeability of an ingredient not contained in the patent with one that was.[46]

---

44. On Demand Mach. Corp. v. Ingram Indus., 442 F.3d 1331, 1333 (Fed. Cir. 2006).
45. TIP Sys., LLC v. Phillips & Brooks/Gladwin, Inc., 529 F.3d 1364 (Fed. Cir. 2008).
46. Warner-Jenkinson Co. v. Hilton Davis Chem. Co., 520 U.S. 17, 24-25, 117 S. Ct. 1040, 1047 (1997) (quoting 339 U.S. at 610).

The test for equivalence is not applied to the invention as a whole, but rather must be applied to each individual element of a claim. This means that even if a device performed the same functions as a patented invention in a similar manner, the device might not infringe the patent. A court must evaluate whether each element of the claim was either present, or when not directly present, an equivalent was present in the device. To make this determination, courts consider whether the element of the device performs substantially the same function in substantially the same way to obtain the same result as the element of the patented invention.[47]

---

47. *See* Graver Tank, 339 U.S. 605 (1950).

Chapter 14

Copyright

By Michael J. Schwab[1]

This chapter discusses the acquisition and protection of copyright, a form of intellectual property protection provided to authors of "original works of authorship" fixed in a tangible form. It covers the legal basis for copyright protection, works eligible for copyright protection, requirements for works to qualify for protection, rights provided to copyright owners, term of protection, requirements for registering a copyright with the U.S. Copyright Office, and infringement claims, defenses, and remedies.

I.   INTRODUCTION

Copyright protects original works of authorship that are fixed in a tangible form of expression. It does not protect ideas, concepts, facts, procedures, systems, techniques, or methods of operation explained, illustrated, or embodied within the work of expression. An "original work of authorship" is an expression of an idea (e.g., novel, magazine articles, computer software, songs, plays, operas, photographs, posters, recordings of music, building designs, etc.) that is independently created and possesses at least some degree of creativity. A work is "fixed" when it is captured in a medium that permits the work to be perceived, reproduced, or communicated for more than a transitory duration.

Copyright law is intended to encourage the creation of art and culture by rewarding creators of original works of authorship with certain exclusive rights. These include the right to make and sell copies of their works, create derivative works, and perform

---

1.   The author wishes to thank Stephen Breidenbach, an associate of Moritt Hock & Hamroff, for his valuable research and assistance with this chapter.

or display their works publicly. These exclusive rights are qualified, however, because copyright protection exists for only a limited period of time and is subject to other limitations.

This chapter provides an overview of the copyright law in the United States, including the following:

- Legal Basis for Copyright Protection
- Copyrightable Subject Matter
- Standards for a Work to Qualify for Copyright Protection
- A Copyright Owner's Rights
- Procedures for Obtaining Copyright Protection
- Duration of Copyright Protection
- Ownership and Transfer of Ownership
- Copyright Registration
- Copyright Infringement (Claims, Defenses, and Remedies)

II. LEGAL BASIS FOR COPYRIGHT PROTECTION

A. Federal Law

In the United States, copyright protection derives from Article I, Section 8 of the U.S. Constitution, which provides Congress with the "[p]ower . . . to promote the Progress of Science and useful Arts, by securing for limited Times to Authors and Inventors the exclusive Right to their respective Writings and Discoveries." The current federal copyright law is the Copyright Act of 1976 (the Copyright Act), which took effect on January 1, 1978.[2] It replaced the Copyright Act of 1909 (the 1909 Act). However, the 1909 Act remains in effect for works created before the effective date of the Copyright Act. Certain significant differences between the Copyright Act and the 1909 Act are highlighted throughout this chapter.

Since its enactment, the Copyright Act has undergone some important amendments, including:

- The enactment of the Orrin G. Hatch-Bob Goodlatte Music Modernization Act on October 11, 2018, which made a number of amendments related to how royalties will be administered and distributed when songs are licensed by digital service providers such as Spotify and Apple Music (the Music Modernization Act).
- To meet certain obligations of the Berne Convention for the Protection of Literary and Artistic Works (the Berne Convention) on March 1, 1989.
- To meet certain obligations of the Agreement on Trade-Related Aspects of Intellectual Property (the TRIPS Agreement) on January 1, 1996.

---

2.   17 U.S.C. §§ 101-1332.

- The enactment of the Sonny Bono Copyright Term Extension Act (effective October 27, 1998) and the Digital Millennium Copyright Act (DMCAA) (effective October 28, 1998).

B. State Law

Before the effective date of the Copyright Act (January 1, 1978), there was a dual system of copyright protection in the United States. The 1909 Act provided federal protection to works that were published or registered. Unpublished and unregistered works were protected, if at all, by state statutory or common law. The Copyright Act preempted most state and common-law protections and established a single system of federal protection.

Generally, the copyright law in effect at the time of a particular act governs the act in question. For example, a dispute concerning a book written in 1975, published in 1980, and copied by an infringer in 2000 would be governed by state or common law for purposes of determining ownership at the time of creation, and the Copyright Act (including the Berne Convention amendments) for purposes of copyright notice and infringement.

C. Copyright Office

The U.S. Copyright Office, a department within the Library of Congress, is the agency of the federal government responsible for the regulation and administration of copyrights. It does not handle dispute resolution or adjudication, but acts as a clearinghouse for registered copyrights. It is responsible for copyright registrations and deposits, recording copyright transfers, and other administrative aspects of the copyright law.

D. International Protection

Copyright laws are national in scope. This means protection against unauthorized use of an original work of expression depends on the law of the country where the unauthorized use occurred. The United States is, however, a party to a number of treaties that generally require member countries to maintain minimum standards for copyright protection under their national laws and provide reciprocal treatment to copyright owners in other member countries. These treaties include the following:

- Berne Convention for Protection of Literary and Artistic Works
- WIPO Copyright Treaty
- WIPO Performance and Phonograms Treaty
- The Universal Copyright Convention
- The Geneva Phonograms Convention
- The TRIPs Agreement

III. COPYRIGHTABLE SUBJECT MATTER

Copyright law protects original "works of authorship," which the Copyright Act[3] defines as including the following categories of works:

- Literary works, which include any works, other than audiovisual works, that are expressed in words, numbers, or other verbal or numerical symbols or indicia such as books, periodicals, manuscripts, manuals, brochures, computer software, and software documentation.

- Musical works, including the accompanying words such as musical compositions and scores and accompanying lyrics, regardless of the medium or form in which they are embodied, whether or not they are in intelligible written form. If a musical work includes both music and lyrics, the copyright protects against the unauthorized use of the integrated work as a whole as well as the words or music alone.

- Dramatic works, including the accompanying music, such as scripts for plays, screenplays, operas, and skits that tell a story though action and dialogue. To be protected, a dramatic work must be fixed in a tangible form of expression. Therefore, a live, improvised performance is not protected unless it is recorded or memorialized in a transcript.

- Pantomimes and choreographic works, which are gestures or dance steps such as ballets, modern dance, and mime works. As with dramatic works, pantomimes and choreographic works must be fixed in a tangible form of expression to obtain copyright protection (e.g., recording the performance on film or digital media, etc.).

- Pictorial, graphic, and sculpture works, such as photographs, posters, maps, globes, diagrams, models, graphic arts, cartoon strips, statues, and works of fine art.

- Motion pictures and other audio-visual works, which are a series of related images that are intended to be shown through the use of a machine or device such as motion pictures, documentaries, and training films.

- Sound recordings, which are works resulting from fixing sounds in a phonorecord[4] and may include musical, spoken performances, and other sounds. Copyright in the sound recording exists separately from the copyright in the underlying musical, literary, or dramatic work and protects only the particular recording.

- Architectural works, which are designs of buildings embodied in any medium, such as architectural plans, drawings, or a constructed building.

---

3. *Id.* § 102.

4. A "phonorecord" is a physical object that contains a sound recording, such as a digital audio file or a compact disc. The term includes any type of object that may be used to store a sound recording, including digital formats such as .mp3 and .wave files. *Id.* § 101.

The Copyright Act[5] provides that copyrightable subject matter also includes the following:

- Compilations, which are works "formed by the collection and assembling of preexisting materials or of data that are selected, coordinated, or arranged in such a way that the resulting work as a whole constitutes an original work of authorship."[6] Examples of compilations include a directory of the best services in a geographical area, a collection of sound recordings from a particular time period, or an academic journal containing articles on a particular topic.
- Derivative works, which are works "based upon one or more preexisting works" in which the earlier work has been transformed, adopted, or recast.[7] Examples of derivative works include translations, dramatizations, condensed versions, and the motion picture version of a book. Derivative works also include works that consist of "editorial revisions, annotations, elaborations, or other modifications which, as a whole represent an original work of authorship."[8]

Copyright protection in compilations and derivative works extends only to the original material contributed by the author. It does not extend to any of the underlying work, and the author does not acquire any rights to the underlying work. Copyright protection in a compilation or derivative work also does not extend to any portion of the work based on preexisting materials that were used "unlawfully."[9] In this context, "unlawful" refers to use of underlying material that was not authorized by the copyright owner or permitted by copyright law.

Practice Pointer

Unless an exception applies, the author of the compilation or derivative work generally must obtain permission, usually in the form of a license, from the owner of the copyright in the underlying work before the work can be used in the compilation or derivative work. Counsel should carefully review all preexisting materials proposed to be used in a compilation or derivative work to determine what, if any, permissions are required to be obtained.

---

5. *Id.* § 103.
6. *Id.* § 101.
7. *Id.*
8. 17 U.S.C. § 101.
9. *Id.* § 103.

The Copyright Act expressly excludes certain works from copyright protection. These include the following:

- Works of the U.S. government.[10] However, the U.S. government may receive and hold copyrights that are transferred to it by assignment, bequest, or otherwise.
- Ideas, procedures, processes, systems, methods of operation, concepts, principals, or discoveries "regardless of the form in which they are described, explained, illustrated or embodied in such work."[11] Copyright protection is limited to the author's expression of ideas and concepts, not the ideas or concepts themselves.

IV.   STANDARDS FOR COPYRIGHT PROTECTION

To receive copyright protection, a work must meet two criteria: originality and fixation.

A.   Originality

Copyright protects "original works of authorship."[12] To be "original," a work must be independently created and possess a minimal degree of creativity. Independently created means the work was not copied. A work does not need to be novel or unique to obtain copyright protection. Two substantially similar or even identical works may each receive copyright protection if both works were created without copying each other or another source. The standard for creativity is low. To be protected, a work must have a minimal amount of creative expression. "All that is needed to satisfy both the Constitution and the statute is that the 'author' contributed something more than a 'merely trivial' variation, something recognizably 'his own.' Originality in this context 'means little more than a prohibition of actual copying.' No matter how poor artistically the 'author's' addition, it is enough if it be his own."[13]

Notwithstanding this low standard for creativity, there are certain works that the Copyright Office and the courts have determined do not contain a sufficient amount of creative expression to qualify for copyright protection. These include the following:

- Titles
- Names

---

10.   *Id.* § 105.

11.   *Id.* § 102(b).

12.   *Id.* § 102(a).

13.   Alfred Bell & Co. v. Catalds Fine Arts, Inc., 191 F.2d 99, 102-02 (2d Cir. 1951); *see also* Feist Publ'ns, Inc. v. Rural Tel Serv., 499 U.S. 230, 345 (1991) ("The *sine qua non* of copyright is originality. To qualify for copyright protection, a work must be original to the author. Original, as the term is used in copyright, means only that the work was independently created by the author (as opposed to copied from other works), and it possesses at least some degree of creativity.").

- Single words or short phrases
- Slogans
- Typeface
- Mere listing of ingredients or contents
- Headlines

Practice Pointer

Some works that do not qualify for copyright protection may, in certain circumstances, qualify for trademark protection (see Chapter 13, Trademarks).

B. Fixation

Copyright protects original works of authorship that are "fixed in any tangible medium of expression."[14] Fixation occurs when the work is embodied by or with the author's permission in a medium that is sufficiently permanent or stable as to permit the work to be perceived, reproduced, or otherwise communicated for a period of more than a transitory duration.[15] Examples of mediums upon which works may be fixed include:

- Ink on paper
- Paint on canvas
- Dictation recorded on tape or digital devices
- Clay molded into a sculpture
- A photograph on film
- Music or motion pictures on video or audio tapes or digital media
- Digital media stored on a computer hard drive, read-only memory, or other electronic, magnetic, or optical media

Fixation can occur on any medium that permits the work to be perceived directly (e.g., book printed on paper) or requires the use of a machine or other device (e.g., an e-book that may only be viewed by the use of an e-reader, computer, or other device). The medium upon which the work is fixed must be sufficiently permanent to permit the work to be communicated for more than a "transitory duration."[16] For example, live television shows are considered to be transitory unless they are recorded simultaneously with the transmission or performance.

---

14. 17 U.S.C. § 102(a).
15. *Id.* § 101.
16. *Id.* "A work consisting of sounds, images or both, that are being transmitted, is 'fixed' . . . if the fixation of the work is being made simultaneously with its transmission."

V. COPYRIGHT OWNER'S EXCLUSIVE RIGHTS

A. Exclusive Rights

A copyright owner is provided with a "bundle" of exclusive rights to protected works.[17] These include the following:

- **Reproduction right.** The right to prevent others from making copies or phonorecords of the work.
- **The right to create derivative works.** The right to make adaptations or derivative works of the work.
- **Distribution rights.** The right to distribute copies or phonorecords of the work to the public. Distribution means the transfer of ownership of copies of the work by any means. This includes the physical transfer of custody, but not ownership, of copies of the work such as through renting, leasing, or lending. Payment or other consideration is not required for a transfer to be considered distribution.
- **Public performance right.** The right to perform the following categories of work publicly: literary works; musical works; dramatic and choreographic works; pantomimes; and motion picture and other audiovisual works. Under the Copyright Act, "perform" means to "recite, render, play, dance, or act [the work], either directly or by means of any device or process or, in the case of a motion picture or other audiovisual work, to show its images in any sequence or to make the sounds accompanying it audible,"[18] and "to perform or display a work publicly" means to perform or display the work in a place that is open to the public or where a substantial number of persons, other than family members or acquaintances, are gathered.[19] A public performance includes the communication or transmission of a work to the public by means of a device regardless of whether members of the public are in the same place or able to receive the performance at the same time. For example, on-demand video is considered a public performance even though it may never be viewed by more than one person at a time.[20]
- **Public display right.** The copyright owner has the exclusive right to display the following categories of work publicly: literary; musical; dramatic and choreographic works; pantomimes; pictorial, graphic and sculpture works; and motion picture and audio visual works, including individual images of motion pictures and other audiovisual works. The criteria for whether a display is public are the same as for a performance.

---

17. *Id.* § 106.
18. *Id.* § 101.
19. *Id.*
20. *See* U.S. v. Am. Soc. of Composers, Authors & Publishers, 627 F.3d 64 (2d Cir. 2010).

B. Exceptions to the Copyright Owner's Exclusive Rights

The Copyright Act contains several exceptions to the exclusive rights provided to copyright owners, such as fair use, the first-sale doctrine, and archival reproductions, that permit certain limited uses of protected works without permission from or payment of a royalty to the copyright owner. The Copyright Act also contains provisions providing for statutory or compulsory licenses that permit certain limited unauthorized uses of protected works subject to the payment of a statutorily defined royalty to the copyright owner.

1. Fair Use

Fair use refers to the legally permissible, unauthorized use of a protected work for certain purposes, such as, but not limited to, commentary, criticism, news reporting, teaching, research, or scholarship.[21] Not all such unauthorized uses of a protected work will be considered to be a fair use. Courts consider the following four factors that are set forth in the Copyright Act when evaluating whether a particular unauthorized use of a copyrighted work is fair:

- **Purpose and character of the use.** This factor considers whether the unauthorized use advances a socially beneficial activity, such as, but not limited to, commentary, criticism, news reporting, teaching, and scholarship. A noncommercial use of a copyrighted work is generally more likely to be found to be fair than a use made for commercial gain. Courts also consider whether the use at issue is "transformative." A work is considered to be "transformative" if it "adds something new, with a further purpose or different character, altering the first use with new expression, meaning or message."[22]
- **Nature of the copyrighted work.** Two issues are generally considered under this factor: whether the copyrighted work is factual or creative, and published or unpublished. Works that are factual and less creative in nature are more susceptible to fair use. This flows from the general concept that copyright protects the expression, not the facts, ideas, or concepts illustrated or embedded within the expression. Unpublished works are generally provided more protection against fair use than published works. This is based on the concept that the author has the right to determine whether the work will be made public.[23]

---

21. 17 U.S.C. § 107.
22. Campbell v. Acuff-Rose Music, Inc., 510 U.S. 569 (1994) ("The central purpose" of the fair-use analysis is "to see . . . whether the new work merely 'supersede[s]' the objects' of the original creation . . . or instead adds something new, with a further purpose and different character altering the first with new expression, meaning, or message . . .").
23. *See* Mattel Inc. v. Walking Mountain Prods., 353 F3d 792, 803 (9th Cir. 2003) ("The second factor in the fair use analysis recognizes that creative works are close to the core of intended copyright protection than informational or functional works.").

- **Amount and substantiality of the portion of the work used.** This factor considers the amount of a protected work used on both a quantitative and qualitative level. Although there is no bright-line rule from a quantitative perspective, the use of a large percentage of the protected work generally weighs against a finding of fair use, whereas the use of a small percentage of the protected work generally weighs in favor of fair use.[24] However, the use of a small percentage of the protected work can weigh against a finding of fair use if the portion used is a qualitatively important part of the protected work.[25]

- **Effect of the use on the potential market value of the copyrighted work.** This factor considers what impact the unlicensed use has on the existing and future market for the protected work. In assessing this factor, courts evaluate both the current market for the original work as well as the future market if the infringing use becomes widespread. The greater the impact on the market for the original work, the less likely a use will be found to be a fair use.[26]

Practice Pointer

The determination of whether a particular use of a protected work is a fair use requires an analysis of all four factors. There is no bright-line rule. The evaluation involves elements of subjective judgment, and it can be difficult to assess whether a particular use will be deemed to be fair or infringing. There is, therefore, an element of risk in relying on fair use to defend the unlicensed use of a protected work.

---

2.   First-Sale Doctrine

Copyright law grants the owner of a copyright with the exclusive rights to distribute and display the protected work. The first-sale doctrine (sometimes referred to as the exhaustion doctrine) is an exception to these rights. Under this doctrine, once the owner of a protected work sells or transfers a work, his or her interest in the material object is exhausted, and the buyer or transferee is generally permitted to resell, rent, gift, or destroy the work without violating the copyright owner's rights. Thus, after a publisher

---

24.   *See* Authors Guild v. Google, 804 F.3d 202 (Fed. Cir. 2015) ("The clear implication of the third factor is that a finding of fair use is more likely when small amounts, or less important passages are copied, than when copying is extensive, or encompasses the most important parts of the original.").

25.   *See* Harper & Row Publishers, Inc. v. Nation Enters., 471 U.S. 539 (1985) (the publication of a 300–400 word passage from Gerald Ford's yet-to-be published memoir was found not be a fair use, in part because the quoted passage, which included Gerald Ford's decision to pardon Richard Nixon, was found to be the "heart" or the most important part of the work).

26.   *See* TCA TV Corp. v. McCollum, 839 F3d 168, 186 (2d Cir. 2016) ("In assessing harm posed to a licensing market, a court's focus is not on possible lost licensing fees from defendants' challenged use. Rather, a court properly considers the challenged use's impact on potential licensing revenues for traditional, reasonable, or likely to be developed markets.").

sells a book, for example, it cannot control the further distribution of that particular copy of the book.[27]

Practice Pointer

The first-sale doctrine relates the distribution of the actual copy of the work sold or transferred. It does not permit the purchaser or transferee to make copies of the work.

There are limited exceptions to the first-sale doctrine related to the rental of phonorecords that embody musical sound recordings and computer programs.[28]

- **Phonorecord rentals.** An owner of a phonorecord that embodies a musical sound recording is prohibited from renting it to the public for direct or indirect commercial gain. This exception is narrow because it was intended to prevent record stores from renting records for home recording. It applies to the rental, not the sale or other transfer of ownership, of sound recordings that contain musical works. It does not apply to sound recordings that contain other content, such as commentary or dialogue (e.g., audio books). Further, libraries and educational institutions are exempt and can rent or loan recordings of musical works.
- **Software rentals.** The owner of a copy of computer software is prohibited from renting it for direct or indirect commercial gain. This prohibition is limited and does not apply to rentals by nonprofit libraries, provided the library affixes an appropriate warning to the copy. The prohibition also does not apply to software that is embodied in a: (1) machine and cannot be copied during the ordinary use of the machine; or (2) limited-purpose computer designed for playing video games that may also be used for other purposes.

3.   Other Exceptions

Other exceptions in the Copyright Act to the copyright owner's exclusive rights include, but are not limited to, the following:

- Certain reproduction and distribution rights provided to libraries and archives[29] and other, mostly noncommercial public performances and displays.[30] For example, in certain circumstances, teachers and pupils in the course of face-to-face instruction in a classroom may display copyrighted works.

---

27.   *See* Kirtsaeng v. John Wiley & Sons, Inc., 568 U.S. 519 (2013) (the first-sale doctrine applied to copyrighted books legal made and first sold outside the United States).

28.   17 U.S.C. § 109.

29.   *Id.* § 108.

30.   *Id.* § 110.

- An owner of a copy of a computer program may make or authorize the making of a copy of that program if the copy is: (1) an essential step in the utilization of the program, and the copy is not used in any other manner; or (2) for archival purposes, and all archival copies are destroyed if the continued use and possession of the program ceases to be lawful.[31]
- Copyrighted works may be reproduced in Braille, audio, electronic, web-Braille, or other formats for use by the blind and other persons with disabilities.[32]
- Under the 1998 DMCA amendments to the Copyright Act, an online service provider (OSP) that meets certain requirements will not be liable for a claim of copyright infringement based on materials or links posted to its website by third parties. To obtain this "safe harbor," the OSP must comply with the following administrative requirements: (1) designate a copyright agent to receive take-down notices; (2) post the agent's contact information on the OSP's website; (3) register the agent with the Copyright Office; (4) adopt and communicate to users a copyright infringement policy; and (5) respond to notices of claimed infringements.[33]

C. Compulsory and Statutory Licenses

Statutory and compulsory licenses are exceptions to the general rule that the copyright owner's permission is required to reproduce, perform, or distribute a copyrighted work. In some circumstances, a copyrighted work can be used without the copyright owner's permission, but only if the user pays certain required fees and complies with other administrative requirements. There are a number of statutory or compulsory license provisions in the Copyright Act. These include provisions related to nondramatic musical compositions,[34] public broadcasting,[35] retransmissions by cable and satellite television systems,[36] and nonsubscription digital audio transmissions (e.g., internet radio).[37] An example is the compulsory license for nondramatic musical compositions which permits the distribution of a new sound recording of a musical work that was previously distributed to the public by or under the authority of the copyright owner. To take advantage of this compulsory license, the artist must send a notice to the copyright owner or, if the copyright owner is unknown, to the Copyright Office within 30 days of the recoding, but before any distribution and pay royalties as determined by the copyright law. Although a compulsory license allows for the production and distribution of physical copies of the song, the copyright owner remains in control of the public performance rights to the song, including its transmission over the radio or internet. In certain circumstances, a public performance license for the song can be obtained from

---

31. *Id.* § 117.
32. *Id.* § 110.
33. *Id.* § 512.
34. 17 U.S.C. § 115.
35. *Id.* § 118.
36. *Id.* § 119.
37. *Id.* § 114(d)(1).

the various "performance rights societies,"[38] such ASCAP, BMI, and SESAC. When fully implemented, the Music Modernization Act will amend the process by which royalties charged by the performance rights societies are determined and create a process by which mechanical licenses for songs are determined, paid, and distributed.

VI. MORAL RIGHTS

Moral rights refer to the personal, noneconomic rights of artists to control the alteration of their creative works and the use of their name. These are generally referred to as the rights of "attribution" and "integrity." Attribution is the right to be identified or not identified as the creator of a work. Integrity is the right to control modifications to and/or the destruction of the work. Moral rights are distinct from copyright and exist regardless of who owns the copyright to the work.

Many countries, particularly those in Western Europe, broadly protect moral rights. Historically, moral rights were not recognized in the United States; however, to meet certain obligations under the Berne Convention, the United States adopted the Visual Artists Rights Act (VARA)[39] in 1990, which provides limited moral-rights protection to artists of "works of visual arts" that are produced in a single copy or in signed and numbered limited editions of 200 or less. The rights provided to artists under VARA include the right to: (1) claim or disclaim ownership of the work; (2) prevent the intentional distortion, modification, or mutilation of the work if such acts will harm the artist's honor or reputation; and (3) prevent the destruction of a work if it is of a "recognized stature."[40] VARA does not apply to works made for hire, and the rights provided are limited by the fair-use exception and other limitations. The rights are not transferrable and exist for the life of the artist (or longer for works created before December 1, 1990). However, an artist may waive his or her moral rights, provided that the waiver is in a writing that specifically identifies the work and the uses for which the waiver is being granted. A waiver by one joint author waives the rights of all authors.

VII. COPYRIGHT OWNERSHIP

Copyright protection exists from the moment a work is created in a fixed form. Unless a work is a "work made for hire," the initial owner of the copyright is the author who is the person that created the original work and fixed it to a tangible form of expression.

---

38. "A 'performance rights society' is an association, corporation, or other entity that licenses the public performance rights of nondramatic musical works such as the American Society of Composers, Authors and Publishers (ASCAP), Broadcast Music, Inc. (BMI) and SESAC, Inc." 17 U.S.C. § 101.

39. *Id.* § 106A.

40. *See* Cheffins v. Stewart, 825 F.3d 588, 592 (9th Cir. 2016) ("the purpose of VARA is to protect two 'moral rights' of authors—the rights of 'integrity' and 'attribution.' The right of integrity allows artists to prevent any deforming or mutilating changes to his work, even after title to the work has been transferred. The right of attribution allows the artist to be recognized by name as the creator of the work.").

Only the author and those deriving their rights through or from the author have the right to claim copyright protection in a work.

A. Works Made for Hire

If the work is a work made for hire, the employer or the party that commissioned the work, not the person who created the work, is deemed to be the author.[41] Under the Copyright Act, a work will be considered a work made for hire if it is:

- Created by an employee within the scope of their employment.

Practice Pointer

Whether a person is "employed" for purposes of determining whether a work is a work made for hire does not always require a formal employment relationship. The issue of whether a work is created within the scope of an employment relationship is determined by general principals of agency law.[42]

- Specifically ordered or commissioned if two conditions are met. First, the work must fit into one of the following nine statutorily defined categories of work: (1) a contribution to a collective work; (2) a part of a motion picture or other audiovisual work; (3) a translation; (4) a supplementary work; (5) a compilation; (6) an instructional text; (7) a test; (8) answer material for a test; and (9) an atlas. Second, the parties expressly agree in writing that the work will be considered a work made for hire.

The determination of whether a work is a work made for hire is different under the 1909 Act. Under the 1990 Act, a work was deemed to be a work made for hire if it was created at the expense of the commissioning party, and the commissioning party retained the right to supervise and control the work. The differences in the two acts can be significant for determining the ownership and duration of a copyright in work created before, but published after, the effective date of the Copyright Act (January 1, 1978).

---

41. 17 U.S.C. § 101.

42. *See* Community for Creative Non-violence v. Reid, 490 U.S. 730 (1989) (with respect to a determination of whether a work is a work made for hire, "ordinary cannons of statutory interpretation indicate that the classification of a particular hired party should be made with reference to agency law"); Metclalf v. Bocho, 294 F.3d 1069, 1072-73 (9th Cir. 2002) ("In the absence of a written agreement, to determine whether a writer of a work is an employee who does not own the work, or instead an independent contractor who does, we apply 'principles of general common law of agency.'").

Practice Pointer

To avoid disputes concerning copyright ownership, all agreements regarding the creation of any works that may be subject to copyright protection such employment, services, and other agreements should be in writing and contain both work-for-hire and copyright assignment provisions (e.g., "Any work performed by Executive during Executive's employment with Company shall be considered a "Work Made for Hire" as defined in the U.S. Copyright laws, and shall be owned by and for the express benefit of Company. In the event it should be established that such work does not qualify as a Work Made for Hire, Executive agrees to and does hereby assign to Company all of Executive's right, title, and interest in such work product including, but not limited to, all copyrights and other proprietary rights.")

B. Joint Authorship and Ownership

A joint work of authorship is a work created by two or more authors in which the contributions of each author are inseparable or interdependent parts of the unitary single work, and the authors intended their contributions to be merged into a single work.[43] To be considered a joint author, the contributor's contribution must meet the standards for copyright protection (originality and fixation). Whether an individual will be considered an author generally depends on whether the individual has some actual input and control over the creative process. An individual that only contributes ideas or direction for a work is generally not considered to be a joint author.

The copyright in a joint work of authorship is initially owned equally and jointly by all the authors; therefore, unless the authors otherwise agree in writing, each author has an undivided equal ownership right in the joint work and can, without permission from the other owners, exploit its rights to the joint work subject only to the obligation to pay to the other owners their share of any profits received from such exploitation. Thus, if one author contributes 90 percent and one author contributes 10 percent to a joint work, each author, unless there is a written agreement indicating otherwise, owns 50 percent of the joint work. In addition, a joint owner does not need permission from the other owners to transfer his or her interest or grant a license to the work, provided, however, that an exclusive license granted by a joint owner is only exclusive with respect to that owner's interest. This means that a licensee who obtains a license from any joint author will not have the right to restrict the other owner's rights to exploit, transfer, or license their own interests in the joint work.

---

43.   17 U.S.C. § 101.

Practice Pointer

Written agreements are essential when two or more parties are creating a copyrightable work.

C. Collective Works

A collective work is a work that consists of a group of separately copyrightable works that are assembled into a collective whole (e.g., periodicals, anthology, or encyclopedia).[44] The copyright in the collective work vests in the person who complied and arranged the preexisting materials.[45] However, the protection extends only to the original work of expression contributed by the complier, such as the selection and arrangement of the preexisting work and any other original material created by the complier and included in the collection (e.g., preface, commentary, etc.). Absent a written assignment, the authors of each of the individual works included in the collection retain the copyright to their work contributed to the collection.

Practice Pointer

Unless an exception applies, permission from the authors of the preexisting works is required before such works can be included in the collective work.

VIII. TRANSFER OF COPYRIGHT OWNERSHIP

Ownership in a copyright may be transferred in the same manner as tangible property. Rights or ownership to a copyright may be acquired by license (exclusive or nonexclusive), assignment, the grant of a security interest, through a will, or a sale connected to a bankruptcy.[46] The transfer may include all or only some of the exclusive rights provided by the copyright. For example, the owner of a copyright in a work may provide a license to perform the work publicly, but not to record or create a derivative work based on the work.

---

44. *Id.*
45. *Id.* § 201(c).
46. *Id.*

Practice Pointer

Assignments of and exclusives licenses to use a copyright must be in writing signed by the transferring party. Nonexclusive licenses do not have to be in writing and can be implied by the circumstances.[47]

A. Recording Transfer with the Copyright Office

The documents evidencing a transfer of rights in a copyright may, but are not required to, be recorded with the Copyright Office. Transfer documents can be recorded regardless of whether the copyright being transferred is registered with the Copyright Office.[48] Advantages of recording a transfer with the Copyright Office include the following: (1) the recording acts as constructive notice of the facts stated on the recorded document if the work is registered and the document identifies the work so that it would be revealed by a search using the work's title or registration number, and (2) the recording establishes priority over another party claiming ownership on the copyright. In addition, recordation is required to perfect a security interest in a registered copyright.

B. Termination Rights

Under certain circumstances, authors or their family members (if the author is deceased) may terminate copyright transfers and licenses. Upon termination, the rights transferred return to the author or his or her descendants.[49] To be effective, the termination must comply with specific and highly technical requirements of the Copyright Act and regulations of the Register of Copyrights. The right to terminate, including when the right may be exercised and the person who may exercise it, depends on a number of factors, such as when the grant was made and when the right to the copyright was first secured.

IX. DURATION OF RIGHTS

Copyright protection begins the moment an original work of authorship is fixed in a tangible form. Determining how long copyright protection will continue to exist for a work can be complicated in that different standards apply depending on when rights to the copyright were secured. The chart below outlines some of the general rules for determining the duration of a copyright.

---

47. *Id.* § 204.
48. *Id.* § 205.
49. *Id.* §§ 203 and 204.

Trigger Date or Period	Trigger Event	Condition	Duration	Law
January 1, 1978	Work created on or after the trigger date	The work was created by single author and is not a work made for hire.	70 years after the author's death	17 U.S.C. § 302
January 1, 1978	Work created on or after the trigger date	The work is a joint authorship and is not a work made for hire.	70 years after the last author's death	17 U.S.C. § 302
January 1, 1978	Work created on or after the trigger date	The work is a work made for hire or a pseudonymous or anonymous work.	Either 120 years after creation or 95 after first publication	17 U.S.C. § 302
January 1, 1978 to March 1, 1989	Work created during the trigger period	The work was published during the trigger period without a proper notice.	None (in the public domain due to the failure to follow notice formalities)	Berne Convention Implementation Act of 1988.
January 1, 1978	Works created but not published or registered before the trigger date		Same as for works created on or after the trigger date	17 U.S.C. § 303
January 1, 1978	Work created before trigger date but not published before the trigger date	The work remains unpublished until December 31, 2002.	Until December 31, 2002	17 U.S.C. § 303
January 1, 1978	Work created before trigger date not published before the trigger date	The work is published by December 31, 2002.	Until December 31, 2047	17 U.S.C. § 303 (reflects a 20-year extension under the Sonny Bono Copyright Term Extension Act)

Trigger Date or Period	Trigger Event	Condition	Duration	Law
1909 to 1977	Work published or registered during the trigger period	The copyright did not expire between January 1, 1978, and October 27, 1998	28 years beginning when the work was first published, or if an unpublished work, registered	1909 Act and the Copyright Act
1909 to 1977	Work published or registered during the trigger period	Copyright expired between January 1, 1978, and October 27, 1998	28 years beginning from the date of publication, or if an unpublished work, registration plus a potential renewal of 47 years	1909 Act and the Copyright Act

X. PUBLICATION

Publication is defined in the Copyright Act as the distribution of copies or phonorecords of a work to the public by sale or other transfer of ownership or by rental, lease, or lending. Offering to distribute copies of phonorecords to a group of people for the purpose of further distribution, public performance, or public display also constitutes publication.[50] Under the 1909 Act, copyright protection extended only to works that were published with a proper notice or registered. Publication is not a requirement for copyright protection under the Copyright Act and has no effect on whether a work is protected. Whether a work is published does, however, have important implications. These include, but are not limited to, the following:

- Whether a work is published could affect the duration of copyright protection.
- The date and nation of first publication may determine whether a foreign work is eligible for copyright protection in the United States.
- A copyright registration provides certain legal presumptions if the work is registered before or within five years after the work was first published.
- A copyright owner may be entitled to claim statutory damages and attorney's fees in a lawsuit for infringement if the work was registered before the infringement began or within three months after the first publication of the work.
- Deposit requirements for registering a published work are different than the requirements for registering an unpublished work.

---

50. *Id.* § 101.

XI. NOTICE

A copyright notice is a statement placed on a work to inform the public that a party is claiming ownership of the work. Use of a copyright notice is not required to obtain copyright protection for unpublished works, foreign works, or works published after March 1, 1989 (the effective date of the Berne Convention Implementation Act). However, use of a notice provides the copyright owner with important benefits, including the following:

- puts potential users on notice that copyright is claimed in the work and may deter infringement;
- may prevent an infringer from seeking to limit liability for damages based on the "innocent infringer defense"; and
- may assist others in locating the copyright owner to obtain permission to use the work.

Use of a copyright notice was required for works published before March 1, 1989, and publishing a work without a proper notice before that date may have caused the work to lose its copyright protection and fall into the public domain.

A proper notice under the Copyright Act must contain the following three elements:

- the symbol © (the letter "C" in a circle), the word "Copyright," or the abbreviation "Copr.";
- the year of first publication (or of creation for unpublished works); and
- the name of the copyright owner, or an abbreviation or an alternative designation by which the owner can be identified.[51]

An example of a proper notice for an article the copyright to which is owned by the author's law firm is "© 2018 Moritt Hock & Hamroff LLP." The notice must be in a size and position sufficient to provide reasonable notice of the claimed copyright.

XII. REGISTRATION

Copyright protection begins from the time an original work is created in a "fixed" form. A copyright registration is not required to have rights in a copyright; however, registration has important benefits, such as the following:

- establishes a public record of the copyright claim;
- allows the owner to file a suit for infringement;
- if made within five years of the first publication, the registration acts as *prima facia* evidence of the validity of the copyright;

---

51. *Id.* § 401.

- if registration is made within three months after the first publication or prior to an infringement, statutory damages and attorney's fees will be available to the copyright owner in a suit for infringement;
- a registration can be filed with U.S. Customs and Border Protection to help stop the importation of infringing works.

An application to register a copyright can be filed by the author, the owner of an exclusive right, the owner of all the exclusive rights, or by an agent on behalf of the author or owner. An application to register a copyright contains three elements:

- a completed application form;
- payment of a nonrefundable filing fee; and
- a nonreturnable deposit, which is a copy of the work "deposited" or filed with the Copyright Office. An acceptable deposit depends on the type of work being registered.

A registration creates a public record of facts concerning the authorship and ownership of the claimed work, including the following: (1) the title of the work; (2) the author of the work; (3) the name and address of the copyright claimant or copyright owner; (4) the year of creation; (5) and information on whether the work was published, previously registered, or includes any preexisting materials.

Although registration is not required under the Copyright Act, registration was required to obtain copyright protection for unpublished works under the 1909 Act. The 1909 Act also required registrations of both published and unpublished works to be renewed at certain times. Registration may have also been necessary to preserve copyright protection in works published with no notice or defective notice between January 1, 1978, and February 28, 1989. This is because the Copyright Act, as initially enacted and before being amended by the Berne Convention Implementation Act, required published works to contain a copyright notice as a condition to copyright protection. Publication without a proper notice resulted in a loss of copyright protection unless only a small number of copies were published without notice, or the work was registered before or within five years after the publication without notice and the owner took reasonable steps to add a notice after discovering the failure to include a notice.

XIII. MANDATORY DEPOSIT

The Copyright Act contains a provision that requires all works published in the United States to be deposited with the Copyright Office.[52] Although an application to register a copyright must include a deposit, a deposit may be made without registration. Failing to make a deposit does not result in the loss of any rights, but may result in a fine or other action by the Copyright Office. The purpose of the requirement is to ensure the Library of Congress obtains a copy of every work published in the United States.

---

52. *Id.* § 407.

The provision generally requires two complete copies of the "best edition" of a work be sent to the Library of Congress within three months of publication. The "best edition" of a work is the edition that was published in the United States at any time before the deposit that the Library of Congress determines to be the most suitable for its purposes.[53]

XIV. COPYRIGHT RENEWAL

The requirements and rules related to renewing a copyright depend on when a work was created. The Copyright Act was amended in 1992 to make renewals automatic for works created on or after January 1, 1978, and optional for works created between January 1, 1964, and December 31, 1977. The benefit of renewing the copyright in these works is that the renewal acts as prima facie evidence of copyright validity for the renewal term. For works created before these dates, renewal was required to maintain rights.

XV. INFRINGEMENT CLAIMS, DEFENSES, AND REMEDIES

Copyright provides the owner with a bundle of certain exclusive rights to make, reproduce, and sell copies of their works, create derivative works, and perform or display their works publicly. If these rights are infringed, the owner can file a copyright infringement action in federal court. Federal courts have exclusive subject matter jurisdiction over copyright matters. Below is an overview of claims, defenses, and remedies that are likely to be at issue in a copyright infringement dispute.

A. Civil Claims—Direct and Indirect Infringement

To prevail in a copyright infringement action, the copyright owner must show ownership of a valid copyright in the work and that the defendant copied the work. Ownership is established by evidence that shows the claimant created or properly acquired the rights to an original work of authorship fixed in a tangible form of expression. A copyright registration, if obtained within five years of the first publication of the work, acts as prima facia evidence of the validity of the copyright and ownership. This shifts the burden of disproving ownership to the defendant. Copying can be shown by direct or indirect evidence. Direct evidence is an admission of copying or testimony from a witness who observed the copying. In most cases, a copyright owner must rely on indirect evidence of copying. This requires evidence that the defendant had access to the copyrighted work and that the defendant's work is substantially similar to the protected work. There is no

---

53. The criteria used to identify the "best edition" for a particular type of work are set forth in the "Best Edition Statement" in Appendix B to Part 202 of the Copyright Office's regulations.

bright-line rule to determine whether two works are substantially similar, and courts have developed a number of tests to evaluate the issue.[54]

A defendant in certain circumstances can also be held liable for indirect copyright infringement under theories of contributory and vicarious infringement. Contributory infringement occurs where the defendant, with knowledge of the infringing activity, induced, caused, or materially contributed to the infringing activity of another party.[55] Vicarious infringement occurs where the defendant has control over the infringer and financially benefits from the infringement.[56]

The statute of limitations for civil infringement claims is three years after the "claim accrued."[57]

B. Criminal Copyright Infringement

Criminal prosecution is available for certain "willful" acts of copyright infringement.[58] The statute of limitations for criminal copyright infringement is five years "after the cause of action arose."[59]

C. Defenses

Possible defenses against a claim of infringement depend on a number of factors, but can include the following:

- The defendant can challenge the validity and ownership of the alleged copyright.
- There was no copying, which means the defendant did not exercise any of the exclusive rights provided to the copyright owner.
- The use of the copyrighted work was a fair use.
- The defendant is an innocent infringer, which means the defendant engaged in infringing activity without knowing the conduct was an infringement. This is not an absolute defense because the intent of the infringer is not an element of

---

54. Most, but not all, courts use one of two tests to evaluate substantial similarity: The "ordinary observer" test (*see* Peter Pan Fabrics, Inc. v. Martin Weiner Corp., 274 F.2d 487 (2d Cir.1960)) and the "extrinsic/intrinsic" test (*see* Sid & Marty Krofft Television Prods., Inc. v. McDonald's Corp., 562 Fd.2d 1157 (9th Cir. 1977)). A third test, the "abstraction-filtration-comparison test," is used in the Tenth Circuit and some other courts (*see* Gates Rubber Co. v. Bando Chem. Indus., Ltd., 9 F.2d 823 (10th Cir. 1993)).

55. *See* Fonovisa, Inc. v. Cherry Auctions, Inc., 76 F.3d 259 (9th Cir. 1996).

56. *See* Shapiro, Bernstein & Co. v. H.L. Green Co., 316 F.2d 304 (2d Cir. 1963).

57. 17 U.S.C. § 507. A copyright ownership claim accrues when "a plaintiff's authorship has been 'expressly repudiated.'" Brownstein v. Lindsey, 742 F.3d 55, 58 (3d Cir. 2014). "A copyright infringement claim accrues when the plaintiff knows of the potential violation or is chargeable with such knowledge. Because each act of infringement is a distinct harm, the statute of limitations bars infringement claims that accrued more than three years before the suit was filed, but does not bar preclude infringement claims that accrued within the statutory period." Roger Miller Music, Inc. v Sony/ATV Publ'g, 477 F.3d 383 (6th Cir. 2007).

58. 17 U.S.C. § 506.

59. *Id.* § 507.

the infringement analysis, but in certain circumstances may reduce the damages awarded to the copyright owner.[60]

D. Remedies

In a lawsuit for copyright infringement, the copyright owner may be entitled to the following remedies:

- preliminary and permanent injunctions against further infringing activity;[61]
- collection and destruction of infringing articles;[62]
- money damages, which may include the following:[63]
  - Actual damages, which is the dollar amount of any demonstrated loss to the copyright owner because of the infringement, such as lost sales, lost licensing revenue, or any other provable financial loss attributable to the infringement.
  - Infringer's profits, which is money made by the infringer as a result of the infringement. This may only be awarded if the infringer's profits exceed the amount of actual damages suffered by the copyright owner.
  - Statutory damages, which are damages set by law and are available only to a copyright owner that registered a work with the Copyright Office within three months of the first publication or before the infringement.

Statutory damages are important because in many cases, actual damages and the infringer's profits are difficult to prove. Statutory damages range from $750 to $30,000 per infringement (unless the infringement is proven to be "innocent" or "intentional"). The amount awarded is in the court's discretion and generally depends on the seriousness of the infringing act. If the infringer is proven to be "innocent," the infringer may pay as little as $1,200. If the infringement is found to be "intentional," however, the infringer may pay as much as $150,000 for a single infringement.

---

60. *Id.* § 504(c)(2).
61. *Id.* § 502.
62. *Id.* § 503.
63. *Id.* § 504.

About the Authors

Megan M. Adeyemo (Chapter 8: The Impact of the Automatic Stay) is a partner in the Dallas office of Gordon Rees Scully Mansukhani LLP. Her practice focuses on Bankruptcy, Restructuring & Creditors' Rights, Business Transactions, Real Estate, Directors, Officers, and Shareholder Litigation, as well as Banking & Finance. Ms. Adeyemo has represented parties in every aspect of bankruptcy, including debtors, debtors-in-possession, secured and unsecured creditors, creditors' committees, and trustees. Her practice spans the United States, including California, Colorado, Florida, and Texas. Ms. Adeyemo previously served as a co-chair of the Mountain-Desert Network of the International Women's Insolvency & Restructuring Confederation and is currently co-chair of the publications and content subcommittee for the Business Bankruptcy Committee of the American Bar Association. She has received numerous awards, including the Rising Star award in the field of Bankruptcy & Creditor/Debtor Rights from 2013 through 2015. Ms. Adeyemo has been frequently published in both local and national publications. Ms. Adeyemo can be reached at madeyemo@grsm.com or (214) 461-4053.

Courtney E. Alvarez (Chapter 11: In-House Counsel's Guide to Insurance Coverage) is Counsel in the Insurance Recovery Group at Lowenstein Sandler LLP. She represents corporate policyholders in complex insurance coverage disputes relating to directors and officers liabilities, government investigations, professional errors and omissions liabilities, products liabilities, and environmental liabilities. She has successfully implemented legal strategies to obtain favorable coverage results for a range of clients, including defense contracting firms, financial services firms, automobile parts manufactures, government-sponsored enterprises, and regulated utilizes, as well as individual directors and officers. Courtney holds a law degree from Howard University School of Law and a Bachelor of Arts degree from Villanova University. She has handled all aspects of insurance coverage claims, from drafting notice letters to responding to insurer investigatory reservation of rights letters and insurer claim denials. She can be reached at calvarez@lowenstein.com or +1 202.753.3760.

Terese L. Arenth (Chapter 12: What Is a Trademark or Service Mark?) is a partner in the Garden City, New York office of Moritt Hock & Hamroff LLP, where she serves as Chair of its Marketing, Advertising & Promotions practice group within its Intellectual Property department. Ms. Arenth concentrates her practice in promotional marketing, advertising and Internet/new media and also has extensive experience in the firm's intellectual property, cybersecurity and unfair competition practice areas. She is an experienced litigator in complex arbitrations and litigation in both State and Federal Courts, focusing on trademarks, copyrights, domain name disputes, TCPA claims and business disputes. Ms. Arenth also regularly handles matters involving a variety of sponsorship, licensing, distribution and general corporate transactions, primarily in connection with the counseling, negotiation and drafting of sponsorship, licensing and distribution agreements, online privacy policies and website terms of use. She has frequently served as a speaker and author on various advertising, marketing, and intellectual property law-related topics. As a member of the Intellectual Property Law Section of the American Bar Association, she has served two terms as Chair of its Promotions & Marketing Law Committee and two terms as Vice-Chair. Ms. Arenth was recognized by Long Island Business News as one of Long Island's Top 50 Most Influential Women in Business for two consecutive years and has been honored by Hofstra University's School of Law as an Outstanding Woman in Law. She can be reached at tarenth@moritthock.com.

Leslie A. Berkoff (Chapter 8: The Impact of the Automatic Stay) is a partner at Moritt Hock & Hamroff LLP, where she serves as Co-Chair of the firm's Litigation and Bankruptcy Practice Group, as well as Co-Chair of the firm's Alternate Dispute Resolution Practice. Ms. Berkoff concentrates her practice in the area of bankruptcy and restructuring litigation and corporate workouts, and she represents a variety of corporate debtors, trustees, creditors and creditor committees both nationally and locally. Her practice also includes an emphasis on equipment leasing and healthcare law. Ms. Berkoff is also an experienced litigator and handles corporate transactions both locally and nationally. In addition, Ms. Berkoff has an active alternate dispute resolution practice and frequently serves as a mediator and arbitrator. Ms. Berkoff serves as a Member of the Dispute Resolution Section Advisory Council of the American Bar Association (ABA), she is also a contributing editor on ADR for the ABA's publication Business Law Today. She is the Vice Chair and Content Director for the ABA's Dispute Resolution Committee, as well as the Membership Chair of the Business Bankruptcy Committee for the Business Law Section of the ABA. Ms. Berkoff is Co-Chair of the Mediation Committee for the New York State Bar Association as well as Co-Chair of the Mediation Committee of the American Bankruptcy Institute and a contributing editor on for the organization's journals on the Mediation Matters column. Ms. Berkoff holds a BA from the State University of New York at Albany, as well as a Juris Doctorate from Hofstra School of Law. Prior to joining Moritt Hock & Hamroff LLP, Ms. Berkoff served as a law clerk to the

Honorable Jerome Feller, United States Bankruptcy Judge in the Eastern District of New York, from 1991 to 1993 and to the Honorable Allyne R. Ross, Federal Magistrate Judge in the Eastern District of New York, from 1990 to 1991. Ms. Berkoff speaks and publishes extensively and is a recognized leader in her field. She can be reached at lberkoff@moritthock.com or 1-516-873-2000.

Thomas E. Best (Chapter 6: Requests for Proposal and Alternative Fee Arrangements as an Effective Tool for Evaluating and Selecting Outside Counsel) is a Deputy General Counsel for The Home Depot, the world's largest home improvement retailer. Tom leads the General Liability and Legal Operations for the Company and advises its Asset Protection, Corporate Security, and Business Continuity functions on strategy. Tom is a certified Six Sigma Green Belt and a trained Six Sigma Black Belt. During Tom's time at the Company, Tom has pioneered several innovative programs that have directly resulted in process improvements and cost savings including the use of National Discovery Counsel, Regionalization and Rationalization of Outside Counsel, Alternative Fee Programs, Early Case Assessment, Pre-Litigation Alternative Dispute, and Medicare Secondary Payer Compliance. Tom serves as Co-Chairperson of the Legal Department's Supplier Diversity efforts and has been a frequent panelist at the State Bar of Georgia's Business Development Symposium. Tom has received several intra-Company awards over the years including being a member of the Company's Associate Leadership Program and Director's Learning Experience (DLX). He has also received the Company's prestigious "Living the Values Award" and executive recognition for his leading role with the Legal Department's Supplier Diversity efforts. Tom is a graduate of the University of Virginia and the Walter F. George School of Law at Mercer University where he served on the Law Review Editorial Board as the Student Writing Editor. He currently serves on the Board of Directors of the Atlanta Volunteer Lawyer's Foundation and has served in past years on various boards of the National Retail and Restaurant Association (NRRDA) and CLM.

Stephen E. Breidenbach (Chapter 13: Patents) is an associate at Moritt Hock & Hamroff LLP. He works hand-in-hand with clients to help them better understand their use of technology and solve the complex legal problems which manifest when law and technology collide. He helps companies meet their compliance obligations under the various cybersecurity, privacy and communications laws. He assists companies in drafting written information security policies (WISPs), privacy policies, terms of use, structuring and reviewing data retention policies, drafting cybersecurity provisions for vendor agreements (such as Business Associate Agreements) and handling cybersecurity incidents (such as phishing attacks, denial of service attacks, etc.), including data breaches. He is also often involved in drafting software development contracts, advising on Americans with Disability Act compliance for websites, reviewing rights issues related to the usage of open source code, handling online defamation, drafting Software as a Service Agreements, handling Digital Millennium

Copyright Act violations, determining compliance obligations for online advertising and protecting the intellectual property rights of clients' electronic assets (such as software). He can be reached at sbreidenbach@moritthock.com or 12122392000.

Lauren H. Cooper (Chapter 10: Electronic Discovery in Civil Litigation) is an associate with Actuate Law, LLC in Chicago, where her practice focuses on representing clients in resolving consumer finance disputes in matters involving compliance with the Fair Debt Collections Practices Act (FDCPA) and the Fair Credit Reporting Act (FCRA) as well as licensing and regulatory matters. Lauren also has expertise in the fields of Data Privacy and Security, Information Governance and Records Management and E-Discovery. Lauren received her law degree from Loyola University of Chicago School of Law and her Undergraduate Degree from the University of Michigan. Lauren can be reached at lauren.cooper@actuatelaw.com or 312-579-3126.

Elizabeth S. Fenton (Chapter 2: Internal Corporate Investigations) practices in the Wilmington, Delaware office of Saul Ewing Arnstein & Lehr LLP. A litigation partner, she focuses on disputes involving corporate and LLC governance, indemnification rights, fiduciary duties, and restrictive covenants. She has led internal investigations of businesses in the financial, healthcare, and manufacturing industries. Subject matters include compliance with the Foreign Corrupt Practices Act, the Commodity Exchange Act, Sarbanes-Oxley and many others. A graduate of the University of Pennsylvania Law School and Brown University, Elizabeth may be reached at elizabeth.fenton@ saul.com or on Twitter @delitigator.

Amy R. Foote (Chapter 3: Conducting a Sexual Harassment Investigation: A Practical Guide) is a partner with StoneTurn, a global advisory firm. She brings nearly 20 years of legal, regulatory, compliance and investigative experience as a prosecutor, internal corporate counsel, and litigator. Amy has advised public and private sector clients on compliance issues, commercial disputes, governance issues, and complex litigation, and investigations. She has supervised compliance engagements, conducted numerous internal investigations, and managed a wide variety of employment disputes and criminal and regulatory matters. Amy also successfully defended clients in criminal and civil matters, including those before the U.S. Department of Justice, the U.S. Securities and Exchange Commission, the New York State Attorney General's Office, and local law enforcement departments. Amy began her legal career as an Assistant District Attorney in the New York County District Attorney's Office. She frequently writes about workplace discrimination issues and sexual harassment. Amy can be reached at afoote@stoneturn.com or +1 646 979 4111.

Susan N. Goodman (Chapter 5: Cybersecurity and Protecting Data Privacy) is a partner at the Tucson firm of Mesch Clark Rothschild, P.C. Ms. Goodman joined the firm in 2013, expanding its' healthcare practice to include regulatory compliance expertise where she focuses her practice on healthcare provider support in contracting, dispute resolution, compliance, governance, and process improvement. She also supports the United States Bankruptcy Trustee as a patient care ombudsman in Chapter 9 and 11 health care reorganizations. Ms. Goodman's other professional experiences include: RN in the cardiac catheterization lab and cardiac critical care unit; cardiac medical device industry experience in clinical education support, sales, marketing, and human resources management; hospice admission team management; revenue and expense hospital-based performance improvement work; and, data analytics.

Lauren E. Jaffe (Chapter 10: Electronic Discovery in Civil Litigation) is an associate in the Chicago office of Riley Safer Holmes & Cancila LLP, a national law firm of litigators, trial lawyers, and transactional attorneys. She has experience in complex commercial litigation, class actions, criminal, and compliance matters, and has practiced from the vantage points of private attorney, federal law clerk, and trial paralegal. Ms. Jaffe graduated with honors from both the University of Chicago Law School, where she received her law degree, and Washington University in St. Louis, where she received her Bachelor of Arts. She is admitted to practice in Illinois, the Sixth and Seventh Circuit Courts of Appeals, the Northern District of Illinois, and the Southern District of Ohio. Ms. Jaffe can be reached at ljaffe@rshc-law.com or 312-471-8726.

Samantha R. Johnson (Chapter 1: Attorney-Client Privilege for the In-House Attorney) is a Senior Associate General Counsel for Grady Health System, one of the largest public academic healthcare systems in the United States. Her practice includes both transactional and litigation matters. She counsels, represents and educates Grady employees and medical staff on issues of patient care, ethics, contracts, human resources, compliance, risk management and regulatory matters. She devotes a substantial portion of her time to advising Grady's Care Management Department, which includes Nurse Case Management and Social Work, and Grady's Emergency Medical Services division. Prior to her in-house career, Ms. Johnson handled civil litigation, insurance coverage, and insurance defense matters. Samantha is an accomplished author and speaker, focusing on legal issues for emergency medical services, EMTALA, guardianships, healthcare law and ethics, and insurance law. She is an adjunct professor for the Georgia State College of Law and the Georgia State J. Mack Robinson College of Business.

Samantha is an active member of both the State Bar of Georgia and the State Bar of South Carolina. A native of Atlanta, Georgia, she is a graduate of The Westminster Schools and Vanderbilt University. She received her law degree from the Georgia State University College of Law in 2003, and her Master of Business Administration and Master of Health Administration from the Georgia State J. Mack Robinson College of Business in 2014. Samantha can be reached at sjohnson@gmh.edu or (404) 616-6238.

Krista L. Kulp (Chapter 8: The Impact of the Automatic Stay) is an associate with Cole Schotz P.C. in Hackensack, New Jersey where she practices in the litigation and bankruptcy departments. She represents businesses in commercial litigation and disputes at the trial and appellate levels. Her experience also includes creditors' rights and bankruptcy. Ms. Kulp has taken key roles in many components of civil litigation, such as writing pleadings and motions, drafting and reviewing discovery, taking and defending depositions, facilitating settlement negotiations, and advocating for clients at hearings and at trial.

Ms. Kulp serves as Editor-in-Chief of the e-newsletter for the Business Bankruptcy Committee for the American Bar Association. Through the Business Bankruptcy Committee, she has participated in panel discussions and webinars and has authored and prepared written materials relating to bankruptcy issues. She co-authored the fourth chapter of *Reorganizing Failing Business*, 3rd Ed., 2017 published by the Business Law Section of the American Bar Association and has been published in the *New York Law Journal* and the *American Bankruptcy Institute Journal*. She also serves as the Communications Co-Chair for IWIRC-NY. Ms. Kulp can be reached at kkulp@coleschotz.com or at 201-525-6317.

Katherine A. Lemire (Chapter 3: Conducting a Sexual Harassment Investigation: a Practical Guide) is a partner with StoneTurn, a global advisory firm. She has more than 20 years of experience advising public and private sector clients on a broad range of compliance and integrity issues, complex investigations, corruption, anti-money laundering, fraud, and risk matters. She brings deep expertise in law enforcement best practices and supervisory, investigative, and oversight skills to tackle corporate malfeasance, money laundering schemes, sexual misconduct in the workplace, cyber fraud, employee theft, and corruption. Katherine previously operated Lemire LLC, a firm specializing in compliance, risk, and investigative matters, and served as an Assistant United States Attorney in the U.S. Attorney's Office for the Southern District of New York. Katherine is a frequent speaker and panelist at industry events on internal investigations, monitorships and regulatory reviews. She has written on issues including sexual harassment, cybersecurity and compliance. Katherine can be reached at: klemire@stoneturn.com or +1 646 979 4101.

John Levitske (Chapter 2: Internal Corporate Investigations) is a Senior Managing Director in the Chicago office of Ankura, a global expert and consulting services firm. John focuses on Business Valuation Dispute Analysis and Complex Financial Disputes. He has over 30 years of experience, including over two decades of Big Four public accounting and international consulting firm experience, in business valuation, financial analysis, economic damage quantification, forensic accounting, retrospective solvency analysis, and post-merger & acquisition accounting calculations. Furthermore, he has provided consulting and expert witness testimony services and has served as a neutral party in arbitration and mediation. He has testified as an expert witness in the US and Europe in depositions, hearings, bench and jury court trials, and domestic and international arbitration (ICC, SCC, AAA, JAMS, FINRA, and ad hoc arbitrations) and has served as a neutral arbitrator. In addition, he currently serves as the Chair of the Dispute Resolution Committee of the Business Law Section of the American Bar Association and is a past National President of the Forensic Expert Witness Association.

Michelle N. Lipkowitz (Chapter 2: Internal Corporate Investigations) is a partner in the Baltimore office of Saul Ewing Arnstein & Lehr LLP, a full-service law firm, where she focuses her practice on commercial litigation, white collar defense, and government investigations. Michelle brings a breadth of litigation experience, including traditional criminal experience, to her practice. Accordingly, Michelle has extensive experience dealing with highly sensitive matters and crisis management, including handling the press. Her practice includes internal and governmental investigations, commercial real estate, shareholder disputes, consumer class actions, construction matters, products liability, and contractual disputes. She represents clients from a broad range of industries, including pharmaceutical, manufacturing, education, financial services, healthcare, construction, technology, retail and telecommunications, as well as governmental entities and nonprofits. Michelle obtained her J.D. from Georgetown Law and her B.A from Harvard University. She can be reached at Michelle.Lipkowitz@ saul.com or + 410-419-5482.

John G. Loughnane (Chapter 5: Cybersecurity and Protecting Data Privacy) is a partner in the Corporate and Transactions Department of Nutter McClennen & Fish LLP in Boston. He helps clients negotiate and implement technology and financing transactions. He also helps clients navigate change and solve problems in today's fast paced innovation economy. Earlier in his career, John served as Regional Corporate Counsel for North America at PTC, an international publicly-traded technology company. John serves on the Executive Board of TMA Global (Turnaround Management Association), on the Board of the Legal Technology Resource Center (LTRC) of the American Bar Association's Law Practice Division, and as Special Projects Leader for the Mediation Committee of the American Bankruptcy Institute. John is a member of the International Association of Privacy Professionals and is a Certified Information Privacy Professional (CIPP/US). John has served as a board member of the George Washington University Law Alumni Association and currently serves as president of the College of the Holy Cross Lawyers Association. He can be reached at jloughnane@nutter.com.

Mark A. McGrath (Chapter 2: Internal Corporate Investigations) is a Senior Managing Director at Ankura, an international firm that provides management consulting and expert services to businesses. He is a Certified Public Accountant and Certified Fraud Examiner with twenty years of accounting, auditing, investigative and internal controls experience. He focuses his practice on assisting legal counsel, corporate clients, boards and audit committees on complex, fact-finding accounting investigations involving whistleblower allegations, SEC enforcement and financial reporting issues. He is also a trusted advisor to clients on matters involving anticorruption and bribery, technical accounting and auditing issues, internal controls assessments and remediation, regulatory compliance, anti-money laundering, and other litigation support needs. He can be reached at mark.mcgrath@ankura.com or 202-251-3275.

Alexandra Morgan (Chapter 7: Managing Regional and National Litigation) is a former Skadden, Arps, Slate, Meagher & Flom LLP litigation associate in Chicago. She currently serves as a law clerk on the U.S. Court of Appeals for the Seventh Circuit. Ms. Morgan earned her J.D. from the University of Chicago, with honors.

Sheila M. Murphy (Chapter 6: Requests for Proposal and Alternative Fee Arrangements as an Effective Tool for Evaluating and Selecting Outside Counsel) is Senior Vice President and Associate General Counsel at MetLife. She leads the U.S. Regulatory and Retail Litigation Group where she provides litigation, regulatory and risk mitigation advice. Sheila focuses on providing proactive, strategic advice to identify and resolve complex issues and protects business interests. Sheila can be reached at smurphy1@metlife.com. Sheila is a graduate of the University of Pennsylvania Law School, where she served on the Comparative Labor Law Journal and the School of Management at the State University of New York at Binghamton where she graduated magna cum laude. Prior to joining MetLife, Sheila was at the law firm of Thacher Proffitt & Wood.

Shelby A. Poteet (Chapter 8: The Impact of the Automatic Stay) is an associate in the San Diego office of Gordon Rees Scully Mansukhani LLP. Her practice focuses on Bankruptcy, Restructuring & Creditors' Rights, Commercial Litigation, Directors, Officers, and Shareholder Litigation, as well as Consumer Protection defense. Ms. Poteet volunteers with the Credit Abuse Resistance Education program, where she teaches high school students about financial literacy. Ms. Poteet can be reached at spoteet@grsm.com or (619) 696-6700.

Daniella Quitt (Chapter 9: Managing Class Actions) is a partner at Glancy Prongay & Murray LLP, a national law firm based in Los Angeles with offices in New York specializing in class action litigation in federal and state courts throughout the country. Ms. Quitt has focused her practice on shareholder rights and ERISA class actions but also handles general commercial and consumer litigation. Ms. Quitt has extensive experience in successfully litigating complex class actions from inception to trial. She graduated from Fordham University School of Law in 1988 and is a member of the Bar of the State of New York, and is also admitted to the United States District Courts for the Southern and Eastern Districts of New York and the United States Court of Appeals for the Second, Fifth, and Ninth Circuits. Ms. Quitt also serves as a member of the S.D.N.Y. ADR Panel. She can be reached at dquitt@glancylaw.com.

Steven S. Rubin (Chapter 13: Patents) is Chief Intellectual Property Counsel for ITT Inc. In this role, he is responsible for leading ITT's intellectual property protection strategy, including assessing the commercial and strategic value of the company's portfolio, identifying the gaps and areas of opportunity and advising senior management of actions to be taken to maximize the value of ITT's intellectual property portfolio. A patent and cybersecurity attorney with more than 20 years of experience, Steve joined ITT in 2018 from Moritt Hock & Hamroff, LLP, where he created and chaired the firm's patent practice and formed and co-chaired its cybersecurity practice. He is currently serving as the co-chair of the Internet of Things (IoT) committee in the Licensing Executives Society and has served in various other roles in other professional organizations. He is a senior member of the Institute of Electrical and Electronics Engineers (IEEE), a Certified Information Privacy Professional (CIPP/US) and active in the American Bar Association Intellectual Property Law section. Steve speaks and publishes frequently on issues and topics related to patent and cybersecurity law and has taught intellectual property and patent law at several New York universities. He holds a Juris Doctorate degree from Hofstra University School of Law and a Bachelor of Science degree in Electrical Engineering from the New York Institute of Technology.

Joseph M. Saka (Chapter 11: In-House Counsel's Guide to Insurance Coverage) is a commercial litigator in the Washington, DC office of Lowenstein Sandler LLP. As Counsel in the firm's Insurance Recovery Group, he has more than ten years of experience in helping legal departments enforce their contractual rights and recover money from breaching parties. His efforts have resulted in more than $100 million in recoveries under all major types of commercial insurance. Joseph is a cum laude graduate of The Catholic University of America, Columbus School of Law, and holds a Bachelor of Arts degree from George Washington University. Prior to entering private practice, Joseph served as a judicial extern for the Honorable Ricardo M. Urbina (retired) of the U.S. District Court for the District of Columbia. His clients include corporations, nonprofit organization, and state-owned enterprises pursuing insurance coverage and contractual indemnification for significant losses and liabilities. He can be reached at jsaka@lowenstein.com or +1 202.753.3758.

Michael J. Schwab (Chapter 14: Copyright) is counsel at Moritt Hock & Hamroff where he handles all facets of soft intellectual property and licensing matters. Mr. Schwab specializes in trademark and copyright counseling, litigation and counseling on regulatory and other issues in the beverage alcohol, dietary supplement and food industries. His practice is diversified and includes all aspects of a domestic and international copyright practice, including registering and enforcing copyrights in the United States and abroad as well as counseling clients on a wide range of issues such as work for hire, fair use, international copyright protection, renewal and termination of rights and recording registrations with customs authorities. He also has extensive experience drafting and negotiating contracts involving copyrighted works such as software licenses, work for hire agreements, publish agreements, assignments, licenses and distribution agreements. His practice also includes all aspects of a domestic and international trademark practice, including, advising, searching the availability of marks, filing and prosecuting trademark applications, handling contested oppositions, cancellations and litigations, managing worldwide trademark portfolios, enforcing trademark rights, including gray market goods, anti-counterfeiting, and monitoring and preventing infringing third party trademarks, internet and related domain name use and advertising compliance. Mr. Schwab can be reached at mschwab@moritthock. com or + 212-239-2000.

Steven P. Seltzer (Chapter 5: Cybersecurity and Protecting Data Privacy) is Deputy General Counsel at Moritt Hock & Hamroff LLP, a full-service New York business law firm with offices in Garden City and Manhattan. Steven is a member of the Commercial Litigation Practice Group and provides advice and counsel on a wide variety of dispute and pre-dispute matters, including issues of cybersecurity. He also provides internal ethics advice to attorneys in the firm. Before joining the firm, Steven enjoyed a 25-year in-house career at MetLife. In that role, Steven similarly handled a broad range of business litigation and pre-litigation matters, as well as having led the department's Global Litigation Unit and coordinated a cross-functional legal team to partner with the company's IT department in enhancing its U.S. cybersecurity preparation and prevention efforts. Steven received his J.D. from NYU School of Law and his undergraduate degree from Emory University. He can be reached at sseltzer@ moritthock.com or 516-873-2000.

Elizabeth J. Shampnoi (Chapter 4: Mediation and Arbitration: How to Prepare Your Company and Yourself) is President of Shampnoi Dispute Resolution and Management Services, Inc. and serves as a mediator, arbitrator, consulting expert and trainer. With 20 years of experience in the field of alternative dispute resolution (ADR), Ms. Shampnoi works with in-house counsel, law firms, and executives providing strategic advice to develop and implement ADR programs to avoid and resolve disputes quickly and efficiently while achieving successful outcomes. Ms. Shampnoi regularly serves as a mediator and arbitrator in commercial and employment disputes and has successfully mediated and arbitrated over 200 disputes. She also provides trainings for companies concerning best practices in all areas of ADR. Ms. Shampnoi's focus in the area of ADR began early in her career when she served as the District Vice President of the New York region of the American Arbitration Association (AAA). Following her tenure at the AAA, Ms. Shampnoi served as a litigator and in-house counsel. Ms. Shampnoi is based in New York City and can be reached at (914) 522-0174 or elizabeth@shampnoiadr.com.

Charles F. Smith (Chapter 7: Managing Regional and National Litigation) is a partner at Skadden, Arps, Slate, Meagher & Flom LLP and leads the litigation and regulatory enforcement group in Chicago. He represents a broad array of U.S. and international companies, as well as their top executives, in complex regulatory investigations, enforcement matters and litigation. Mr. Smith is an experienced trial lawyer, having tried many cases in federal and state courts around the country. These cases typically involve complex securities, accounting, financial or bankruptcy-related issues. He has represented many companies and their officers and directors in securities and derivative litigation. Mr. Smith has also represented financial services firms in SEC, DOJ, CFTC and FINRA enforcement matters. Mr. Smith earned his J.D. from University of Chicago Law School, *cum laude*. He can be reached at charles. smith@skadden.com or +1 312.407.0516.

Penelope M. Taylor (Chapter 6: Requests for Proposal and Alternative Fee Arrangements as an Effective Tool for Evaluating and Selecting Outside Counsel) is a partner at McCarter & English, LLP and is admitted to practice in New Jersey, New York, and Pennsylvania. She has more than 25 years of experience handling complex commercial litigation with a focus on life insurance, annuities, securities, mutual fund, investment, and ERISA litigation. She primarily represents financial services companies, banks, account representatives, brokers, broker-dealers, and corporations in individual and class actions and FINRA arbitrations involving all kinds of business, commercial, and consumer disputes. She can be reached at ptaylor@mccarter.com or + 1 973.639.7947.

Martin T. Tully (Chapter 10: Electronic Discovery in Civil Litigation) is a founding partner of Actuate Law, LLC in Chicago. He is a veteran trial lawyer with over 25 years of national experience representing companies and individuals in complex commercial litigation concerning a broad array of fields and industries. Empowered by his commercial litigation practice, Martin is nationally recognized for his knowledge and experience in the fields of electronic discovery, information governance and data security/data privacy. His expertise helps clients to stay ahead of the curve in each of these fields with respect to developing law, technology, and best practices, whether in the context of active litigation and regulatory matters, or in seeking to avoid them. Martin is also adept at leveraging both technology and strategic partnerships with technologists to achieve client objectives. Martin advances thought-leadership in data law as a member of the Steering Committee of the Sedona Conference Working Group on Electronic Document Retention and Production (WG-1), as an active member of the Sedona Conference Working Group on Data Security and Privacy Liability (WG-11), the 7th Circuit Council on eDiscovery and Digital

Information, the ABA Section of Litigation, Privacy and Data Security Committee, and the International Association of Privacy Professionals (IAPP). In addition, Martin has published and presented extensively on the topics of e-discovery, information governance, cybersecurity, and legal technology; has been recognized by Chambers USA, Nationwide, for Litigation: E-Discovery; and has been acknowledged by Who's Who Legal as being "widely regarded for his 'superior knowledge' of electronic discovery and information governance." Martin is a graduate of the University of Illinois at Chicago and a graduate, with honor, of the DePaul University College of Law. Martin is also devoted to public service, having served as the elected mayor of his hometown of Downers Grove, IL for eight years. He can be reached at martin.tully@actuatelaw.com or 312.579.3128.

Amy Van Gelder (Chapter 7: Managing Regional and National Litigation) is a partner at Skadden, Arps, Slate, Meagher & Flom LLP in Chicago. She represents a wide variety of clients in complex commercial litigation, including securities and consumer fraud class actions, bankruptcy litigation, shareholder derivative suits, and disputes relating to mergers and acquisitions and commercial contracts. Ms. Van Gelder's experience includes counseling clients in federal and state court throughout the country and in all phases of litigation, including trial and appeal. She also has represented corporations in regulatory investigations, including matters before the Department of Justice, the SEC and multiple state regulators. Ms. Van Gelder earned her J.D. from George Washington University, with highest honors. She can be reached at amy.vangelder@skadden.com or +1 312.407.0903.

Chet B. Waldman (Chapter 9: Managing Class Actions) is a partner at Wolf Popper LLP, based in New York City, where he has concentrated in litigating numerous federal and state securities class actions and derivative actions throughout the U.S. He also has extensive experience in litigating complex health care and consumer fraud cases. Prior to working at Wolf Popper, Chet worked at the New York office of Weil, Gotshal & Manges, where he was predominantly involved in antitrust litigation. He has been a member of the Securities Litigation Committee, the Mergers & Acquisition Committee, as well as the Inter-American Affairs Committee of the New York City Bar Association. Chet is a graduate of Cornell University (A.B. 1982) and Boston University School of Law (J.D., 1985) where he was both a G. Joseph Tauro Scholar and a Paul J. Liacos Scholar and was a member of the American Journal of Law and Medicine. He was admitted to the bar in 1986 for the State of New York, the United States District Court, Southern and Eastern Districts of New York in 1988, and the United States Court of Appeals for the First Circuit in 2013. He can be reached at cwaldman@wolfpopper.com or 212-451-9624.

Kelly M. Warner (Chapter 10: Electronic Discovery in Civil Litigation) is a partner in the Chicago office of Riley Safer Holmes & Cancila LLP. Kelly conducts internal investigations, responds to regulators' inquiries, advises clients on corporate compliance, and represents clients in prosecuting and defending complex civil and criminal litigation matters. Kelly has significant experience consulting with clients and colleagues on eDiscovery obligations and litigation readiness. She has served as adjunct professor of law at the Loyola University Chicago School of Law. Kelly is a member of The Sedona Conference Working Group 1 on Electronic Document Retention and Production (WG1). She is the co-chair of the Education Sub-Committee of the 7th Circuit Council on eDiscovery and Digital Information (formerly the Seventh Circuit Pilot Program on Electronic Discovery), and also trained as an eMediator under the Council's eMediation program. Kelly can be reached at kwarner@rshc-law.com or 312-471-8740.

Index

B

D

E

L

S